Contemporary Japanese Thought

WEATHERHEAD BOOKS ON ASIA

WEATHERHEAD BOOKS ON ASIA
Columbia University

LITERATURE
David Der-wei Wang, Editor

Ye Zhaoyan, *Nanjing 1937: A Love Story*, translated by Michael Berry
Makoto Oda, *The Breaking Jewel*, translated by Donald Keene
Han Shaogong, *A Dictionary of Maqiao*, translated by Julia Lovell
Takahashi Takako, *Lonely Woman*, translated by Maryellen Toman Mori
Chen Ran, *A Private Life*, translated by John Howard-Gibbon
Takeuchi Yoshimi, *What Is Modernity? Writings of Takeuchi Yoshimi*,
translated by Richard Calichman
Eileen Chang, *Written on Water*, translated by Andrew F. Jones
David McCann, editor, *The Columbia Anthology of Modern Korean Poetry*
Amy D. Dooling, editor, *Writing Women in Modern China:
The Revolutionary Years, 1936–1976*

HISTORY, SOCIETY, AND CULTURE
Carol Gluck, Editor

Contemporary Japanese Thought

Edited by Richard F. Calichman

COLUMBIA UNIVERSITY PRESS

NEW YORK

Columbia University Press
Publishers Since 1893
New York   Chichester, West Sussex
Copyright © 2005 Columbia University Press
All rights reserved

This publication has been supported by the
Richard W. Weatherhead Publication Fund
of the East Asian Institute, Columbia University.

Library of Congress Cataloging-in-Publication Data
Contemporary Japanese thought /
edited by Richard F. Calichman.
p. cm. — (Weatherhead books on Asia)
Includes bibliographical references and index.
ISBN 0–231–13620–X (cloth : alk. paper)
ISBN 0–231–13621–8 (pbk. : alk. paper)
ISBN 0–231–50988–X (elec.)
1. Japan—Civilization—1945–
I. Calichman, Richard. II. Series.
DS822.5.C656   2005
952. 04—dc22   2004065672

Printed in the United States of America
c 10 9 8 7 6 5 4 3 2 1
p 10 9 8 7 6 5 4 3 2 1

CONTENTS

ACKNOWLEDGMENTS

This book is above all the product of several friendships begun while I was conducting postdoctoral research in Tokyo from the years 1999 to 2001. Nishitani Osamu (Tokyo University of Foreign Studies) was kind enough to act as my adviser during this time. In addition to the various seminars offered by Professor Nishitani, I also attended those given by Takahashi Tetsuya (University of Tokyo) and Ukai Satoshi (Hitotsubashi University). These seminars were a source of great inspiration for me, and I am happy to thank Professors Nishitani, Takahashi, and Ukai for discussions that took place both within and outside of them. I would also like to express my gratitude to Professor Iwasaki Minoru (Tokyo University of Foreign Studies), whose Hegel seminar with its unorthodox mixture of Japanese, German, and French remains a model for me of intellectual inquiry and camaraderie.

More generally, I am grateful to all of the book's contributors—in addition to those named here, Professors Ehara Yumiko, Kang Sangjung, Karatani Kōjin, and Ueno Chizuko—for their generous participation in this project. I am no less thankful to the translators of these essays for their fine work here.

This project would not have been possible without the work of Naoki Sakai, with whom I first began reading contemporary Japanese thought. Carol Gluck has provided consistent support for this project, and I am indebted to her kindness. This work has also benefited from two reviewers, one of whom remains anonymous; the other, Mark Anderson, read the manuscript carefully and offered suggestions and encouragement, both of which were quite welcome. Takeshi Kimoto performed a valuable service in checking over several translations with his usual expertise. Finally, thanks go to Madge Huntington of the East Asian Institute at Columbia University and Jennifer Crewe of Columbia University Press.

The book is dedicated to M: *xiexie*.

Contemporary Japanese Thought

INTRODUCTION

A book on contemporary Japanese thought might at first glance appear surprising, given that "thought" — or "theory," as it is often called — has in the modern era generally been linked with the West as its proper provenance. One readily speaks, for example, of French theory or German theory, and these references are more or less directly understood without raising much question. Despite the presence of numerous theoretical writings by so-called non-Western thinkers in non-Western languages, these texts have hitherto done little to drive a wedge between the notions of "West" and "thought," thereby provoking discussion as to the meaning of these terms both in themselves and in combination with one another. The question arises, then, as to how to best categorize or classify such concrete examples of modern non-Western thought — for surely academia has thus far appeared unwilling to grant currency to such categories as, say, Chinese theory or Indian theory. Rather the common response to these texts has been to see them as necessarily derivative of the West, such that the West retains its position as the center of intellectual production and the non-West becomes the mere recipient of that influence. Even in the field of Asian Studies, the notion of "Western theory" has gone largely unchallenged. The question has not been whether this term any longer makes sense, if indeed it ever did, but rather whether such thought or theory can legitimately be *applied* to Asian texts, as these latter are assumed to be inherently devoid of any theoretical properties.

In other words, theoretical readings of non-Western works are still in many cases seen to be misreadings, since the application of Western theory presumably brings to these texts certain abstract elements that are strictly foreign to them. Now this assumption is problematic for several reasons, but it is especially so in the case of Japan. For the fact is that modern Japanese thought has long been at the forefront of theoretical inquiry and scholarship. In this context, it is perhaps important to recall that Japanese thinkers have since the beginning of the twentieth century participated in the latest philosophical developments in, for example, phenomenology, life-philosophy *(Lebensphilosophie)*, dialectics, and hermeneutics. Much of this work coalesced around the group of philosophers collectively known as the Kyoto School, as led by Nishida Kitarō (1870–1945) and Tanabe Hajime (1885–1962). This group, although highly diverse in nature, set forth many important insights regarding the status of such notions as history, praxis, technology, aesthetics, and religion. But from today's standpoint, it is arguably the study of the relation between subjectivity and negativity that has come to be regarded as their most significant intellectual legacy. While it is not the aim of this introduction to examine the achievements of the Kyoto School, it should be mentioned that these philosophers were, in one way or another, invariably confronted with the question of their own positionality vis-à-vis "Western thought." The secondary scholarship on modern Japanese philosophy has followed this lead, as can be seen in the representation of the texts of the Kyoto School as striving for a dialogue or even synthesis between East and West, the former determined primarily along the lines of Zen Buddhism and the latter in terms of the grand philosophical tradition that stretches from Plato to Heidegger. From our own perspective, however, there seems to be little reason to determine thought on the basis of its geographical or cultural background. This point will be more fully explored in the following pages, but for the moment it is sufficient to note that contemporary Japanese thought can trace its beginnings back not only to previous Western thinkers and traditions, but also to those of Japan. Indeed, given the extreme complexity and convoluted nature of such affiliations, it might be worthwhile to question the very possibility of assigning to thinkers and their thought any fixed regional properties.

Contemporary Japanese thought centrally takes up this question of regional identification in the context of nationalism, which is why even the otherwise standard reference to "Japanese thought" must be made with circumspection. Many of the essays in this volume explicitly address this question; others, however, pursue quite different paths that raise equally important questions. Yet taken as a whole, these essays can be said to offer a more or less fair or accurate representation of Japanese thought as it has flourished these past two decades or so. As goes without saying, this collection makes no claim to be *the* definitive text on contemporary thought in Japan, for one can easily imagine other collections with their own equally valid principles of inclusion (and, therefore, exclusion) regarding individual contributors, common thematics, dates of essays, university and journal affiliations, political inclinations, etc. Clearly there can be no such thing as a perfectly neutral or objective collection of this type, for the criteria brought to bear upon the field of Japanese thought ineluctably transform any simple representation of it into an active intervention. Here we must accept responsibility for the principles underlying our own editorial choices. In particular, let us name two of these principles (among others) and their effect upon the overall composition of the volume:

1. *The principle of practice.* Among contemporary thinkers in Japan, priority has been given to those whose attention to theoretical issues has explicitly focused on their practical dimensions. It is this indissociability of the theoretical and practical that grounds for these thinkers the political thrust of their writings. To read their works is to understand that scholarship is not to be undertaken simply for the purpose of acquiring knowledge, but also to effect a change in contemporary social practices, both in Japan and beyond and in academia and beyond. Such thinking is fully consistent with the aim of this volume, which is to present an introduction to contemporary thought in Japan while at the same time provoking reflection as to the very meaning of this notion of "Japanese thought."

2. *The principle of gender.* In Japan, generally speaking, the term *shisō,* or "thought," does not include feminism, which on the contrary stands as its own category. The inclusion of feminist writings in a book on contemporary Japanese thought, therefore, might strike some readers as odd or inappropriate. However, it was felt that a reflection of this exclusion of feminist theory from the category of thought would only perpetuate certain problematic assumptions at work within intellectual circles in Japan, and this we were unwilling to do. Gender issues occupy an undeniably significant place in contemporary thought and practice, and the composition of this volume attests to that fact.

Finally, let us not fail to mention certain concrete circumstances surrounding the organization of this collection. After the initial plan for the book had been conceived and a publisher secured, contributors were contacted and asked to provide essays of approximately 10,000 words in length (in the form of either one long essay or two shorter ones). Translators were assigned to these essays, which, upon being translated, were then edited so as to ensure maximum fidelity and readability. Rather than group the essays thematically, a decision was made to simply pair them with their respective authors, who are listed here in alphabetical order.

I

In a volume such as the present one, it might be helpful to begin thinking about the disciplinary or institutional space known as "Japanese thought" through reference to the celebrated Meiji writer Natsume Sōseki. For traditionally Sōseki's works have been determined to exist *outside* of this space: while it is readily granted that Sōseki fulfills the criterion of Japaneseness on account of his birth and parentage, he is nevertheless primarily read as an author of literature rather than as a thinker, or *shisōka*, thereby placing him in the category of Japanese literature as opposed to that of Japanese thought. Such an understanding, however, seems to be refuted or at the very least troubled by the fact of his inclusion in the recent Iwanami *Tetsugaku shisō jiten* [Dictionary of philosophy and thought], where Sōseki, who appears in that text as "someone who is more than just a writer" but, indeed, a "thinker," is credited for the depth and complexity of his reflections on such topics as desire, ethics, and East-West relations.[1] I mention this not so as to resolve the question of Sōseki's institutional belonging in favor of thought over literature, for example—thus allowing me to present him as a forebear to contemporary Japanese thought, of which the eight writers assembled here would be representatives—but rather to draw attention to a certain irreducible contingency that inheres within this space of "Japanese thought." This contingency reveals itself in the very criteria by which to judge the nature of Japanese thought, that is to say, what it is and what it is not. If there can exist some degree of uncertainty or confusion over whether to situate such a monumental figure as Sōseki either within or without the institution of Japanese thought, then clearly this institution cannot be understood as in any way natural or necessary. In other words, the institution of Japanese thought must be seen as properly devoid of anything that could enable it to constitute itself as such. Sōseki's inclusion within or exclusion from Japanese thought depends, rather, on a contingent decision. If there are those who see him as rightly occupying this space, then there are also those who see him as just as firmly outside of it. In the absence of any objective criteria according to which we could determine the parameters of Japanese thought in its distinction from, say, Japanese literature or, conversely, from French thought or Chinese thought, we are left simply to *judge* what belongs to the space of Japanese thought and what does not. In the case of Sōseki, it is, of course, the aspect of "thought" that is most immediately in question. Yet if the notion of thought can be shown to surrender its apparent necessity or naturalness, then so too could the notion of "Japanese." If the institution of Japanese *thought* must distinguish itself from that which, while Japanese, is nevertheless not properly classifiable as thought, then this same institution must also distance or differentiate itself from that kind of thought which does not present itself as *Japanese*. Here, as well, the absence of anything that could be objectively determined as Japan or Japanese means that we are forced to decide the nature and extent of these boundaries ourselves. This decision, let us repeat, is necessarily a contingent one, given that there is nothing that announces itself as intrinsically Japanese.

We are perhaps now better prepared to read Sōseki, and so discover the strange lesson he helps teach us about the nature of Japanese thought. The following passage is to be found in the opening part of Sōseki's well-known lecture "Gendai Nihon no kaika" [The civilization of modern-day Japan], delivered in Wakayama on August 15, 1911:

> But if you ask me what we're supposed to *do* (*dō suru noda*) about this present-day civilization of ours, I won't have an answer for you. I merely plan to explain (*tada setsumei wo shite*) what "civilization" means and leave the rest to you. Well, then, what do we mean by "civilization"? My guess is that you do not understand the civilization of modern-day Japan. By this I mean no disrespect toward you. None of us really understands it, and that includes me. I just happen to be in a position that gives me more time than you to think about such matters, and this lecture allows me to share my thoughts with you. All of you are Japanese, and so am I (*anata gata mo watakushi mo Nihonjin*); we live in the modern age, not the past or the future, and our civilization influences us all; it is obvious that the three words "modern," "Japan," and "civilization" bind us together inseparably (*dōshitemo kittemo kirenai hanasubekarazaru missetsu na kankei ga aru*). If, however, we remain unconscious of the civilization of modern-day Japan, or if we do not have a clear understanding of what it means, this can adversely affect everything we do. We will all be better off, I believe, if, together, we study this concept and help each other understand it.[2]

Apart from the fact that these lines derive from the thought of a Japanese thinker or perhaps literary writer, they do not seem to directly touch upon the institution of Japanese thought. Nonetheless, they are highly important in helping us better understand that aspect of Japaneseness without which Japanese thought would be, according to its very definition, impossible. Sōseki's aim here is to clarify the meaning of modern Japanese civilization, a phrase which, if only hazily understood at the time, was nevertheless no less widespread and thus powerful for all that. In order to clarify this meaning, he recognizes, it is first necessary to break up this phrase or concept into its component parts, which are then very briefly described in terms of their relevance to his lecture. Hence, in the order Sōseki himself lays out: Japan ("All of you are Japanese, and so am I"); modern ("we live in the modern age, not the past or the future"); and civilization ("our civilization influences us all"). Sōseki's particular focus throughout the essay is on this last term, civilization, as he appears to believe that the first two terms, Japan and modern, present in their immediacy far less difficulty of comprehension. He is, moreover, careful to remind his audience of the lecture's modest intentions, for he wishes only to describe or "explain" the meaning of civilization, and thus of modern Japanese civilization, rather than prescribe a course of action in regard to this civilization ("But if you ask me what we're sup-posed to *do* about this present-day civilization of ours, I won't have an answer for you. I merely plan to explain what 'civilization' means and leave the rest to you"). In this way, Sōseki implicitly reveals his belief that explanation can be cleanly separated from prescription, that, in other words, language can be used to convey the meaning of something without thereby producing any concomi-tant effects, either on the object being explained or on those being addressed. Modern Japanese civilization is thus viewed as something that, preexisting in its reality Sōseki's explanation of it, offers itself simply as the object that is repeated or represented through that explanation.

How then are we to understand Sōseki's stated refusal to supply a prescrip-tion regarding modern Japanese civilization? This gesture reflects, at its most fundamental level (that is to say, even prior to any literary or historical analysis of his works), a refusal to recognize the prescriptive force of his own utterances. In his positing of a modern Japanese civilization, Sōseki essentially denies his own contribution to the *formation* of such entity through the effects of his lan-guage. For, contrary to what one might believe, that which is called "modern Japanese civilization" (and so too, following this same argument, "contempo-rary Japanese thought") exists nowhere else but in the inscriptions that at each instant institute or found modern Japanese civilization. It is through the force of such instituting inscriptions that modern Japanese civilization comes into being, precisely, as an institution, i.e., a body or form which does not exist nat-urally. Nowhere is this more apparent in this context than in the entity Japan, which for our purposes functions to highlight the difficulty of the concept of contemporary Japanese thought. For Sōseki, the aspect of Japaneseness within the phrase "modern Japanese civilization" appears to be self-evident: "All of you are Japanese, and so am I," he tells his audience, and there the matter is laid to rest. But the truth of the matter is that, however unwittingly or unconsciously, Sōseki is actually *doing* something through these words; his language in its per-formativity is creating effects that function to institute or sustain a sense of Japaneseness, one which does not otherwise exist naturally. In his haste to focus on the notion of civilization, Sōseki fails to consider that the Japanese identity he claims to share with his audience does not derive from the fact that they are, in reality, all Japanese. This claim rather has its source in a kind of decision Sōseki makes to establish a sense of ethnic or national communality by identifying himself together with his audience *as* Japanese. Given its status as a non-natural institution, Japaneseness cannot be understood as representative of a preexisting reality that is Japan. Referring not to any past reality but rather to the present instant of Sōseki's statement or utterance, "Japan" reveals itself to be irreducibly temporal in nature: it is in time that "Japan" emerges through its inscriptions.

Clearly, the consequences of this insight for any introduction to contemporary Japanese thought are enormous. For the institution of Japanese thought must now be recognized as having no transcendent status that can be appealed to beyond its inscriptions, or markings, in time and space. This institution, *qua* institution, is entirely subject to those inscriptions that form it retroactively, or *jigoteki ni*, hence forcing us to rethink both our relation to the past and our present institutional belonging. The scholar Abe Masao can be said to demonstrate this point in his introduction to the English translation of Nishida Kitarō's 1911 *Zen no kenkyū* when, in responding to the question of whether there can be found in Japan a philosophical tradition, he cites the works of such thinkers as Kūkai, Shinran, Dōgen, and Itō Jinsai as proof of its existence.[3] Leaving aside the problematic structure of address here (in which Abe writes from the enunciative position of a Japanese writing about a fellow Japanese for the benefit of a readership that he identifies as "Western"), we can point out that Japanese philosophy comes in this act of language to be projected back onto a past in which it did not originally exist. It is in this way that institutions come to be naturalized, that is, shorn of those present instances of inscription upon which they are, in fact, fully dependent. In the context of Japanese thought, there have historically, of course, been thousands of thinkers and texts that can be subsumed under this category. Yet it must be acknowledged that this category emerged only *after* the appearance of these diverse instances, not prior to them. Japanese thought constitutes itself as an institution or disciplinary field by retroactively gathering these multiple instances together and sublating their difference through recognizing, or remarking, them as now parts within an ideal whole. Let us point out that the success of this operation of forming Japanese thought as a unified and integral entity depends, crucially, on a passage from empiricity to transcendentality. Given its status as ideal object, that which is called "Japanese thought" should have no worldly existence in and of itself. If it is true that this thought is instantiated or concretized by those multiple instances that appear in its name, one must nevertheless make a radical distinction between these merely empirical events and Japanese thought as such, which is properly transcendental. However, taking into account the retroactive nature of ideal objects, which are formed by remarking past inscriptions on the basis of the present—such that, for example, Kūkai, Shinran, Dōgen, and Itō Jinsai come to be seen *ex post facto* as the forefathers of Japanese philosophy or perhaps Japanese thought—we cannot but conclude that transcendentality, far from simply governing those empirical instances that appear in its name, actually depends upon them. Empiricity, that is to say, reveals itself in its marking to be nothing less than the condition upon which the transcendental first becomes possible. Meaning this, more simply stated: that what is called "Japanese thought" is devoid of any reality other than that which is bestowed upon it (retrospectively) through the instituting or founding acts of inscription.

However, given the radical difference of time within which all empirical inscriptions necessarily take place, those instances that otherwise purely instantiate Japanese thought must be seen to be utterly dissimilar to one another. In this sense, such thinkers as Kūkai, Shinran, Dōgen, and Itō Jinsai are, prior to their collective identity as Japanese philosophers—which identity, let us repeat, is accomplished strictly through the retroactive *act* of identification—marked most immediately by their mutual difference. Identity is arrived at by passing through this difference, and from this we may infer that identity is, far from being primal or originary, in truth wholly derivative of difference; it is what can appropriately be called an *effect* of difference. And here we might refer to Heidegger, given his tremendous importance for twentieth-century "Japanese thought" (both in the Kyoto School and beyond), and specifically Heidegger's suggestion that identity is derivative of a more originary instance, that which he calls "the Same."[4] In thus recognizing that difference is constitutive of identity rather than the reverse, we can also see—and indeed by the same token—that difference threatens this identity essentially. If Japanese thought is what it is by virtue of its differential inscriptions in all their worldliness or empiricity, then this is tantamount to saying that Japanese thought is always already different from itself. Inhabiting all identity from its very inception, this difference must nevertheless be rigorously understood to be structural or formal as opposed to merely empirical. Were difference to be nothing more than empirical, it would be impossible to formulate how the unity of Japanese thought comes to be constituted, just as it would be impossible to account for the inscription of difference in all idealities. Such an essential (or virtually essential, given the terms of our argument) understanding of difference is indispensable in grasping how actual instances of "Japanese thought" can always not be either "Japanese" or "thought" as well as, conversely, how instances that are traditionally situated outside of this thought can always be remarked as belonging within it. For example, the same criteria that might disqualify Sōseki from identification as a figure of Japanese *thought* (despite the considerable complexity of his ideas, as elaborated in both his fiction and his essays)[5] would surely exclude, say, Heidegger from the category of *Japanese* thought (despite his sustained influence on Japanese thinkers, from Miki Kiyoshi to the present, and despite the appearance of his works in Japanese translation).[6] In order to fully appreciate the contingency upon which such criteria are based, however, it is necessary to realize that the differential inscriptions upon which the ideality of Japanese thought is grounded, or made possible, function simultaneously to unground it or render it impossible as well.

One would be mistaken in viewing this insight into the relation between identity and difference, or transcendentality and empiricity, as either irrelevant to or excessively abstract in respect to a proper understanding of Japanese thought, which is after all the aim we have set for ourselves in this introduction. A very similar logic of empiricity in its double movement of appropriation within and resistance against conceptual thought can be read, for example, in the works of the postwar critic and sinologist Takeuchi Yoshimi, where it appears as the necessary (un)grounding of what is called the "place of contemplation" (*kansō no ba*) by or within the "place of action" (*kōi no ba*).[7] It would not be too much, I believe, to claim that this logic represents the very obverse of abstraction. For what is at stake here is the process by which institutions come to be formed in their revealed unnaturality or derivativeness through present acts of inscription. These acts are *decisive* both in the sense that they leave behind them a mark or incision (from *caedere*, meaning "to cut") and in that they announce a decision. This decision is made in the face of all contingency and carries with it a prescriptive force: whether one wishes to or not, the decision transforms (or remarks) reality, instituting in its place a new and entirely unprecedented reality. As opposed to the view that institutions exist objectively, or in and of themselves outside of human intervention—what phenomenology refers to critically as the "natural attitude" (*natürliche Einstellung, shizenteki taido*)—an awareness of the prescriptive force of one's decisions reveals that institutions can at any time be changed or altered, for in order to be what they are they must remain essentially open to human activity. The institution of Japanese thought, for example, appears to be closed off *in principle* from that which does not present itself as either "Japanese" or "thought." Yet since both of these notions acquire meaning only in being remarked, they are *in fact* susceptible to transformation. The impact of decision on existing reality takes place against the background of time, which, in its constant change, naturally threatens institutions that can maintain themselves only by being identically remarked. In this regard, we can better perceive the considerable weight of decision in its relation to the maintenance of institutions. For, given that institutions attain their autonomy and self-functioning only as an *effect* of the differential inscriptions that are decision, their opening to this latter is nothing less than an opening to the possibility of change.

This strange need for entities to inscribe themselves so as to present and preserve themselves as such has recently been examined by the philosopher Jean-Luc Nancy. As Nancy writes in his essay "Le soi-disant peuple,"

> The people can only say *self* to itself as a *so-called/self-saying (soi-disant) people*. The subject of enunciation enunciates itself as subject of the enunciated . . . but its real presence is attendant upon the execution of the content of the enunciated: the people will appear when the principles of the constitution take effect, since it is the constitution that constitutes the people. Yet the constitution only constitutes them as subject of its enunciated, leaving them missing as subject of the enunciation. The instituted people lack the instituting people, unless it be the reverse.[8]

Here we see very clearly that a people do not exist naturally but rather come into being derivatively only at the instant of their self-inscription, what Nancy refers to here as a "self-saying." This term plays upon the double meaning of *soi-disant*, which in common parlance means simply "so-called" but can also more literally be read as "self-saying": a people (for example, Americans, Japanese, etc.) can never be other than so-called, that is, not really a people because they arrive at this identity only through the act of identifying themselves collectively *as* a people. There is thus an insurmountable delay in the formation of identity, since it departs from a self that is however not yet a self so as to reflexively arrive at itself through the force of its self-articulation. This passage that is the movement of self-formation furthermore creates a split between the people as, on the one hand, instituting (or that which actively posits itself in its collectivity) and, on the other, instituted (that which the people are posited as being—or rather, in retroactive fashion, as *having been*). For Nancy, this split is necessarily an irreparable one.

Given what we believe to be the central importance of this point for any understanding of "Japanese thought" *in its own terms*, let us refer back now to the passage from Natsume Sōseki that we quoted earlier for purposes of illustration. In order for Sōseki to establish what he calls an "inseparable binding" (literally, an "intimate relation that can in no way be cut or divided") with his audience, he must first appeal to their common or shared identity as Japanese. It is perhaps not insignificant in this respect to point out that the movement of unification or collectivization that Sōseki is here effecting by his language manifests itself only in tension with its opposite movement. This countermovement, as it were, can be seen in the set of distinctions he draws, first between himself and his audience ("My guess is that *you* do not understand the civilization of modern-day Japan" whereas "*I* just happen to be in a position that gives *me* more time than *you* have to think about such matters") and then, secondly, between the three terms that together comprise the topic of his lecture ("it is obvious that the three words 'modern,' 'Japan,' and 'civilization' bind us together insepara- bly").[9] However, these two movements of unification and differentiation should not be regarded as simply equivalent to one another. Rather it is more accurate to say that the identity Sōseki is attempting here to effect is articulated in relief against the background of that difference to which he calls attention. This dif- ference is, to use the word Sōseki himself uses in the essay "Bungei no tetsug- akuteki kiso" cited below, a kind of "fact" *(jijitsu)*. It is from this initial fact of difference that he draws distinctions between people and words; in this way he simultaneously acknowledges the presence of difference *and* begins to negate it by actively figuring it in the form of distinct entities (I-you, modern-Japan- civilization). This negation of difference is then finally itself negated by the for- mation of collective unities, in which difference is now synthesized as part within the whole. Hence, despite the difference that originally underlies them: the "inseparable binding" that ties together "we Japanese" as well as the title and topic of Sōseki's lecture. What must be emphasized here is that it is language that functions as the medium through which the relation between identity and difference comes to be organized. Focusing strictly on the collective Japanese identity that Sōseki posits in these lines, we can see that this identity must have recourse to a "self-saying" in order to come into being. This strange need to say the words *anata gata mo watakushi mo Nihonjin* derives from the absence of any substantial community of Japanese people, an absence which these words para- doxically attempt to conceal as well as to compensate for. Sōseki fails to realize that the Japanese whom he invokes are nothing more than a "so-called people," constituted *not* by any fictionally shared experience of modern civilization or by any other empirical criteria (linguistic, cultural, ethnic, racial, etc.) but rather simply by the force of its "self-saying." It is this self-saying that, while producing a split within the subject between the instituting and instituted, nevertheless also effectively transforms the original "fact" of difference into distinct and artic- ulated parts which are then taken up within the communal whole.

We are now better able to understand the danger of speaking of "Japanese thought" as if these words referred back beyond language to the thought of a Japanese community or people understood as *substance (jittai)*. The problem here, however, is that such a substantialist notion of identity still thoroughly informs the field of Japan Studies, and this despite certain recent theoretical advances to the contrary. In this respect, it is important to note that the formation of Japanese identity as undertaken, for example, by Sōseki (and this would be but one of thousands of possible examples that could be examined here, for Sōseki is in no way alone in this project) finds full support on the part of "non-Japanese" writers as well. Indeed, it makes little difference whether one is an actual Japanese citizen or national in this case since what is most crucial to this project is the inscriptive act of identification, in which one is essentially anonymous.[10] This directs our attention back to the need for recognizing the irreducibly prescriptive force of one's statements given that, as we have discussed, the notion of Japaneseness comes to the fore only in its being remarked. It is for this reason not an innocent act to write on *Japanese* history, *Japanese* literature, or *Japanese* thought, etc., for, as we saw in the case of Sōseki, descriptions or explanations simultaneously constitute their object in the course of their activity. It is in this light that we must view the paradoxical status of "theory" in the Japan Studies field. For this term is traditionally applied to any discussion which inquires not merely into the Japanese object itself, but rather into the conditions of possibility of that objective knowledge. It is at this more fundamental level of inquiry that one understands that objects of cognition can have no natural existence outside of consciousness, that, on the contrary, consciousness is necessary in order to disclose the objective world as meaningful or significant. This is not to say, of course, that consciousness produces the world in the manner of God. Rather it discovers itself as already situated in the world, one which is inherently hostile to its interests, and it seeks to domesticate this hostility by revealing things as meaningful. As is well known, this insight represents the very departure point of phenomenology.[11] What is most relevant for our purposes here is the lesson that things in their natural existence are meaningless in and of themselves; objective meaning is something that can by right be *arrived at* only through the participation of consciousness in its repeated acts of inscription. As such, it represents absurdity itself to speak of things as if the property or quality of Japaneseness inhered naturally within them. And this same, of course, holds true in thinking of Japan itself as a thing to which properties originally belong. "Japan is *nothing*" (*Nihon wa nanimono demo nai*), as Takeuchi Yoshimi famously declares in the 1948 essay "Kindai towa nanika" [What is modernity?], meaning in this context that no substantial reality can precede the operation in which Japan comes to be temporally inscribed or marked up as meaningful.[12] In the present case, for example, it is in the act of writing *on* "Japanese thought" that one actually comes to write Japanese thought. Given the prescriptive force of one's statements, there can be no theoretical distance on the part of the Japan scholar between himself and his object of study. In this way we can see that what in the Japan Studies field is called "theory," which is generally derided for its excessive abstraction, represents in fact the most concrete form of inquiry. For here there can be recognition that the field is formed on the basis of one's decision to write on those objects internal to it, thereby constituting their very objectivity and interiority. This recognition opens up the possibility, then, to transform or even deform the field in its very formation.

Before finally turning our attention to the eight thinkers whose works are represented in this volume, I would like to conclude this discussion on the problematic nature of "Japanese thought" through reference to the well-known literary and arts critic Kobayashi Hideo. In the course of a roundtable discussion during the "Overcoming Modernity" symposium held in Tokyo in the summer of 1942, Kobayashi addresses some challenging remarks to the Kyoto School religious philosopher Nishitani Keiji regarding the relation between Japanese philosophy and the Japanese language:

> To slightly change the topic, both your essay and that of Yoshimitsu [Yoshihiko] are extremely difficult. I would go so far as to say that these essays lack the sensuality of the Japanese people's language. We feel that philosophers are truly indifferent to our fate of writing in the national language. Since this language is the traditional language of Japan, no matter how sincerely and logically expressed, its flavor must appear in one's style as that which can only be achieved by Japanese people. This is what writers always aim for in their trade. It is linked to literary reality, and so either moves people or leaves them unmoved. Thought is contained within this literary reality. Philosophers are extremely nonchalant in this regard. If this attitude is not overcome, however, it strikes me that Japanese philosophy will never truly be reborn as Japanese philosophy. What are your thoughts on this?[13]

What is perhaps most evident in these lines is the tension not simply between Japanese literature and Japanese thought or philosophy, but rather, even prior to this, between the notions of Japanese and non-Japanese themselves. In this respect, the disciplines of literature and philosophy function as the vehicles in which the quality of Japaneseness is conveyed. For Kobayashi, this quality is seen to be manifested most properly or immediately in the Japanese language. In this way, Japanese literature and philosophy can be judged as to the degree of their embodiment of Japaneseness on the basis of the criteria present within the Japanese language, or "national language" (*kokugo*) as Kobayashi refers to it. Here philosophical writing is found deficient, as it lacks that "sensuality" (or "suggestiveness": *nikkan*) believed to be inherent to Japanese, and thus, in marked contrast to literature, fails to consider the emotive effects it produces on its readers (which "either moves people or leaves them unmoved"). In its apparent unconcern for that language from which it springs and with which it is forced to negotiate in the course of its self-expression, Japanese philosophy runs the risk of losing that quality which makes it most authentically Japanese. In which case, whatever the measure of its *philosophical* achievements, it will properly speaking no longer be *Japanese* philosophy.

In his desire to see produced a Japanese philosophy that is as fully Japanese as Japanese literature, Kobayashi is forced to conflate the notion of the Japanese language with that of the Japanese people. Let us point out that the rhetorical force of this conflation derives from what is implicitly set forth as the logical or necessary relation between these two entities. As Kobayashi argues, "Since *(ijō)* this language is the traditional language of Japan . . . its flavor must appear in one's style as that which can only be achieved by Japanese people." The underlying assumption of this (false) cause-and-effect relation is that mastery of the Japanese language is possible only by Japanese people. Such sentiment reflects a widespread if tacit misunderstanding concerning the relation between language and people, which can be very simply formulated as follows: *if* one is Japanese, *then* one speaks the Japanese language; or conversely, *if* one speaks the Japanese language, *then* one is Japanese. (This conflation can in fact be seen operating in the English word "Japanese," which signifies both Japanese people and the Japanese language). Grasped in these terms, it is clear that precisely this same logic of identity underlies the institution of Japanese thought, just as it does those of Japanese history and literature. The principles that govern these institutions generally require, for example, that what is called "Japanese thought" be produced by Japanese people in the medium of the Japanese language. While such requirements appear to be commonsensical, it must be remembered that they are the result of a decision, and hence profoundly contingent. Three points should be mentioned in this connection.

1. The decision that institutes and maintains the institution is a necessarily violent one. We can perceive this violence very clearly in Kobayashi's remarks to Nishitani, particularly when he warns of an impending threat to Japanese philosophy if it continues to remain "indifferent" to what he believes to be the "fate" *(shukumei)* of Japanese writers to write in the Japanese language ("If this attitude is not overcome, however, it strikes me that Japanese philosophy will never truly be reborn as Japanese philosophy"). Yet this violence may be said to reflect an even deeper violence, one that is inseparable from all institutions, for institutions preserve themselves strictly on the basis of exclusion. As we demonstrated earlier, for example, the institution of Japanese thought must exclude from itself both those Japanese discourses that lack the status of *thought* (e.g., literature) and those discourses of thought that derive from outside of *Japan* (e.g., German thought or Chinese thought). However, this is not to suggest that the

institution of Japanese thought be *simply* or *immediately* done away with in the hope of avoiding such exclusionary violence, a notion that calls to mind nothing so much as Hegel's figure of the "beautiful soul."[14] (For it can never be a question of withdrawing oneself entirely from participation in institutions. In the case of Japanese thought, this institution has proved invaluable in the production and interpretation of Japanese texts, and this work should be supported as vigorously as possible. At the same time, however, there is no reason that this institutional attention to Japanese texts must continue on the basis of their putative Japaneseness, with all the exclusions that this concept entails). Rather, it is first of all to draw attention to the inescapably violent nature of institutionality, an understanding of which may be said to open up possibilities for institutional change, a chance to render institutions *less* exclusive and more receptive to difference or alterity. In, for instance, the present volume on Japanese thought, we can, I believe, observe a powerful critique of the notions of Japanese people and Japanese language upon which this institution has traditionally been grounded.

2. Kobayashi's determination of the Japanese language (literally, "the language of the Japanese people," or *Nihonjin no kotoba*) as inherently "sensual" alerts us to a certain essentialism or ahistoricality in his thought, a point to which many scholars have, in fact, critically drawn attention. All too often, however, this criticism is set forth solely in respect of Kobayashi's attempt to attribute an essential meaning to what is yet insufficiently regarded as the historically shifting nature of the Japanese language. In other words, the argument here still focuses too exclusively on Kobayashi's *subjective* act of essentialization without taking into account the equally essentialist nature of the Japanese *object* as implicitly posited by the scholar himself. For if one fully recognizes the temporal or historical character of the Japanese language, then it becomes impossible to speak of this entity as simply having a history; rather this language's thoroughly historical being threatens its unity or integrity so fundamentally that it becomes necessary to inquire into the very possibility of employing it as a legitimate object of study. Here again we uncover another point of commonality between Kobayashi and the Japan Studies field as a whole, given the latter's deeply entrenched aversion to such essential questioning as might place in jeopardy the identity of the Japanese object. In the particular context of Kobayashi, his stated desire to eliminate from Japanese philosophy the abstract and unsensual elements of its language so as to restore its properly Japanese character is, we believe, profoundly reminiscent of Motoori Norinaga's project in the eighteenth century to restore Japan to what he believed to be its originally natural being, in all its concreteness and immediacy, prior to its contamination and resulting abstraction through contact with China. It is in this regard no coincidence that Kobayashi would so strongly identify his own thought with that of

Motoori, resulting in his major work, *Motoori Norinaga*, to which he devoted fully eleven years of his life before finally completing it in 1976.[15] The series of hierarchical oppositions that Motoori established between immediacy and abstraction, nature and history, purity and contamination, and Japan and China, all of which are represented in the binary terms *yamatogokoro* (Japanese mind/heart) and *karagokoro* (Chinese mind/heart), finds expression here nearly two hundred years later in Kobayashi's condemnation of Japanese philosophy (with the significant exception, of course, that the Japan-China binary has now been replaced by the Japan-West binary).[16]

3. The operation of returning Japanese philosophy to its proper source in Japan, from which it has become unmoored and thus rendered inauthentic, takes place entirely on the basis of the whole-part relation. We can glimpse a sign of this in Kobayashi's remark that "thought is contained within this literary reality" *(bungaku no riariti . . . no naka ni shisō ga fukumareru)*, for the logic which enables thought to be reduced to a mere part within the totality that is "literary reality" (and it is unclear what Kobayashi means by this term) is precisely the same logic which states that Japanese philosophy can be subsumed within the totality that is Japan. Here Japanese philosophy is determined strictly in terms of specific difference, in which it coexists alongside Japanese literature as species whose dissimilarity from one another is ultimately negated by their common subsumption within the genus Japan. (And here we might recall Sōseki's rhetorical gesture of distinguishing himself from his audience so as to determine the parameters of that specific difference internal to the genus of "we Japanese").

In response to this move by Kobayashi, we can make two observations. First, despite the fact that Japanese philosophy is seen together with Japanese literature as instances of specific difference, there is nevertheless an implicit hierarchy between these two fields. For it is literature that is understood to maintain a more intimate relation with the Japanese language, which for Kobayashi is after all the most immediate embodiment or manifestation of Japaneseness. Without this hierarchy, it would be impossible for thought, which informs philosophy, to be "contained within this literary reality." Hence the opposition that Kobayashi posits between Japanese literature and philosophy, in which he positions himself very clearly as on the side of literature, is one in which literature is judged to be superior. However, the problem that immediately arises here is that Kobayashi is forced to appeal to, or draw upon the resources of, philosophy so as to establish this superiority of literature. In grounding his argument on the very classical notion of the whole-part relation, according to which Japan functions as the whole that comprehends within itself both philosophy and literature as its distinct parts or species, Kobayashi is in effect arguing against himself in asserting that the priority that literature enjoys over philosophy is ultimately grounded upon philosophy itself. Even more important, however, we can see in this demonstration that the whole-part relation of philosophy grounds the very relation between Japan (whole) and Japanese philosophy (part) itself. One lesson that can be gleaned from this is that the part, or that which is (to use Kobayashi's word) "contained" within the whole, can nevertheless always come to exceed this latter, thereby threatening the very structure of the whole-part relation and particularly the notion of belonging so central to it. The consequences of this lesson for any thinking of "Japanese thought" should be evident, as thought is perhaps now not so easily contained within that national genus. As we will see, the present collection very explicitly bears witness to this fact.

Second, the logic of the whole-part relation that informs the containment (or belonging) of Japanese philosophy and literature within the whole that is Japan as well as the containment of "thought" within "literary reality" comes to be called into question by Kobayashi's own language. Let us recall here that the entire exchange with Nishitani centers on a critique of Japanese philosophy for its "nonchalance" and "indifference" to what Kobayashi describes as the "fate" of Japanese writers to write in Japanese. Through reminding Japanese philosophers that thought is ultimately contained within literary reality, it is hoped that they will become more attentive to that "sensuality" or "suggestiveness" putatively inherent in the Japanese language. The notion of literary reality thus represents for Kobayashi a kind of linguistic purity, in which the particular properties of Japanese (sensuality, etc.) reveal themselves in all their fullness and immediacy. Strangely enough, however, Kobayashi chooses to designate this space of pure Japaneseness with *gairaigo*, or what is referred to commonly as a "loanword," meaning a term that originally derives from outside Japan. Kobayashi speaks here of *bungaku no* riariti, significantly, *not bungaku no* genjitsu or *bungaku no* jitsuzaisei. As someone deeply versed in French literature and thought, of course, such usage would have been quite natural for Kobayashi (and indeed, for many others without that training). Yet the point here is not simply to focus on the circumstances surrounding Kobayashi's manner of speech. Rather his choice of a loanword in this context is noteworthy in that it points to an *outside* of Japan. If the phrase *bungaku no riariti . . . no naka ni shisō ga fukumareru* can be said to illustrate the logic of the whole-part relation which enables, in turn, the comprehension of Japanese philosophy and literature within Japan, then the true "reality" of this logic is that philosophy and literature—and, let us add, "Japanese thought"—can never be contained within Japan. Or rather: such containment takes place on the basis of an outside that both allows it and disallows it. In which case, all *Japanese* thought, *Japanese* philosophy, *Japanese* literature, and *Japanese* history can be said to refer most originally to this outside. The reference to Japan is strictly derivative or secondary, that is to say, contingent; it is dependent upon a decision.

II

It will perhaps not come as a surprise that Nishitani's response to Kobayashi takes a very different form from the one we have sketched out above. Nishitani defends Japanese philosophy against Kobayashi's criticism by arguing, more or less, as follows: We are fully aware that the abstractness of philosophical writing poses a problem; this abstractness derives primarily from the fact that Japanese philosophers are engaging with the texts of Western philosophy, which present both conceptual and terminological difficulties that cannot be resolved simply through recourse to traditional Japanese usage or phraseology, as this would indeed lead to even greater confusion; lacking the time to write in such a way as to make our texts more easily comprehensible to the average Japanese reader, we in fact see ourselves as participating in a dialogue with Western thinkers, whose ideas we seek to advance beyond; and finally the linguistic "sensuality" or "suggestiveness" as referred to by Kobayashi differs between the fields of literature and philosophy.[17] This response is as one might expect, but it is nevertheless unfortunate (and, of course, deeply revealing) that Nishitani fails to more fundamentally call into question the subsumptive relation between Japanese philosophy and Japan, as maintained here by Kobayashi. (And Nishitani was no doubt fully in agreement with Kobayashi on this point, whatever their other differences). Yet even here we can begin to perceive some of the cracks or strains of this relation, almost as if it were asked to bear an excessive amount of weight. For if, as Nishitani indicates, Japanese philosophy conducts its philosophical dialogue most urgently *beyond* as opposed to *within* Japan's own national borders, then perhaps the very notion of thought as "contained" by or within a nation (national culture, national language, etc.) must be reexamined. Such a reexamination, let us point out, would not simply take as its goal the opening of Japanese philosophy or thought to its outside. On the contrary, that opening must be understood as having *already taken place* from the very moment Japanese philosophy or thought forms itself as such. In this sense, the empirical event of Japanese philosophy going beyond itself and encountering its exterior (for example, Nishitani's own period of research in Germany from 1924 to 1926 immediately upon graduation from Kyoto University, where he famously studied under Nishida) can be said to repeat or remark that more essential movement of difference within which it is necessarily caught up. Because of this movement, that which is called "Japanese philosophy" can, rigorously speaking, be referred to only with quotation marks.

What, then, might an institution of "Japanese" thought look like that was more conscious of its (unsublatable, unsubsumable) internal differences, and hence more receptive to the event of alterity? In the present volume, for example, we have gathered together eight thinkers whose works have for at least the past decade or so constituted an important critical force in the Japanese *shisōkai*, or "domain of ideas," broadly understood. For a variety of reasons, these thinkers may be said to challenge some of the principles or premises upon which Japanese thought has traditionally, if merely implicitly—given the extent to which these principles have become naturalized—grounded itself. We can refer here to the range of empirical criteria used to determine the category of Japaneseness, primary among which are those of race, ethnicity, language, culture, and geographic location. In the past, these distinct sets of criteria were frequently conflated with one another (as, for instance, we saw in the case of Kobayashi Hideo), such that a Japanese person was defined, naturally enough, as a racial and ethnic Japanese who resided in Japan and spoke the Japanese language. Recent scholarship on cultural theory has valuably shown that such notions of national identity are entirely *fabricated*, in the double sense here of construction and deception. Paradoxically, however, these insights have if anything tended to strengthen those fields of research that are grounded upon national identity, as for example the field of Japan Studies. In this regard, the appropriative ability of institutions must be reckoned with in all of its force. Here we confront one of the greatest difficulties in our own project, for the general heading of "contemporary Japanese thought" appears capable of reducing all of the thinkers represented here into mere *examples* of this national discourse, hence confirming their belonging to Japan in the very gesture by which they are otherwise shown to exceed or undermine it. In terms of this nonbelonging, we might remark that not all of the thinkers brought together in this volume reside in Japan, not all are what are traditionally considered to be "ethnically" Japanese (once again, reminding ourselves of the utterly fabricated nature of this concept),[18] and not all of their works are originally written in the Japanese language. (And furthermore, in respect of the historically male-dominated institution of Japanese thought, not all of these thinkers are men). In, for example, the instance of language, the fact that works are produced that are written initially in, say, English or French (as is in fact the case here with some of the essays) might conceivably disqualify them from inclusion within the category of Japanese thought. Such tension between national identity and national language has, of course, a long and varied history, as we see quite clearly in the field of literature when considering such modern writers as Conrad, Kafka, and Nabokov as well as Kazuo Ishiguro, despite the considerable differences between them.[19] Even beyond such empirical facts as those relating to biographical circumstances and textual production, however, it is significant that the thinkers assembled here attempt more or less explicitly to work out a logic with which to dismantle this notion of national identity. No doubt these attempts are quite diverse from one another, responding each in its own way to different historical exigencies that generate, in turn, a plurality of reading strategies (methodologies, objects of inquiry, etc.). Yet there can nevertheless be seen in these texts a sustained thinking of resistance against that movement of unification or collectivization that seeks to reduce difference to nothing more than disparate instances of identity. If then it must be recognized that it is always possible to appropriate these essays back within the posited whole or totality that is contemporary Japanese thought, it must on the other hand also be acknowledged that such operation contravenes the logic that is actively being worked out within them.

From our perspective, the essays of the sociocultural theorist Kang Sangjung can perhaps best be approached as a critique of the denial or disavowal of history, which takes here two distinct (if interrelated) forms. First, this critique directs itself against the institution of Oriental Studies *(Tōyōgaku)*, as established in Japan in the late nineteenth and early twentieth centuries by the colonial administrator Gotō Shinpei together with the scholar of Oriental history *(Tōyōshigaku)* Shiratori Kurakichi. History is denied by this institution in its attempt to set forth distinct and internally unified geopolitical entities whose relation to one another is based strictly upon oppositionality. It is this dimension of oppositionality, which belongs properly to logic rather than to history itself, that reveals the ahistoricality inherent in the Orientalist project. Hence the notion of Oriental history must be seen as a contradiction in terms since, as Kang notes, "the very category of the 'Orient' is nothing but an 'imaginary time and space,' one that emerged from the suffering common to non-Western societies in their attempt to reconcile civilization and culture, difference and identity."[20] Following the West in the construction of the image of the Orient so as to better reflect itself (what Kang refers to in the context of collective cultural and national identity as "narcissism," or *jiko tōsui*), Japan also went about erecting an entire network of Orientalist knowledge only to discover that the oppositionality upon which that knowledge was grounded ultimately gave way before that force of history which it had sought to repress. If we visualize history in this sense as exerting a violent and relentless pressure against identity, then it might help us better understand Kang's own role in his textual practice as both a reader and producer of those "cracks" *(wareme)* and "internal fissures" *(uchigawa kara hokorobi)* that mark the opening of geopolitical entities to alterity.[21]

Second, the critique draws support from both history and philosophy in its attack on the notion of essence, as employed by various nation-states in the service of national ideology. Kang condemns here both the cultural essentialism of the United States ("The unity and communal identity of the American state are being defined once again by inciting antagonisms of cultural essentialism") and the Japanese emperor system understood as "national essence" *(kokuminteki honsei)*.[22] In the specific context of the latter, the emperor system comes to be seen as an integral part of Japanese modernization, thus functioning as the thread that ties together the entirety of post-Meiji history as, properly, *Japanese* modern history. In its essential grounding, which enables the nation to preserve its identity despite the flux of historical difference (and these two terms *dōitsu-sei* and *saisei* are, let us point out, crucial for Kang's thinking of history), all traces of violence can be effaced from the "national narrative" as mere accidents and exceptions, or what Kang calls "temporary deviations" *(ichijiteki na itsu-datsu)*.[23] Violence is in this way situated outside Japan in its self-formation as a modern nation, whereby it is opposed to modernity, and this opposition between modernity and violence comes to be conceived in philosophical (or metaphysical) terms according to the classical distinction between essence and accident. That is to say, the entire history of colonial violence that brought about, in successive fashion, the 1895 Sino-Japanese War, the 1905 Russo-Japanese War and, most destructively, the 1931–1945 Fifteen-Year War is regarded now as inessential to Japan's original nature, which on the contrary (tautologically enough) is defined by its opposition to and against such violence. This disavowal of history very effectively served to perpetuate the myth of the postwar, at which time, it was claimed, Japan could finally overcome the "temporary deviation" or aberration of militarist violence (i.e., history) and return to its true course of progressive modernization (essence): "The postwar signified a reversal of that history of insanity and a return *(fukki)* to the healthy and transparent nationalism of the Meiji state."[24] Frighteningly enough, as Kang reports, polls suggest that over eighty percent of Japanese citizens now accept this kind of national narrative as true. It is precisely against such collective amnesia, as it were, that the importance of rigorously thinking about history emerges in all of its force.

For Ueno Chizuko, the noted sociologist and feminist scholar whose works have been instrumental in fostering an understanding of Japanese feminism for some two decades now, it is necessary to think of questions of gender and sexuality without any recourse to the notion of nature. For, indeed, nature must be understood in some sense as a *notion*, because of which it becomes possible to claim that there is nothing natural about nature, that it is already to some degree exposed to, or permeated by, history. The importance of this insight is perhaps best measured by the degree to which the notion of nature has traditionally informed the common or everyday understanding of gender. According to this understanding, women's natural (or innate) weakness, passivity, and irrationality are to be sharply distinguished from men's natural strength, will, and capacity for reason. As Ueno points out, however, such an attribution of differential qualities "tells us more about those who attribute than those who are attributed."[25] Here we discern two principles that may be described as central to Ueno's thought:

1. The transition that is to be effected from the *attributed* to the *attributor* corresponds with a decisive shift in focus from object to subject. In this shift, the object is revealed to be irreducibly other to those significations that come in history to be attached to, and thus ultimately conflated with, it. What must be remembered is that the object exists on a radically different level from those significations that first open it, for better or worse, to the world of meaning. Failure to recognize that the object, existing originally prior to meaning, thereby resists those significations inevitably leads to a naturalized view of the meaningful object. In response to this process of naturalization, Ueno insists that it is history that is responsible for making objects what they are. Recognition of the force of historical significations to shape social reality introduces within this latter an element of contingency, and it is on the basis of such contingency that political change (e.g., changes in gender politics) becomes possible. As, for instance, Ueno writes in the context of the notion of motherhood, perhaps one of the most naturalized concepts in modern society, "The concept of 'Mothers' . . . is thus in no sense *necessary*. . . . [T]he category of 'Mothers' is a manufactured one that can be discontinued at any time."[26] It is precisely because of this absence of necessity in regard to the historically sedimented meanings around the notion of motherhood that this notion can be signified otherwise, thus opening up new and even subversive possibilities for—as another scholar of Japanese feminism might put it—acting *like* a mother.[27]

2. The critique of what commonly appears to be natural is not simply made from a position that is external to this latter, since natural attributes or properties reveal themselves to be directly opposed to those other attributes or properties set against them. Thus, in the case of gender, it is clear that female qualities are posited in opposition to male qualities. What is necessary, then, is to examine putatively natural entities in terms of these qualities so as to uncover the logic that in fact informs them through and through. This logic, which of course lacks any natural status, is one of binarity; although hidden from view, it is central in determining objects that are otherwise merely different from one another as now "binary oppositions," as Ueno writes. It should be remarked here that Ueno, who has written a book on structuralism, is especially sensitive to such

binary operations as well as to the motivation behind them, given that one term comes always to be tacitly privileged over the other (male over female, Occident over Orient, etc.).[28] Rather than simply reverse this hierarchy and declare the historically deprivileged term as now in fact superior (which would be the position of a certain dialectics), Ueno instead undertakes a kind of genealogy so as to reveal the historically changing nature of these terms. Hence the reading strategy she adopts in the context of Japanese mothers consists in carefully following this concept throughout its itinerary in postwar Japanese fiction, from Yasuoka Shōtarō in the 1950s to Yamada Eimi in the 1980s. This reading demonstrates the impossibility of reducing the enormously complex social phenomenon of motherhood to any fixed or comprehensive meaning, either through binary logic, cultural determinism, or sociobiological destiny.

Finally, let us not fail to call attention to the importance of Ueno's attack against Japanese particularism, as to be found most transparently in *Nihonjin-ron* discourse. Here focus is directed to the works of such otherwise extremely disparate writers as the conservative scholar Hasegawa Michiko, the psychiatrist Doi Takeo (author of the 1971 *Amae no kōzō* [The anatomy of dependence]) and the literature and social critic Karatani Kōjin. Ueno's profound interest in history prevents the critique of Japanese particularism from grounding itself in Western universalism—a charge which has in fact frequently been leveled against Japanese feminism, and one which she strongly refutes. Ueno is correct in seeing within Japanese particularism (especially in its more overt nationalist overtones) a certain reactionism: it is strictly in response to the threat of Western universalism that a desire emerges to posit and preserve a fictitious uniqueness to Japanese culture, for this uniqueness, it is believed, protects the sovereignty of Japan from the comprehension of the West. What must be underscored here, however, is that the paradoxical effect of reinforcing a sense of national-cultural particularism is the overall strengthening of universalism itself. For, as can be seen most clearly in Hegel, the part is necessarily both part and whole. Despite its particularism, Japan as a nation-state is capable of self-differentiation, and in this process precisely the same relation between the West and Japan is replicated between Japan and its own parts (citizens, national institutions, etc.). As such, it is ultimately insufficient (despite the importance of its political strategy, which must also be taken into account) to claim a space *proper* to Japanese feminism, as when Ueno argues against the universalism of Western feminism: "Japanese feminism has its own *raison d'être*, its own history, and its own voice."[29] What is perhaps more valuable in this context is to remain vigilant against those "binary oppositions" whose presence Ueno helps teach us to detect, as for example the binary between Japan and the West.

Ehara Yumiko is another sociologist and feminist scholar whose works are instructive both in illustrating some of the problematics and methodologies current within the institution of feminism in Japan, and also in investigating those discourses of power that come to create the modern self. For Ehara, the process by which this self is shaped or created necessarily involves questions of time and place as well as of gender. As she writes in her study of the political theorist Maruyama Masao,

> Rather I would like to ask how, as a subject *(shutai)* with the sexed body of a woman who is located within the time of the present and the locus of Japan, one might be able to question the various powers that have constructed the self *(mizukara)*. . . . [T]he question is how to understand the concrete operations of the various powers that encircle my body, or the subject called myself.[30]

We can see in these lines that Ehara rejects any notion of the self that would designate a space of pure subjective interiority; on the contrary, the self is "constructed" (or "constituted": *kōsei shitekita*), and this construction in its very sociality brings into play various relations of power. There can thus be no simple conflict between self and society, as has been maintained in traditional sociological discourse, since the self is at its inception already opened up to the social. Yet such a notion of the self as existing in some sense before or outside of the social can be seen to linger in Maruyama's otherwise astute analyses of sociopolitical phenomena. The "free, decision-making agent" whose absence Maruyama condemns in the context of Japanese ultranationalism during the Fifteen-Year War is considered as characteristic of the modern West, in contrast to which Japan in its uniqueness or particularity *(Nihonteki tokushitsu)* must be grasped as strictly premodern, hence producing citizens whose lack of freedom and "sense of subjective responsibility" results in a violent "transfer of oppression." Part of Ehara's critique of Maruyama derives from this difference of situating the self in its sociality.

Ehara's focus on the self in its social constructedness leads her to examine those power relations that, in politically determined contexts, repress certain individuals while privileging certain others. Here it becomes necessary to locate those structures whose presence is so ubiquitous in society as to avoid calling attention to themselves, hence making their effects all the more powerful. The everyday phenomenon of teasing, for example, is revealed by Ehara to contain an extremely intricate system of rules and dynamics that govern the relation between the teaser and the teased. This "logic" of teasing, as it is called, naturalizes the violence that is perpetrated on the teased by ensuring that it is seen as nothing more than a form of play, thus effectively preventing any condemnation of this behavior. Such structural analysis is important when one tries to understand the historical reception of the women's liberation movement in Japan during the 1970s, when women who participated in the movement were openly scorned and ridiculed in the mass media. Because this treatment was cloaked in humor, however, the violence that motivated it came to be obfuscated. In order to first reveal this violence *as* violence, then, Ehara is forced to abstract from the immediate historical circumstances surrounding this denigration of feminism (which were at this point of such an immediacy as to provoke only reactions of denial concerning this violence) and highlight those structural aspects of teasing that function to keep it subordinated. By making explicit those inequalities inherent in the social—or, as she writes elsewhere, that "power contained in social structures themselves, whose workings cannot be reduced to the intentions of specific individuals"[31]—Ehara effectively opens up new possibilities for social relations, especially those relations in which gender and sexuality are most at stake.

The works of Karatani Kōjin, the widely recognized dean of criticism in Japan, have long been influential in generating discussion on such contemporary philosophical notions as those of alterity *(tashasei)*, exteriority *(gaibusei)* and singularity *(tandokusei)*, to name but a few. Karatani brings to his theoretical analyses an unusually broad range of knowledge and interests. So, for example, in his reading of Sōseki here, the opening discussion alone touches upon such otherwise historically diverse figures as Ōoka Shōhei, Masaoka Shiki, Roland Barthes, Northrop Frye, Origuchi Shinobu, Rousseau, Saint Augustine, and Arai Hakuseki.[32] This gesture of summoning an array of writers and thinkers in the course of following the thought of a single figure (which gesture must be described as a characteristic feature of Karatani's writing, and is in no way limited to his texts on Sōseki) is an exciting one, but it would be wrong not to see here an expression of what is in fact a powerful theoretical insight since, for Karatani, focus on *one* thinker is possible only through focus on *others*. No doubt such a reading strategy produces quite dispersive effects at times, and yet these effects are precisely what Karatani aims for in showing the ultimate grounding of all thought in alterity. In other words, this strategy has its roots in—and therefore cannot rigorously be understood outside of—his thinking of the relation between the one and the other, in which the latter must first be traversed in order to arrive at the former, and because of which attention on this one can at any time be disrupted by those elements of which, in a double sense, it is *a-part* (that is, both belonging to and different from itself).

Another feature of Karatani's work that bears emphasis is his inflection of certain terms or concepts for the purpose of bringing the complex relation between philosophy and history more sharply into focus. One example of this can be seen in the notion of *bun*, meaning "writing," through which he comes to approach Sōseki's text. Here Karatani attempts to think this notion in such a way that it functions as a kind of center around which a dialogue is staged between Sōseki, the writer Ōoka Shōhei (author of the 1952 antiwar novel *Nobi* [Fires on the plain]), Roland Barthes, and Jacques Derrida. (Derrida, who is not named in the essay, appears only implicitly, in contrast to these other three writers.) Now on the one hand, *bun* existed in the Meiji period as a literary genre, as Karatani cites Ōoka writing in regard to Sōseki, and this can of course be seen in Masaoka Shiki's distinctive use of *shaseibun*, which Karatani views as a sub-genre of *bun*. On the other hand, however, *bun* reveals itself to be far greater than a specific literary genre that emerged at a specific point in history. Rather it is, as Karatani writes, "that 'degree zero' which contains all possibilities; it is *écriture*, to use Barthes's terms."[33] In this merging of *bun* with *écriture*, a historically delimited literary form is radically opened up so as to signify something like an original site of *possibility (kanōsei)*, from which it then becomes possible to launch a critique of *actuality (genjitsusei)*. And this is precisely what Karatani does in this context, as when he turns his attention now back to the specific historical possibilities that offered themselves during the second decade of the Meiji period. These possibilities were unfortunately never realized, but what is of significance here is the pivot Karatani makes from history (the genre of *bun*) to philosophy (*écriture qua* general possibility) and then back again to history (those specific possibilities available in early Meiji). In this pivot, the meaning of "writing" comes to be considerably transformed so as to refer no longer simply to either Ōoka's *bun* or Barthes's *écriture*, as this latter usage designates primarily the formal conditions established by a writer in relation to his work.[34] Indeed, *bun/écriture qua* possibility must properly be seen as that which newly emerges or takes place as a result of Karatani's putting into relation two otherwise distinct fields, writers and historical contexts. Yet the necessity of this strategy reveals itself in Karatani's critique of modern Japan in its betrayal or perhaps neglect of those possibilities inherent at its inception, possibilities which were subsequently foreclosed by such factors as its modernist ideology, the nation-state system, and the genre of the novel.[35]

The notion of aesthetics undergoes a similar metamorphosis in Karatani's study of the "Overcoming Modernity" symposium, where his reading diverges quite sharply from both Takeuchi Yoshimi's 1959 essay "Kindai no chōkoku" and the philosopher Hiromatsu Wataru's 1989 book *"Kindai no chōkoku" ron*. This notion refers, in various parts of the paper, to Kant, Hegel, Nishida Kitarō, the Marxist philosopher Tosaka Jun, the *burai-ha* writer Sakaguchi Ango, Paul Valéry, and Kobayashi Hideo (this last makes reference during the symposium to what he calls "Bergsonian aesthetics"). Karatani defines aesthetics most clearly as "that which surmounts and unifies actual contradictions at an imaginary level." He continues: "Conversely, 'aesthetics' becomes dominant in those places where it is impossible to actually surmount actual contradictions. This explains why aesthetics never developed in England. . . . On the other hand, German idealism is basically an 'aesthetics'—as is modern Japanese philosophy as well."[36] Karatani is attempting here to show why the participants of the symposium all but avoided any discussion of England or the United States during the proceedings, despite the fact that Japan was then at war with these two countries, and chose instead to focus on the philosophy and literature of Germany and France. He finds his answer in aesthetics, which he defines essentially as an overcoming of contradictions. As with the case of Karatani's use of the Barthesian term *écriture*, however, this definition of aesthetics differs substantially from those of Kant and Hegel, to which he nonetheless makes reference. To further complicate matters, Karatani seems at times to indicate by this notion mere aesthetic objects or activities (as for example when he speaks of those fields of study that tend to draw Japanese students to France, such as literature, philosophy, cooking, and fashion).[37] In point of fact, this difficulty of defining aesthetics can also be seen in both Kant and Hegel, but there the tension revolves most centrally around the two meanings of this word (from the Greek *aisthēsis*, "perception") as, on the one hand, the study of perception or sensibility and, on the other, the study of art or beauty. Karatani avoids this ambiguity by lifting the term from this debate and making it function primarily in relation to the notion of contradiction. The merits of this move can be debated, but the political intent is admirable, as Karatani seeks to demonstrate that the symposium's "overcoming of modernity" was purely imaginary in its failure to resolve the actual contradictions at hand.

Like Karatani, Naoki Sakai writes very much *across* the disciplinary borders of history, philosophy, and literature, as well as across the geopolitical borders of Japan and the United States. Much of Sakai's work can be described on the basis of a question rhetorically posed by the philosopher Philippe Lacoue-Labarthe, "Why would the problem of identification not be, in general, the essential problem of the political?"[38] This attention to the problem of identification functions in Sakai's thought as nothing less than a kind of ethical imperative, which can be formulated in its most basic terms as follows: Act in such a way as to resist the desire for identification. Now the difficulty that immediately becomes apparent here is that, as Nietzsche famously remarked of Kant's categorical imperative, such a command "smells of cruelty."[39] This cruelty lies in the fact that one must resist not merely such external mechanisms of identification as, for example, the State and its various institutions, but rather, precisely because such institutions have already become remarked or internalized by the subject in its interiority, one must learn to resist *one's own* desire for identification. While there is in this rejection of subjective desire a certain ascetic quality, one must nevertheless be careful not to explain this quality in terms of the—admittedly dense—theoretical nature of Sakai's work. (In Japan as well as in the United States, Sakai's works have often been accused of being excessively theoretical, thereby provoking both misunderstanding and antipathy). On the contrary, following the classical philosophical distinction between *theōria*, *praxis*, and *poiēsis*, this work reveals itself to be concerned most fundamentally with acting, or *praxis*, rather than with theory. (In the context of the essay included below, moreover, it is the notion of *poiēsis*, or "making, producing," that receives the greatest attention). Nowhere is this resistance against identification manifested more palpably than in the critique of national or cultural identification, which provides in turn the groundwork for the comparative analysis of what Sakai calls "imperial nationalism" undertaken here.

Explication of the process of identification requires a combination of broad historical knowledge and acute psychological insight, given that the subjective desire for national or cultural identity is produced above all objectively, meaning in this instance as a result of the convergence of certain historical forces that exist outside the self. If these forces first produce the subjective desire for identification, however, they nevertheless require the subject's *response* to them, in which the subject comes now to confirm or claim this desire as his own, and acts according to it. Sakai sketches out the various forms that this response generally takes, and discovers at their core the presence of a binary logic that determines identification strictly along the coordinates of "the negation-affirmation axis," as he writes.[40] So for example, in his reading of John Okada's 1957 novel *No-No Boy*, Sakai locates the desire on the part of the Japanese-American minority subject to *either* embrace his sense of belonging to the United States through self-identification as an American citizen, despite the very real racial discrimination and inequality he encounters there, *or* to reject such self-identification because of those injustices and instead identify himself as Japanese. In both cases, however, the negation of identification with one national culture takes place only the better to effect an affirmation with the other, as this other national culture is seen as the symmetrical opposite of the first. Precisely the same phenomenon can be seen in wartime Japan with respect to those Taiwanese colonials who were violently submitted to the integrationist policies *(kōminka seisaku)* of the imperial nation, which demanded that they identify themselves as Japanese despite their clearly inferior social status.[41] As Sakai shows in his examination of several Japanese-language literary texts produced in Taiwan during that period, certain Taiwanese identified themselves with the colonized (thereby falling into the trap of the modernization = civilization paradigm) while others, in their otherwise politically important gesture of resisting Japanese colonial violence, nevertheless grounded this resistance on their sense of native Taiwanese identity (thereby falling into the converse—and hence complicitous—trap of *minzokushugi*, or ethnic-nationalism). Sakai's reading of these works is guided throughout by an interest in undermining these complementary desires for identification, which are based equally in narcissism, so as to open up a kind of "cruel" (because ethical) form of relationality that takes place beyond any transference and sense of belonging.

One final, related point: Sakai would surely describe the emergence of Japanese nationalism, and particularly that of its past imperial nationalism, in much the same way that certain contemporary philosophers have described German nationalism, "as the long history of the *appropriation of means of identification*."[42] (And the opening part of his paper here represents an attack against this same mechanism of appropriation within American nationalism, particularly that of its current imperial nationalism). Significantly, however, Sakai chooses to problematize the identificatory processes utilized by or rather inherent in imperial nationalism by focusing on what he calls "subjective technology" (*shutaiteki gijutsu*). This notion, which refers back to Nishida's reading of Aristotle and the problem of *technē*, is briefly defined elsewhere as the process "whereby the subject *(shutai)* constitutes and manufactures itself," in contrast to the more widespread meaning of technology, in which the subject *(shukan)* creates or works on an object that exists simply outside itself, thereby not resulting in the subject's own self-production.[43] What must be emphasized here is, first, the close relationship between the notions of *technē* and *poiēsis*, given that they both refer to a making or manufacturing of the subject; and, second, the extremely valuable insight into everyday sociopolitical processes that this understanding of subjective manufacturing affords Sakai. (It is the latter that represents Sakai's very marked political departure from Nishida, despite the clear debt to his thought). For if imperial nationalism—in the context of either Japan or the United States—establishes certain technologies through which to effectively produce national subjects, then a rigorous understanding of this process might help us better resist it.

It is highly instructive to read the works of the philosopher Takahashi Tetsuya alongside those of Sakai, for while they are both among the foremost practitioners of deconstruction in Japanese criticism, their approaches nevertheless differ considerably from one another. As the author of one of the leading books on Derrida in Japan, Takahashi's relation to deconstruction is perhaps the more clearly delineated.[44] At any rate, the two essays included in this volume are noteworthy in providing us a glimpse into the dynamics of intellectual debate taking place in Japan today. These essays may be said to form a set in that, despite the fact that they were originally published separately, they are both essentially critiques of the literary critic Katō Norihiro with respect to the problem of nationalism.[45] What may perhaps seem surprising here is Takahashi's particular manner of critique, for the logical rigor with which he reads Katō presents itself hand in hand with an emphasis on the importance of *content*. In philosophy, generally speaking, an appeal to logic is associated with a denigration or at least deprivileging of the role of content, and with this of course a corresponding stress on the notion of *form*, and yet in Takahashi precisely the reverse can be seen. How can we explain this unexpected turn of events? One way to do so would be to detect in Takahashi's thought a certain kind of logic that remains yet intimately bound up with the worldliness or empiricity indicated by the term "content" *(naiyō)*. The complex nature of this binding is such as to allow Takahashi to condemn Katō's argument for its excessive formalism without, however, thereby falling into the trap of historicism, i.e., the reduction of things (phenomena, concepts, etc.) to determined empirico-historical events. When, for example, Takahashi, in quoting Katō, remarks that "while such statements may appear to be 'correct' in a formalistic sense *(keishikiron toshite)*, they are not at all self-evident when seen in the context of concrete historical situations," he is *not*, let us emphasize, merely privileging content over form, the concrete over the abstract, and history over the transcendental.[46] If these first terms may be said to occupy pride of place in Takahashi's thought, they do so only by virtue of their *relation to* those second terms to which they are otherwise opposed. For in truth Takahashi's critique could be easily recuperated were it to do no more than simply counter Katō's formalism — which notion is also expressed in the language of these essays by such terms as "fundamentalism" *(genrishugi)* and "pure" *(junsui)* — with an appeal to the concreteness of historical situations. (Let us mention in passing here that while such critiques are not infrequently made against philosophy on the part of historians, they remain very much indebted to an underlying, and unexamined, empiricism). This explains why Takahashi attempts to situate his discourse *both* prior *and* posterior to that of Katō: it is prior in the sense that it formulates certain concepts whose universality or generality is able to take into account Katō's formalism, and yet it is also posterior in that it focuses on those singular historical circumstances which Katō neglects. However, this double move that Takahashi takes reveals itself to be in fact one and the same move, since he is primarily concerned to show how the "Japanese 'national subject' as closed community" *(tojirareta . . . kyōdōtai toshite Nihon no 'kokumin shutai')* that Katō wishes to construct is from the beginning already opened up to its other.[47] It is this opening that, taking place originally prior to the formation of this community as such, in a sense foretells the event of those *in*cursions or *in*fringements from which it will actually come to suffer. The concepts that Takahashi employs to demonstrate this exposure of the community to its otherwise excluded outside include that of originary impurity (or "impurity of origins," *shutsuji no fujunsa*), the trace of the other *(tasha no konseki)*, responsibility (which is glossed elsewhere more fully and more literally as *ōtō kanōsei toshite no sekinin*),[48] and democracy to come *(kitaru beki minshushugi)*.

While this is obviously not the place to examine these concepts in depth, we can nevertheless make several brief remarks regarding Takahashi's charge of nationalism against Katō. As with many of the best critics of nationalism, Takahashi follows Heidegger's statement in his 1947 "Letter on Humanism" that nationalism is to be understood most properly as subjectivism.[49] The national subject that Katō aims to construct, according to Takahashi's reading, is one necessarily based on unity, internal homogeneity, and self-representation. This unity can be seen primarily negatively, as Katō mourns its loss in the postwar period in the form of what he refers to as the nation's "personality split." Takahashi rightly discerns in such language a nostalgic desire to repair this split, thereby allowing Japan to recover its putatively original oneness and state of normalcy. Although Katō's desire here takes shape in order to offer a unified apology to Japan's war victims in Asia, Takahashi argues that it is this very national unity that lies at the root of the problem of nationalism. Hence Katō's proposal of a unified national apology would represent something like a "rational nationalism" as distinct from the wartime "irrational nationalism," as Takahashi critically cites the political analyst Alain Minc saying in regard to the difference between French and German nationalism. For Takahashi, such distinctions are merely cosmetic, for they leave entirely in place the violent structure of nationalism itself. The issues of internal homogeneity and national self-representation come together in Takahashi's view in what he calls "the politics of national symbols," meaning here the *Hinomaru* national flag and *Kimigayo* national anthem.[50] Responding to Katō's rejection of this anthem because it does not emotionally resonate with many Japanese citizens, Takahashi points out that it is precisely in such emotional identification that national homogeneity comes to be created. Even if such identification is effected in the name of apologizing to Japan's Asian war victims, it invariably excludes this Asian other in the process of nation formation and thus remains violent at its core.

Addressing this same issue of Japan's national flag and anthem, the scholar of modern French literature and thought Ukai Satoshi argues that the attack against the *Kimigayo* as based on its relative estrangement from the lives of most Japanese people harbors within it, in fact, a desire for national identification that is necessarily of a piece with fascism: "When we seek a point of contact with the masses as based on a sense of unease with the *Kimigayo*, we become absorbed by the [oppositional] movement's unwitting progressivism. We thus succumb to the temptation of overcoming the situation at the mountain's lowest point, to use an old-fashioned expression. [Walter] Benjamin would certainly see here an opening for fascism."[51] Ukai is in this context concerned to show some of the faults that have unfortunately dogged the opposition in its protest against the passage of the National Flag and Anthem Law *(kokki kokka hō)* in the summer of 1999. To this end he reads Benjamin alongside the poet and writer Tanigawa Gan so as to arrive at a more rigorous thinking of *teikō*, or "resistance," one that remains sensitive to the theoretical trap inherent in the notion of opposition, to which perhaps resistance always remains vulnerable. For the oppositional stance enacts its reversal strictly by accepting the terms upon which the debate takes place, hence blinding itself both to the deeply problematic nature of these terms themselves and to the manner in which the opposed and opposing sides remain entirely controlled by them. In for example the debate around the Japanese national flag and anthem, opposition comes to be articulated on the basis of a progressivist ideology that shares much in common with the logic of nationalism, with the result that the sense of Japanese national identity becomes, ironically enough, strengthened by that opposition. Although clearly sympathetic to such movements in their struggle against conservative forces, Ukai nevertheless seeks to expose and interrogate those otherwise hidden theoretical grounds that all too often condemn political and social opposition elements to replicate that violence which they wish to prevent. In this work, an internal questioning of the notion of opposition is commenced, through which Ukai extends to his readers something like an "invitation to resistance."[52]

This important difference between the notions of opposition and resistance can be seen to inform Ukai's thinking of what he calls the "two-in-one" (meaning: necessarily interrelated) problems of colonialism and modernity. He develops this thinking through an ambitious examination of the writings of Takeuchi Yoshimi, the Chinese writer Lu Xun, Frantz Fanon, and Derrida, interweaving these very disparate texts together against the shared background of Hegel's dialectic of the master-slave relation. Both Takeuchi (aided by his reading of Lu Xun) and Fanon conceive of the phenomenon of colonialism in terms of the master-slave dialectic, which is in turn mapped onto the geopolitical relation between the West ("Europe") and the non-West. Ukai provides a generous interpretation of these two writers in their efforts to set forth resistance against European colonization, and yet ultimately he rejects this dialectic between the master and the slave as too limiting in its binarity, since "questions of colonialism and modernity, as well as questions concerning the essence of Europe, must necessarily disrupt the thought that depends on this master/slave dichotomy *(nibunhō)*."[53] It is highly significant that the rejection of this dialectic does not simply originate in Ukai's own "subjective" decision. On the contrary, the reading of Takeuchi and Fanon that he undertakes here remains guided throughout by these "objects" of his inquiry, who precisely for this reason (i.e., the fact that objects in their alterity *precede* the fixed division between subject and object necessary for all scholarly inquiry) are both more than and less than objects. Hence the texts of Takeuchi and Fanon give themselves to be read in such a way that the participation in a certain traditional dialectics comes to the fore while, at the same time, these texts offer themselves up to be read otherwise, now resisting that dialectical interplay of opposites within which they seem to be caught up. Must we stress that it is this very reading strategy that Ukai adopts which powerfully bears upon the question of colonialism that lies at the heart of this essay? For the opposition against colonialism generally takes as its theoretical departure point the opposition between the West (Europe) and the non-West, because of which resistance comes to be reduced to nothing more than the stance adopted by this latter entity against the former. To this, however, Ukai asks if the notion of resistance might not be more originary, or general, than that of the opposition which underlies the distinction between these two entities. If so—and clearly this is what Ukai believes—then it becomes no longer possible to speak simply of these oppositional entities as such, and this in turn calls for an entire rethinking of the phenomenon of colonialism. As Ukai writes, with reference to Derrida and, further back, to Lu Xun: "Colonialism does not begin between Europe and its outside. It has always already begun (and is moreover not finished) in the 'inside' of Europe's geographical boundaries and in the midst of its history. Europe itself is in a sense a colony, and this is why colonialism constitutes its essence."[54]

Nishitani Osamu, who, like Ukai, is also a scholar of modern French literature and thought, turns his attention in the essay "'Fushi' no wandārando" [The wonderland of "immortality"] to the complex relation between human subjectivity and death in the light of recent advances in medical technology. This essay represents an attempt to open up a dialogue with Heidegger (specifically the early Heidegger, for whom the thinking of death appears most urgent), to whom any thinking of subjectivity and death is of course enormously indebted. In this regard, the following passage from *Being and Time* will perhaps help us better understand the general thrust of Nishitani's reading:

> Death does not just "belong" to one's own Dasein in an undifferentiated way; death *lays claim* to it as an *individual* Dasein. The non-relational character of death, as understood in anticipation, individualizes Dasein down to itself. This individualizing is a way in which the "there" is disclosed for existence. It makes manifest that all Being-alongside the things

with which we concern ourselves, and all Being-with Others, will fail us when our ownmost potentiality-for-Being is the issue.[55]

The relevance of these lines for Nishitani's dialogue with Heidegger lies in the notion of individuality and corresponding neglect of the question of the other that marks, in a certain sense, Heidegger's thinking of death. That I must die alone since no one can possibly die in my place establishes, for Heidegger, the importance of individuality in the context of death. It is in this context that the individual Dasein can break free from its subjection to the "they" (*das Man*) of everyday existence and finally recover its self in its "ownmost potentiality-for-Being," as he writes. Thus the opening of Being that takes place through an authentic "anticipation" of the possibility of one's own death not only offers itself to the individual Dasein; it is indeed that which individualizes Dasein in the first place.

Now Nishitani takes extremely seriously this role of death in bringing Dasein forth in all the fullness of its individuality. His response to Heidegger, to whom he is at once respectful and critical (and this attitude, let us quickly note, differs sharply from that found in other areas of the Japan Studies field, where the attack against Heidegger's "politics" takes place with only the most cursory understanding of his thought), is to confront the conceptual dyad of death and individuality with that of immortality *(fushi)* and communality *(kyōdōsei)*, as effected by what Nishitani calls, in an unusual phrase, "compositing" *(fuku-gōka*: literally, the making composite or compound). Here Nishitani refers to the technology of organ transplantation, which appears to decisively break up the individual's integrity or wholeness—that is to say, its status as *unit*—by introducing others' organs or bodily parts within the otherwise proper space of the physical self. In this instance, death would no longer belong to me; or rather, it would be mine now only insofar as I exist as constituted by others. As Nishitani writes, "The exchangeability *(kōkan kanōsei)* of parts renders individuality *(kotaisei)* itself composite, thus changing the meaning of the event of 'death,' which completes the individual as absolute unit *(zettaiteki tani)*. In the world of the individual as exchangeable composite, even death comes to be cheated in the formation of new composites. Death occurs only with the individual, but this individual is now variable and recombinable."[56] In response to this point, it is conceivable that Heidegger would argue that Nishitani forces the discussion of death into a narrow biological-empirical interpretation, for what is at stake in *Being and Time* is *not* the event of physical death itself but rather, crucially, the attitude of anticipation one adopts vis-à-vis the *possibility of death*, that is to say, the possibility of the very impossibility of existence for Dasein. Furthermore, Heidegger might protest that it is precisely in the anticipation of death *qua* possibility that one is able to free oneself from the hold of the "they" of everyday existence and recover that being with others that is essentially part of Dasein. In which case, anticipation in its individualization of Dasein would paradoxically also be that which most opens it up to Being in its fundamental alterity; that is to say, this strange "individuality" of Dasein is one in which it would be in fact *least* individual because *most* fully ex-posed to the presence of the other.[57]

Yet it is important to emphasize that Nishitani is not merely attempting here to use contemporary medical technology as the means by which to refute Heidegger's thinking about death, despite his claim that the latter "was in a sense blind to modern 'death.'"[58] On the contrary, for Nishitani the emergence of this technology forces us to recognize that the subject can never be proper *(koyū)* to itself, that even when confronted with the possibility of its own death, it remains strictly anonymous *(mumei)* and impersonal *(hininshōteki, hijinkakuteki)*, nothing more than "scattered and dispersed existence," as he puts it.[59] And this is why Nishitani seems to privilege the example of cellular reproduction, in which an organism divides to become two in what is simultaneously an event of birth and death. As he points out, it is senseless here to assign death to a single identity, since this latter is itself the product of the births and deaths of countless other single-celled organisms. The technology of organ transplantation appears to follow more or less this same principle, which might be called something like "originary multiplicity" in that the individual unit is revealed to contain within itself traces of the other. (In this respect, it is surely no accident that Nishitani makes several references throughout the essay to *saen*, or *différance*). What must be understood here, however, is that for Nishitani the significance of transplant technology lies at its basis in *movement* (i.e., the "trans-" of transplant, the *i* or *utsuru* of *ishoku*). It is this notion of movement, which he conceives both here and elsewhere in both a philosophical and a historical sense,[60] that accounts for the fact that the subject is necessarily a composite or compound *(fukugō)*. Hence, *contra* Heidegger (or rather a certain reading of Heidegger), even prior to the individualizing moment that man comes to authentically anticipate the possibility of his own death, he is already exposed to the alterity of others in such a way that his subsequent individuality will always be compromised or haunted by them. Or rather, since, to be fair, Heidegger is foremost a thinker of movement, the anticipation with which authentic Dasein moves outside or ahead of itself to its own death is reexamined by Nishitani on the basis of another kind of movement, one that is coeval with this one but which is less "vertical" than "horizontal" since the inexorable movement to my own death is always shared or divided by those others with whom I am in relation, and who indeed partially die *with* me and I *with* them. In this sense, Nishitani performs an invaluable service for us in beginning to draw out the infinite implications of the *with*.

Notes

1. Hiromatsu Wataru et al., eds., *Tetsugaku shisō jiten* (Tokyo: Iwanami Shoten, 1998), pp. 1200–1201.

2. In *Natsume Sōseki zenshū* (Tokyo: Iwanami Shoten, 1995), vol. 16, pp. 416–417; trans. Jay Rubin, *Kokoro: A Novel and Selected Essays* (Lanham, Md: Madison Books, 1992), pp. 258–259.

3. Nishida Kitarō, *An Inquiry into the Good*, trans. Masao Abe and Christopher Ives (New Haven: Yale University Press, 1990), p. viii.

4. Martin Heidegger, *Identity and Difference*, trans. Joan Stambaugh (New York: Harper & Row, 1969), pp. 28 ff.

5. Karatani Kōjin, whose work on Sōseki is represented in this volume, has long been instrumental in analyzing the conceptual density inherent in his texts. Many of these essays appear in the collection *Sōseki ron shūsei* (Tokyo: Daisan Bunmeisha, 2001). One might also refer here to the important readings undertaken by the literary critic and theorist Komori Yōichi, as, for example, his *Sōseki wo yominaosu* (Tokyo: Chikuma Shobō, 1995) and *Seikimatsu no yogensha: Natsume Sōseki* (Tokyo: Kōdansha, 1999).

6. This engagement with Heidegger can be seen in several of the thinkers presented here, most immediately in the works of Nishitani Osamu: *Fushi no wandārando: sensō no seiki wo koete* (Tokyo: Kōdansha Gakujutsu Bunko, 1996); Naoki Sakai: *Translation and Subjectivity: On "Japan" and Cultural Nationalism* (Minneapolis: University of Minnesota Press, 1997); Takahashi Tetsuya—*Gyakkō no rogosu: gendai tetsugaku no kontekusuto* (Tokyo: Miraisha, 1992), esp. pp. 75–108; and Karatani Kōjin: *Kotoba to higeki* (Tokyo: Kōdansha Gakujutsu Bunko, 2001), esp. pp. 327–352.

   It bears emphasizing that the approaches and strategies that constitute these engagements with Heidegger are entirely dissimilar from one another, and indeed have on occasion functioned as the site of active criticism and debate between these thinkers. For this reason there can be no such thing as the "Japanese" reception or understanding of Heidegger, despite the prevalence of such phrases in Japanese philosophical and intellectual historical scholarship.

7. In *Ro Jin nyūmon* (1953), as collected in *Takeuchi Yoshimi zenshū* (Tokyo: Chikuma Shobō, 1980), vol. 2, p. 39. These notions can be traced back equally to Nishida Kitarō and to the Chinese writer Lu Xun, whose writings Takeuchi assiduously worked to introduce in Japan.

   I elaborate this reading of Takeuchi in *Takeuchi Yoshimi: Displacing the West* (Ithaca: Cornell East Asia Series, 2004).

8. Jean-Luc Nancy, "Le soi-disant peuple," in *Traces: A Multilingual Journal of Cultural Theory*, vol. 4. (I would like to thank Jon Solomon for introducing me to this text.)

   In this connection, it might be apposite to call attention to the fact that Nishi-

tani Osamu is also known in Japan as the translator of Nancy's influential work
The Inoperative Community, trans. *Mui no kyōdōtai: tetsugaku wo toinaosu bunyū
no shikō* (Tokyo: Ibunsha, 2001).

9. No doubt there will be readers who accuse us of overinterpreting Sōseki on this
point, as if these distinctions he is making derive more from our own reading
than from the Sōseki text "itself." In support of our reading, then, let us refer to
Sōseki himself. As he writes in the essay "Bungei no tetsugakuteki kiso" (1907),
"In the first place, I am standing here and you are all sitting there. I am standing
in a low place and you are all sitting in a high place. That I am standing and you
are sitting represents a fact. If we were to express this fact differently, we could say
that I am a 'self' (*watakushi wa ware toiu mono*) and you are my 'exterior'
(*watakushi ni taishite watakushi igai no mono to iu*). Using a more difficult
expression, this fact is one of 'self-object opposition' (*butsuga tairitsu*). That is to
say, the world comes into being on the basis of the dual or relative relation (*sōtai
no kankei*) between self and object." (In *Natsume Sōseki zenshū*, vol. 16, pp.
67–68). On the basis of these lines, written four years earlier than the "Gendai
Nihon no kaika" essay we are following here, it should be evident just how much
is at stake in Sōseki's otherwise unremarkable gesture of distinguishing himself
from his audience.

10. Hence it is necessary to make a transition from the notion of natural identity to
that of enunciative positionality (*hatsuwa no tachiba*) since, as Naoki Sakai points
out in his essay "The Problem of 'Japanese Thought': The Formation of 'Japan'
and the Schema of Cofiguration," "'Japanese' is not a natural attribute to an individual but an identity constituted relationally within a specific discourse in each
instance." In *Translation and Subjectivity*, p. 47.

11. Let us take the occasion to note here that phenomenology has historically in
Japan maintained very open relations with the various discourses of the human
sciences, thus producing works in which empirical research manages to avoid the
pitfalls of naturalism by allowing itself to be shaped by the insight into the intentional nature of consciousness. One example of such work would be Ehara
Yumiko's early text on the sociology of the life-world (*Lebenswelt*), *Seikatsu sekai
no shakaigaku* (Tokyo: Keisō Shobō, 1985). In a more explicitly philosophical context, Takahashi Tetsuya examines the work of Husserl in his discussion of the relation between history, violence, and reason in *Gyakkō no rogosu*, pp. 16–74. Kang
Sangjung also refers to Husserl and the phenomenological critique of naturalism
and historicism in his work on Max Weber, *Max Weber to kindai* (Tokyo: Ochan-
omizu Shobō, 1986), pp. 147–181.

In the field of literature, Kamei Hideo has provided a phenomenological
analysis of Meiji-period texts in his *Transformations of Sensibility: The Phenomenology of Meiji Literature*, trans. Michael Bourdaghs et al. (Ann Arbor: University
of Michigan Center for Japanese Studies, 2002).

12. *Takeuchi Yoshimi zenshū*, vol. 4, p. 145; italics ours. This essay is discussed by
Ukai Satoshi in his "Colonialism and Modernity" paper included in this collec-

tion. Significantly enough, it is also taken up elsewhere in a very similar context by both Kang Sangjung, in "Datsu orientarizumu no shikō," in *Orientarizumu no kanata he* (Tokyo: Iwanami Shoten, 1996), pp. 198–200, and Sakai, in "Modernity and its Critique: The Problem of Universalism and Particularism," in *Translation and Subjectivity*, pp. 170–176).

13. In *Kindai no chōkoku* (Tokyo: Fuzanbō Hyakka Bunko, 1999), pp. 247–248. These lines are also cited and discussed by Karatani in his "Overcoming Modernity" paper below.

   For English-language accounts of the "Overcoming Modernity" symposium, see Harry Harootunian, *Overcome by Modernity: History, Culture, and Community in Interwar Japan* (Princeton: Princeton University Press, 2000), pp. 34–94; and Minamoto Ryōen's essay "The Symposium on 'Overcoming Modernity'" in *Rude Awakenings: Zen, the Kyoto School, and the Question of Nationalism*, ed. James W. Heisig and John C. Maraldo (Honolulu: University of Hawaii Press, 1995), pp. 197–229.

   Kobayashi Hideo's writings on literature have been made available in translation in Paul Anderer, *Literature of the Lost Home: Kobayashi Hideo — Literary Criticism 1924–1939* (Stanford: Stanford University Press, 1995).

14. This figure "lives in dread of besmirching the splendour of its inner being by action and an existence; and, in order to preserve the purity of its heart, it flees from contact with the actual world, and persists in its self-willed impotence to renounce its self which is reduced to the extreme of ultimate abstraction." G. W. F. Hegel, *Phenomenology of Spirit*, trans. A. V. Miller (Oxford: Oxford University Press, 1977), p. 400.

15. In *Kobayashi Hideo zenshū* (Tokyo: Shinchōsha, 2001), vol. 14, pp. 25–523.

16. Ueno Chizuko discusses Motoori's notions of *yamatogokoro* and *karagokoro* in her essay "In the Feminine Guise: A Trap of Reverse Orientalism," as included below.

17. *Kindai no chōkoku*, pp. 248–249.

18. Or what Etienne Balibar has called "fictive ethnicity," in *Race, Nation, Class: Ambiguous Identities* (London: Verso, 1992), p. 10.

19. Ishiguro was born in Japan in 1954 but has lived in England since age five. In the course of a revealing dialogue between Ishiguro and the novelist Ōe Kenzaburō held in Japan in 1989, Ōe remarks upon Ishiguro's qualities as a representative *English* (as opposed to Japanese) writer as based upon a very problematic notion of national character: "When your books first began to appear in Japan, that was how they were introduced [as peaceful and gentle, like Japanese art]. You were described as a very quiet and peaceful author, and, therefore, a very Japanese author. But from the first I doubted that. I felt that this was an author with a tough intelligence. . . . I also felt that this kind of strength was not very Japanese, that this person was, rather, from England." "The Novelist in Today's World: A Conversation," in *Japan in the World*, ed. Masao Miyoshi and H. D. Harootunian (Durham: Duke University Press, 1993), pp. 168–169.

It is unfortunate that Ōe, despite his great importance as a writer, fails to understand that a plurality of possible national identities available to an individual does not necessitate choosing one true identity from among them. On the contrary, this very plurality points to the original absence of such identity. What is more, this absence of identity opens up in turn the possibility of identification, but the necessary consequence of this transition from identity to identification means that the latter is now radically contingent.

20. Kang Sangjung, " 'Tōyō' no hakken to orientarizumu," in *Orientarizumu no kanata he*, p. 136. And again, several pages later: "The well-known term 'Orient' (or Asia) came to be defined as a geopolitical order due to the Japanese colonial empire's invasion following the first Sino-Japanese War. Prior to this invasion, there existed no fixed geopolitical-cultural space in the region, thereby rendering any sense of Asian unity impossible" (p. 146).

21. "Kokumin no shinshō chiri to datsu-kokuminteki katari," in *Nashonaru hisutorī wo koete*, ed. Komori Yōichi and Takahashi Tetsuya (Tokyo: Tokyo Daigaku Shuppankai, 1998), pp. 150 and 154.

22. *Nashonaru hisutoī wo koete*, p. 145, and *Orientarizumu no kanata he*, p. 143, respectively.

23 *Orientarizumu no kanata he*, p. 123. This logic of "deviation," which grounds difference upon identity so as to negate or neutralize its otherwise dispersive effects, is also worked out by Takahashi Tetsuya in the course of his critique of Katō Norihiro, in *Sengo sekinin ron* (Tokyo: Kōdansha, 1999), pp. 132–133 (included below).

   For an exchange of views between Kang and Takahashi regarding such topics as nationalism, civilization, and barbarism, see *Shikō wo hiraku* (Tokyo: Iwanami Shoten, 2002), esp. pp. 3–50.

24. *Nashonaru hisutorī wo koete*, p. 149.

25. "In the Feminine Guise: A Trap of Reverse Orientalism," in *U.S.-Japan Women's Journal*, English supplement no. 13, 1997, p. 3.

26. "Collapse of 'Japanese Mothers,' " in *U.S.-Japan Women's Journal*, English supplement no. 10, 1996, p. 5. Italics ours.

27. Ayako Kano, *Acting Like a Woman in Modern Japan* (New York: Palgrave, 2001). As Kano (whose work is cited by Ueno in a note to "In the Feminine Guise") writes, "Acting like a woman does not come naturally. It has to be taught, learned, rehearsed, and repeated. It does not arise from a moment of inspiration, but from many years of persistent inculcation. In an acting woman, the cultural and social desires of an age are concentrated, molding her every gesture, every glance" (p. 3).

28. Ueno Chizuko, *Kōzōshugi no bōken* (Tokyo: Keisō Shobō, 1985). Regarding this privileging of one term over another in the binary relation, Ueno aptly points out that it is the privileged term that actually sets forth the deprivileged term "as its residual category." In "Collapse of 'Japanese Mothers,' " p. 11.

29. "In the Feminine Guise," p. 10.

30. "Feminizumu kara mita Maruyama Masao no kindai," in *Feminizumu no paradokkusu: teichaku ni yoru kakusan* (Tokyo: Keisō Shobō, 2000), p. 100.

31. *Feminizumu to kenryoku sayō* (Tokyo: Keisō Shobō, 1988), p. 32.
32. "Sōseki no tayōsei: 'Kokoro' wo megutte," in *Kotoba to higeki*, pp. 40–42.
33. Ibid., p. 41. For a more extended treatment of this notion of *bun* in regard to Sōseki's works, see Karatani's *Sōseki ron shūsei*, pp. 233–260 and 357–361.
34. As Barthes writes, "[W]riting is thus essentially the morality of form, the choice of that social area within which the writer elects to situate the Nature of his language." *Writing Degree Zero*, trans. Annette Lavers and Colin Smith (New York: The Noonday Press, 1967), p. 15.

    The Barthesian notion of *écriture* has been examined by Jonathan Culler as follows: "As opposed to his language, which an author inherits, and his style, which Barthes defines as a personal and subconscious network of verbal obsessions, an *écriture* or mode of writing is something an author adopts: a function he gives his language, a set of institutional conventions within which the activity of writing can take place." *Structuralist Poetics: Structuralism, Linguistics and the Study of Literature* (Ithaca: Cornell University Press, 1975), p. 134.
35. Let us point out here the massive importance of this notion of possibility in Karatani's thought, as can be seen for example in *Tankyū II* (Tokyo: Kōdansha Gakujutsu Bunko, 2001), pp. 52–67; in "Ango sono kanōsei no chūshin," in *Kotoba to higeki* (Tokyo: Kōdansha Gakujutsu Bunko, 2001), pp. 399–420; and in *Marukusu sono kanōsei no chūshin* (Tokyo: Kōdansha, 1978).
36. "Kindai no chōkoku," in *"Senzen" no shikō* (Tokyo: Kōdansha Gakujutsu Bunko, 2001), pp. 121–122.
37. Ibid., p. 108.
38. "Transcendence Ends in Politics," in *Typography: Mimesis, Philosophy, Politics*, ed. Christopher Fynsk (Cambridge: Harvard University Press, 1989), p. 300. (Let us note that Sakai himself refers to this important work several times in *Translation and Subjectivity*).
39. Friedrich Nietzsche, *On the Genealogy of Morals*, trans. Walter Kaufmann and R. J. Hollingdale (New York: Vintage Books, 1989), p. 65.
40. "Two Negations: The Fear of Being Excluded and the Logic of Self-Esteem," p. 42 (previously unpublished manuscript).
41. For a recent example of English-language scholarship on this issue, see Leo Ching's *Becoming "Japanese": Colonial Taiwan and the Politics of Identity Formation* (Berkeley: University of California Press, 2001).
42. Philippe Lacoue-Labarthe and Jean-Luc Nancy, *Le mythe Nazi* (La Tour d'Aigues: Éditions de l'Aube, 1998), p. 39. Emphasis in the original. We cite Nancy here at least partly to emphasize how important his thought, and particularly the notions of community, identification, and exposure so central to it, has been for Sakai's own thinking. It is regrettable, let us add parenthetically, that the works of Lacoue-Labarthe and Nancy have remained largely unread in the Japan Studies field, given the considerable implications of their thought for much cultural studies research being done today.
43. *Translation and Subjectivity*, p. 24.

44. *Derida: datsukōchiku* (Tokyo: Kōdansha, 1998). In addition, Takahashi has translated (with Ukai Satoshi) Derrida's 1991 text *L'autre cap* as *Ta no misaki: Yōroppa to minshushugi* (Tokyo: Misuzu Shobō, 1993) as well as the 1977 "Limited Inc a b c . . . " as *Yūgen sekinin kaisha* (Tokyo: Hōsei Daigaku Shuppankyoku, 2003).
45. Katō's works are not especially well known in the United States. Harry Harootunian refers to his 1985 text *Amerika no kage* in "America's Japan/Japan's Japan" (*Japan in the World*, p. 199); Norma Field also refers to this text in "*Somehow*: The Postmodern as Atmosphere" (*Postmodernism and Japan*, ed. Masao Miyoshi and H. D. Harootunian (Durham: Duke University Press, 1997), pp. 170–171).
46. "Nihon no neonashonarizumu 2: Katō Norihiro shi 'Haisengo ron' wo hihan suru," in *Sengo sekinin ron*, p. 136.
47. Ibid., p. 151.
48. "'Sengo sekinin' saikō," in Ibid., pp. 23–30. See on this notion of responsibility also the dialogue between Takahashi and the writer Suh Kyungsik in *Danzetsu no seiki shōgen no jidai: sensō no kioku wo meguru taiwa* (Tokyo: Iwanami Shoten, 2001), pp. 90–148.
49. Martin Heidegger, *Basic Writings*, ed. David Farrell Krell (New York: Harper & Row, 1977), p. 221. As Heidegger (who would of course fall subject to his own critique here) writes, "Every nationalism is metaphysically an anthropologism, and as such subjectivism. Nationalism is not overcome by mere internationalism; it is rather expanded and elevated thereby into a system."
     Takahashi discusses the problem of Heidegger's nationalism (alongside the nationalism of the philosopher Watsuji Tetsurō, who was strongly influenced by Heidegger) in "Kaiki no hō to kyōdōtai: sonzai he no toi to rinrigaku no aida," in *Gyakkō no rogosu*, pp. 75–108.
50. "Hinomaru-kimigayo kara shōchō tennōsei he," in *Sengo sekinin ron*, p. 251.
51. "Hata no kanata no kaisō: naze Hinomaru wa 'omedetai' no ka," in *Impaction* (March 2000), no. 118, pp. 30–31.
52. *Teikō he no shōtai* (Tokyo: Misuzu Shobō, 1997). In this collection of writings, Ukai attempts to forge a thinking of resistance through a reading of a wide range of topics as well as of such authors as Jean Genet, Edward Said, Derrida, and Kant.
53. "Koroniarizumu to modaniti," in *Tenkanki no bungaku*, ed. Mishima Kenichi and Kinoshita Yasumitsu (Tokyo: Minerva Shobō, 1999), p. 210.
54. Ibid., p. 223.
55. Martin Heidegger, *Being and Time*, trans. John Macquarrie and Edward Robinson (New York: Harper & Row, 1962), p. 308. Italics in the original.
56. "'Fushi' no wandārando," in *Fushi no wandārando: sensō no seiki wo koete*, p. 293.
57. On this and related questions, see Christopher Fynsk, *Heidegger: Thought and Historicity* (Ithaca: Cornell University Press, 1993), pp. 28–54; and Jean-Luc Nancy, "The Decision of Existence," in *The Birth to Presence*, trans. Brian Holmes (Stanford: Stanford University Press, 1993), pp. 82–109.

58. *Fushi no wandārando*, p. 280. Interestingly enough, Heidegger is here compared unfavorably with Hegel, for whom, as Nishitani writes, "human activity is from the beginning bound up with 'death.'"

59. Ibid., p. 273. In this context it becomes clear that Nishitani is trying to work out a notion of man in all his bareness as mere "bodily existence" (*shintai no seizon*), but what is equally noteworthy is that such bodily existence represents for him precisely the opening for *ethics*, or what he calls the "subject as 'ethicality'" ('*rinrisei*' *toshite no shutai*) (p. 256).

60. See for example *Ridatsu to idō: Bataille, Blanchot, Duras* (Tokyo: Serika Shobō, 1997), pp. 7–18.

Chapter 1

THE POLITICS OF TEASING

Ehara Yumiko

1. Introduction

Ever since the women's liberation movement first appeared in Japan in the early 1970s, its treatment by the mass media has been characterized by "teasing" and "ridicule." "'Viragoes' Sexual Sensibilities Revealed in the Journal *Woman-Eros*," "The Frightful Contents of the Lib Calendar," "Women on Top in Preventing Rape and Pregnancy, Proclaims this Brainy Women's Libber," "Four Days at a Women's Lib Retreat: 'Men are Better After All,'" "The 'Adorable Aspects' of Amazons Assembled for the Jamboree"—these are some representative titles of articles dealing with "women's lib" in weekly magazines.[1] Of course there were articles that presented the movement straightforwardly, and this treatment of course differed depending on the nature of the media.[2] But we can still say that the media's mainstream attitude was one of "teasing" and "ridicule."

As goes without saying, this attitude of "teasing" has deeply offended women in the lib movement. "We know they will tease us whenever we do or say anything, but we will just grit our teeth and go on anyway."[3] "Ever since women calling themselves women's lib started appearing in Tokyo last October, the articles have been filled with jeering laughter and mockery. In a word, they portray us as 'ugly women making a fuss.'"[4] "Why do you immediately caricature someone when you hear the word 'lib'?" one woman protested to a reporter.[5]

It had been no different in the United States. Jo Freeman summarizes the media response to the women's liberation movement of the 1960s and 1970s as follows: "Most of the media compounded this problem by treating early women's liberation activities with a mixture of humor, ridicule, and disbelief."[6] Whereas reporters had examined the political message underlying the parodic antics of the Yippies,[7] "they just glanced at the surface of the women's actions and used them to illustrate how silly women were. The press treated women's liberation much as society treats women—as entertainment not to be taken seriously."[8] Likewise, in looking at the history of women's liberation movements in general, we can say that society's basic response has always been one of teasing and ridicule. The radical activities of the British and American suffragists as well as the Japanese Blue Stockings were confronted repeatedly by "mocking" and "teasing."

Based on these facts, we could censure journalists' attitudes and criticize their innate predispositions. In this article, however, I would like to consider this "teasing" of the women's liberation movement as a political expression and examine the logic and meaning of its rhetoric.

For the way "teasing" is expressed has a particular quality that goes beyond mere criticism, attack, or harassment. We can see this, for example, in the fact that the angry response of the "teased" women differs from the response to a mere attack. It is a kind of anger that seems to turn inward and be deprived of an outlet. Such anger would not arise in response to an intentional attack. We could thus say that this anger arises in response to the way "teasing" is expressed, rather than in response to the intentions behind the criticism or attack.

Of course, as Freeman states, "teasing" has its roots in the contempt for women in general. But disdain does not necessarily breed "teasing": coolly ignoring women or blatantly insulting them would be other possible consequences of contempt. When other groups of disdained people stood up to demand an end to discrimination, they did not encounter the kind of concentrated barrage of "teasing," "ridicule," and "mocking" that the women's movement encountered. Instead they were either treated with blatant hostility or ignored completely.

We can thus surmise the existence of a kind of deep "categorization" at work, one that is hidden from our consciousness. We can suppose that there exists some kind of "interpretive framework" that makes us react to some groups with "teasing" and to others with "blatant hostility." This interpretive framework operates unconsciously, on the side of both the "teased" and the "teaser."

Together with this deeper "categorization," "teasing" adds a meaning that goes beyond the content as expressed in words. This added meaning is a structural one inherent in the rhetoric of "teasing." Because it is not clearly verbal-ized, it works as if it were a "trap" or "bind" that constrains interaction. As a result, those who are "teased" are positioned within the "teasing" itself, where they can find no outlet, and have no choice but to let their undirected anger simmer inwardly.

Because of this process, "teasing" comes to have a strong if tacit political power. In Japan, the mass media's response of "teasing" has had a significant effect of psychologically distancing many women from the lib movement. Precisely because this effect has been achieved tacitly, however, any critique of such teasing has so far failed to be persuasive.

In this article, I would like to take up the "structure of teasing" itself, examining the various "categories" to which "teasing" is applied and considering why and how "teasing" comes to have political effects. In such a brief space, of course, I cannot explore this "structure" too deeply. What follows is thus merely one attempt to expose the political effects of "teasing" from an immanent analysis. In this way, we can begin to clarify why the lib movement was faced with such a fusillade of "teasing" as well as uncover the extent of its political effects.

2. The Structure of Teasing

What then is "teasing"? As seen from one side of this act, it is a form of interaction. "Teasing" is an act that is directed from the "teaser" to the "teased," and is usually accompanied by words. In this section, I would like to consider the verbal dimension of "teasing."

In general, words have dual meanings: the meaning of their content itself and that of their particular context or situation, i.e., the way words should be taken. The same is true of "teasing."

Let us begin with the latter. "Teasing" words are situated in the context of "play," that is, they are not meant to be taken "seriously" or literally. As part of "play," these are words of ease and latitude, and so escape the responsibility that words customarily hold in daily life.

Hence "teasing" is usually accompanied by certain kinds of markers, as for example snickering, a certain tone of voice or gesture, and suggestive winking. These markers are not necessarily exhibited directly to the "teased." They might be exhibited to a third party, instead. There are of course instances in which the "teased" person is "unaware" of such markers. Whenever anyone recognizes the markers as such, however, these words are then proclaimed to be "teasing" and "play."

"Teasing" prevents the specification of the utterance's agent of responsibility precisely because it is not regarded as "serious." It is of course clear in a face-to-face situation who is speaking, but the content of the teasing statement is expressed *as if it were hearsay or a self-evident fact*. We do not feel teased by statements that take the form of "*I think* you are X," in which content is ascribed to the speaker's thoughts and intentions, for here the location of responsibility is clear. But since "teasing" is "play," it is unnecessary to clarify responsibility. The rules of "play" render this unnecessary.

Hence "teasing" words are made "universal" and "anonymous" so as not to be ascribed to the individual's intentions.

In, for instance, magazine articles in which "teasing" is conducted by words alone, the markers are given through the sentences' tone, vocabulary, and style. What is important here is to leave the subject of the sentence ambiguous and "anonymous." Thus one writes, "Wow! How frightening! Don't go near them!" etc.

When "teasing" arises within a group, everyone present is compelled to be complicit in it unless there is a particular reason to object, for such "teasing" is "play" and a form of "joking." As "play," it would be the greatest sacrilege to break the rules. Everyone present is thus forced into a passive complicity, that of not breaking the rules. It not only takes a great deal of courage to break the rules, it also requires a legitimate reason to persuade everyone present.

On the other hand, the person who initiates the "teasing" tries to establish the game by actively involving others. In this way, the teaser successfully renders "teasing" words more "anonymous."

The double meanings and contexts of these words clearly show that "teasing" presupposes not only the existence of the "teased," but also that of an audience as third party. Principally or structurally, "teasing" words maintain a stance of "play" to the audience and one of "universal, anonymous, self-evident statements" to the "teased." Yet this fact does not prevent the following: first, that both these meanings are read by the two different parties, each of whom must nonetheless continue to act according to their given script; and second, that even with no audience, such words represent "teasing" since the "teased" person can always also act as audience. The "teased" can always proceed according to the script as if there were an audience, as can the "teaser" as well.

This double meaning is fundamentally the structure of "teasing" itself. Anything can be "teasing" insofar as it contains this structure. Lying to someone who has forgotten that it is April Fool's Day and ridiculing their response, sticking a rude note on someone's back, telling horror stories to children and enjoying their reaction—these are all acts of "teasing" that arise between someone who knows this is "play" and another who mistakes it as "truth." In all such cases, the audience is shown that this is a "game" or "play," yet such is concealed from the "teased."

Let us next consider the content of "teasing" words. While, of course, anything can become a target of "teasing," such words reveal a few obvious patterns based on their content. The most important of these is to shift the intent or motivation of the "teased" onto an unintended or only privately expressed context.

When, for instance, the "teased" is enthusiastic or passionately involved in some act, "teasing" "mocks" these acts or words by placing them in a different context. One example would be to call a domestic dispute a "friendly tussle." "Seriousness" and "enthusiasm" make excellent targets for "mocking."

Another tactic is to ascribe a more base motivation, one different from that which is publicly expressed, to the actions and words of the "teased." Examples can be found in ascribing mercenary motives to moral or ethical claims, or finding signs of romance in a couple's innocent behavior. In such cases, the "teaser" claims to know the real intentions better than the "teased." The motivations and intentions ascribed to the "teased" are those that would normally be considered "shameful" or "embarrassing" to express publicly, and yet might very generally or universally be held by anyone. Hence it can be claimed at one and the same time that it is only natural for the "teased" both to have and to "hide" such motivations.

In their content, then, "teasing" words can make some kind of claim about the acts and attributes of the "teased." Since this claim is made within the context of "teasing," however, such words are declared to be "play."

From this analysis, we can see that the pattern of social interaction called "teasing" has the following characteristics. First, by fundamentally belonging to the context of "play," "teasing" actions and words avoid the responsibility of "serious" social interactions. Second, its words must nonetheless be presented to the "teased" as "anonymous, universal, and self-evident" in order for this game to exist. Through this double meaning, the "teaser" stands in a superior position to the "teased." Third, "teasing" words can in their content make some kind of claim about the actions and attributes of the "teased."

3. The Function of Teasing

"Teasing" may possess various functions, the most important of which is its ability to confirm "familiarity."

"Teasing" is usually not deployed with strangers. Rather it takes place between two familiar parties, and functions to confirm that our relationship is of such familiarity that we can "tease one another." For it is difficult to "tease" without expecting to be forgiven, since otherwise the act's disingenuous nature may incite the anger of the "teased." "Familiarity" is confirmed when the "teased" acknowledges the "teaser's" expectation to be forgiven.

Such mutual "teasing" might arise among those in a familiar and equal relationship, or in a relationship between cohorts. Here "teasing" is indeed a pastime or game, much like children's "play."

However, "teasing" will have various other meanings when one side is clearly dominant over the other or is in a role of protecting the other. Let us consider a relation between a stronger and weaker party, in which the former is clearly dominant, and examine its various aspects.

In such a relationship, "teasing" obviously has the function of confirming that the two parties are in a relation of "familiarity" as well. In this familiar relation between a stronger and weaker party, there exists a "mutual teasing" that is a kind of "expression of affection." Here the weaker party's act of "teasing" the stronger serves to confirm that the latter's protection or affection is indeed turned toward the former, while the stronger party's "teasing" of the weaker shows the former's "leniency" and affirms his affection for the latter.

Yet those who are generally considered to be in a socially weaker position tend to receive "teasing" from absolute strangers. Children are one example. This kind of "teasing" is often the expression of "familiarity." Adults who "tease" children rarely have malicious intentions. Children are sometimes highly offended by such "teasing," however, not despite but precisely because this "familiarity" comes from a stranger. For such "teasing" occurs without regard to the child's own intentions. The very fact that a stranger has judged the child's intentions as insignificant is a sign that he has slighted the "teased" child as inferior. This, in turn, can be "deployed" as a tactic to disparage the other. To use a nickname or term of familiarity with someone with whom one is not really familiar, or with a stranger, clearly conveys an intent to disparage.

In a relationship between a stronger and weaker party, "teasing" often performs the function of veiling those actions in which the actual intent is to attack, criticize, or punish. Here "teasing" is deployed for this very purpose.

Since "teasing" exists in the context of "play," it can be "deployed" to hide one's aggressiveness. In society, competition and fighting are restricted except in institutionally sanctioned modes. In unsanctioned fights, then, it becomes necessary to cloak one's aggressiveness. Particularly in relationships where it is clear which side is stronger and which weaker, the outcome of the fight is clear from the beginning. To confront each other "seriously" in such a case would be disadvantageous not only to the weaker side, but to the stronger side as well since it would arouse the censure of society. This is when "teasing" is "deployed" as a useful tactic because it is positioned within the context of "play" and yet can still present information about the other's actions or attributes. Such deployment of "teasing" not only occurs among parties who know each other, but is widely practiced between those who are stronger and weaker in terms of social categorization.

When the weaker side adopts the form of "teasing" to critique or attack the stronger, this usually has the purpose of restraining the latter's reactive aggression and of protecting itself. Since the weaker side might be easily crushed by the stronger side's counterattack, it tries to hide the intentions of its own attack or critique within the format of "teasing." Since "teasing" is "play," social norms restrict countering it with actual attacks, which would be considered "breaking the rules." Even in "teasing" among equals, to actually become angry in response to "teasing" would be considered "immature." For the stronger side to become angry and attack the weaker in response to such "teasing" would be truly "unbecoming." Since the weaker side recognizes this, it tries to avoid attack from the stronger by placing its own critique or attack in the context of "teasing." The fact that "teasing" is a kind of "anonymous" expression also works to the weaker side's advantage, for it can express its critical intentions without revealing itself as an individual actor on stage. Because of its nature as a game, "teasing" can draw many members of the audience into complicity.

To critique or attack a stronger party by adopting the form of "teasing" is also to reconfirm the existence of the stronger-weaker relation through the use of this form itself. By using the tactic of "teasing," the teaser redefines himself as the weaker side, as unworthy of being taken seriously. As a result, the stronger side is compelled to submit to the norm of leniency. This explains why the jester is allowed to make very biting critiques of those in power. The self-definition of Edo period writers of *gesaku* fiction can also be understood from this perspective. By defining their own work as "playful writing," these writers positioned themselves as unworthy of being taken seriously, and as a consequence gained the right to "tease," "mock," and "parody" everything.

On the other hand, the stronger side's "teasing" of the weaker is often deployed in order to hide the former's intentions of attacking the latter, thus avoiding social censure. The side that is clearly more powerful would lose face by fighting "seriously" against the weaker. By presenting its aggressive intentions via the circuitous route of the "play" called "teasing," the stronger can show its "leniency" and "composure" and uphold appearances.

Yet this tactic can be "deployed" as a way to disparage the other. For the very use of the form of "teasing" defines the other as unworthy of being taken seriously.

The above analysis has thus shown the following: "teasing" performs the function of acknowledging "familiarity" by confirming that the two parties can mutually "forgive" one another. But in stronger-weaker relations, "teasing" can be "deployed" as a social act that realizes actual intentions of disparagement, attack, or critique. Conversely, through the form of "teasing," one can define oneself as "unworthy of being taken seriously" and define the other as "not worth taking seriously."

I hope to have shown that when it comes to the meaning and function of "teasing," factors such as the degree of familiarity and the social categories of stronger and weaker play an implicit role. While "teasing" can drastically change its meaning and function depending on the mutual relation of these categories, these are always related to the meanings of "contempt" and "familiarity."

4. The Bind of Teasing

Based on the fundamental characteristics of "teasing" as analyzed above, let us now attempt to answer the following question: How might one be able to object to the information presented in the form of "teasing"? On the one hand, there are cases when "teasing" might simply be a form of "play" to be enjoyed by all. As mentioned in section 2, above, however, there are also cases when this involves actual attacks or disparagement. When the "teased" party feels it has been disparaged or unreasonably censured, how would it be possible to object?

Objecting is difficult, for "teasing" insists that it is "play" and proclaims that its actions and words escape conventional social responsibility. As stated previously, a reaction of criticism and "serious" objection would only violate the rules of "play," resulting in a failure to persuade the audience.

Perhaps such objection would only lead to further snickering as "immature," or to being treated with silent contempt as inappropriate, or to incurring anger or critique as "unreasonable."

Insofar as the structure of "teasing" is established, objections must inevitably be judged as rule-breaking. Hence the objections to "teasing" must assume the additional task of dismantling its very structure.

Such dismantling is achieved by "proving" that "teasing" is not "play" but rather an intentional attack on the part of specific individuals or groups. By "proving" this, it might be possible to pull the audience—the potential accomplice of the "teaser"—toward the "teased." As a result, "teasing" words could be taken out of the context of "play" and reread as the intention or ideas of a specific individual or group. Only in this way can the content of these words be critiqued.

However, the responsibility for such rereading rests with those who object to "teasing." In contrast to one who objects to censure or attack, then, one cannot object to "teasing" by remaining "innocent." For this rereading is tantamount to attributing ill will or aggression to the "teaser," and such attribution is in itself a declaration of a hostile relationship. Hence the "teased" or objecting party is also performing a hostile act through objecting. What makes matters worse is that the objecting party is in this way the first to declare hostility. Such objection thus cannot take the form of an innocent insistence on having been "unreasonably attacked," such as would be the case with objecting to overt censure or attack. Rather it must take the form of aggressively pointing out and attacking the other side's ill will or shortcomings. The objecting party cannot object without thereby sullying its own hands. Since it cannot make its own innocence the grounds of validity, then, this objection at most only provides the locus for further debate. The "teaser" can easily argue against the objector on the basis of the fact that the latter broke the rules.

Regardless of the anger it feels toward this "teasing," the "teased" party finds it difficult to discover an outlet for its emotions. Its anger will thus turn inward. The desire to object is dulled simply by imagining the various difficulties that an objection to "teasing" would encounter. One might come to feel that the best strategy would be to totally ignore this "teasing."

It is in this sense that being "teased" can feel more devastating than being censured or attacked. Censure or attack against beliefs and ideologies can in fact end up strengthening these, but since "teasing" does not provide an outlet for anger, it leads to a sense of emptiness, as if one were wrestling against oneself. The person entangled in the structure of "teasing" is caught in its bind. Attempting to disentangle oneself is like struggling to escape from a quagmire.

5. The Politics of Teasing: The Case of Sexual Discrimination and the Women's Liberation Movement

Finally, let us consider the "teasing" of the women's liberation movement as based on the above analysis.

Freeman has correctly identified the essence of this "teasing," finding that the tone is equivalent to that which society in general uses to treat women. Based on this insight, let us first consider "teasing" against women in general.

First, women are on a daily basis made the objects of "sexual teasing." It is a common occurrence for young women walking down the street to be whistled at by strange men or to have rude jokes made at their expense.

Sexual matters are very important as material for "teasing." As sex is the most *familiar* matter for human beings, it is difficult for consciousness to express it. Sex is customarily an area of taboo for expression. It is thus generally only possible to talk about it in a very twisted form. The snickering that accompanies such talk is proof of the twisted relation between the body and expression. Hence, to be subjected to sexual language inevitably calls forth embarrassment and confusion. This makes sexual matters privileged material for "teasing."

In this society, men are seen as the superior sex. For men, women represent the sexual other, and any woman can be reread in this way. A man and woman in a sexual relationship are recognized by society as being in the most "familiar" of relationships. "Teasing" is an act that would be allowed in such relations, and is an expression of such "familiarity." Yet since all women are potentially sexual objects, "familiarity" is attributed to all women at the level of fantasy. As a result, "sexual teasing" can be directed at any unknown woman.

Second, women are seen, like children, as belonging to a socially inferior category. Like children and the elderly, women are considered to be in need of protection. Those in such need are seen as lacking the right to reject the attention of others, since they might potentially require this help at any time. From another perspective, this means that there are believed to be fewer barriers against approaching someone who belongs to this inferior category. As a result, greater "familiarity" tends to be attributed to those who belong to this category.

Consequently, women in general tend to more easily become objects of "teasing." It is rare for a woman to be treated "seriously" and more common for her to be treated "lightly," as something trivial.

All of this results in fantasies of "private life" and "familiarity" being attributed to women. Thus, as Freeman notes, society in general comes to treat women as a kind of entertainment.

It goes without saying that the "teasing" directed at the women's liberation movement is based on such "teasing" of women in general. Yet we might also understand it as a more complex kind of defensive reaction.

First, we must ask why the women's liberation movement became the *same kind* of target of a fusillade of "teasing" as that directed at women in general, for the mass media usually refrain from "teasing" active women with "serious intentions." Housewives involved in the peace movement and mothers advocating children's happiness generally avoid becoming the targets of "teasing." Why then did the women's movement (especially that of the early 1970s) become the same kind of target of a fusillade of "teasing" as that directed at women in general? First, because women insisted on their rights as women. Second, because the lib movement presented the sexual realm as an issue. For these reasons, the mass media treated the movement as "women's behavior."

As a result, all of the claims of the women's liberation movement came to be reread. Such rereading is very easily achieved once the women of this movement are treated as sexual objects. Seen in this way, these women are now defined as physically unattractive. Their claims can then be interpreted as "frustrations on the part of sexually unfulfilled women," or "the sad musings of ugly, unpopular women." Thus it was said that women would shout about independence, freedom, and liberation because they couldn't find decent men.

Once women are treated as sexual objects, those who censure and critique men are seen as "viragoes" and "amazons" who reject the "familiarity" of sexual relationships. Conversely, the physical characteristics of women involved in the women's liberation movement are imagined as stereotypes: they must be man-like women with "unkempt hair" or "severe hairstyles." When interviews were held based on these created images, it was found that these women were "surprisingly" "quite attractive" and "unexpectedly feminine."

However, the fact that the women's liberation movement could be treated in the same way as women in general reveals the strength and depth of the root of sexual discrimination. We all unconsciously commit various acts of "discrimination."[9] When an antidiscrimination movement arises that problematizes this phenomenon, however, we become conscious of such "discrimination" and are made to transform ourselves. Yet such a change of attitude was not prevalent in response to the women's liberation movement.

This is first of all because the category of women is considered (like that of children) to be a natural category, and second because women are too close to men. As a result, sexual discrimination is less likely to be recognized as "discrimination," and the women's liberation movement that insists on abolishing such "discrimination" is not received "seriously."

Yet here we can grasp society's (and especially men's) panic in relation to the women's liberation movement. For men, women are others who are positioned in the fantasy of "familiarity" and in a relation of "indulgence." Criticism on the part of this "familiar other" perhaps touched off a panic among men who "did not know how to deal with" these women. Thus, rather than clearly critiquing or censuring the movement, these men sought to "dodge" it through "teasing." For one can always deploy "teasing" as a tactic of attack even when one cannot logically justify one's own position.

Yet the negative effects of such "teasing" of the women's liberation movement were much greater than any possible critique or censure. First, by discussing the movement only in the context of "teasing," the impression was created that it was not worth treating "seriously." It was said that "it is no use getting upset at what women are saying," just as "it is no use fighting with children." Without in any way critiquing or debating the points in question, then, the persuasiveness and effects of the movement's claims were weakened.

Second, and more important, the impression was created among women in general that the kind of women involved in the women's liberation movement deserved to be "treated sexually." In this society, "serious" women, like "housewives" and "mothers," are exempt from becoming "objects of sexual teasing" when they are *treated individually in public situations*. Even if they are objects of "sexual teasing" on a daily basis, few women are treated that way in public situations. In the mass media, even fewer women are treated this way. Thus, in fact, such women are seen as having reasons for "deserving such treatment." By treating women in the women's liberation movement as objects of "sexual teasing," the mass media were able to create the impression that these were extremely peculiar women. As a result, the majority of women in general would want to position themselves as different from them. For to be "treated as sexual objects" in public situations would signify a kind of "diminished status." This would represent a kind of sanction against women who have "fallen" from the position of such "respectable women" as "mothers" and "housewives."

The lib movement questioned the very division of women between the "sacred image" of the "mother" and the "secular image" of the "female." It consequently chose the standpoint of "woman." Yet this choice provided much ammunition for "teasing."

If this "teasing" clearly bore negative political effects on the claims of the women's liberation movement, women activists would naturally feel intense anger toward it. Yet since "teasing" was positioned in the context of "play," it was extremely difficult to object to it. The more one objected, the greater the chances of supporting the "teasing" claims of "hysteria." Even when one sensed here the existence of a deep-rooted "discriminatory consciousness" against women, little could be done except to continue one's "futile resistance" within the "trap of teasing."

Translated by Ayako Kano

Notes

Ehara Yumiko, "Karakai no seijigaku," in *Josei kaihō to iu shisō* [The thought of women's liberation] (Tokyo: Keisō Shobō, 1985), pp. 172–194. First published in the journal *Josei no shakai mondai* [Women's social issues], no. 4 (1981). Author's note: This essay owes much to the works of Ervin Goffman.

1. *Playboy* (Japanese edition), February 12, 1974; *Asahi geinō* [Asahi entertainment], July 3, 1975; *Shūkan taishū* [Popular weekly], September 7, 1972; *Shūkan sankei* [Sankei weekly], May 19, 1972.
2. Inoue Teruko has analyzed the differences in media treatment of the lib movement in *Joseigaku to sono shūhen* [Women's studies and its margins] (Tokyo: Keisō Shobō, 1980).
3. Yoshitake Teruko, *Shūkan sankei*, November 20, 1975.
4. Ozawa Ryōko, *Fujin kōron* [Women's forum], January 1, 1971.
5. *Kono michi hitosuji* [Straight on this path], ed. Shinjuku Lib Center, no. 2, March 1, 1973.

6. Jo Freeman, *The Politics of Women's Liberation: A Case Study of an Emerging Social Movement and its Relation to the Policy Process* (New York: Longman, 1975), p. 111.

7. Yippies were members of the Youth International Party, politically active hippies. More clearly political than hippies, yippies engaged in antiestablishment activities during the 1960s. —*Trans.*

8. Freeman, p. 112.

9. See Ehara's analysis of the concept and practices of "discrimination" in her *Josei kaihō to iu shisō*, pp. 61–97. —*Trans.*

A FEMINIST VIEW OF
MARUYAMA MASAO'S MODERNITY

1. The Feminist Critique of Japanese Particularity

Many people would agree that Maruyama Masao's political thought is still sufficiently effective for decoding the sociopolitical situation of contemporary
Japan. At the very least, many people would agree that his ideas can be easily
recycled for describing such problems.

In his 1946 "Chōkokkashugi no ronri to shinri" [Theory and psychology of
ultranationalism],[1] Maruyama pointed out that in Japan, "The entire national
order is constructed like a chain, with the Emperor as the absolute value entity;
and at each link in the chain the intensity of vertical political control varies in
proportion to the distance from the Emperor." There exists no "free, decision-
making agent" and hence no "despotism as a concept." This lack of "despotism
as a concept" has led to the fact that, "though it was our country that plunged
the world into the terrible conflagration in the Pacific, it has been impossible
to find any individuals or groups that are conscious of having started the war."
This shows that there was an absence of a "sense of responsibility," in other
words, that this state of affairs "impeded the development of a sense of subjective responsibility."

The actions of Japanese war leaders were "not circumscribed by the dictates
of conscience," but were, rather, "regulated by the existence of people in a

higher class." Hence, even the prime minister, who "held greater power than any of his predecessors," revealed the "psychology of a timidly faithful Japanese subject: what instantly came to his mind was a proud feeling of superiority, based on the knowledge of being close to the ultimate authority, and a keen sense of being burdened by the spiritual weight of this authority." In other words, the justification of domination based on the relative distance from the center gave rise to "a phenomenon that may be described as the maintenance of equilibrium by the transfer of oppression." By "exercising arbitrary power on those who are below, people manage to transfer in a downward direction the sense of oppression that comes from above." Individuals who are situated within this system, even those "who in ordinary civilian or military life have no object to which they can transfer the oppression," are "driven by an explosive impulse to free themselves at a stroke from the pressure that has been hanging over them" once they are in a position of superiority.

Here Maruyama found one of the reasons for the insidiousness of Japanese military culture in which lynching was pervasive, as well as for the military's "acts of brutality" in China and the Philippines. It is easy to find the same (or a similar) kind of psychology at work in the various social problems of contemporary Japan, such as bullying in the classroom or corporal punishment by teachers.

In his 1949 "Gunkoku shihaisha no seishin keitai" [Thought and behavior patterns of Japan's wartime leaders],[2] Maruyama also pointed out the existence of two "thought patterns": "submission to *faits accomplis*" and "refuge in one's competence or jurisdiction." "Submission to *faits accomplis*" refers to "the point of view that because something has happened one is obliged ipso facto to approve of it." "Refuge in one's competence or jurisdiction" derives from the argument that one's actions are based on one's assigned line of duty, that judging the rightness of one's actions is not included within the jurisdiction of that duty, and that therefore "responsibility" for those actions does not exist in oneself.

As Maruyama points out, this logic of self-vindication in the end results in the same kind of absence of responsibility in the ruling class as described above, thus revealing the "dwarfishness of Japanese fascism." The same kind of thought patterns or logic of self-vindication is easily found in the political logic that reduces such issues as the liberalization of the rice market to the question of foreign pressure or, again, in the self-vindicating logic that defendants use in construction-industry bribery scandals.

The same can be said with regard to Japanese feminism. The idea of Japanese political society's premodernity, as described by Maruyama, is still repeatedly reproduced within Japanese feminist discourse.

For example, Suzuki Yumi has pointed out that sexual harassment in Japan tends to be predominantly of the gender-role coercion type. As a characteristic of this type, the agent of action is not specified, specific individuals are not held responsible, and the corporations themselves tend to "allow license to men on the presumption of women's sacrifice."[3] "In a workplace environment that regards the corporation as 'one big family,' there is little recognition that women and men as free individuals have entered into an employment contract with the company, and many of the male workers in particular identify strongly with the company as a 'community sharing a common destiny.'"

Therefore, there is little inclination on the part of any organization to hold the perpetrators of sexual harassment responsible, and the perpetrators themselves have little sense of responsibility. This has the tendency of turning an organization's response to sexual harassment not toward punishing the perpetrator and aiding the victim, but rather toward censuring the victim's act of accusation and excluding the accuser. The victim suffers from the sense of isolation that comes from feeling she would have to fight against the whole organization if she were to risk raising her voice in accusation. She is practically forced to choose "between either staying in the company and enduring in silence or leaving."

Suzuki points out that these characteristics of sexual harassment in Japan reflect the "premodern mode of relationship between the organization and individual in Japanese society." It is easy to perceive in this observation the same lack of a "free, decision-making agent" and "sense of subjective responsibility." In other words, one perceives here the same kind of transferring "in a downward direction the sense of oppression that comes from above," as described by Maruyama.

This becomes even clearer in the case of the military comfort-women issue. Historical details seem to show that this issue is closely related to a characteristic inherent in the Japanese military, which might be called the archetypal Japanese organization. It is said that the massive roundup of military comfort women began with the Nanjing Massacre. Maruyama argues that the Japanese military's acts of brutality were committed by rank-and-file soldiers: "Men who at home were 'mere subjects' and who in the barracks were second-rank privates found themselves in a new role when they arrived overseas: as members of the emperor's forces they were linked to the ultimate value and accordingly enjoyed a position of infinite superiority." The atrocities were the results of soldiers "driven by an explosive impulse to free themselves at a stroke from the pressure that has been hanging over them."[4] If the mobilization of military comfort women was a strategy to mitigate this "explosive impulse," then the "atrocities" suffered by these women were indeed grounded in the psychology of "transfer of oppression." For military comfort women, predominantly women of the Korean peninsula, had been chosen for the intra-military "management" of this psychology, which would otherwise have been directed towards the Asian populace in the colonies:

> In the rapid succession of the wars of aggression onto the continent, such behavior of the Japanese military in the occupied areas as looting, arson, assault, and rape can be considered as acts of sexual aggression, of releasing sexual frustrations against weaker persons, though in this case money was not paid. . . . Without reflecting on this fundamental mistake, military comfort women were unprecedentedly supplied through public funds in the name of preventing soldiers from raping the local women.[5]

Of course, it was not merely the problem of the Japanese military organization that gave rise to the military comfort-women issue. "It is clear that things got out of the control of certain conscientious military officers, as the problem of the war of aggression was compounded with the sexual consciousness of men who had become accustomed to the policy of licensed prostitution."[6] In other words, it is valid to regard the "particularity" inherent in the sexual consciousness of Japanese society as being in the background of this problem.

Minamoto Atsuko ascribes this "particularity" of Japanese society's sexual consciousness to the "thought and culture of rejecting sex," as transmitted "even in the transition of historical society from the early modern to the modern era."[7] "In the modern era, the modern rational spirit of the West greatly transformed Japan's cultural climate," and yet, "while encountering the West, the various layers of modernized Japanese culture still retained large 'traces' of the early modern era." This kind of "actuality of Japanese modernity" is indeed "the actuality of Japanese modernity as analyzed in Maruyama's *Nihon seiji shisōshi kenkyū* [Studies in the intellectual history of Tokugawa Japan]." For Minamoto, moreover, this actuality meant that "cultural layers concerning 'women' also maintained traces of the early modern era," or even that "those traces were further reinforced."

Such statements seem to argue that the most urgent task of Japanese feminism is to describe the nature of "Japanese sexuality" as based on a framework shared with Maruyama, that of the traces of early modernity in Japanese modernity. For the various layers of Japanese society confronting Japanese feminism would inherently involve problems related to Japanese sexuality (and gender), which would in some sense retain the traces of early modernity.

Each time it has confronted various concrete aspects of sexual discrimination in Japan, therefore, Japanese feminism finds qualities particular to Japan that are different from those of Europe and the United States. It has understood this Japanese particularity as retaining the traces of early modernity, that is, as an example of Japan's premodernity. We could say that Maruyama's political thought has been one of the theoretical sources providing the basis for such epistemology. In this sense, we are still caught within Maruyama's sphere of influence.

But although this epistemology bears a certain effectiveness, we must also question its validity. To understand Japanese particularity as premodernity will have the tendency to take on a sheen of modernizationism when evaluated negatively, and one of anti-modernizationism when evaluated positively.

However, it seems to me that this makes it especially difficult in Japan for a subject gendered as female to question modernity. In what follows, I would like to propose several points for considering Maruyama's "modernity" from a feminist perspective by elucidating the distortion found in postmodern feminism in Japan.

2. The Distortion of Postmodern Feminism in Japan

Unlike the first wave of feminism, the second wave maintains as its keynote a strong mistrust of modernity. This is because of the contradictory position offered to women in modern society. In modernity, women have been defined as being at once equal to men as human beings and as being "women," who are essentially different from men. Within this double definition, women end up being placed in a liminal position. As the normative values of male-female equality became more clearly established, the liminality of women was even further reinforced, especially after the achievement of women's suffrage. The second wave of feminism in advanced capitalist states was based on this kind of liminality in modern society, particularly after the achievement of suffrage.[8]

Second-wave feminist theory has thus developed as one of its main points the duality of modern society, or the separation of the public and private domains, and the subordination of the latter domain to the former. The separation of the public domain (such as corporate, political, and state organizations) from the private (such as family life and personal life) implicitly positions members of society into one or the other domain, depending on their sex. Nonetheless, modernization theory, which understands modern society to mean the modernization of consciousness and normative values, has argued away this positioning as universal and based on the natural order of the sexes. The logical outcome of this is that the hierarchy within the private domain—in which women are predominantly placed—is obscured as a natural order, with this domain being subordinated to the public one.

Hence, despite the professed principle of "modernity" that forbids discrimination based on attributes, women are clearly discriminated against in the "public domain" (women as second-class citizens!). Within the "private domain," moreover, they also face discrimination, such as the imposition of unpaid housework and child-care labor as well as the denial of the right of sexual self-determination. All of these have been justified as based on the natural order of women's sex (and, therefore, not a form of discrimination). Women who were dissatisfied with such discrimination were told to resent nature rather than society. The systematic duplicity of modernity signifies none other than these kinds of experiences as suffered by women.

For this reason, second-wave feminist theory has fundamentally maintained a mistrust of modern society, especially with regard to the kinds of modern consciousness and normative values that promote modernization. On the one hand, modern consciousness and normative values purport to define women as human beings and reject sexual discrimination, but on the other, they define men as the standard for human beings and recognize women as a special privilege only when they fit these masculine standards. This is, in the end, nothing but the most insidious form of androcentrism.

In other words, this reinforces the sense that sexual difference exists only for women. Also it creates divisions between women: it grants the privilege of being considered human only to those who fit the masculine standard whereas to others it affixes the label of remaining within the natural order of their sex; i.e., it marks them with the natural sex of "woman." As a result, being female becomes a negative symbol for women; it becomes that which they must deny as much as possible in order to be human.

Postmodern feminism in Europe and the United States most clearly presents this basic understanding of second-wave feminism. It states that the universalism of modern consciousness and normative values is exactly the kind of knowledge that has reduced women to nature and physicality as well as obscured their social and cultural construction. It states that in order to elucidate this mechanism of knowledge, we must describe the way universalistic discourse—which acts as if sexual difference did not exist—ends up constructing difference.

This basic position of postmodern feminism, insofar as it is within the bounds of Euro-American feminism, coincides also with the relativizing of modern Western culture. After all, modernity that posits the West as universal had also treated with the same kind of duplicity people from non-Western cultures, minorities from non-Western cultural backgrounds, people of color, the non-middle classes, those with disabilities, etc.

The same can be said in the case of such minority, ethnic, class, and disability issues as in women's issues. By acting as if these various people's differences do not exist, modern universalism differentiates those who do not fit the Western standard (the standard of white middle-class able-bodied males) and reifies these differences as natural. Such differences have been reified as natural differences inherent in the body, that is, as differences (in abilities, etc.) that represent these people's essential attributes. Through this knowledge, the cause of discrimination is thus thrown back upon the discriminated as their own problem. In this way, postmodern feminism claims to be able to act in solidarity with various other movements by confronting Western modernity ("universalism" indeed!) in its reification of these differences.[9]

In the case of Japanese feminism, however, such a critical perspective of modernity results in a strange distortion. This is because Japan is not the West. Insofar as one situates oneself in the West, the postmodern position will simultaneously lead to a critical investigation of one's own society and culture. Yet this is not the case insofar as one situates oneself in Japan. In limiting oneself to the social changes developing in Japan, one can of course point to trends of "modernization" and "Westernization." In this sense, modernity has, even in Japanese feminism, become the target of relativization. Yet at the same time, modernity in Japan means the West, and from this perspective, modernity's relativization would mean not the relativizing of Japanese modernity but rather the relativizing of the West. In this regard, the relativization of modernity would not automatically lead to a critical examination of one's own society and culture, but could lead to an argument reappraising and affirming Japanese society and culture.

Because of this ambiguity, Japanese feminism has always warned against the Japanese reception, or transformation, of postmodernism. It has thus critiqued so-called Japanism. Yet despite this consensus, or precisely because of it, a strange distortion has also existed, as I will explain below.

This distortion is related to the question of how one understands the difference between Japan and the West. According to postmodern thought, difference is not essential but rather constructed through various linguistic and social practices. In other words, what exists is not difference per se but rather practices of differentiation. In this way, what gives birth to the difference between Japan and the West are those practices that emphasize this difference and attempt to give some kind of political meaning to it.

As such, a postmodern critic of Japanism cannot be satisfied simply by critiquing those ideas that praise Japan. Even if one were to consider Japan critically, one would also fall into Japanism by presupposing Japan's difference from the West, emphasizing that difference, and privileging such an oppositional axis. From this standpoint, the schema that posits any kind of Japanese particularity must itself become a target of critique.

However, this standpoint might come to resemble that of the universalist or modernizationist, who acts as if the difference between Japan and the West did not exist. If we deny the positing of Japanese particularity itself, we might end up constraining critical investigations into our own society and culture. This is precisely why critiques are leveled from the standpoint that regards as *truly* postmodern the critical investigation of one's own society and culture as well as the discovery of modernity's multi-layeredness. This would run counter to the standpoint that is satisfied merely to question the existence of the Japan-West opposition.

As Ōgoshi Aiko points out, "We must guard against the facile reduction of everything to cultural determinism, but the attempt to solve problems through universalism without considering cultural background is also a futile play of abstractions."[10] In Japan, "postmodernism lacks confrontation and struggle against its own cultural climate. . . . This is a problem common to Japanese postmodernists, for whom postmodernism is no more than a critique of Western modernity. But unless there is a critical perspective against the existing cultural climate, Japanese-style postmodernism will remain nothing more than a reactionary play of abstractions."[11]

However, this latter postmodernist position as espoused by Ōgoshi paradoxically comes to resemble Maryuama's modernization theory, which posited Western modernity as the ideal type with which to remonstrate against the premodernity of Japanese society. It is easy to see here a revival of Maruyama, as Ōgoshi assumes the continuity of Japanese sexual culture from premodernity. Also she critiques Japanese-style feminism by comparing it to Western modernity, accusing this feminism of "negating the autonomous individual while leaving the Japanese cultural climate unquestioned."

I see in the entanglement of these arguments the strange distortion of postmodern feminism in Japan. From the standpoint of the former, the latter are no different from those Japanists who posit Japan as the particular by presupposing the continuity and uniqueness of the Japanese cultural climate. At the same time, however, the latter can be seen as modernizationists who advocate Japan's modernization according to the standards of Western modernity. Yet from the latter's standpoint, the former can be critiqued in much the same way: the former can be called universalists and modernizationists who act as if the difference in cultural backgrounds between Japan and the West did not exist, and yet precisely because of this they can be seen as Japanists in implicitly affirming the Japanese cultural climate.

What is this strange distortion in which two opposing arguments can critique each other in the same terms, those of Japanism and modernizationism? How can we understand this situation? We cannot avoid this question if we, as subjects positioned in the locus called Japan, propose a postmodern feminism (which was more or less the basic position of Japanese second-wave feminism) that takes a critical perspective on modernity. What is at stake here is indeed the very possibility of a feminism that questions modernity from the position of a subject situated in the locus called Japan.

3. *A Feminist View of Maruyama Masao's Modernity*

It is my belief that this strange distortion inherent in Japanese feminism's post-modern standpoint can inversely throw into relief the mechanism of knowledge inherent in the concepts of modernity itself, as argued by such "modernization advocates" and "civil society advocates" as Maruyama Masao. Without unraveling this mechanism of "knowledge," our very questioning of modernity as a gendered female positioned in the locus of Japan is to unwittingly invite accusations of being a Japanist or modernizationist, hence making the accomplishment of our endeavor all the more difficult.

What I wish to question here are of course not the words "Japanism" or "modernizationism" themselves. These words could avoid unnecessary confusion if defined clearly. This would be a more important task for those who wish to posit Japanists or modernizationists as hypothetical enemies, or for those who wish to employ these terms to make an argument.

But this is not my point here. Rather I would like to ask how, as a subject with the sexed body of a woman who is located within the time of the present and the locus of Japan, one might be able to question the various powers that have constructed the self. Regardless of whether these powers be called modernizationism or Japanism, the question is how to understand the concrete operations of the various powers that encircle my body, or the subject called myself. This is also to ask how the confusion of the connotations of modernizationism and Japanism as brought about by the questioning of modernity in Japan makes it difficult to ask that very question. In order to ask these questions, we must take as our task the unraveling of the mechanism of knowledge in Maruyama's modernity.

Many have already described this mechanism in Maruyama's political thought. For example, Yabuno Yūzō has stated that while "American political thought projects its future as an extension of the present," Maruyama's political thought "projects its future as an extension of the negation of present society."[12] Modernization theory in American sociology, such as that of Talcott Parsons, was a framework for describing contemporary society and forecasting the future on the basis thereof. But modernity in Maruyama's thought is a framework for showing what is still missing in Japan, and is thus used for negating contemporary society. Because modernity in Maruyama represented such a benchmark of absence, it could end up being purified and formalized as the "ideal of Western modernity."

Although modern European society was itself "an extremely multifaceted and multilayered society,"[13] Maruyama's modernity is posited where such complexities are abstracted. As a result, those aspects of Japanese political discourse that do not fit the abstracted ideal of Western modernity are seen negatively, as manifestations of Japan's premodernity. By assuming a historical view that progresses from premodernity to modernity, and by positioning Japan and the West along this axis, the abstracted ideal of Western modernity—which is retroactively positioned in the temporal axis of the modern—is deployed as a basis to negate the political practices of contemporary Japan.

Yet at the same time, since the modernity that is still missing in Japan is posited as the universality that ought to be achieved, it is seen as that which ought to be equated with Japan. Japan and modernity are opposed to each other and yet equated with each other. This duality is the same as that which modernity forced upon women. In this sense, Maruyama Masao is indeed a modernizationist.

Yet this is not all. There is another aspect that I would like to point out in what follows.

One of the criticisms against the mechanism of knowledge in Maruyama's political thought is that it allows him to claim a privileged position in discussing Japanese society.

> Maruyama puts himself and only himself in the position of the West, and from this position criticizes Japanese backwardness as well as the irresponsibility of that emperor system fascism which arises from it. But isn't this questionable? I mean, isn't it a bit underhanded to put oneself in such a privileged position and critique Japan's present situation through idealized Western thought?[14]

However, I believe that the greatest problem inherent in this mechanism is not that it allows Maruyama to put himself in a privileged position. Maruyama would probably reply to such a critique by saying, "No, this is not true. I myself have the same backwardness as a Japanese person, which is precisely why I have provided the kind of description that resembles a willful excavation of my own pain." He would say, "I am Japanese, as should be evident. It should be obvious that there is no way I can avoid my own critique." But herein lies precisely the problem, for what Maruyama accomplishes by deploying the concept of modernity is to present the (fantasy of) belonging to this implicitly presupposed homogeneous Japaneseness.

This problem can be considered from two directions. One is the issue of the reification of Japaneseness that results from equating modern Western society with the ideal of Western modernity. If one were to compare the various realities of modern societies that developed in various places against the ideal of Western modernity, one would surely find differences. In short, elements of premodernity would surely be found in any modern society.

As such, there is no guarantee that those aspects of difference in modern Japanese society, which were discovered by being measured against the ideal standard of modernity, are indeed particular to Japan. Elements of premodernity could potentially be discovered in Korea, China, or even Europe itself. Yet Maruyama's political thought nullifies this possibility by equating modern European society with the ideal of Western modernity. This makes it possible to equate the discovered premodernity with Japanese particularity, thus making it easy to discuss—and to reify—Japan.

Second, rather than allowing Maruyama to put himself in a privileged position, this reification of Japan makes it possible to homogeneously dilute the problem of Japanese fascism into the problem of Japanese backwardness. Let us recall how Japanese fascism, as described by Maruyama, was that of a homogenous society, covered from top to bottom by the same logic of the transfer of oppression. Yet between those positioned at the top of emperor-system fascism and those at the bottom, there must have existed tremendous differences in the significance of this logic in actual daily life. For those soldiers at the very bottom ranks of military hierarchy, the resistance of oppression from above would surely have meant risking death.

Before a term like "system of irresponsibility" can be homogeneously applied to Japanese society, then, what must be questioned is the possible extent to which subjects in various positions can actually resist. By pointing out that the lowest-ranking soldiers committed atrocities against the Asian populace, however, Maruyama presents a magnificently homogenous Japan. This is a Japan in which everyone from top to bottom is lacking in a sense of subjective responsibility and is covered by the psychology of transfer of oppression. Maruyama accuses and the Japanese people collectively repent. Here the ground for accusation is modernity as an ideal that does not exist anywhere in actuality. . . . Haven't we encountered this scene before?

Indeed, Maruyama is at one and the same time a Japanist and a modernizationist. It is true that he takes the universal standpoint of the ideal of Western modernity. In its Eurocentrism, however, such universalism can depict Japan only as particularity. In this sense, Maruyama is a modernizationist, for better or worse. Yet precisely by taking this standpoint of modernizationism, he portrays

Japan as a homogenous society. He creates Japan by positing the absent center of the ideal of Western modernity. When regarded from the continuity of these kinds of linguistic practices in Japan, Maruyama is indeed revealed to be a Japanist. Hence, regardless of whether we agree with him or not, we should not be surprised to find ourselves at once modernizationist and Japanist.

But what makes this scene even more depressing is the fact that Maruyama's mechanism of knowledge renders it difficult for various subjects, who are variously differentiated and positioned in Japanese society, to seriously question the experiences of war and fascism as well as other aspects of modern society.

What is most lacking here is the point regarding "women." It is no coincidence that women rarely appear in Maruyama's descriptions. Where, if anywhere, are women located in emperor-system fascism? Were "women" situated like men within the transfer-of-oppression system? Did the difference between women and men not exist in this system? If so, how is one to understand the military comfort-women issue? Or is it the case that women did not exist in Japan as conceived by Maruyama? Were women mere victims, located outside of Japan? Is Maruyama's gender blindness a result of his modernizationism or Japanism?

This last question misses the point, for the two are actually one. It is because one posits the ideal of Western modernity as standard that a homogeneous space called Japan can be created. Both Western modernity as standard and the Japan that is differentiated from this standard are worlds that are implicitly gendered, and yet are posited as if gender did not exist. Both modernizationist universalism (which neglects the specificity of the Japanese cultural climate) and the theory of Japanese particularity (which paints a homogenous Japan) can function as an apparatus that erases the specific experiences of subjects positioned in the category of woman.

Rather than patterns of thought, Maruyama should have questioned the various differences in experience that these patterns forced on subjects in varied situations. It is only on the basis of such experience that one can concretely formulate a political society that is not a system of irresponsibility.

Within Maruyama's clever logic, I perceive a parallel with both the reification of the category of woman that universalism forced in modernity and the homogenization of women as forced by such reification. In its struggles, second-wave feminism explained why modernizationism created the category of woman as that which bears exactly the opposite characteristics of modernity. Thus it is precisely Japanese feminism that should be in a position to unravel the clever mechanism of Maruyama's political thought.

Rather than realizing this potential, however, Japanese feminism seems to be caught within Maruyama's mechanism of knowledge. This mechanism is extremely powerful and defies the efforts of Japanese feminism to escape from it. Yet clearly it will be difficult for us to question modernity as women positioned in the locus of Japan insofar as we remain caught within its parameters.

Translated by Ayako Kano

Notes

Ehara Yumiko, "Feminizumu kara mita Maruyama Masao no kindai," in *Feminizumu no paradokkusu: teichaku ni yoru kakusan* [The paradox of feminism: Diffusion through fixture] (Tokyo: Keisō Shobō, 2000), pp. 87–107. Originally published in *Gendai shisō*, vol. 22, no. 1 (January 1994), pp. 208–217.

1. *Thought and Behaviour in Modern Japanese Politics*, 2nd edition, trans. Ivan Morris (Oxford: Oxford University Press, 1969), pp. 1–24. Quotations are from pp. 16–19.
2. In *Thought and Behaviour in Modern Japanese Politics*, pp. 84–134. Quotations are from p. 103.
3. Suzuki Yumi, "Sekushuaru harasumento no kihon kōzō to sono Nihonteki tokushitsu" [The basic structure of sexual harassment and its Japanese particularity], in *Sekushuaru harasumento wa naze mondai ka: genjō bunseki to rironteki apurōchi* [Why is sexual harassment a problem?—Current analyses and theoretical approaches], ed. Kanegae Haruhiko and Hirose Hiroko (Tokyo: Asahi Shoten, 1994).
4. Maruyama, "Theory and Psychology of Ultra-Nationalism." Both quotations are from p. 19.
5. Yamashita Akiko, "Sei shinryaku, sei bōryoku no rekishi to kōzō" [The history and structure of sexual aggression and violence], in *Nihonteki sekushuariti* [Japanese sexuality], ed. Yamashita Akiko (Tokyo: Hōzōkan, 1992), pp. 5–76. The quotation is from pp. 41–42.
6. Ibid.
7. Minamoto Atsuko, "Nihon no hinkon naru sei fūdo" [Japan's indigent sexual climate], in *Nihonteki sekushuariti*, pp. 79–128. The quotations are from p. 82.
8. Lynda M. Glennon, *Women and Dualism: A Sociology of Knowledge Analysis* (New York: Longman, 1979).
9. On the relationship between postmodernism and feminism, see also Linda Nicholson, "On Postmodern Barricades: Feminism, Politics, and Theory," in *Postmodernism and Social Theory: The Debate Over General Theory*, ed. Steven Seidman and David G. Wagner (London: Basil Blackwell, 1992), pp. 82–100.

10. Ōgoshi Aiko, "Feminizumu wa ai to sei o katareru ka" [Can feminism speak of love and sex?], in *Nihonteki sekushuariti*, pp. 131–202. The quotation is from p. 157.

11. Ibid., p. 193. The quotation in the next paragraph is also from p. 193.

12. Yabuno Yūzō, *Kindaikaron no hōhō: gendai seijigaku to rekishi ishiki* [Modernizationist methods: Current politics and historical consciousness] (Tokyo: Miraisha, 1994).

13. From Saeki Keishi's statements in "Zadankai: kindai no hakken" [Roundtable discussion: The discovery of modernity], in *Kanagawa daigaku hyōron* [Kanagawa University Review], no. 16 (1993).

14. Ibid.

Chapter 2

THE IMAGINARY GEOGRAPHY OF A NATION AND DENATIONALIZED NARRATIVE

Kang Sangjung

Geopolitical Vertigo and Redefining the Nation

Since when have retrogressive "masturbatory views of history," as represented by the "liberal view of history," come to dominate bookstore shelves? They became noticeable around the time of the Gulf War. In fact, Fujioka Nobukatsu, the leading proponent of this "liberal history," begins both his *Kingendaishi kyōiku no kaikaku* [Reforming modern history education] (1996) and *Ojoku no kingendaishi* [A modern history of shame] (1996), with prologues describing the impact of this war.

For example: "Many Japanese, relying on the idealism of the Constitution's Article Nine, were able to steep themselves completely in sentimental pacifism." Or again: "The Gulf War was a shocking event that showed that the ideal of 'pacifism' as contained within Article Nine, and upon which 'peace education' was based, failed in the face of the reality of international politics." In short, according to Fujioka's recollections, the Gulf War was a sensational event that exposed the defects of Japan's "postwar democracy."

What, then, are the fatal defects of "postwar democracy?" Fujioka lists five:

1. The conviction that democracy and (State) power are as incompatible as oil and water.

2. The absence of decisive leadership in the administration of the State.
3. The complacent acceptance of peace defined solely in terms of "isolated pacifism" and the resulting neglect of problems relating to national security.
4. The uneven distortion caused by the enlargement of individual rights and extreme minimalization of national duties.
5. Blind faith in a "democracy" that neglects liberalism.

These represent the defects of "postwar democracy" as rejected by Fujioka.

What emerges when we invert this defective "postwar democracy"? Fujioka wants to say only this: that Japan should "free" the Leviathan of the State from the chains of "postwar democracy," especially the peace Constitution at its foundation, thus allowing the nation to become a major player in post–Cold War international politics, as based on the clear determination of State will.

What is required for this to occur? As perhaps suggested in Fujioka's fourth defect of "postwar democracy," it is the "remaking" of national consciousness.

Why is this requirement important? To borrow the words of Shiba Ryōtarō, for whom Fujioka expresses great admiration, if the modern State consists of an equivalence between the State and the nation or people, then this equivalence represents "a State wherein the nation or people identifies itself with the State, and also where the people regard each other as homogeneous."[1] It is thus necessary for such a people to actively identify with the State and transform itself in such a way that it "willingly fights for the nation."

For Fujioka, a concrete image of this kind of State is conveyed in an episode in Shiba's novel depicting the Russo-Japanese War, *Saka no ue no kumo* [Clouds above the hill], which provided the decisive impetus behind Fujioka's allegiance to the "Shiba view of history." Referring to the heroic efforts of the workers who repaired Admiral Tōgō Heihachirō's flagship *Shikishima* in time to face the Russian Baltic fleet, Fujioka writes, "In addition to the soldiers at the battlefront, the lowly shipyard workers also worked desperately for the sake of the nation at this time of crisis. Postwar Japanese, fundamentally robbed of the idea of the 'State,' can no longer recognize that spirit for what it was."[2] Following the trauma of the Gulf War, it is this idea of the State that Fujioka wishes to recapture.

According to Fujioka, however, postwar Japan's inclination toward economic value alone has resulted in such spiritual decline that it has forgotten the idea of the State and even lost sight of the public sphere itself. It is precisely such mind control that, propelling this "spiritual dismantling of the State," becomes the perverted, masochistic view of history that "humiliates, disdains, and disparages one's own nation and ethnicity." In concrete terms, this represents the "Tokyo Tribunal cum Comintern view of history."

Indeed, Fujioka appears to define the "liberalism" of the "liberal view of history" in terms of a historical reexamination that is free of all dogma and prejudice. In fact, he has sought to balance and criticize several versions of Hayashi Fusao's affirmation of the Greater East Asian War, which is considered to be the opposite extreme of the "Tokyo Tribunal cum Comintern view of history." Yet a look at *Ojoku no kingendaishi*, published after *Kingendaishi kyōiku no kaikaku*, clearly reflects Fujioka's unequaled disdain for this latter view. It is not at all clear whether such a view of history exists and what it exactly means. In essence, it refers to all "anti-Japanese" historical views that hinder the self-formation of the people *qua* Japanese and deny pride in one's own national history.

As is clear here, Fujioka has since the Gulf War focused the most actual point of debate on the question of the people's historical memory. This is amply reflected in such statements as the following: "The most important thing produced by the people is their own national modern history education," and "The main hero of modern history is the nation's people and the State they produce. Modern history is above all the narrative of the life of the people and their State."

Bergson referred to memory that could not be externalized into information devices as "pure memory," the ability to recall and recognize. If it is precisely this recollecting memory that holds special meaning for man, then historical memory also depends on such ability to recall and recognize. Unlike habitualized memory, which can be externalized, pure memory represents a creative (re-creative) act that first becomes possible within the actuality of the "here and now." Despite its status as a discourse of successive clichés, the "liberal view of history" has succeeded in expanding the repercussions of debate because it confronts us with the most actual problem of historical memory. In other words, it necessarily forces each of us to reconfirm the meaning of the "here and now." This process is accompanied by the danger of reconfirming one's own position within the discursive space of the postwar period, where perspective arrangements have collapsed. Awareness of this danger can be called "geopolitical vertigo," but this phenomenon is in no way unique to Japan.

In more global terms, geopolitical vertigo is not unrelated to the dramatic post–Cold War economic and ideological "deterritorialization" of the geopolitical world order that was established under American hegemony as well as the incipient destabilization of the sociospatial triad (sovereign states, territorial unity, and communal identity) that characterized the interstate system. For this very reason, there has come about an opportunity for the emergence of a kind of fundamentalism.

One scholar of geopolitics has formulated these twisted relations as follows:

This implosion of the geopolitical order of the Cold War starkly foregrounded the degree to which the post–World War II world order had come apart and placed the meaning of the "West," "Europe," and "United States" as sociospatial identities in crisis, thus provoking the experience of vertigo we have noted. But every deterritorialization creates the conditions for a reterritorialization of order using fragments of the beliefs, customs, practices, and narratives of the old splintered world order. Out of the experience of vertigo, newly imagined visions of state, territory, and community are projected in an effort to restabilize and reterritorialize identity amid global flux.[3]

In the United States, the representative discourse would be Samuel Huntington's "clash of civilizations." As can also be seen in Huntington's recent essay, "The Erosion of American National Interests,"[4] this is nothing other than a project of global "reterritorialization" that projects the *Kulturkampf* against the "inner enemy" and "unwanted 'other'" that threatens America's traditional national interests and identity. The unity and communal identity of the American State are being defined once again by inciting antagonisms of cultural essentialism.

In Japan, it is the attempt to create an "official history" as the people's past record that represents this project of reterritorialization. The term "official history" is a key word in the appeal of the Society for the Reform of History Textbooks, of which Fujioka is a leading member. It is also noteworthy that writers and essayists of a relatively younger generation have echoed the desire to rescue the memory of the people or nation, now identified with that of the State, from the ruins of the past and decorate it with the laurels of "official history." It is clear that the desire for "official history" seeks to redefine the people by drawing a line between "citizen" and "noncitizen." To use an extreme expression, this implies the beginning of a "civil war" fought over historical memory.

I would like to reconfirm that, fifty years after the war, Japan's discursive space has deteriorated to the point of this chilling spectacle. This is in no way a mere accident, however. Rather it must be understood as developing from the origins of the postwar period.

The Myth of the Beginning and the Forgetting of Empire

Carol Gluck, the American scholar of Japan, points out that Japan's "postwar" represents a composite of several different postwars,[5] the most dominant narratives of which are the "postwar as mythical history" and the "postwar as inversion of the prewar."

The "postwar as myth" is the myth of an absolute discontinuity, a "zero hour" marking a rupture between wartime and postwar that began exactly at noon, August 15, 1945, with the emperor's radio address announcing the surrender. This "August revolution theory" claimed liberation from the prewar, antifeudal militarist system and all its spiritual supports, which led Japan into a devastating war. The postwar was thus considered an "anti-past" wherein such prewar phenomena were inverted.

Inheriting this type of postwar narrative, the "progressive postwar," which extended from communism to leftist liberalism, came to bear the burden for democratic reform and the ideas and movement of pacifism. The "postwar of the middle-class," which initially sympathized with this postwar but clearly parted ways with the arrival of high economic growth, came to envelop the vast majority of the nation. This signified a democracy that consisted of a homogenous middle-class society. The goal of equality in material and social wealth in fact accelerated the liberation of "private" life and fixed the image of a single "lantern-type society" that was bloated with no neck or base. It was precisely this large-scale devotion to Americanism that, to borrow the words of Maruyama Masao, represented the postwar version of modern Japan's aporia, consisting of a polarization between nationalism and the liberation of an apolitical sensibility. The inclination toward economic value alone that Fujioka laments as the cause of spiritual deterioration, in which the idea of the state is forgotten, generally corresponds with this point.

This movement toward a monologic Americanism didn't take place across the board, however. In being filtered through the various negotiations of daily life, its penetration proceeded by mixing with "Japanese phenomena." Conversely, "Japanese phenomena" were rediscovered in being affected by Americanism, thus widening the scope of cultural nationalism. The postwar of the middle class leveraged the representation of the Japanese people = nation as a monolithic image into defining new gender roles and marginalizing heterogeneous minorities, especially those from the former colonies. In this sense, postwar nationalism, having lost its prewar core as the "national polity," disintegrated and flowed back to its old social haunts, losing its direct centripetal attraction to the state while maintaining the idea of ethnic homogeneity.

It was the international conditions at the time that made possible this middle-class postwar—in other words, the "postwar as Cold War." By choosing "subordinate independence" under the United States, Japan placed itself in the international environment of a "peace within walls." Despite the fact that fierce fighting and civil wars were waged repeatedly throughout the region outside these walls, from the Korean War to the end of the Vietnam War, the postwar middle class was able to enjoy the prosperity of "private" life. This arrangement marked Japan as an economic power to the extent that "the United States, so manifestly 'the winner' of the Far Eastern War in 1945, could by the 1970s be seen as having been in certain senses the greatest of its long-term 'losers.'"[6] Yet the distortion between Japan's "subordinate independence" and the peace and prosperity centered on "private" life remained unresolved.

The overlapping of the end of the Cold War and the fiftieth anniversary of Japan's postwar era, along with the recognition that modernity as a goal was not a mirage but an already accomplished reality, at once brought this distortion to its breaking point. At the same time, the mythological nature of the first type of postwar was laid bare.

John Dower, the American historian of the "Fifteen-Year War," has discussed the positive inheritance from the empire that aided Japan's postwar recovery, while in Japan there has emerged a "revisionist" reading (that of Yamanouchi Yasushi) of the 1930s that clarifies the historical relation between the forced "modernization" of the wartime mobilization system and postwar system society on the basis of world-historical contemporaneity.

These discussions suggest that modern warfare, especially world war and its wartime system, forcibly brings about systemic change, regardless of the war's purpose or ideology. Relating this point to the history of wartime and postwar systems surrounding modern Japan and Asia, from the Sino-Japanese and Russo-Japanese Wars to World Wars I and II, the historian Mitani Taichirō makes the following observation:

> The thesis that "war is the extension of revolution" appears to possess a generality that applies to all modern wars. Japan is perhaps no exception to this. In modern Japanese history, war has in many senses produced revolutionary effects upon the prewar system, both domestically and in terms of international relations. Domestically, these effects have appeared in the form of democratization and militarization (and conversely, demilitarization); while internationally, they have appeared as colonization (and conversely, decolonization) and internationalization[7]

In this regard, Shiba Ryōtarō's commonly appealing view of history that sees the "season of evil" stretching from 1905 (the Russo-Japanese War) to 1945 (the surrender) as the "demon child" of modern Japan represents an attempt to reedit modern Japan's path through numerous wartime and postwar systems into a comfortable national history.[8]

For Shiba, the forty years that transformed the shape of the Meiji state were merely the "demon child carelessly conceived by the legal system under the Meiji Constitution." In this sense, the postwar signified a reversal of that history of insanity and a return to the healthy and transparent nationalism of the Meiji state. In a certain sense, Shiba's historical view as a "national writer" can be said to represent the most popular form of postwar historical narrative. He breaks down the myth of the postwar's beginning into easily digestible pieces. That is to say, both the emperor and the people or nation are seen as victims of militarism, while the postwar comes to correspond with the Allied story of a peaceful government being established in accordance with the "freely expressed will of the people" through "the revival and education of the Japanese people's democratic tendencies."[9]

At the same time, this story also fits perfectly with the emperor's so-called declaration of humanity that took place in early 1946, before MacArthur's Constitution draft was announced. The declaration, as if tallying up with the Allied story line as described by the GHQ, begins with the "Charter Oath" of 1868 and declares the composite of the discontinuity and continuity of 1945 in the following fashion: "The binds uniting us and the people have always been tied with mutual trust, respect and affection, not with mere myth or legend. They are not founded upon the fictional concepts of the Emperor's divinity, the superiority of the Japanese people over others or the fate to rule the world."[10]

The third opening of the country that was the postwar was thus converted into a national history that completed the second opening left unfinished by the Meiji state. As a result, the memory of the beginnings of colonial rule and the "Greater East Asian War" were clearly elided. The war was renamed the "Pacific War" and an "adroit moral equation" established, in which the attack on Pearl Harbor and the nuclear bombing canceled each other out. It was inevitable that this historical narrative, which highlighted parts of the past while obscuring others in the background, would bring about a "striking amnesia of the (colonial) empire." This forgotten memory remained frozen within the Cold War, abandoned for fifty years of the postwar period.

It is clear that the myth of a beginning to the postwar period and the national history of Japanese modernity turn a blind eye toward a broader perspective that includes both the wartime and the postwar systems, a perspective that would rupture their narratives. As is amply reflected in the words "one hundred million hearts as one" and "one hundred million people," language used in the two edicts declaring war and surrender, the wartime system could not have operated for even one instant without mobilizing the nearly one-third of the one hundred million "imperial subjects" comprising other colonized ethnic groups. In this sense, postwar national history has barely maintained itself by excluding these alien ethnic groups and forgetting the history of that exclusion.

In the case of Japan, the domestic effects of decolonization were relatively small, as compared to demilitarization. In other words, the problems endemic to decolonization were dissolved into the general problems of demilitarization. Moreover, the process of decolonization overlapped with the course of the Cold War. The political and economic reconstruction of Japan that followed the change in Occupation policy came in response to the demands of the Cold War. This in turn influenced the decolonization of Japan's former colonies and occupied territories. According to the strategic necessities of the Cold War, decolonization was frozen to the extent that it would not hinder Japan's role in the Cold War. Now, with the end of the Cold War, we should understand the unfinished process of Japan's decolonization (i.e., the second stage of the decolonizing process) to have begun.[11]

This problematic proposed by Mitani is directed toward those cracks that have formed within the frozen memory of the war.

What, then, would a historical narrative be like that is able to respond to this problematic?

The Imaginary Geography of a Nation and Denationalized Narrative

I have in my hands now the three volumes of *Senjika zainichi Chōsenjin shiryō shū* [Wartime resident Korean documents], published in 1997. It contains the records of a resident Korean organization's print media that began in January 1935 and ran until the height of the "Greater East Asian War" in October 1943.[12] This was distributed not only within Japan "proper," but also to the main cities of the Korean peninsula, "Manchuria," and regions of China. With the exception of the main official newspapers of the Korean peninsula, the Japanese *Keijō nippō* [Seoul news] and the Korean *Mainichi shinpō* [Daily News], it was quite rare for Korean print media to be allowed to publish for such a long time. In keeping with the official policy of creating imperial subjects out of Koreans, the paper frequently carried stories of the Harmony Association's activities and announcements of wartime mobilization policies from the governor-general's office, thus making its "pro-Japanese" position obvious to all. Clearly, the newspaper did not represent the voice of the wartime Korean people.

Despite the newspaper's support for imperialization policy in certain sections, it is by no means impossible to read the frustrated ethnic consciousness and anguish of resident Koreans in other sections. There is, for example, the following record of impressions on the part of those Korean youth who enlisted as Imperial soldiers (November 25, 1939). In between the headings of "Peninsular volunteer soldiers' impressions of Japan proper" and "Taking to heart the joy of being born in the Empire," the following explanation is inserted:

> This is the moving record of impressions of Japan proper as formed by three hundred Korean volunteer soldier trainees who crossed the far sea and entered the imperial capital early on the sixth. These are the scarlet letters of patriotism in which the emotions of our vigorous peninsular youth, whose crimson hearts are enveloped in khaki uniforms, are hastily recorded.

The record of the "vigorous peninsular youth" reads as follows:

> The purpose of our travel to Japan proper is entirely different from a school trip. One purpose is to worship at Ise Shrine and worship the Imperial Palace from afar. Another is to present ourselves to the people of Japan and achieve an ever stronger unity between Japan and Korea. We prayed for the hallowed divine nation Japan and for its continued prosperity, and ever more firmly confirmed our desire to repay the sacred debt of the Emperor's benevolent gaze that is bestowed equally upon us. We worshipped the east every morning at our training center and recited our oath as imperial subjects as if standing before the Emperor, thus strengthening our conviction as subjects. . . . In respectfully worshipping before the Nijūbashi Bridge, we simply wept tears of gratitude.

To be certain, the fervent desire to become "Japanese" could not arise without the forceful and oppressive reality of the colony. Yet it cannot be denied that the desire of the colonial "peninsulars" to become ever better "imperial subjects" was based not only on mere coercion but also on voluntary motives.

In reality, however, one can glimpse almost everywhere in the *Tōa shinbun* [East Asia news] interviews in which "Japanese from Japan proper" confessed their discrimination as well as articles in which "peninsulars who had become good imperial subjects" were "confused" and greatly disappointed by the discriminatory language on the part of these Japanese. There can be seen an anticipatory resolution to die as "Japanese" as well as the daily discrimination that so unavoidably affected Koreans. In seeking to overcome this antinomy by becoming more "Japanese" than the "Japanese from Japan proper," a fierce desire to imitate was laid bare, as in the unrequited love of the Korean volunteer soldiers. While the tone of *Tōa shinbun* encouraged the policy of imperialization, in reality "radical and fierce views that even policymakers couldn't voice" were expressed as well.

To be sure, here the possibility emerges that "peninsulars" could be more patriotic "Japanese" than those "Japanese from Japan proper." This possibility was continually betrayed, however, and the imagined community of "Japanese" could do nothing but idealize the "Japanese from Japan proper." "Peninsulars," who were not "Japanese from Japan proper," came to repeat an infinite process of *ekstasis* in pursuit of that unattainable ideal of being "Japanese." The blatant and undeniable reality of ethnic discrimination was such that the "Japanese from Japan proper" never believed the "peninsulars" could become "Japanese," which means that it was precisely these "Japanese from Japan proper" who were the prisoners of that "Japanism of Japan proper"[13] in their status as "Japanese." No doubt the unattainable *ekstatic* desire leading to the anticipatory resolution to become "Japanese" grew ever stronger on account of this discrimination.

The wartime empire accomplished its integration when this desperate leap to become "Japanese" on the part of the "peninsulars" became their own autonomous desire. Viewed ideally, however, there always existed the possibility of a rupture in this notion of "Japanese." Such possibility was also the instant of exposure in terms of how much this "Japanese interiority" was protected by an arbitrary boundary. For any "Japanese nationalism of Japan proper" that equated the notion of "Japanese" with that of "Japanese from Japan proper" would necessarily have caused the integration of the empire to fail. The mono-ethnic national history of the postwar would thus have been unable to come into being as the ideal of an imperial nation.

In this connection, the Ministry of Education's *Jinjō shōgaku chirisho I* [Elementary school geography, vol. 1] of March 1938, the plainest account of the imagined geography of the "Japanese" people, opens its first chapter, "The Great Japanese Empire," with the following words: "Our Great Japanese Empire lies in the east of the Asian continent and consists of the Japanese islands and Korean peninsula." As regards the people, it provides the following explanation:

> The people number approximately one hundred million. While most are ethnically of Yamato origin, Korea holds about twenty-three million Koreans and Taiwan about five million ethnic Chinese and some one-hundred thousand natives. Hokkaidō also contains a small number of Ainu, as does Karafuto along with some other natives. Approximately one million people of Yamato ethnic origin have immigrated to other countries.

In terms of regions, "Honshū is divided into the five regions of Kantō, Ōu, Chūbu, Kinki, and Chūgoku. To this is added the regions of Shikoku, Kyūshū, Hokkaidō, Taiwan, and Korea." The nation is divided into eleven regions in total.

This geographic space as imperial "icons for the people" supported both the aforementioned "impressions of Japan proper on the part of the peninsular volunteer soldiers" and the imaginary geography of the "Japanese people" who were their contemporaries. Such assimilation of the "peninsulars" into "Japan proper" by worshipping at Ise Shrine and the Imperial Palace were state rituals that deeply inscribed these "Japanese" icons into their bodies. When a subject desiring "rebirth" as "Japanese" emerged among the "peninsulars" through these rituals, the psychological device supporting imperial integration succeeded in projecting outward the moment of its internal division.

Even if it was only a matter of principle, however, this was also the instant at which the internal fissures of national history *qua* the history and memory of the "Japanese from Japan proper" (i.e., the "Japanese people") were necessarily revealed. The history of the war, therefore, was a succession of dangerous moments wherein the critical point of the national could be exposed.

Without question, the beginning of the postwar violently contracted the mixed composition of the people into a "Japanism based on Japan proper" while returning it to a composition that preceded the colonial empire. The aforementioned "Emperor's Declaration of Humanity" represented the state's manifesto of this contraction. If the "evil season" of forty years was the "demon child" for national history, as Shiba's historical view would have it, then the "Japanese" who were abandoned at the "war's end" as others—as nothing more than "peninsulars"—must also be forgotten "demon children." The memory of these "demon children" lost its place in the face of that violent forgetting and "reterritorialization" of the national, and was thus forced to continuously wander about. The memory of "Korean B- and C-class war criminals" may perhaps be described as a grave-post for the beginning of that cruel postwar.

I sometimes recall a single photograph of my father's younger brother, a person who may have followed a similar path in the postwar period as those war criminals. The faded photograph captures the tense expression of a "peninsular" wearing the armband of the military police and holding a Japanese sword. Next to him stands his wife, a "Japanese from Japan proper," who is wearing a sad expression and carrying an infant. This was a final photograph taken during the "war's end," as people prepared for "suicide." The "peninsular" survived and returned to the "peninsula," leaving behind his wife and child in "Japan proper." Amidst the upheaval, he lost contact with them and was forced to live the postwar period alone. Former "Japanese" who began to pursue a new history of liberation, civil war, and military rule had their memories of "Japan proper" completely erased and lived as ethnic-nationalists in the newborn nation-state. This episode is in no way uncommon, however; rather it represents the postwar experience of those "peninsulars" who were caught up in this tumult. The opportunity to ask my uncle about his memory of the war has now been lost forever. Only one thing is certain: that it was "Japanese" national history that obliterated that memory.

Might not the "season of evil" refer less to an imperial era than to one that intoxicates itself with the sweet narrative of national history and attempts to revive it by completely excluding the alterity of others? Whether one likes it or not, the memory of history is formed in a place that bursts through all nationality. Both the "Japanese from Japan proper" and the "peninsulars" must discover anew ways to narrate this memory in order to avoid "reterritorializing" the global "geopolitical vertigo" into yet another national history.

Translated by Trent Maxey

Notes

Kang Sangjung, "Kokumin no shinshō chiri to datsu-kokuminteki katari," in *Nashonaru hisutorī wo koete* [Beyond national history], ed. Komori Yōichi and Takahashi Tetsuya (Tokyo: Tokyo Daigaku Shuppankai, 1998), pp. 141–156.

1. Shiba Ryōtarō, *Kono kuni no katachi II* [The form of this nation II] (Tokyo: Bunshun Bunko, 1993), p. 16.
2. Fujioka Nobukatsu, *Kingendaishi kyōiku no kaikaku: zendama akudama shikan wo koete* [Reforming modern history education: Beyond the hero-villain view of history] (Tokyo: Meiji Tosho, 1996), p. 100.
3. Gearóid Ó. Tuathail, *Critical Geopolitics: The Politics of Writing Global Space* (Minneapolis: University of Minnesota Press, 1996), p. 230.
4. *Foreign Affairs*, October 1997, p. 10.
5. Carol Gluck, "Kindai toshite no nijū seiki: Nihon no 'sengo' wo kangaeru" [The twentieth century as modern: Reflections on Japan's "postwar"], *Sekai* [World], November 1997.
6. Christopher Thorne, *The Issue of War: States, Societies, and the Far Eastern Conflict of 1941–1945* (London: Hamish Hamilton, 1985), p. 325.
7. Mitani Taichirō, *Kindai Nihon no sensō to seiji* [War and politics of modern Japan] (Tokyo: Iwanami Shoten, 1997), p. 31.
8. Shiba Ryōtarō, "'Zakkaya' no teikokushugi" [The imperialism of the 'general store'], in *Kono kuni no katachi I* [The form of this nation I] (Tokyo: Bunshun Bunko, 1993).
9. "The Potsdam Declaration" (July 26, 1945), in *Nihonshi shiryō: gendai* [Japanese historical data: The present age], ed. Research Association of Historiography (Tokyo: Iwanami Shoten, 1997), p. 145.

10. "Tennō no ningen sengen" [The emperor's declaration of humanity] (January 1, 1946), in *Nihonshi shiryō: gendai*, pp. 162–163; and Yonetani Tadashi, "Maruyama Masao to sengo Nihon" [Maruyama Masao and postwar Japan], in *Maruyama Masao wo yomu* [Reading Maruyama Masao] (Tokyo: Jōkyō Shuppan, 1997), p. 137.
11. Mitani Taichirō, pp. 76–77.
12. Sotoyama Dai, *"Tōa shinbun* kaisetsu" [East Asian news commentary], in *Senjika zainichi Chōsenjin shiryō shū* (Tokyo: Ryokuin Shobō, 1997), vol. 3, pp. 247–253.
13. Sakai Naoki, "Nihonjin de aru koto" [Being Japanese], *Shisō* [Thought] no. 882 (1997).

THE DISCOVERY OF THE "ORIENT" AND ORIENTALISM

I. The Postwar and the Repetition of History

A line from a scene in Luchino Visconti's masterpiece *The Leopard* runs, "Everything must change in order not to change." These words brilliantly express the paradoxical continuity between Japan's prewar and postwar periods, in contrast to the flood of narratives on the "fifty years of postwar."

The "postwar" period was in many nations discussed domestically until the 1950s, when it was replaced by the term "contemporary." In the case of Japan, why has the homogeneity that is the postwar era been unconditionally accepted for over fifty years now? Like heavy clouds, the postwar myth known as the "discontinuity" of 1945 has concealed everything. Along with this metahistory, various polls reveal that the overwhelming majority of Japanese (over 80 percent) have in one way or another affirmatively accepted the postwar. Here we can see a narrative of the "postwar as conservatism," according to which "things are fine the way they are." This is, so to speak, a narrative of the "postwar as talisman."[1]

Should this "vagueness" be perceived as the brightness of the early postwar period, right after the canopy of the nation-state had collapsed? Should one understand it as an empty shell of the vital spirit of reform and freedom that the postwar initially expressed? Or is it the result of the routinization of such reform and freedom? If none of these is true, must one think that the postwar was from its very beginning ironically bound up with the prewar? If so, then surely the key to redefining Japan in the larger context of the twentieth century lies precisely in the "modernization narratives" that were repeated both before and after World War II.

In fact, the postwar Shōwa era has been newly interpreted as the second leap of Japanese modernization, following the Meiji Restoration. In other words, the odious "Fifteen-Year War" is seen as a temporary deviation from the golden road to modern Japan. The nation returned to the initial track of modernization in the postwar period, which began with defeat and reconstruction. Such an analogy has proved to be a brilliant success: the modernization narratives repeated throughout the Meiji, Taishō, and Shōwa periods obliterated all wartime memories, while the nationwide "conversions" (tenkō) before and after 1945 were facilitated by both the persecution of war criminals at the International Military Tribunal and the people's "victim consciousness."

What has been excluded or concealed in this discursive space of the postwar? Carol Gluck, the North American scholar of Japan, has described the United States and the emperor system as postwar Japan's "ghosts at the historical feast." I should add here that "Asia" too was such a ghost, for the narrative of Japanese modernization and development has dragged along behind it the "shadow of Asia" while positioning the postwar in the comparative context of the Meiji Restoration.

In a sense, Japan's view of foreign countries makes up an "important part of the nation's spiritual territory, which has a profound relationship with both domestic and foreign activities and practices." Alongside the escalation of actual geographic violence as represented by colonial rule, Japan's imaginary geography of Asia as mapped out during the Russo-Japanese and first Sino-Japanese wars—especially the ideas and images of Taiwan, Korea, and China (Shina)—marked a decisive turn. In order to understand how deeply this imaginary geography was related to the Orientalism of the imperialist West, one need only see how Japanese colonies were discussed in analogy with Islam, which was central to Western Orientalism. As Tokutomi Roka writes, "The time of Mohammad is long gone. Islamic countries . . . will undeniably fall if they do not depart from Mohammad. I said before that the Korean Renaissance would begin when the Koreans abandon their white robes. Today I proclaim that the Renaissance of the Near East will begin when the Turks take off their red hats."[2]

Such a view of Asia runs throughout Japan's postwar national memory like an undercurrent. This becomes evident if one examines Yoshida Shigeru, who played a pivotal role in bridging the prewar and postwar eras. Yoshida, whom even Konoe Fumimaro referred to as a conservative politician of the old generation, was nevertheless the most important figure of Japan's ruling elite after 1948, and even became a symbol of his generation. This represents postwar Japan's obvious paradox.

Yoshida's political reemergence signifies that the defeat did not destroy the bedrock of preexisting conservative forces. One should analyze Yoshida's case in order to understand the Japanese empire and its imperial consciousness. Here is an essential element that links the prewar and postwar periods. As both the prewar "manager of the empire" and the "postwar architect of Japan–U.S. military relations," Yoshida actually viewed the San Francisco Treaty (which brought postwar Japan under external control) in terms of the realization of "cooperative imperialism." This notion clearly reflects Yoshida's abundant experience of "imperial management." Yoshida "did not easily accept the idea that Japan's militarism was an immanent part of the Meiji Restoration, even after 1945." Rather he boasted of the overall unity of Japan's "principle of foreign policy ever since the opening of the country":

> Previous politicians from the time of the Meiji Restoration ran the government during a period of turmoil, but still achieved great deeds for the prosperity of the nation. From today's perspective, the remains of their arduous management are clear. The basic course of diplomacy after the opening of the country was, in sum, the close alignment with England. But after tiny Japan gained its miraculous victory in the Sino-Japanese War in 1895, England—which had significant interests in the Far East— inevitably recognized our country's authority and voluntarily initiated a pro-Japanese policy.[3]

As should be clear in these recollections, Yoshida "belonged to the first post–Sino-Japanese War generation, which was deliberately inspired by emperor-centered nationalism and the resilient policies of imperialist expansion." Yoshida's impressions both repeat and reconfirm Japan's modernization narratives as centered upon the "national polity." This represents the conservative mindset that seeks to repair the dissolution of the empire (the war defeat) and the failure of official history through the power of repetition, as sustained by "genealogical and procreative metaphors." In this sense, history is even in the postwar repeated as the "present past."

What kinds of assimilation and distortion did the representation of Asia undergo through this repetition? I would like to consider this question by focusing on the field of Oriental History (Oriental Studies).

II. Colonies and Oriental Studies

Japanese discursive space from the late nineteenth century to the twentieth century is filled with ideologies of colonial imperialism. As cited above, Yoshida's nostalgic recollections were repeated on the horizon of this same space. When Yoshida was finishing up his formal education, Japan had just won the first Sino-Japanese War and had begun to pursue the "aggressive idea of building a colonial empire equal to those of the Great Powers." In 1897 Yoshida entered Gakushūin University, where he came to be inspired by the ideas of "Japanism" and "national polity" while also developing a great interest in Asia. The president of Gakushūin was Konoe Atsumaro, whose predecessor was Miura Gorō. It is well known that Miura was an avid advocate of the invasion of the Asian mainland. He even played a central role in the assassination of the Korean empress while acting as residential official and legation attaché in Korea.

It is highly symbolic that Miura established the field of "Oriental History" while president of Gakushūin, for Shiratori Kurakichi, who would later become a pioneer in this field, took a post at this university in 1890 after graduating from Tokyo Imperial University. This reveals the process that intellectual domination and cultural hegemony distilled in the geographic violence of the colonial empire. Such interaction between knowledge and power can be observed in Shiratori's commentary on the relation between Gotō Shinpei, the "founder of colonial business," and "Oriental Studies." Shiratori explains Gotō's academic achievements as follows:

> The Count (Gotō) stands out among other politicians and entrepreneurs. He respects scholarship and conducts thorough research when engaging in practical politics and economic management. His enthusiasm even extends to other remotely related matters. On each issue, the Count not only planned and led academic research, he also looked after the data. Everyone knows that while in charge of Taiwan's civil administration he gathered many scholars, set aside an enormous budget and led detailed investigations of Taiwan's legal system, local customs and languages, etc. His achievements still shine forth, even in academic circles.[4]

This passage vividly describes the very beginning of the enormous system of knowledge and power as jointly produced by colonialism and Orientalism in Taiwan, the "(first) laboratory of colonial rule." Along with the expansion of territory gained in winning the Russo-Japanese War, the results of Taiwan's "live experiment" of "scientific colonialism" would be applied to Manchuria, Korea, and the Chinese mainland. Yoshida Shigeru later enthusiastically recalled that Gotō, who became the largest organizer of business in the colonial empire as president of the South Manchurian Railroad Company, "demonstrated such competence and authority as comparable to that of England's former East Indian Company"

Gotō consistently emphasized the importance of field research. Wherever he went, he invariably "left behind research instituions and scientific studies," which can be seen, for example, in the massive archives of the South Manchurian Railroad Company. Gotō's idea of "scientific colonialism" can be traced back to his experience studying policy as a hygiene technician in the Department of the Interior. His *Kokka eisei genri* [Principles of national hygiene], published in 1890, systematically explains the concept of "scientific colonialism." This concept belongs to the administrative system of state affairs, as based upon the *Medizinalpolizei* (hygiene police) and hygiene administration—or what Michel Foucault refers to as *Polizeiwissenschaft* (the science of political administration).

Gotō was keenly aware of the necessity of "demographic investigation" and statistical "observations of social life" in order to facilitate the expansion of national resources by "integrating residents under the principle of marginal utility." Gotō perceived Taiwan as the "training ground for colonial administration." His science was realized in his large-scale "statistical research studies of the Taiwanese population and its changes, crimes, educational affairs, communication, agriculture and industries (such as the sugarcane industry)." Moreover, the results of his studies of "physiographic conditions" and local customs would later play a major role in bringing about the "new principles of territorial rule." (Gotō held up these "new principles" and avoided "the words 'colonial policy'"). As Gotō later wrote in his *Nihon bōchō ron* [Theory on Japanese expansion], as if boasting of his success:

> I spent barely ten years in Taiwan, yet the experience I acquired there was my pride and glory. . . . As soon as I took a post in Taiwan, I conducted various experiments, thus deepening my awareness. But my work environment was so full of bustling that I could not pursue my goals as I wished. Nonetheless, my conviction that every political strategy should be built on biological principles was validated through actual experiments in Taiwan. Heaven assigned me the task of totalizing the irregularities of human life and rewarded me with the great gift of accurately interpreting their nature, meanings and principles.[5]

With the expansion of Japan's geographic violence into the "Manchuria-Korea" region, "Colonial Governor" Gotō's notion of "scientific colonialism" grew into a large-scale project.[6] Shiratori's Oriental History had prepared the authoritative academic discourse that would support Gotō's project. In this sense, the encounter between Shiratori and Gotō was a symbolic event that intimately tied Orientalist discourse to the idea of a "powerful society through well-regulated economic and political systems." Elsewhere Shiratori explains that the "Research Division of Manchurian History and Geography" was set up at the South Manchurian Railroad Company with substantial help from Gotō. In this institution, Shiratori led a research group whose members included Yanai Watari, Matsui Hitoshi, Inaba Iwakichi, Tsuda Sōkichi, and Ikeuchi Hiroshi. This group published such studies as *Manshū rekishi chiri* [Manchurian history and geography], *Bunroku Keichō no eki* [The battle of the Bunroku and Keichō], and *Chōsen rekishi chiri* [Korean history and geography]. Through these studies, the group institutionalized academic discourse on Manchuria, Korea, and China. Conversely, however, this process shows that colonialism's "formation of power" acquired intellectual authority by appearing in various discourses and institutions (academic societies, schools, libraries, diplomatic organizations, etc.). Herein lies the source of Oriental History (Oriental Studies) in Japan. As if following European history, the intellectual domination of this "Japan-styled" Orientalism sought to enclose Asia within a "classification system of discipline and training," with Japan as standard.

Yet Japan was haunted by an unavoidable dilemma. For despite the invention of various techniques and disciplines used to observe, dominate, and maintain Asia in such a way that Japan was posited as transcendental subject, no one could deny that Japan was itself part of this Asian *topos*. The question, then, was how Japanese culture could distance itself from Asia—which was a kind of proxy for Japan, even its own "hidden self"—and at the same time acquire the force and identity with which to establish an equal dialogue with the West as other. This is where the field of Oriental History came in. Shiratori must have been fully aware of this connection. It was made clear to him by Japan's expansion into "Manchuria-Korea":

> I returned to Japan at the end of 1903. Around that time, Russo-Japanese relations had started to become tense. The climate was unpredictable. War finally broke out in the following February, and the whole world watched zealously. Fortunately, our troops steadily pushed the Russian troops out of the fields of Manchuria-Korea, finally gaining victory. In any case, the impressions I received during my study in Europe grew increasingly stronger. I came to the conclusion that Orientals must

lead the research of the Orient. The fact is, however, that westerners had pioneered most of this research, leaving hardly anything for Japanese scholars to take up. The exception to this was Manchuria-Korea, a region over which previous wars had been fought and which Japan was about to conquer. Western scholarship on this region was still scarce. While some research of course existed, such as several useful language studies, issues of geography, history and archeology yet remained unexamined. Given the new political circumstances brought about by the war, the Japanese must conduct fundamental academic research on this region.[7]

When Shiratori writes that "Orientals must lead the research of the Orient," he means of course the Japanese. In other words, "Orientals" incapable of self-representation would be represented by the Japanese, who were however also "Orientals." The Japanese would then inform the West (the other) about "them." It was in this twisted Orientalism that Oriental History found its reason for being. Furthermore, the domain of Oriental History expanded in the form of "savage lands" (Manchuria-Korea) to be explored together with the escalation of actual geographic violence. Here we can see the growth of Shiratori's academic passions and expectations. The South Manchurian Railroad Company's "Research Division of Manchurian History and Geography" became the site where "scholars from different fields could work together."

Here it should be clear that the academic discourse of Oriental History was produced, repeated, and developed in various exchanges with political power, as could be seen in Japan's imperial and colonial systems.

If we are to understand Orientalism as a "system of citation between writers," then Oriental History can be said to have expressed (either fully or with partial modification) the persistence and tenacity of Japanese Orientalism in the postwar period. In other words, Oriental History demonstrates in an extremely condensed manner the way Japan used Orientalism for its modernization. Oriental History was the ultimate form of knowledge that responded to the historical question of how Japan could modernize while escaping from the objective category of the Orient. Likewise, it responded to the question of how Japan could impose an Orientalist cultural hegemony over Asia while preserving its identity with it. Japan constructed such an identity in terms of the relation between its idea of the "Orient" (which was discovered or created by both its identity with and difference from the West) and its imaginary geography and history of Korea, Manchuria, and China. Herein lies the aporia that was repeated throughout Japan's process of modernization. It is in this sense that we must problematize the field of Oriental History and its pioneer figure, Shiratori. For what is expressed as an extremely refined system of academic discourse is how modern forms of knowledge were bound up with power in Japan's modernization narratives, how the relation between "self" and "other" (Asia and the West) was created, and finally what kinds of ironic results were produced therefrom. As goes without saying, the problems of Shiratori's Oriental History still haunt the public memory of "fifty years of postwar."

III. The Discovery of the "Orient" and the Creation of History

If we are to understand the nation itself as narrative, then narrative power (as well as the power to deter the formation and emergence of other narratives) occupies an extremely important position for culture and imperialism. As Shiratori writes:

> Today the Manchurian Empire looks forward to a bright future as Japan's neighbor. Is it right that many Japanese are ignorant of its history? We predicted around 1908 that research on Manchuria would be necessary, and I can console myself that our efforts have not been wasted. . . . Westerners still perceive Manchuria with a jaundiced eye. We must teach them about its basic history so that they realize that Manchuria has not simply been established as Japan's puppet-state. In this regard, I believe it is necessary for not only historians but indeed laymen to conduct purely academic studies of Manchurian ancient history.[8]

After the Manchurian Incident, Shiratori's ambitions for Oriental History greatly expanded in step with the founding of the Manchurian state and the invasion of the Chinese mainland. When Shiratori spoke of "Manchuria" or "Manchuria-Korea," however, this imaginary geography did not include the actual inhabitants or ethnic groups of these regions. Rather his historical investigations focused only on the "location of castles, wartime military routes, traffic routes, and territories." Shiratori's project sought to establish a relation between Japan and "Manchuria-Korean" history as well as to clarify Japanese national identity and its historical mission. This project was only possible as based upon the "silence of the natives" in the face of the Japanese colonial empire's overwhelming influence. In this respect, Shiratori complacently accepted the "assimilation" of the colonized through both Japanese historical narratives and the ideology of "universal brotherhood" (*isshi dōjin*). The waning geopolitical-cultural territory of the "Orient" was appropriated within Japan (which had become the "Orient's" sole "flourishing power"), and its existence was recognized only as a corollary of Japanese history.

Despite the rhetoric of "universal brotherhood," there was of course no mixing or harmony between the Japanese and the "subordinated races" as based on mutual respect and affinity. I will say more about this later but, in Shiratori's case, both the "origin" of the Japanese people and the emperor system as unchanged and yet ceaselessly changing "national essence" (national polity) assumed a "religiosity" similar to that of Protestantism in the historical studies of Leopold von Ranke (whom Shiratori saw as a model). In this way, the possibility of granting equal rights and responsibilities to those colonized ethnic groups who had become "Japanized" as "imperial subjects" was foreclosed in advance. Here it must be understood how Shiratori's discourse on the "Orient" was made possible by the twisted relations of identity and difference.

Furthermore, as should be clear from Shiratori's remarks above, the "other" for Japan was the West. It was expected that the dialogue with history could take place, and indeed necessarily had to take place, only between Japan and the West. In other words, Shiratori tried here as well to undertake the question of Japan's identity with and difference from the West. After the Manchurian Incident, however, Japan's dialogue with the West became impossible, thus leaving Japan's narrative as only "monologue." To what extent was Shiratori aware of this aporia? If he was unable to see it, then what immanent problems existed within his thought and Oriental History?

From just prior to the Meiji Restoration to the outbreak of the Pacific War, Shiratori's life was, as he himself relates, a "happy life in a happy age." "Occasionally the Professor (Shiratori) remarked that he was very grateful for having, in the brief span of time from the Meiji and Taishō eras to the glorious era of Shōwa, witnessed the nation's unprecedented prosperity and the striking development of Japanese life and culture. The Professor believed that his happy life was truly a gift of this age." From the Manchurian Incident to the Pacific War, Shiratori lacked even the slightest doubt about the Japanese modernization (or progress) narrative that ran throughout the Meiji, Taishō, and Shōwa eras. It can thus be said that this great scholar gave no thought even to the "deviation" that was the "Fifteen-Year War." This was perhaps the aporia encountered by Oriental History when, during the war, its mission had finally run its course.

When Shiratori pushed to its end the Japan-"Orient" distinction and described the West (the "other") as the reverse image of Japan's ideal, modern Japanese history devolved into "monologue" and lost sight of its dialogic "other." Having largely achieved its goal of forming a nation-state in the Meiji era, the Japanese empire had by the Taishō era already come to regard its "Westernized" modernization as a "mechanical Trojan horse," one that would confuse and disrupt those sociocultural structures "proper" to Japan. Here the attainment of modernization with its mixture of disillusionment cast a complicated shadow. This is clear in Gotō's *Nihon bōchō ron*. Angry with Japan's deadlock in foreign relations and confused domestic conditions after World War I, Gotō complained that "Europe shows no good-will, China betrays us, negotiations with Russia are at a standstill, and the U.S. has recently passed anti-Japanese immigration laws. We must recognize that Japan faces a rough road ahead. Now is the time for national reflection." Gotō then attributes these hardships to Japan's forgetting of itself and "fascination with imitating Western civilization" such as to neglect the "nation's true self": "We have been so dazzled by the external radiance of Western civilization that, with no regard to its substance, we value the West and demean ourselves." The pendulum thus swings over to narcissistic national identity: "The Japanese nation deserves the highest award at the World National History Exhibit. Japan possesses the greatest glory and authority in respect to its prodigious capacity to incorporate, absorb, comprehend and assimilate, and particularly in regard to its organic absolutism as centered upon the Imperial family."[9]

Gotō's claim pervades the new motif of Shiratori's Oriental History. Oriental History attempted now to separate itself from the West, just as *kokugaku*, or Japanese Classical Studies, sought to do so previously with China. Here the West came to be seen as an infirm "outside"; it was deprived of value and regarded as that which Japan must not become. Like the "succession of a bloodline," Oriental History thus simply repeated its "monologic" history.

What was reflected in this term "Oriental History" was the ambiguity of modern Japan's view of its position in the world. For the very category of the "Orient" is nothing but an "imaginary time and space," one that emerged from the suffering common to non-Western societies in their attempt to reconcile civilization and culture, difference and identity. It is for this reason that Oriental History replaced China with the term *Shina*, thereby relativizing it by positioning it within a broader time-space than the "Orient," and sought to discover within the "Orient" the origin of Japan's historical narrative. This was at the same time supposed to open up the possibility of an equal dialogue with the West. For since the "Orient" was also the origin of the West, Japan's focus on it in regard to its own past made this site a common ground where it could compare and compete with the West. By thus distinguishing both the West and Asia as other, Oriental History sought to create a sense of Japan as a modern "Oriental" nation.

It was of course impossible to treat both the "Orient" and the West within Europe's unilinear temporal framework. Shiratori rejected this notion of time and yet maintained the West's academic (scientific) epistemology. His achievement lay in this intellectual feat while drawing on Ranke's historical studies.

IV. Japan Within Identity and Difference

Shiratori, who belonged to the first generation of History and Liberal Arts students at the Imperial University, studied historical criticism in 1887 (Meiji 20) with Ranke's disciple Ludwig Riese. He thus became acquainted with positivist history in its emphasis on facts, objectivity, and respect for data, as based on "how things originally were." This differed from the technical methodology of Ernst Bernheim as introduced by Tsuboi Kumezō, who became professor of History and Liberal Arts after Shiratori graduated. Shiratori's interest in Ranke was prompted less by the data and methodology of his historical criticism than by his ideas of history and original interpretations of spirit as illustrated by this criticism.

> In Ranke's historical philosophy, each nation's history leads to God. Shiratori sought to discover in this philosophy the individuality and specificity of the Japanese nation as well as the synthetic principle through which Japan acquired its own particular historical reality. "Having spent his college years when German nationalist thought was being introduced to Japan, witnessing the promulgations of the Imperial Constitution and Rescript on Education and finally receiving a nobleman's education at Gakushūin under Miura Gorō," Shiratori sought a way to guarantee Japan's particular identity while grounding the idea of the Japanese ethnos on a historical idea (the emperor system). At the same time, what utterly distinguished him from Ranke was his view that the emperor system, in its historical being as manifestation of the universal spirit, was (like a transcendental entity) an object of absolute devotion. It was the emperor system, at once historical and suprahistorical, which was the ultimate source of Japan's "progress."

In 1913 (Taishō 2), after the annexation of Korea and with the growing invasion of Manchuria, Shiratori remarked that "Japan, according to Oriental History, is characterized by progress." He explains the cause of this progress as follows:

> The Japanese race stands alone in Asia. There is no other nation like Japan, whose character is utterly different from that of China, India, Persia and Egypt. . . . Situated in Asia's easternmost corner, Japan is flourishing brilliantly. There can be no question of this. Japan is in a position to absorb all the world's strengths.[10]

Shiratori concludes that just as Japan was able to skillfully incorporate only those aspects of "Confucian fundamentalism" that were compatible with "our national polity," so too can it do the same thing with "Western culture."

The certainty that Japan could now follow the same course of "progress" as the West without losing its identity was based on both historical and suprahistorical ideas. While part of the "Orient," Japan was yet able to pursue the same course of "progress as civilization" as the West by "maintaining the framework of Oriental civilization" and combining "Oriental" and Western cultures. We can describe this notion of Japanese history as informed by Shiratori's "Oriental History" as a narcissistic "discourse of Japanese heterogeneity."

For Shiratori, there was an urgent need to elucidate Japan's "origin" in its relation to Asian history. Here he could not ignore the massive amounts of Western Orientalist scholarship. Nevertheless, he sought to establish a "dialogue" with the West by elevating "Japan's Orient" to the world stage through his own geo-historical dynamics.[11]

Shiratori's dynamics consisted of a dualism between "North" and "South," which calls to mind Herbert Spencer's dualism between military and civil society. Such dynamics not only explained the rise and fall of various nations, it also confirmed the "Orient" as a mediated existence between Japan and the West as well as provided a general framework situating Japan's past within Asia. Shiratori's ambition to make the Eurasian continent the world's geo-historical focal point, thereby reducing the West to its mere peninsula, sought its foothold in the affinity between Japan and Korea as well as the problem of this affinity's "origin."

At the beginning of the first Sino-Japanese War, Shiratori had published "Tangun kō" [A study of Tangun, the legendary founder of Korea] in issue 28 of *Gakushūin hojinkai zasshi* [*Journal of the Gakushūin Society of Academic Brotherhood*]. Later he avidly researched Korean history, employing methods from comparative linguistics to prove that both Japanese and Korean were Ural-Altaic languages, with the former belonging to the Mongolian group and the latter to the Tungus group. Shiratori explains the aims of his research at the beginning of his "Kokugo to gaikokugo to no hikaku kenkyū" [Comparative study of Japanese and foreign languages] (1905): "This comparative study of Japanese and foreign languages is motivated by my desire to find the source of the Japanese language as well as to elucidate the origins of the Yamato race." Here his intentions are quite clear.

The very concept and system of the "Japanese language" is impossible without the formation of the nation-state as "imaginary community." Nevertheless, Shiratori sought to fulfill his desire for the language's "pure origin":

Nothing resembling the Japanese language can be found in other Asian nations, which proves that Japanese is a solitary language. Previously I believed that Korean and Japanese must share the same origin, and even presented several papers arguing this point. After much reflection, however, I came to realize that the two languages are absolutely unrelated. The more I examined Japanese in comparison with other Far Eastern languages, the clearer it became that Japanese is unlike these. It is now plain to me that there is no similar language anywhere in the world.

In the end, Shiratori's desire for "origin" became enclosed within "monologue," where it simply repeated its own self-identity within a world devoid of any dialogic "other."

It was at this point that Shiratori abandoned his research of Korea (which "today is possessed of a uniqueness that is neither Mongolian nor Manchurian"), even in order to demonstrate the intimate relation between the Japanese and Korean languages. Korea now came to be confined within the geopolitical and cultural ideology of "Manchuria-Korea." This signified that Korea was not a nation but rather a mere geographic area. Yet such a view was in no way unusual. Similar accounts can be found, for example, in the "blighted Korea" of Nitobe Inazō, who had served in colonial Taiwan under Gotō Shinpei as government-general engineer.

Nonetheless, Shiratori stands out in regard to the scope of his geo-historical research, which stretched from Korea to "Manchuria," central Asia, India, and Eastern Europe. He tried to explain the decline of Korea and China on the basis of a "North-South dualism" that operated throughout the entire "Orient," and prove systematically that Japan differed from the other "Oriental" nations. This represented a challenge to Western Orientalist taxonomy and the formation of a new taxonomic system that would transform Asia's past from the West's Orient to "Japan's Orient."

Shiratori's theory of "North-South dualism" began to take shape during the Russo-Japanese War, and clearly reflects Japan's own awareness of itself as a burgeoning colonial empire. This is clear from the fact that Shiratori discusses the dualism of "Oriental History" within the "North-South opposition" in terms of the political opposition between Russia and England on the Asian continent.

For years I have claimed that the basic trend of Oriental History derives from the opposition between the two great powers of North and South. In ancient times, the rise and fall of the Han race of the South and the so-called "Northern Barbarians" generally shaped the central stage of Oriental history. This same formation lives on in modernity in the opposition between England (South) and Russia (North). I believe that the history of the Far East is fundamentally shaped by such opposition. If one observes the facts of history according to this dualism, then one can very accurately interpret the rise and fall of all cultures from Central Asia in the West to Manchuria, Korea and even Japan in the East.[12]

For Shiratori, China's decline was no accident. Rather it was caused by the loss of equilibrium in the opposition and strife between the North (the military society of the "Northern barbarians") and South (the civil society of the Hans). Such dualism also accounts for the vertiginous rise and fall as experienced in such peripheral areas of the Chinese mainland as the Korean peninsula.

This was Shiratori's basic schema of knowledge in regard to both China and Korea. To this extent, it was inevitable that such ethnic groups or nation-states were excluded from civilization's "progress" and defined in terms of stagnation and decline. In contrast, there had existed in Japan "Northern barbarians known as the Ainu who sought the rich soil of the South," but the "Japanese of the South" had "repelled" the Ainu and "driven them back," eventually forming an ideal culture that combined both North and South. As Shiratori confidently concludes, "This North-South opposition is the basic structure underlying Oriental history and Asia's political framework. I believe that one can clearly grasp the core of history in this manner. This is my brief answer regarding the proper way to view Oriental History as a whole."[13]

The aim of Shiratori's "Oriental History" was to ground the integration of "Japan's unique" dualism upon the simultaneously historical and suprahistorical "national essence" (the emperor system). This also explains why the question of Japanese culture's "origin" assumed such decisive importance. However, historical beginnings are to be found in "diverse differences" rather than in the inviolable identity of the "origin" (*Ursprung*). As Foucault writes, "Only metaphysicians seek the spirit of history in the faraway ideal of the 'origin'":

> It is no longer origin that gives rise to historicity; it is historicity that, in its very fabric, makes possible the necessity of an origin which must be both internal and foreign to it: like the virtual tip of a cone in which all differences, all dispersions, all discontinuities would be knitted together so as to form no more than a single point of identity, the impalpable figure of the Same, yet possessing the power, nevertheless, to burst open upon itself and become Other.[14]

Undoubtedly captivated by the "chimera of Japan's pure origin," Shiratori forgot that history teaches us how to laugh at the "gravity of origin." Although he required the physician that is history to exorcise the shadow from Japan's spirit, as it were, Shiratori nevertheless returned to the world of myth by integrating all the differences, dispersions, and discontinuities within the single identity of Japan's "origin." As I have repeatedly pointed out, Shiratori left behind merely the empty principle of identity with no "other."

Shiratori no doubt believed that only this notion of Oriental History could free Japan from the Eurocentric world order and its inferior status therein. Ultimately, however, this notion was nothing more than an attempt to elevate Japan to the rank of the Great Powers. In this regard, "Japan's Orient" represented a Japan-centered "totality" that replaced that of the West. Shiratori never witnessed the way "Japan's Orient" later became the "Greater East Asia Co-Prosperity Sphere" and ended in self-destruction. As Tsuda Sōkichi remarked, Shiratori was a "happy man in a happy age." For the "Orient," however, that age was an unhappy one.

The shadows of the past clinging to Shiratori's "Oriental History" possess a real meaning that goes beyond mere historical reflection. For, as goes without saying, Asia's stunning growth has brought about in Japan a desire to "return to Asia." It is no longer unusual now to discuss the theory of "Escape from the West and Enter Asia" rather than that of "Escape from Asia and Enter the West" as a new alternative to Japan's "Cold Peace" with the United States. Is Japan part of Asia? This at once old and new question has returned at a time when Japan's national identity is linked with changes in domestic politics.

The postwar conservatives (as represented by Yoshida's generation) who established Japan's 1955 domestic political structure understood the San Francisco Peace Treaty as a "cooperative imperialism" that would enable the nation to, alongside the West, "peacefully" exploit Asia. This has since resulted in a rift between these conservatives and their followers. With the growing exhaustion of Japan's postwar foreign and domestic systems, there has been a reemergence of certain historical memories evoking "Japan's Orient" of the past. What does this reemergence signify?

As our examination of Oriental History reveals, the well-known term "Orient" (or Asia) came to be defined as a geopolitical order because of the Japanese colonial empire's invasion following the first Sino-Japanese War. Prior to that invasion, there existed no fixed geopolitical-cultural space in the region, thereby rendering any sense of Asian unity impossible. In one stroke, Japan's control of Taiwan and its invasion and colonization of the Korean peninsula as well as its expansion into the mainland raised Asia to the level of collective existence in international relations. A shared consciousness of a geopolitical-cultural order thus gradually came into being, with dispersed regions and countries now seeking their own identity in Asia.[15] The "Orient" or Asia is, therefore, nothing but a regional order formed by Japan's imperialist invasion.

Together with Japan's history of imperialism, Shiratori's "Oriental History" was fated to rise and fall with equal speed. Paradoxically, however, the United States came to replace prewar Japan in sustaining the regional order of the "Orient" during the Cold War. That is to say, rather than overturn "Japan's Orient" as in a sense established by prewar Japan, the war defeat and consequent American rule actually repeated this regional order in the form of an "enforced regionalism from above," as led by the United States. The fact that postwar Japan was, under the aegis of the United States, able to repeat its overwhelming economic force in the region is further proof that this notion of an Asian regional order has survived in a new form. In this regard, we have not yet fully broken the spell of "Oriental History" as an academic system institutionalized from the time of the first Sino-Japanese War to the beginning of this past century as an intellectual authority on the "Orient."

Translated by Shu Kuge

Notes

Kang Sangjung, "'Tōyō' no hakken to orientarizumu," in *Orientarizumu no kanata he* [Beyond Orientalism] (Tokyo: Iwanami Shoten, 1996), pp. 122–146. Originally published as "Saīdo: orientarizumu igo" [Said: After Orientalism], in *Gendai shisō* [Contemporary thought], 23:03 (1995).

1. Carol Gluck, "The Past in the Present," in *Postwar Japan as History,* ed. Andrew Gordon (Berkeley: University of California Press, 1993), pp. 64–95.
2. Quoted in Sugita Hideaki, *Nihonjin no Chūtō hakken* [The Japanese discovery of the Middle East] (Tokyo: Tokyo Daigaku Shuppankai, 1995), p. 152.
3. Yoshida Shigeru, *Kaisō no jūnen* [Recollection of the last ten years] (Tokyo: Shinchōsha, 1957), vol. 1, p. 25.
4. Shiratori Kurakichi, *Shiratori Kurakichi zenshū* [Complete works of Shiratori Kurakichi] (Tokyo: Iwanami Shoten, 1971), vol. 10, p. 358.
5. Gotō Shinpei, *Nihon bōchō ron* (Tokyo: Dai-Nihon Yūbenkai, 1924), pp. 1–4.
6. Mark R. Peattie, "Japanese Attitudes toward Colonialism," in *The Japanese Colonial Empire, 1895–1945* (Princeton: Princeton University Press, 1984), p. 85.
7. Shiratori Kurakichi, *Shiratori Kurakichi zenshū,* vol. 10, pp. 376–377.
8. Ibid., p. 407.
9. Gotō Shinpei, *Nihon bōchō ron,* pp. 162–163. This expression of Gotō's excessive nationalism reflects his deep dissatisfaction with the restraints placed on Japan's imperialist and colonial policies by the West, as he believed that the nation

should be accorded a position commensurate with its strength. Here we can see a rhetoric that renders Japan's vital "force of assimilation' equivalent to "Oriental civilization" as well as paraphrases the confrontation between Japan and the West as an opposition between "Oriental civilization" and "Occidental civilization."

10. Shiratori Kurakichi, *Shiratori Kurakichi zenshū*, vol. 9, p. 186.

11. This passage is inspired by Stefan Tanaka's *Japan's Orient: Rendering Pasts into History* (Berkeley: University of California Press, 1993). In his reading of the academic discourse of Shiratori's Oriental History, Tanaka shows that the link between reality and scientific knowledge is not a necessary one, as it is formed through the mediation of contingent power.

12. Shiratori Kurakichi, *Shiratori Kurakichi zenshū*, vol. 8, p. 69.

13. Ibid., vol. 9, p. 253.

14. Michel Foucault, *The Order of Things: An Archaeology of the Human Sciences* (New York: Vintage Books, 1994), pp. 329–330.

15. Regarding the manner in which the geopolitical category of Asia was "repeated" in U.S. Cold War policy, see John W. Dower, *War and Peace in Japan* (New York: W.W. Norton & Co., 1993). See also Irie Akira, "Nihon to Ajia—hyakunen no omomi" [Japan and Asia: The weight of a hundred years], in *Sekai* [World], 606 (1995): 45–53.

Chapter 3

OVERCOMING MODERNITY

Karatani Kōjin

I. The Opposition Between Two "Aesthetics"

Today I will speak of the famous "Overcoming Modernity" symposium, which was held in 1942 (Shōwa 17), following the outbreak of hostilities between Japan and the United States. While a careful study of this symposium could not possibly be undertaken in such a short lecture as this, I in fact plan to spend the next year on this topic in the course of a university seminar. Today I can speak of only one aspect of the symposium.

A diverse group of people participated in the "Overcoming Modernity" symposium (which includes here the presented papers). The symposium basically consisted of three groups: the *Bungakkai* [Literary World] group, the Japanese Romantics, and the Kyoto School, but there were also present a natural scientist, a Catholic theologian, and a film critic. In a larger sense, however, those who did not participate in the symposium should not be overlooked. For example, while Kobayashi Hideo of *Bungakkai* was present, neither Yasuda Yojūrō of the Romantics nor Nishida Kitarō of the Kyoto School was involved. In his article "Kindai no chōkoku" [Overcoming modernity], Takeuchi Yoshimi focuses primarily on Yasuda Yojūrō, one of these nonparticipants. Likwise, Hiromatsu Wataru discusses such figures as Nishida Kitarō and Miki Kiyoshi, who were also absent from the symposium.

It must thus be said that the thinking of "overcoming modernity" comes out most fully before the early 1940s, that it was already present in the 1930s in the minds of various thinkers. Even looking at the symposium in this broader fashion, however, we can see that one of its most obvious traits lies in the fact that the participants were primarily influenced by German and French philosophy and literature. This fact is highly significant when we consider that the symposium took place at the beginning of the war between Japan and the United States. The war was not fought against Germany and France, but rather against England and the United States. Nevertheless, there was hardly any discussion of these latter countries during the symposium.

I would like to draw attention to the fact that the "Overcoming Modernity" symposium took place at a specific time through the organization of a specific journal. The time was after the outbreak of the Japan-U.S. War and the journal was *Bungakkai*, edited by such people as Kobayashi Hideo and Kawakami Tetsutarō. For example, members of the Kyoto School conducted the "Sekaishiteki tachiba to Nihon" [The world-historical standpoint and Japan] roundtable discussions that appeared in the journal *Chūōkōron*. In these discussions, there is a very clear standpoint that regards the Japan-U.S. War as "world-historical." The Kyoto School sought to provide a philosophical grounding of both the Greater East Asia Co-Prosperity Sphere and the Japan-U.S. War. In contrast, what is conspicuous about the "Overcoming Modernity" symposium is that it never arrived at such a clear conclusion, but rather avoided one. Indeed, this symposium not only toned down such a political standpoint, it also seems to have criticized that philosophical standpoint.

The notoriety of the "Overcoming Modernity" symposium stems from the fact that its standpoint is seen as identical to that of the Kyoto School and of Yasuda Yojūrō. Those who write on the symposium generally claim that it lacked anything coherent, and so they focus instead on those absent Kyoto School members or on Yasuda, who was likewise absent. Yet this lack of any coherent conclusions is seen as the fault of such kind of Japanese-style roundtable discussions. Or again it is attributed to the great number of writers in attendance, because of which discussion remained intuitive and inconsistent. I disagree with such views. The symposium's inconsistency or incoherency was actually foreseen from the start by its organizers. As Kawakami Tetsutarō writes in his "Ketsugo" [Concluding remarks]:

> Symposiums of a similar format were held about ten years ago at the League of Nations by the "Committee for Intellectual Cooperation," with several chaired by Paul Valéry. There one could see the mobilization of intellectuals as a stopgap measure of the Treaty of Versailles, whose con-

tradictions had already begun to be exposed. Toward this end, it was skill-fully contrived that the topic for discussion be "How are Europeans pos-sible?" First-rate intellectuals thus exhausted their minds in trying to strip the body from the intellect. The attempt to ban political statements from the proceedings succeeded remarkably in the end in strengthening the political effects of their discourse as a whole. Although versed in intellec-tual etiquette, the participants' chorus sounded empty amid the emascu-lated if apparently rich and glorious harmony. Their forlorn hopes are revealed today by the real state of European politics. (*Kindai no chōkoku*, Fuzanbō Bunko)

It is clear that Kawakami had Valéry's "Committee for Intellectual Cooper-ation" in mind when he organized the "Overcoming Modernity" symposium. Of course Kawakami criticized that project as "empty," but I don't think we should take this criticism at face value since such comments were commonly made during this time of censorship. In fact, Kawakami "attempted to ban political statements from the proceedings" of the symposium. Whether this attempt "succeeded remarkably in the end in strengthening the political effects of [the participants'] discourse as a whole" is of course another question. But it is clear that, to say the least, Kawakami knew the political effectiveness of the apolitical.

Takeuchi Yoshimi writes the following: "In my view, the greatest legacy of the 'Overcoming Modernity' symposium was not its status as war and fascist ideol-ogy. Rather it lies in the fact that the symposium failed to achieve even this, and that its attempt at intellectual formation resulted in intellectual loss" ("Kindai no chōkoku"). Yet the symposium did not aim at "intellectual formation," as Takeuchi puts it. If we take up the Kyoto School and the Japanese Romantics individually, we can certainly see some "intellectual formation." But by arrang-ing these two groups relatively in a row, the "symposium" came to "result in intellectual loss." It is for this reason that the symposium still bears reading even today, or rather this is why it appears as a "riddle."

For example, as I have mentioned, the "Sekaishiteki tachiba to Nihon" sym-posium actively sought to give meaning to Japan's standpoint. That is, both the Greater East Asia Co-Prosperity Sphere and the Greater East Asia War came to be endowed there with philosophical significance. But the most dominant fea-ture of the "Overcoming Modernity" symposium is what can be described as its derision of such significance. This attitude can be seen not only in Kobayashi Hideo, but also in Nakamura Mitsuo, who, however, spoke little during the pro-ceedings. In other words, this was the attitude of the journal *Bungakkai*. As Nakamura Mitsuo writes in his symposium paper:

When they (Europeans) reject or negate the human spiritual-intellectual order (or disorder) that is modernity, we can see their implicit conviction that they themselves have lived through that order (or disorder) to its end. When they claim that nothing more can be expected from modernity, their despair stands alongside their confidence that they have accomplished virtually everything that modernity allows. . . . Now in reflecting upon this question, do we have such a healthy despair or confidence about "modernity," one that is rooted in our very lives?

("'Kindai' he no giwaku" [Doubts about "modernity"]).

Nakamura Mitsuo is clearly critical of the symposium. Rather than reject it, however, he attempts to position it as the very site of criticism. For example, Nakamura states that he too was aware of Valéry's Committee for Intellectual Cooperation, having attended Valéry's lectures while studying in France before the war. When such scholars of French literature as Kawakami Tetsutarō and Nakamura Mitsuo refer to "Europeans," they mean France. At the time of the symposium, however, France was occupied by Germany, and Europe (with the exception of England) was "unified" by the Nazis. Thus it is natural that Kawakami would say that Valéry's committee "sounded empty." Nevertheless, Kawakami seems to have tried to align himself with the *esprit* of the defeated French.

There is no question that Valéry envisioned his Committee for Intellectual Cooperation as an opposition against the fascism that was then spreading throughout Italy, Spain, Finland, and Germany. But this opposition was quickly defeated. It is hardly possible that Kawakami and Nakamura were happy with this defeat. At the same time, however, they were fully aware of Valéry's powerlessness. I think that their "hopeless hope" lay in their desire not to suffer a similar fate.

As represented by Heidegger, the notion of "overcoming modernity" was actively discussed in Germany, even if this exact phrase was not used. For example, the realization of a *Grossraum* or "large area" (the European community) that would transcend modern sovereign states was part of this notion of "overcoming modernity." But Germany was Japan's ally, not its enemy. Rather it can be said that the framework for the "overcoming modernity" debate in Japan (as put forth by the Kyoto School and the Japanese Romantics) came from Germany. Thus we can say that one of the characteristics of the "Overcoming Modernity" symposium was its criticism of such German thought. In other words, the symposium's opposition was in a sense an opposition between German thought and French thought. Which is to say, it represented a conflict between the camps of philosophy and literature. As Kobayashi Hideo writes:

> In effect, the overcoming of modernity is really a question of overcoming western modernity. It is easy to speak of Japanese modernity. To slightly change the topic, both your (i.e., Nishitani Keiji) essay and that of Yoshimitsu [Yoshihiko] are extremely difficult. I would go so far as to say that these essays lack the sensuality of the Japanese people's language. We feel that philosophers are truly indifferent to our fate of writing in the national language. Since this language is the traditional language of Japan, no matter how sincerely and logically expressed, its flavor must appear in one's style as that which can only be achieved by Japanese people. This is what writers always aim for in their trade. It is linked to literary reality, and so either moves people or leaves them unmoved. Thought is contained within this literary reality. Philosophers are extremely nonchalant in this regard. If this attitude is not overcome, however, it strikes me that Japanese philosophy will never truly be reborn as Japanese philosophy. What are your thoughts on this?

In a sense, such a view still remains today. For example, Hiromatsu Wataru points out that in the postwar period the "Overcoming Modernity" symposium is discussed only in terms of literary criticism, thereby neglecting the role of the Kyoto School. Yet there are certain reasons for this. The Kyoto School's remarks were extremely crude and empty—although this is in no way a characteristic of "philosophy" as such, but rather of a certain kind of philosophy. This point can be grasped by looking at Hiromatsu's own prose. Modern Japanese philosophy has been formed by the vocabulary and ways of thinking of German Idealism. It is this that has come to be seen as "philosophy." Yet philosophy must consist of clear thinking that is based on one's life and experience. In this sense, it is precisely the "literary critics" who were the more philosophical. Yet these men were primarily affiliated with French literature and philosophy.

Hence it must be said that the opposition between literature and philosophy was really an opposition between two kinds of philosophy. Conversely, however, this can also be described as an opposition between two kinds of "literature" or "aesthetics." For example, Kobayashi Hideo set "Bergsonian aesthetics" against the German Romantics' notion of aesthetics. What is crucial is that, first, both of these were nothing more than "aesthetics"; and secondly, England and the United States, with whom Japan was then at war, were completely omitted here. Such omission is closely connected to the fact that these writers were "aesthetic."

II. The Difference Between "Political Freedom" and "Literary Freedom"

It is said that Japan has been "Westernized" since the Meiji era, but the meaning of the "West" here is generally confusing. I would like to consider the West in terms of the division between England and the United States on the one hand and France and Germany on the other. This distinction can be clearly seen particularly among intellectuals. The most representative thinker of the early Meiji era, Fukuzawa Yukichi, belongs to the English-American tradition. As a practical issue, English has now come to be adopted in the schools as a required language. Yet the Meiji state was modeled on Bismarck Germany, and German was indispensable in such state discourses as law, medicine, and philosophy. Since Inoue Tetsujirō, Japanese "philosophy" has centered on German Idealism. Meanwhile, French established itself as the language of literature in the latter half of Meiji. For example, both the Naturalists and the Shirakaba School were exclusively devoted to France.

Let us here place Natsume Sōseki between these two spaces. As goes without saying, Sōseki was a scholar of English literature, and yet he was ordered to study not English literature but rather the English language when sent to England by the Ministry of Education in 1900 (Meiji 33). Sōseki then inquired of Ueda Kazutoshi whether this meant that he was not to study English literature. Since matters were of course not so strict, "I realized that I had some room to change things according to my own judgment." These words appear in the preface of Sōseki's *Bungakuron* [Theory of literature]. Or rather, Sōseki could not but expressly write them. Yet why was he ordered to study the English language? This question is deeply related to his work *Bungakuron*.

German was the "state" language while English was the language of the economy and practical matters. This is clear from the fact that English has now come to be the required language in schools. At the time, English was a global language that circulated throughout the British Empire and the United States. Precisely for that reason, however, it became difficult to make English the language of literature. Kant says that interest must be discarded in aesthetic judgments, and there is too much interest at stake in English. Even now, to study English literature is to study the English language, which will be useful later on. Among the many students in English literature departments, there are few who enter to study literature. However, this is not the case with students in French literature departments. Even with a college degree, it is difficult to make a living with French. For example, while there are many who study abroad simply in order to master English, this is all but impossible in the case of French. Those who go to France do so in order to study such things as literature and philosophy or cooking and fashion. In a broad sense, moreover, these are all related to "aesthetics."

Such an atmosphere in fact already existed when Sōseki was studying in England. French literature was then dominant not only in Japan, but in England as well. In other words, to study literature at that time represented both opposition to the state and a renunciation of economic interest. However, to Sōseki, having studied English literature, the meaning of "literature" was far from clear. He was unable to simply separate it from the useful, the moral, and the intellectual. *Bungakuron* represents Sōseki's attempt to inquire into what literature fundamentally is. Yet he perhaps would not have asked this question had he studied something other than English literature. Those of his contemporaries who studied French literature or German philosophy were far more sanguine. From the perspective of these latter disciplines, English literature and philosophy seemed empirical, lacking in depth and coherence.

However, in the eighteenth century, England was the most developed modern society in the world. In both its bourgeois economy and its political form, England brought forth from its own experience things that belonged uniquely to it. In Sōseki's words, the country achieved a "spontaneous" development. For example, in England Sōseki cherished and studied the eighteenth-century writers Jonathan Swift and Laurence Sterne. But England at that time was under the influence of French literature, and neither Swift nor Sterne was considered literary. Similarly, Sōseki's work *Wagahai wa neko dearu* [I am a cat] was also seen as nonliterary by the Japanese literary establishment at that time, which was dominated by French Naturalism. For in this work there can be seen all kinds of discussion, from politics, economics, and science to cultural critique.

If England is "spontaneous" (*naihatsuteki*), then other areas must be "externally motivated" (*gaihatsuteki*). For example, it can be said that French Enlightenment thinkers idealized (*rinenka*) what England experienced, while German intellectuals grasped it in a more ideal (*kannenteki*) form. Here the distinctions between England, France, and Germany are not important; rather, we should refer to things as English, German, or French. These terms archetypally express three types of spiritual attitude.

For example, it is often said that Marx's thought has its roots in Germany (philosophy), France (socialism), and England (economics). But Marx moved from Germany to France and then on to England. His ideology critique was originally a critique of the process by which a "problem" is grasped and "overcome" merely as an idea when no problem actually exists. This is the reason that German and French philosophy found acceptance in Japan. Here modern society was ideally grasped and even "overcome" where no modern society actually existed.

For example, the thought of "freedom" (*jiyū*) did not originally come from philosophy but rather from economics. As Tosaka Jun writes in his 1935 (Shōwa 10) text *Nihon ideorogīron* [On Japanese ideology]:

> As goes without saying, liberalism (*jiyūshugi*) first began as economic lib-eralism. The departure point of such liberalism was the rejection of state intervention as based upon the Physiocrats and subsequent classical eco-nomics (whereas state intervention was grounded upon mercantilism). This economic liberalism, with its economic policies and theories of free trade and open competition, soon gave birth to political liberalism and all that went with it. Political liberalism consisted of freedom and equal-ity (as the social position of citizens) as well as the specific political con-cept of democracy (i.e., bourgeois democracy) as based upon freedom and equality.

We can cite, for example, Ishibashi Tanzan as a Japanese economic liberal. In his early Taishō period essay "Dai Nihonshugi no gensō" [The fantasy of great Japanism], Ishibashi called for the relinquishing of such colonies as Korea and Taiwan. There was no need for a Great Japan, he said, when a smaller Japan would be sufficient. Arguing for free trade, Ishibashi wrote that Korea and Japan would willingly participate in such trade if Japan were to voluntarily liberate them. This position is one of liberalism as based upon Adam Smith. Ishibashi continued to immerse himself in such liberal thought, but he was of course in the minority. In a way, Natsume Sōseki was an English liberal, as can be seen in his lecture "Watakushi no kojinshugi" [My individualism]. It can perhaps be said that Sōseki's philosophical standpoint was that of Hume.

However, such intellectuals have been extremely rare in Japanese history, and they have all been treated with contempt. For example, even those figures of "Taishō democracy" were already mere "political liberals" as compared with Ishibashi. They saw the colonies as a self-evident premise. Yet what of "liberal-ism" in the Shōwa period, when even the possibility of "political liberalism" had disappeared?

As Tosaka writes, "But the third phase of liberalism was created out of these economic and political liberalisms, or perhaps it was grounded upon or corre-sponded with these. For convenience' sake, let us call this phase *cultural liber-alism*" (*Nihon ideorogīron*). For Tosaka,

> The very meaning of such liberalism is literary, it must be a liberalism that is decisively cut off from liberalism in the sense of political action (which would necessarily lead to the pursuit of democracy). Even in its political

aspect, it is here nothing more than liberalism as a literary concept, one that utterly transcends politics. . . . Now surprisingly enough, such literary liberalism contains a path that runs through fascism.

Tosaka's analysis is extremely important.

The notion of "aesthetics" that I previously spoke of refers to this "literary liberalism." In an environment in which the Left had been destroyed and political and economic liberalisms themselves had been hunted down, the journal *Bungakkai* represented the standpoint of "cultural liberalism." The "Overcoming Modernity" symposium was not so pernicious as some have claimed without, however, having actually read it. Rather it is shocking that such statements were possible during this time of war. In other words, *Bungakkai* was perhaps the sole journal that sought to preserve "freedom" of speech.

The phrase "end of modernity" was popular around the year 1935 (Shōwa 10). While these words are similar to the "end of history" phrase that one hears today, it should be noted that Marxism was at that time completely suppressed in Japan. With the destruction of the Left, Kobayashi Hideo's *Bungakkai* was envisioned as a site of intellectual resistance as based upon liberalism. In fact, the Marxist thinker Miki Kiyoshi participated in its activities, and Kobayashi even actively recruited Nakano Shigeharu as a member, despite his break with them. However, to claim that *Bungakkai* had to be the site of liberalism is precisely to say that liberalism at this time could only be literary liberalism. That is, in a Japan that utterly lacked any actual liberalism, "freedom" here was realized at an imaginary level, and so could only be "aesthetic."

III. The Standpoints of Yasuda Yojūrō and Nishida Kitarō

As Kant states, aesthetic judgment is based upon "judgment" (imagination), which surmounts and unifies the contradiction between sensation and idea. In Kant, this notion of aesthetic judgment is in the end merely an appearance. With the Romantics who followed Kant, however, aesthetic judgment was placed at the foundation of all judgment. In this way, "aesthetics" became the foundation of philosophy. Since the Romantics, philosophy has in fact meant aesthetics.

More concretely, "aesthetics" is that which surmounts the various contradictions of everyday life and politics. Such contradictions would include, for example, those between the personal and the communal and between the individualistic and the totalistic. These contradictions always appear in capitalist economies. In political terms, this represents the opposition between liberalist economies and state interventionist (socialist) economies. It also represents the contradiction between the imperialist invasion of Asia and the struggle for Asia's liberation from such Western imperialism.

As Takeuchi Yoshimi writes,

> In a way, the "Overcoming Modernity" symposium represented a con-
> densed version of the aporias of modern Japanese history. Faced with the
> urgent intellectual task of interpreting the idea of eternal warfare at a time
> of total war, the symposium marked the explosion of such traditional
> oppositions as that of reactionaryism and restoration, reverence for the
> Emperor and exclusion of foreigners, isolationism and the opening of the
> country, ultranationalism and "civilization and enlightenment," and East
> and West.

But it was "aesthetics" alone that sought to "intellectually" surmount these actual aporias. Of course aesthetics can be of several types. One such type is Hegelian dialectics, that is, a dialectics that sublates contradictions in practical fashion. Hegelian dialectics is aesthetic in its belief that the two contradictory terms were originally one. So-called Marxism is an adherent of Hegelianism, but here dialectics at least contains as its premise a *telos* that is to be realized. Marxism also sets forth the notions of actual change and progress.

But the "aesthetics" that emerged after the destruction of Marxism rejected the very notion that something should be actively realized. Whereas Kant says that beauty exists as separate from interest, so-called post-Romantic "aesthetics" believed that it was precisely the negation of actual interest that was indispensable for the realization of beauty. This is what Yasuda Yojūrō meant by the notion of *romantische Ironie*. For Yasuda, it was precisely "dialectics" that had to be negated in its actual surmounting of actual contradictions. Although "dialectics" first of all meant Marxism, Yasuda sought more fundamentally to negate the notion of "civilization and enlightenment" itself. He saw Marxism as simply the final stage of "civilization and enlightenment."

In effect, what Yasuda called "dialectics" was the attitude whereby one sought to make something actual, whereas "irony" represented the opposition to this. Of course Yasuda also applied these notions to Japan's war. For him, the ideologues' various war aims and realizations had to be negated. He did not care if Japan lost the war if poetry could be realized in the process. The actual con-sisted only of the "occasional causes" of poetry or beauty. This attitude differs from jingoism. For example, Yasuda praised Uchimura Kanzō for his pacifism during the Russo-Japanese War, and it was in fact rumored that Yasuda was listed as a security risk by the state authorities.

Yet Yasuda's attitude was not all that strange. Takeuchi Yoshimi wrote that "the intellectual role played by Yasuda was that of eradicating thought through the destruction of all categories," but this was entirely characteristic of that "irony" of the German Romantics. What is crucial here is that irony was to be used against "dialectics," i.e., the notion of active realization. Perhaps this was the reason Yasuda did not participate in the "Overcoming Modernity" symposium.

Yasuda's notion of "irony" so fascinated people (including Mishima Yukio) because it maintained that interest always dogged those who sought to realize something. Such attempts at realization were thus impure and not "aesthetic." In concrete terms, the *tōsei-ha* military authorities were impure in their attitude toward the punished *kōdō-ha* (who supported the Emperor), since their own interests were at stake. The nation's youths who were fated to die in the war knew that they were actually part of the interests of monopoly capital, regardless of whether the war was justified or not. Hence the Japanese Romantics, to whom these youths were committed, represented a form of aesthetic resistance. Incidentally, this notion of interest is related to Mishima Yukio's expressions of sympathy for the *Zenkyōtō* movement in the 1960s as well as Yasuda Yojūrō's praise for the Red Guards during the Chinese Cultural Revolution. Both Mishima and Yasuda saw in *Zenkyōtō* and the Red Guards, respectively, an indifference to interest and active realization.

Perhaps actual interest must be abandoned at such moments when death is unavoidable. Akutagawa Ryūnosuke coined the phrase "dying eyes," which was later widely taken up by Kawabata Yasunari. Landscape is beautiful as seen from "dying eyes" since there is no longer the interest at stake while one still has life. For Yasuda Yojūrō, "beauty" emerges only when one abandons the attempt to actively realize something.

There exists another attitude regarding actual contradictions: Nishida Kitarō's "logic of nothingness." Simply put, this logic represents a negation of the Hegelian surmounting of contradictions through struggle. What appears to people as contradiction in fact depends upon a superficial viewpoint, since these contradictions are fundamentally unified as what Nishida calls "absolute contradictory self-identity." All contradictions are "sublated" by this logic. However, Nishida's logic is also an "aesthetics."

Such thinking could already be seen in Okakura Tenshin's *Tōyō no risō* [The ideals of the East]. There Okakura writes that "Asia is one," but this oneness refers to the Oriental arts. That is to say, Asia's identity is not to be found in its economy, politics, or religion. Criticizing Hegelian dialectics in its focus on contradiction, Okakura saw in Asia the principle of *Advaita* (nondualism), which represents an identity of contradictories. Although developmental, West-

ern history was based upon incessant strife, whereas the Orient, despite its character of stagnation, represented peace and was based on "love." Yasuda also
grounded his argument on Okakura's "aesthetics."

However, such nondualism is the same as Nishida's notion of "absolute contradictory self-identity." That is to say, Nishida's philosophy is an aesthetics. As
Nishida's student Tosaka Jun sharply observes, Nishida philosophy is Romantic
and aesthetic:

> While it may seem that Nishida's recent philosophy has lost some of its
> Romantic-aesthetic coloring, this is rather due to its establishing of
> Romantic-aesthetic methods (i.e., its manner of organizing the world of
> meanings and images). These methods have begun to be called
> "Nishida philosophy" by Professor Sōda. . . . As I have said, Nishida phi-
> losophy is in no way based upon feudal, gothic methods; rather it repre-
> sents the very essence of modern Romanticism. Nothing is more suited
> to endorse the cultural consciousness of the modern man of culture.
> Here modern man's capitalist education finds a spokesman for its own
> culturally *free* (*jiyū*) *consciousness*, whereupon it becomes a representa-
> tive of the philosophy of cultural liberalism (*jiyūshugi*) (in contrast to
> economic or political liberalism). Herein lies the popularity of Nishida
> philosophy.
>
> ("Mu no ronri ha ronri dearu ka" [Is the logic of nothingness a logic],
> in *Nihon ideorogii ron*)

What I would like to call attention to here is that, in Nishida and still more
in the Kyoto School as a whole, this "logic" acted as something that "logically"
surmounted actual contradictions. For example, the state-controlled economy
was "interpreted" in terms of a "cooperatism" that surmounted both liberalism
and communism, or individualism and totalitarianism (Miki Kiyoshi). Likewise, the Greater East Asia Co-Prosperity Sphere was "interpreted" as something that surmounted both the modern nation-state and Soviet-style internationalism. In other words, every kind of contradiction was seen as "already"
sublated. This "logic" thus came to affirm every established fact, which was
wonderfully beautified in the minds of these philosophers.

As Tosaka Jun remarked, such "logic" was thus aesthetic. In this regard, it
must be said that the *Bungakkai* group sought to critique not merely "philosophy" but "aesthetics," as I have already mentioned. Yet Kobayashi Hideo, who
opposed this logic, nevertheless also remained dependant upon "aesthetics." As
he writes,

Nor is it the case that I do not understand the philosophers' viewpoint. Earlier we discussed the appropriateness of the term "aesthetics" over that of "historical philosophy." While I have never really studied aesthetics, I have been most influenced these days by Bergson's aesthetics—despite the fact that he did not particularly write on this. What I find so interesting in Bergson's aesthetics is his lack of ambiguity, as can be seen so often in the writings of other philosophers. Bergson writes extremely clearly, without any such vague terms as for example that of "concrete universal".. . . . Seeing historical and social man as masked, he directly constructs a metaphysics from pure perceptual analysis. Although Bergson was once popular in the past, the time will again surely come in our country when he is seriously read. What an empty dream! When seen from the perspective of our efforts to attain reality, the massive historical schemes and maps that we moderns stuff into our heads are really demons that must be destroyed and abandoned.

Since the Eleatic School, there can be seen such paradoxes as "Achilles cannot overtake a turtle" or "An arrow in flight doesn't fly." It can be said that such paradoxes have inspired philosophy. Hegel believed that the arrow was in "contradiction" in that it was simultaneously in flight and at rest, and that this contradiction produced movement. In contrast, Bergson held that the arrow appeared contradictory only because time was spatialized and seen analytically. Time was rather *durée*, or "duration," and the "now" was not a point but a manifold. Generally speaking, this is what Bergson thought.

In order to come in contact with "reality," Kobayashi Hideo believed that man should not concern himself with such "aesthetics" as "concrete universals," but rather abandon the restrictions that shadow our thought and participate within such actuality. In other words, Kobayashi held that we should reject the Hegelian program and teleological history and at the same time surmount actual contradictions through an "aesthetic" attitude. This represented an affirmation of the "present" as "duration," which merges with the future in the past. Of course Kobayashi's thinking is also an "aesthetics." In fact, Kobayashi's notions are very close to what Nishida Kitarō called "pure experience" in his *Zen no kenkyū* [An inquiry into the good]. What Kobayashi rejected was simply Nishida's terminology.

Kobayashi Hideo rejected any attribution of meaning (i.e., interpretation) to the Greater East Asia War: "I gradually came to understand that 'history' remains indifferent to the modern interpretations of us moderns. And I first realized that therein lay history's beauty." Please note here Kobayashi's use of the phrase "history's beauty." The Greater East Asia War could not be interpreted by any theory whatsoever; rather it achieved "beauty" only through one's participation in it as "fate." It was thus already seen through "dying eyes."

Although Kobayashi still conceived of the possibility of resistance when he formed *Bungakkai,* he had now reached the point of resignation. Criticizing the war ideology (including that of the Kyoto School), he took the position of those who could do nothing in the war but die, somehow trying to see "freedom" in this.

IV. The Viewpoint of Sakaguchi Ango

It should be clear from the foregoing that the differences and oppositions among those who participated in the "Overcoming Modernity" symposium were fundamentally "aesthetic." We can see there the struggle between France and Germany, as it were, or again between literature and philosophy. As I have already mentioned, however, "Europe" was unified by the fascist powers Germany and Italy, which had formed an alliance with Japan, and so Japan's enemies were strictly England and the United States. The symposium's participants had all reflected on Europe's "depth," and either ignored or entirely dismissed England and the United States. This was due to the lack of "aesthetics" in those two countries.

I stated earlier that "aesthetics" is that which surmounts and unifies actual contradictions at an imaginary level. Conversely, "aesthetics" becomes dominant in those places where it is impossible to actually surmount actual contradictions. This explains why aesthetics never developed in England, despite the fact that it owes its modern form to such eighteenth-century Englishmen as the Earl of Shaftesbury and Edmund Burke. On the other hand, as I have said, German idealism is basically an "aesthetics,"as is modern Japanese philosophy as well.

The "Overcoming Modernity" symposium realized "literary liberalism" to its highest degree. As I have said, this "literary liberalism" differed from the countless trash pieces that were written by ideologues at around this same time (and which are unbearable to read today). Nevertheless, it was nothing more than simple "aesthetic" discussions. With the exception of the contributions of Shimomura Toratarō and one physicist, what stands out in the symposium is its general contempt for technology. Such topics as "culture" and "spirit" were seriously discussed in its place. Yet this is rather odd considering that people like Kobayashi Hideo, Kawakami Tetsutarō, and Nakamura Mitsuo had all read Valéry.

At the beginning of the twentieth century, for example, Valéry had written an essay titled "The Crisis of the Mind." Asking the question "What is Europe?" he said that he only first became conscious of Europe in 1894 with the Sino-Japanese War and in 1898 with the Spanish-American War. Until that time he believed that Europe was the "world," in which there existed such countries as France and Germany. What made Valéry realize that Europe was only one world was the Sino-Japanese War and the Spanish-American War—that is, from Europe's perspective, the Japan of the far East and the United States of the far West. Moreover, these two countries made free use of the technology that had come from Europe to win these wars. Valéry acutely realized that Europe was now only one world when Japan and the United States, making use of European technology, stood against it.

In other words, what allowed Valéry to realize that Europe was only one world was not the existence of other, heterogeneous worlds. He says in fact that it was Europe's own product that came to turn against it. This was technology. Valéry did not conceive of Europe in terms of "culture" or "spiritual depth," but rather as "technology." Thus technology represented an applicability outside Europe, it was something that could corner Europe. In fact, technology later came to corner the United States just as it will someday corner Japan, and this is because technology is applicability. If technology is a European product, then, Europe has conquered the world, even if Europe were to be destroyed by it.

Valéry had astonishing prescience to speak of the United States and Japan in this way at the end of the nineteenth century, for these countries have, alongside Europe, formed the world's tripartite structure, which survives even today. Valéry's insight is related to his rejection of "aesthetics," as it were. As a critic, he focused on "poetics," i.e., the question of "technique" or "technology." Kawakami Tetsutarō criticized Valéry at the symposium as a "mystic of machinery," but he was of course not a mystic at all. Rather he began his work by becoming conscious of the apparently mystical process of creation itself. In other words, Valéry tried to see all mysticism in terms of its technical or technological form.

Now what was rather unique in the symposium were the remarks of the film critic Tsumura Hideo. Tsumura regarded Americanism as the greatest threat. He stood apart from the other participants in that he studied film: "As goes without saying, film is an artistic form that first emerged with the end of modernity." In other words, there is something postmodern about film itself, and this cannot be separated from the question of technology. As Tsumura writes:

Since the Meiji period, Japan has massively absorbed Europe's modern spirit and modern culture. There can be no question of this. Since the Taishō period, however, Japan has also massively absorbed Americanism. . . . What is most frightening about American materialist civilization is the production and furnishing of a lifestyle that fits the present day. It is here that the "masses" have been most influenced and tainted. One would be mistaken to think that only the ignorant masses have been so influenced, and not the intellectuals. . . . I don't believe there is anything of value in Americanism that needs to be handed down. Nevertheless, it is treacherous in the ease, inevitability and familiarity with which it infects people.

The dominant opinion at the symposium was that the United States had no "culture," or only a very superficial one. If this were true, however, why had American culture so strongly permeated Japan? The infectiousness of Americanism was based on the applicability of "technology," which for Valéry originated in Europe. Yet everyone at the symposium, including Tsumura Hideo, criticized American "materialist civilization" and praised the depth of European "culture." Even today, for example, "Japanese culture" is associated with such things as Noh drama, kabuki, the tea ceremony, and flower arrangement, but what has spread throughout the globe are the country's computer games, animation, manga comics and manga-type novels for young girls. Both Western and Asian intellectuals who are opposed to this spread of "Japanese culture" warn against "the ease, inevitability, and familiarity with which it infects people," exactly as the Japanese of the past ridiculed "American culture."

But it would be foolish to view "culture" or "spirit" with such scorn. Given that the "Overcoming Modernity" symposium was conceived at the beginning of the war with the United States, what is the significance of the fact that both the United States and England were all but ignored there? Putting aside the question of what the participants of the symposium actually thought, it seems to me that they were simply convinced that Japan had no hope of winning the war. Perhaps it was the case that any interest in the war's outcome would be un-"aesthetic" or un-"spiritual."

In closing, I would like to quote from an essay that was written shortly before the symposium and was unconnected to it: this is Sakaguchi Ango's March 1942 "Nihon bunka shikan" [My view of Japanese culture]. The essay is a critique of the German architect Bruno Taut's book *The Rediscovery of Japanese Culture.* Taut's argument is that "Japanese culture" is something that exists beyond the fall of Western modernity. Such a thesis was considered to be supportive of Japan's "Overcoming Modernity" discourse at the time. Yet Sakaguchi rejects that sort of "Japanese culture discourse." As he writes,

However, there is a gap that remains entirely unknown to Taut between his discovery of Japan and the beauty of Japanese tradition and the fact that we, despite our neglect of this tradition, are actually Japanese. That is to say, Taut could only discover Japan whereas we, who are actually Japanese, have no need to discover it. While it may be true that we have neglected classical Japanese culture, it is impossible for us to neglect Japan. For us, there is no need to discuss such questions as "What is the Japanese spirit?" Japan is not born from such an explained spirit, nor is that explanation part of this spirit. If the everyday life of Japanese people is healthy, then Japan itself is healthy.

These words do not necessarily apply to Taut alone, as such "explanations" can be seen in every Japanese discussion of "Japan." The same can be said for every discussion of "tradition" in the "Overcoming Modernity" symposium. Moreover, Ango's remarks are a rejection of discourse that describes our alienation and loss of self in modern society. He says that there is no original state to be restored. Ango is speaking here of "beauty," but he stands poles apart from such notions as that of "dying eyes." For him, beauty is what "living" and its "necessity" alone create:

> What is only superficially stylish cannot become truly beautiful. Everything is a question of substance. Beauty for its own sake is stiff and ultimately inauthentic. In short, such beauty is empty. Empty things can never strike one like true things, but are simply indifferent things. It makes no difference whatsoever if the Hōryūji or Byōdōin temples are burnt down. If necessary, it would be best to destroy Hōryūji and build a parking lot in its place. . . . If that were truly necessary, then true beauty would certainly emerge there as well, for true everyday life exists there. Insofar as everyday life is lived truly, there is nothing to be ashamed about blind imitation. Insofar as such imitation represents true everyday life, it is just as superior as originality.

In reading Ango's essay, everything about the "Overcoming Modernity" discussion comes to seem utterly empty. At first glance, Ango's view appears to be that of "modernism." But his despair runs far deeper than that of any of the "Overcoming Modernity" participants. Ango says that such discussions about overcoming the modern or returning to the premodern are vacuous, that we are in any case living therein, and that such "life" is to be affirmed. This is precisely what it means to "overcome modernity," as it were. Yet Ango never explained it like this.

Translated by Richard F. Calichman

Note

Karatani Kōjin, "Kindai no chōkoku," in *'Senzen' no shikō* ["Prewar" thoughts] (Tokyo: Kōdansha Gakujutsu Bunko, 2001), pp. 99–128. Originally given as a public lecture in April 1993 in Yokohama.

SŌSEKI'S DIVERSITY: ON *KOKORO*

I

In addition to his haiku and Chinese-style poetry, Sōseki's writings extend from such early fiction as *Wagahai wa neko dearu* [I am a cat], *Botchan* [The young master], *Yōkyoshū* [Drifting in space], and *Kusamakura* [Grass pillow], to *Meian* [Light and darkness]. These writings, in other words, encompass a great variety of different styles and genres. Such a writer is unique in both Japan and abroad. How was Sōseki's diversity possible? This is a great mystery. For example, Sōseki scholars have sought to discover the mystery of his texts in his personal life, and particularly in his romantic experiences—but this hardly merits the name "mystery." Such linguistic diversity cannot be explained away as mere versatility or literary talent, for ultimately it is related to the question of "history." Regardless of future literary talent, Sōseki's achievements will never again be repeated.

Sōseki's works are generally read as a process of development, or deepening, from such early period writings as *Wagahai wa neko dearu* and *Kusamakura* to *Meian*. Certainly these early works are different from modern novels. Yet it is questionable to even use the term "early period" here in regard to a writer who was nearly forty years old at the time, had already written his "theory of literature," and had only twelve years of life remaining, for it is highly unlikely that

Sōseki substantially changed his views during those final years. It is thus a mistake to regard him in terms of a linear development of his works, or from a modern-novel-centered viewpoint that places *Meian* at the apex. Rather what is essential is the mystery of how Sōseki's linguistic diversity became possible.

One thing that can be said is that Sōseki studied eighteenth-century English literature, which preceded the notion of "literature" as established in mid-nineteenth century France—a notion that was formative of Sōseki's own literary world in Japan at that time. Furthermore, as Ōoka Shōhei points out, the genre of *bun*, or writing, existed when Sōseki began his literary work, and he composed such works as "Rondon tō" [London tower] not as a short novel but rather as "writing." Of course Masaoka Shiki's notion of *shaseibun*, or literary sketching, is also a form of "writing." Such literary sketching could become meaningful only because "writing" already existed as a genre in the first place. "Writing" is not necessarily related to realism, nor is it merely the germination thereof. Sōseki's "writing" was later read as a short novel, but it is no such thing. Sōseki would have known this, as he was already deeply familiar with the Western novel.

What is the significance, then, of Sōseki's adherence to "writing"? Perhaps his novels and indeed the great variety of his works were derived from "writing." Sōseki did not begin composing novels, as *Wagahai wa neko dearu* is an example of "writing." It was while working on this book that his creative activity suddenly began, and for the next decade he would compose an enormous body of works. "Writing" can be described as that "degree zero" which contains all possibilities; it is *écriture*, to use Barthes's terms. I think that Sōseki saw in "writing" those possibilities excluded by the modern novel in its attempts at self-purification.

Now Northrop Frye has examined fiction (including nonfiction) by dividing it into four genres. In Frye's definition, fiction contains all prose writing. The first genre is the novel. Since we are already familiar with this genre, I shall speak of the other three—but let me simply note here that the novel is different from the other genres. The first of these others is the "romance," which can also be called *monogatari*, or narrative. In the romance, the protagonist is not an ordinary person; rather he or she is beautiful, heroic, and possessed of superhuman abilities. In this regard, one can even say that the modern novel consists of ordinary people becoming protagonists. The romance also possesses a certain structure, which can perhaps be described along the lines of what Origuchi Shinobu called the "wandering noble narrative." This is not the prosaic world but rather one that has as its topological structure the existence of another or different world.

The next genre is the "confession." The confession did not begin with such modern writers as Rousseau; rather its traditions are those of, for example,

Augustine's *Confessions.* Noteworthy here is the intellectual nature of this genre. Such tradition also exists in Japan, as for instance can be seen in Arai Hakuseki's *Oritaku shiba no ki* [Told around a brushwood fire]. The following genre is what Frye calls "anatomy." This includes such works as encyclopedic texts, pedantic texts, and satires. In Western literature, anatomy refers to writers like Rabelais, Swift, and Laurence Sterne. The eighteenth-century English literature (including Swift) that Sōseki studied belongs to this genre rather than that of the novel.

Now what is remarkable is that Sōseki wrote in all of these genres. *Yōkyoshū* is literally a romance, *Wagahai wa neko dearu* is satire, or what may also be called pedantic anatomy, *Botchan* is picaresque, and *Kusamakura* is not a "novel," as Sōseki himself had intended. What then of *Kokoro* [The heart], which I wish to speak of today? In my view, *Kokoro* is a "confession"—but this is not to say that the work is confessional, as would be the case with *Michikusa* [Grass on the wayside]. In *Kokoro*, Sensei's letter reads as follows: "My own past, which made me what I am, is a part of human experience. Only I can tell it. I do not think that my effort to do so honestly has been entirely purposeless. If my story helps you and others to understand even a part of what we are, I shall be satisfied."[1] And again: "I want both the good and bad things in my past to serve as an example to others. But my wife is the one exception—I do not want her to know about any of this."[2]

We can see how true to form this is from the perspective of such "confessions" as those of Augustine and Rousseau. The "confession" contains intellectual reflection, which distinguishes it from the autobiographical novel. Indeed, a work like *Kokoro* becomes possible by adopting such a premodern novel form. This form is also rather old-fashioned, as we can see in *Kokoro* in the focus on Sensei's letter, which appears in the latter half of the book. The epistolary form was used widely in eighteenth-century English literature, for the modern novel's narrative form had not yet been established. As soon as this narrative form emerged, however, the epistolary form appeared antiquated. Because of this, *Kokoro* has not been highly regarded in the Japanese literary world, nor have the other works I mentioned. Those works have generally been widely read and quite popular, and it is for precisely this reason that they have been dismissed. They have come to be seen as early works written prior to such novels as *Meian*. Yet Sōseki's greatness lies in the fact that he wrote in all of these genres.

Now although Frye arranges these fictional genres in this manner, the fact is that they are not all equal. The "modern novel" has been the most dominant genre since the nineteenth century, while the others have been marginalized. Despite this dominance, however, these other genres are always necessary. This is very much like the state of affairs since the emergence of industrial capitalism, in which not all modes of production have been capitalized—as others, such as agriculture, still continue—and which even presupposes as indispensable those things that cannot be capitalized.

In contemporary Japan, the anatomy and *monogatari* (narrative) are the most popular. This is related to the fact that the idea of the modern novel has come under suspicion. Yet these cannot replace the modern novel. No matter how the anatomy and *monogatari* are revived, such revival takes place strictly "within" the modern novel—and in this way the novel is activated and lives on. This process can already be seen in Sōseki. Despite the fact that he wrote in all of the different genres, Sōseki already belonged to the world of the modern novel, and thus tried to revive those things that were excluded from that world.

II

Kokoro is such a famous work that it is particularly unnecessary to explain its plot, but let us here simply review its main points.

In the first half of the book, the student known only as *watakushi* meets Sensei at the Kamakura seaside. Finding himself somehow attracted to Sensei, *watakushi* draws closer only to discover that there is something about him that he cannot understand. *Watakushi*'s father falls ill without him having discovered Sensei's secret, and while he is back home, Sensei dies. The second half of the book takes the form of a testament Sensei has written to *watakushi*. While in school, Sensei was betrayed by an uncle, who stole the property left him by his father, and this causes him to grow suspicious of people and suffer a kind of nervous breakdown. At the private boardinghouse where he lives there is a woman and her daughter, and during his convalescence he becomes acquainted with them. He grows fond of the daughter, but his feelings have not yet reached the stage of love.

Sensei has a friend named K, whom he both venerates and finds slightly comical. Sensei wishes to help K in his financial difficulties as well as to ease the nervous exhaustion from which K suffers. On the other hand, however, Sensei wishes to destroy K's sense of ascetic idealism, which he himself cannot attain. "In an attempt to make him more human, then, I tried to encourage him to spend as much time as possible with the two ladies,"[3] and thus Sensei brings K to his lodgings. This action is a sign of both friendship and malice, as Sensei is here attempting to seduce K, as it were.

Once K moves in, however, things become increasingly strange. K confesses to Sensei that he loves the daughter, and yet, even prior to this, Sensei had begun to grow conscious of his own love for the girl because of K's presence, in other words, through his envy of K. Sensei is forced to hear K declare his love for the girl first, and although Sensei should have replied at that time, "No, it is I who loved her first," he is unable to do so. This failure to speak, or "delay," will have grave consequences, and yet such "delay" was actually present from the very beginning. For example, Sensei fell in love with the daughter only after K came to stay with him. Since Sensei first became conscious of his love while suspecting that K might also be in love with her, his claim that he loved her "first" is a lie. There is something about Sensei's "delay" that cannot be explained away as a mere failure to speak. More essentially, this "delay" represents a certain unavoidable condition for man in his relation to the other. I shall speak more about this later.

After hearing K's confession, Sensei one day feigns illness and stays in his room, telling the woman, "I want to marry your daughter."[4] This request is of course granted, but Sensei is unable to tell K. Completely ignorant of K's feelings, the woman goes ahead and tells him the news, as a result of which K commits suicide. Guilt-ridden, Sensei yet remains unable to share his feelings with the "daughter," whom he has married, i.e., his wife. He confesses only to the young student (*watakushi*), whom he swears to absolute secrecy in regard to his wife.

Upon the death of the Meiji Emperor, Sensei tells his wife, "As people of the Meiji era we have now become anachronisms," to which she suddenly and quite inexplicably replies, "Well then, self-immolation is the solution to your problem." He is struck by this term "self-immolation," which by that time was hardly in use, and responds, "I will commit self-immolation if you like; but in my case, it will be through loyalty to the spirit of the Meiji era."[5] One month later, however, General Nogi actually commits this act. This prompts Sensei to make his own decision, and he begins to seriously consider suicide. He writes his confession as a testament during the ten days prior to his death. This, then, is a synopsis of *Kokoro*.

I would like to touch upon the question of "delay" that I mentioned earlier. Sensei conceives this "delay" as his own baseness, and is consumed by guilt because of it. But is this really the case? Could this "delay" have been avoided if Sensei were utterly honest and compassionate? Could it have been avoided if he were clearly aware of his own consciousness and desires? The answer is no. For example, Sensei fell in love with the daughter only after K had moved in with him—or rather, after K had fallen in love with her. If K had not been present, no amount of reflection would have revealed to Sensei his own love for the girl. For that love did not yet exist, but only first came into being through K's mediation. Sensei's consciousness of this love thus arose when he was already in such a position that K had to be sacrificed. This is not the mere anguish of the triangular relation, since love itself is first formed through such triangularity.

For example, let's say there is an unwanted toy lying in the corner of a child's room. Another child enters, sees the toy, and wants it. At that point, the first child suddenly clings to the toy, declaring, "No, it's mine!" When another child wants something that is usually neglected or ignored, the first child clings to it as if nothing were more important. And yet he loses interest in it when that second child gives up and leaves. Is this child merely being spiteful? He might later think that he did something wrong; but at that moment he was not lying, he really valued the toy. Later, however, having lost interest in the toy, he thinks that he lied and did something spiteful.

This is not so different from Sensei's feelings in *Kokoro*. That is to say, without once lying to himself, Sensei nevertheless comes to lie to and betray K. At no point does Sensei lie, nor is he unaware. Effectively, however, he comes to deceive K. After his father's death, an uncle deceives Sensei and steals his property. Sensei grows suspicious of people and suffers a nervous breakdown, but recovers through his contact with the woman and her daughter at the boardinghouse. He should have thus hated all deception, but still he betrays a close friend. Why did this happen?

Sensei excitedly shouts to *watakushi* that people suddenly change: "People will suddenly change when it comes to the question of money. I myself have witnessed such a change."[6] But I wonder about this. For example, even if the uncle appears to Sensei to suddenly change, others would perhaps not be so surprised. People who know the uncle well might think that he was capable of such behavior. The problem is that Sensei, who believes to the very marrow that he would never betray someone as his uncle did, nevertheless "suddenly changes." What is important is not the object that causes such change, whether this be money or women. People can "suddenly change" over other things as well. Noteworthy here is that this "change" is not something of which one can be conscious, or that consciousness occurs too late. Now, then, why is this so?

III

Let us think about this question philosophically. Hegel states that desire is the other person's desire, that is, it is the desire for this other's recognition. There is here a distinction between need and desire. For example, wanting to eat because one is hungry represents need, whereas wanting to eat fine food or dine at nice restaurants already signifies another's desire. The sexual urge is also seen as a physical need, but having such urges only with beautiful women signifies desire.

The standard for "beautiful women" does not exist objectively, but rather changes according to culture, ethnicity, and history. A "beautiful woman" is someone whom other people find beautiful. Since then the acquisition of a beautiful woman is really the acquisition of something deemed valuable by others, this desire is ultimately nothing but the desire for these others' recognition. Yet it is difficult to change one's feelings. Pure need is actually quite rare. In extreme situations it is possible that one would eat and drink anything, but otherwise we exist fundamentally within desire—that is, where the other already mediates.

We often say that one should not imitate but be original and spontaneous. When we aim at something, however, we always see someone as a model. This is the same as saying that our desires are mediated by other people. We often speak of spontaneity and subjectivity, but it must be said that the self and the subject are already formed by incorporating the relation with the other.

Making use of Hegel's ideas, René Girard has examined the notions of desire, imitation, triangular relations, and the exclusion of the third person. In Japan, Girard's views have been applied by Sakuta Keiichi in his discussion of such figures as Natsume Sōseki. Please read here Sakuta's *Kojinshugi no unmei—kindai shōsetsu to shakaigaku* [The fate of individualism—The modern novel and sociology]. Sakuta provides a lucid analysis of *Kokoro* in terms of Sensei's relations with both *watakushi* and K. He reinterprets these relations, which psychologists have previously seen as "homosexual," along the lines of a model-rival theory. For example, Sakuta writes:

> "Sensei" relates in his testament that he brought K back to his home out of a sense of friendship, that he wanted to ease this student's hardships. Yet there remains something in this explanation that is difficult to understand. In my interpretation, "Sensei" wishes to have the respected K guarantee that the daughter is worthy of marriage, even if "Sensei" himself comes to be sacrificed by his own tactics. At the same time, "Sensei" wants to boast to K that he plans to marry her.[7]

And again: "K is the model to whom 'Sensei' turns for judgment, for Sensei's choice of spouse is first justified by K's attraction to her. And yet K can in this way also become 'Sensei's' rival, for if he finds her attractive he will fight 'Sensei' over her."[8]

Sensei's love for the daughter certainly requires K's presence, and yet this third person must be excluded. Even if it appears otherwise, love potentially contains the triangular relation. The same holds true even if the third person is not a concrete individual but a vague entity, like the public. For example, those who wish to marry celebrities want to possess the object of many others' desires.

It can be said that they desire the other, not the celebrity. This is also one instance of the triangular relation.

Moreover, there is in Sensei's friendship for K something ambivalent. Sensei respects K, and yet, while he sees K as a model, he feels that he cannot go to the same lengths. Because of this, Sensei wants to drag K down and corrupt him—and this is what Sensei means when he speaks of "humanizing him." There is nothing forced in such a reading. Elsewhere Sensei says to *watakushi*, who continues to respect him, "At any rate, don't put too much trust in me. You will learn to regret it if you do. And if you ever allow yourself to feel betrayed, you will then find yourself being cruelly vindictive."[9] And again: "The memory that you once sat at my feet will begin to haunt you and, in bitterness and shame, you will want to degrade me. I do not want your admiration now, because I do not want your insults in the future."[10] In other words, the relation with one's model changes from respect to hatred both when one outdoes him and when one realizes one will never be his equal.

What I would like to consider, however, concerns the question of "delay" that I mentioned earlier. Our consciousness and desire, which appear to us as immediate (or unmediated), are already mediated by the other—and this too is a kind of "delay." Even if one clearly reflects upon oneself beyond all doubt, it is each time already mediated. In this sense, the "present" is always "delayed." The title *Kokoro* is ironic, for there is here no attempt to peer within the "heart." Or rather, such peering yields nothing, for our actions derive not from the "heart" but from the relation with the other. Regardless of how one thinks about the heart, then, there is a void there that cannot be filled. This point can perhaps be explained by psychoanalysis, but there is always a "delay" that can never be cleared up.

This issue is related to "history," for in fact *Kokoro* has come to be widely read not only because of its focus on love and triangular relations, but also because of its treatment of historical problems. For example: "Then, at the height of the summer, Emperor Meiji passed away. I felt as though the spirit of the Meiji era had begun with the Emperor and had ended with him. I was overcome with the feeling that I and the others, who had been brought up in that era, were now left behind to live as anachronisms."[11] This notion of "anachronism" (*jisei okure*) does not simply refer to the fact that one is old and out of date; rather it is actually related to a certain "delay" (*okure*).

What does Sensei mean here by the words "Meiji" and "Meiji spirit"? We must not think of Meiji simply as an historical era. Previously I spoke of K as an ascetic idealist. In *Kokoro* we find the following passage:

> Having grown up under the influence of Buddhist doctrines, he seemed to regard respect for material comfort as some kind of immorality. Also,

having read stories of great priests and Christian saints who were long since dead, he was wont to regard the body and the soul as entities which had to be forced asunder. Indeed, he seemed at times to think that mistreatment of the body was necessary for the glorification of the soul.[12]

In this description, K appears simply like the type of young seeker of truth from long ago. But it must be said that such an extreme type as K is characteristic of a certain period, one that differed from past and future periods in regard to both Buddhism and Christianity. For example, by the end of the second decade of the Meiji era, Kitamura Tōkoku turned toward Christianity while Nishida Kitarō turned toward Zen Buddhism. Like K, both these men were extreme types (K also read the Bible).

These men became confined within such absolute interiority because the possibilities that were present during the Meiji Restoration were by this time becoming closed off. On the other hand, their confinement can be attributed to the institutional establishment of the modern nation-state system. That is to say, defeated in their respective political battles, these men sought to express their opposition by rejecting the secular and privileging the spiritual, or interior. Yet Tōkoku committed suicide and Nishida returned to the humiliation of becoming an imperial university nondegree student. Similarly, K's suicide was not prompted by mere heartbreak or a friend's betrayal, as Sensei later realized. For in his very attraction to the opposite sex, K perceived the collapse of such spiritual resistance.

IV

Sōseki himself perhaps experienced something similar to this. Although not committed to any political movements, he doubtless felt that in the second decade of the Meiji era there must be a deepening of revolution as an extension of the Meiji Restoration. At this time Sōseki thought that he would devote his life to the "Chinese classics," and yet he came to study English literature. In the preface of his *Bungakuron* [Theory of literature], moreover, he wrote something to the effect that he felt betrayed by English literature. There the "Chinese classics" are not seen as something from the Edo period, and thus old-fashioned. Rather they were bound up with the very thought and character of those students of that second Meiji decade. English literature, meanwhile, was part of the imperial university system; it was something that one studied in order to achieve worldly success. Sōseki in fact highly distinguished himself in this literature, yet he always felt the urge to escape it. This explains why he left the imperial university and became a novelist, which was considered at that time a rather disreputable profession.

In this regard, we can see that the "spirit of Meiji" Sensei refers to ("I will commit self-immolation if you like; but in my case, it will be through loyalty to the spirit of the Meiji era") has nothing to do with the so-called Meiji *Zeitgeist*. Rather this "spirit of Meiji" signifies the diverse range of possibilities during the "second Meiji decade." For example, what struck Sensei about General Nogi's suicide letter was not his way of thinking but rather that, having lost his banner in the 1877 Seinan War, "he had been wanting to redeem his honor through death."[13] The people of the "second Meiji decade" in fact considered the Seinan War as the "second Meiji Restoration" in its pursuit of the Restoration's ideas. Saigō Takamori became the symbol of this movement, and was also the symbol of the later "Shōwa Restoration." Although Sōseki himself never ceased denouncing the "elder statesmen of Meiji," he also said that he wished to pit himself against the novel "like the Meiji Restoration patriots."

Thus what Sōseki called the "spirit of Meiji" can be understood as the diverse "possibilities" excluded from the modern nation-state system that would be established during the third decade of Meiji. In other words, "history," as I am trying to define it here, refers to those things that are now concealed and forgotten. From another standpoint, these possibilities are also the various possibilities of literature, as I spoke of earlier. Literature does not consist solely of the modern novel of the nineteenth-century West, nor does the movement toward the novel represent development. Perhaps Sōseki resisted this novel-centered notion of literature or its repressive nature. We must not see such resistance merely in terms of Sōseki's own tastes and temperament, nor should we see it as nostalgia for the Orient or Edo period. For it is actually the opposite of these.

In the tragic work that is *Kokoro*, Sōseki may have been trying to separate himself from the past by evoking it so intensely. Marx also said that tragedy was a means to happily part with the past. In fact, Sōseki wrote *Michikusa* after *Kokoro*, and this work won praise from the Naturalists who then dominated Japan's literary world. Sōseki had finally written a novelistic novel, they said. He also set to work on *Meian*, but died before completing it.

Meian has been praised up to the present day as Sōseki's most genuine modern novel, but this is really quite ironic. It is said that Sōseki wrote *Meian* in the morning and "Chinese-style poetry" in the afternoon. Perhaps this book was not all that he had hoped, but that, having lived so far, he felt that he could only follow this path as thoroughly as possible. We should not regard Sōseki's works in linear terms, with *Meian* at the apex. What is concealed within such a history is precisely what I have called "history."

Translated by Richard F. Calichman

Notes

Karatani Kōjin, "Sōseki no tayōsei: 'Kokoro' wo megutte," in *Kotoba to higeki* [Language and tragedy] (Tokyo: Kōdansha Gakujutsu Bunko, 2001), pp. 40–57. Originally given as a public lecture on February 27, 1985, in the city of Kawaguchi.

1. Natsume Soseki, *Kokoro*, trans. Edwin McClellan (Washington, D.C.: Regnery Gateway, 1989), p. 247.
2. Ibid., p. 248.
3. Ibid., p. 180.
4. Ibid., p. 222. Translation slightly modified.
5. Ibid. This entire exchange can be found on p. 245. Translation slightly modified.
6. Karatani seems here to be paraphrasing Sensei's remarks made in ibid., p. 61.
7. Sakuta Keiichi, *Kojinshugi no unmei—kindai shōsetsu to shakaigaku* (Tokyo: Iwanami Shinsho, 1981), p. 137.
8. Ibid., pp. 137–138.
9. *Kokoro*, p. 30.
10. Ibid., p. 30.
11. Ibid., p. 245.
12. Ibid., p. 176.
13. Ibid., p. 246.

Chapter 4

THE WONDERLAND OF "IMMORTALITY"

Nishitani Osamu

"Death" in the Present

Understood as the greatest violence or disaster that can befall us, death has long been man's greatest source of anxiety and fear. We implicitly resign ourselves to death as an absurd yet unavoidable fate, and precisely because this deprivation or extinguishing of existence is our inevitable lot, we seek to assuage our anxiety through belief in the immortality of the soul. Often we envision an eternal afterlife that offers salvation from the misery of a life tormented by anxiety. In regarding such an afterlife as truly immortal life, we turn the pain of death into a condition for salvation. Alternatively, we may not depend upon such a desire for eternal life or the afterlife, but try to work out a kind of wisdom that excludes from life's reality any worry over death as utterly meaningless. Either way, death is the manifestation of a power that peremptorily outstrips human will and authority. Because it transcends human force, man is all the more tightly caught in its grip and thus cherishes a deep desire to be released from it.

Yet when we can no longer believe either in the immortality of the soul or in God's salvation—that there exists an external authority upon which to rely—death paradoxically becomes the most important aspect of human existence. Death concludes life, so that life without death remains unfinished. Death is brought into life as the ultimate possibility, and through this, human autonomy and the completion of life are first guaranteed. Unless death, which completes life, becomes human, human autonomy does not arise as absolute subjectivity. In other words, as Dostoevsky's Kirilov believed, death must become "my life" since transcendence, or "God," is done away with. If death isn't "mine" and something "I" control, then what begins at birth and ends in "my death" can never become "mine." Death is thus not an external accident that befalls "me" as fate or simply extinguishes "me"; rather, it must be something that, through a certain dialectics, inheres within "me." Rilke, for example, wonders if death is not the fruit of life that has grown to maturity within his body, and he assiduously tries to observe it. Death is that which has not yet been realized but inexorably comes ever closer to belonging to "me": it is "my death" which must complete "me." For moderns such as Rilke, death is the final and primordial possibility of one's life; it is that which grounds the irreplaceable propriety of "my" existence.

The philosophers and writers who spoke of "existence" believed that it was the relationship to death — considered as one's own death — that made existence "authentic" or "true." Bataille set out on the "journey to the limits of the possible," and created a project that rendered impossible the very "project" (pro-ject) of shaping existence as possibility. Blanchot exposed himself without reservation to the inoperable act of "writing," which is an act devoted to nonreality rather than an activity of presence that produces and serves reality (in the Hegelian sense), and then reflected upon this experience. Levinas attempted to rethink existence by passing through the "night of insomnia" that extinguishes the "I" and destroys the "world" in the fire of history. No matter how much strength I show in drawing death to me, it can never become "mine." Indeed, the final act in which I try to make death my own forever throws me into the impossibility of "my death." In this sense, death is a deception, a trap into which human beings fall. Unable to die one's own death, man's inescapable fear is not that of dying but rather that he cannot die. Death can never be the goal of an act. Man is not truly related to death in his status as subject. Losing the power to form a proper "I," that is, losing the power to maintain death as "my death," man is in the dissolution of this propriety consumed within death and enfolded by its radical foreignness. In the end, man disappears without possessing death and without completing it as subject. Thus the thinkers of "existence" taught both the *impossibility of death* and the *incompleteness of existence*.

Let me simply add that, as goes without saying, this impossibility of death and the incompleteness of existence do not come to again subordinate man to "God." Rather, such a mode of existence is disclosed *precisely because of the absence of any God*. It is not that the individual's finitude can be compensated only by "God's" infinity; rather the conditions of human existence are disclosed as finite in themselves. The death that is therein disclosed spreads throughout as unrecoverable. This is a death that is ultimately unrelated to man and into which he vanishes. Thus it can also be described as the death of God himself. Yet this death is not something that belongs to God; rather it is the death of God himself, the extinction of all transcendent and universal authority. In this absence of an authority that governs itself through "death," man is returned to his own finite life. With nothing to possess it, this anonymous "death" envelops the world as something "public" that belongs to no one. It spreads imperceptibly throughout, surrounding near and far.

It is said that with the death of God, "man" also died. That may very well be the case. But if this means the extinction of the autonomous and subjective human being, it would actually imply that man has become dispersed and has lost the power to die, that is to say, lost the power to fulfill or complete himself. In fact, this would expose man to a situation in which he *cannot die* his own death—such an *unknown* situation must be called something like the "loss of death." However, the most incisive response to this situation came from a thinking that, with a sense of crisis, braced itself against the "unknown" through recourse to a notion of "homeland." Such thinking regarded this "loss of death" in terms of "falling" (*Verfallen*), as brought about by man's depersonalization in the "mass" age and the neutralization of communality that is "publicness" (*Öffentlichkeit*). This thinking sought a way to restore the propriety of "death" in this superficial "falling." After the "disaster" which presently ensued, all humanity stood amidst the ruins, and the phrase "being towards death" (*Sein zum Tode*) spread throughout as the tritest of catchwords. People became intoxicated with reckless thoughts about "freedom," as brought about by the sense of their "own death." Somewhat removed from the commotion of that age, several strands of radical thought confronted a kind of "limit situation" in their attempt to transform "humanism." They gave themselves over to this unknown situation and sought out the most appropriate words to describe it. For such thinkers, the relation to "death" that they experienced and came to express represented the basic condition of existence that subtly but unmistakably surrounds contemporary man.

Death in Reserve

Since the emergence of nuclear weapons, a technology that is the literal embodiment of "useless negativity," the death of mankind has been collectively secured. Just as the sky envelops the earth, this "death" completely enfolds our environment as foreign and unknown, out of the hands of individuals. "Death" is here unrelated to individual will or action, and is reserved equally for all. On the one hand, technology, which makes possible death's universal reserve, also substantially suspends "war," restricting future wars to limited warfare in the form of "test sites." On the other hand, technology creates massive opportunities for such localized deaths as those resulting from airplane or nuclear power-plant accidents. Depriving men of the propriety of their individual deaths, technology everywhere and in every way makes death increasingly foreign and contingent. In this respect, our daily environment is surrounded by isolated "death" in a remote, alienated manner. Regardless of our greater chances of accidental death (which are always announced as "numbers"), on balance the rewards outweigh the risks, for human life spans have gradually increased with improved living conditions and advances in medical technology. While the average life span was once fifty years, many people now exceed eighty. Moreover, the enormous productivity of today's world has increased the time spent on living itself rather than that spent on acquiring the means to live. There has been a significant expansion in the possibilities and conditions for those activities and pleasures that fill the time of "living." Indeed, the question of how idly surplus time is spent has even become a social topic. "Life" has thus come to assume an aspect of utter amusement and the world has been transformed into a bustling playground. We enjoy our "eternal Sundays" in this insipid space, as if obliged to do so.

It seems that "war" has been suspended indefinitely, thus eliminating the violent deaths that it causes. For the time being, people are able to live oblivious to the likelihood of death. "Death"-related issues now take the form of an "inability to die," as though the universal reserve of "death" and solidification of the sphere of "life" had robbed man of death. It was once said that the anxiety of death constricts life, or that the readiness to die brings fulfillment to life, but now, within a life made easy, "death" has become so diluted that, uncannily, it reigns only as something external to "life." If technology makes possible the universal reserve of death, it also increases our life span. In either case, technology distances man from death. Strictly speaking, it distances man from, or tries to rob him of, a proper death. The fact that "death" in many ways remains an issue today is due to the endless dilution of its meaning, even if "dying" has by no means disappeared. "Death" has become something "public" over which the state has authority, such that the dying no longer have any relation to their own "death."

In this era of nuclear-deterrent "peace," the "making-public of death" now appears in a different form. Medical technology has pushed death ever further away, delaying and deterring it. This technology seeks only to deter death provisionally, but that sometimes creates what are considered useless psychological and economic burdens for individuals and societies. Hence people have come up with the notion of " death with dignity." The intent here is to return death to those who have lost sight of life and would otherwise be robbed of death, to end the delaying of death and remove its deterrence—as when life-support machines are disconnected. In this way, "death" seems to be returned to the dying. But it is not always certain if he who must accept "death" actually has the ability to do so. Rather "death" here becomes an object to be manipulated, one that is unrelated to the dying; it occurs only among "others" as an abstract event apart from the dying person. As goes without saying, the return of "death" to the dying is effected by "public approval," that is, this "death" is a "public death." (A desirable death! some might claim. But I hasten to add that one must consider for whom it is desirable, whose "comfort"—*anraku*—and "dignity" are at stake here? Such terms as "euthanasia"—*anrakushi*—and "death with dignity" are questionable in that they definitely make things out to be self-evident. This death is of course not self-evident for the person in question, nor is it undertaken for the "public good." When man becomes just "anyone" and death something public, there arises within this publicness a "someone" as subject of responsibility—not a subject of rights. Then once again this "anyone" becomes a subject who is able to say "I." Doesn't "ethics" lie in the acceptance of being this "I"? Therein resides the possibility of the subject as "ethicality").

Now the more difficult and dangerous issue of "brain death" no longer even concerns the event of "death." In order for medicine, in its self-development, to obtain "corpses" as its necessary material resources, death must be redefined. This is not simply to manipulate or manage "death" externally, entirely apart from the dying person. Rather death, which was once the all-powerful ground of human authority, is now in the unprecedented position of being determined by man and applied to various ends. "Death" has finally become something "artificial," such as to deny it as such. In this way, the dying lose "death," and this lost death is managed as something denied or negated, something foreign to the dying. Even if the old truth that we all die someday still holds true for now, man's "death" can nevertheless no longer be proper to him.

No one can die in place of another. Even if this were possible, however, that other could still not escape his own death. Because of this self-evident truth, death is seen as man's "ownmost possibility" (Heidegger), that which he can never dispose of or hand over. Now, however, all death is at least potentially "accidental death," that is, contingent death, such that no one's relation to death is proper. On the contrary, "death" has become an object to be manipulated without regard for the dying. Although once seen as the absolute authority in the sense of an ultimate event that determines everything, death has now been transformed into a relative phenomenon determined for other ends. This is precisely why there are debates about death: it is not that death has become an urgent question for man, one whose meaning is now increasingly important, but rather that "death" in its ubiquitousness has become diluted and estranged (it is through its quantification that "death" most clearly reveals its own ubiquitous and diluted nature), and its meaning grown increasingly empty. Confronted with death's dispersal and the "inability to die," however, we grasp these negatively as loss or deprivation. Rather than retrospectively wish for a restoration of "proper death," what if we were to see in this loss of death a surfacing of "immortality"?

The Nomadization of "Immortality"

Technology now envisions "immortality" as within its range, at least in principle. While protein synthesis and genetic engineering manipulate the origins of life, death is gradually pushed back through various life-preservation methods as well as by organ exchange in cases of impaired functioning (whether artificial organs or organ transplants). This gradual delaying of death brings the cyborg dream (or nightmare) ever closer to reality. Of course this is not to say that death simply vanishes. Rather several "deaths" are necessary for every "prolongation of life." These deaths are in any case unavoidable, however, and through their utilization—that is, through the use of the corpses left behind (or produced?) by "death" as material resources—other deaths can be delayed. Thus even if "death" is already present, there still remains the merit of prolonging life in view of "immortality." On balance, this will be seen as an increase in life span, as such utilization of death contributes to the "benefit of mankind." It can be said that man has advanced one step toward "immortality" by making the utilization of death possible. Yet despite the fact that this "prolongation of life" brings about an extension of individual life, it is possible only by introducing "parts" that do not belong to the individual and are essentially exchangeable. Thus the decisive nature of "immortality" is already announced.

To say that man has an afterlife, as has long been believed, is not the same thing as saying that he has "immortality." The continuation of life after death is envisioned through the finitude of life in this world in a kind of springboard effect. Because this life is finite, its negation is envisioned as eternal life after death or as eternal life that continues from past lives to future lives. Time is often regarded as a sign that accompanies a falling or loss, and the finitude of this world is seen as a result of a fall within time. Eternity is imagined to exist outside of this world, that is, outside of the world of time; it represents the nullity of that time with which it alternates (as if, just as light erases darkness, either this world has no past lives or future lives, or eternal life returns to erase this world). Thus the finitude of this world comes to be relativized.

Such "belief" cannot simply be described as an irrational illusion. Advances in technology do not eliminate fantasies of the "world beyond." Notions of a four-dimensional world, theories of antiprotons and antimatter, black holes, the big bang, new scientific conceptions of the universe, or even actual human experiences of outer space that go beyond laboratory research and theoretical inquiry—none of these in any way turns the notion of a "world beyond" into an outdated illusion. On the contrary, they increasingly provide theoretical and sensory material for this notion. The experience of a universe without light or darkness, front or back, left or right, or up or down (to say nothing of the fact that this vast universe is not uniform, or that time and space are mutually inter-changeable) illuminates in inverse fashion the claim that "this world" in which we live is a temporal world sealed within an extremely delimited space, or that it is a world within the capsule of "time." This experience has provided a sen-sory ground for that fantasy which seeks to understand the world from the per-spective of the dark, timeless expanse of infinity. By looking at photographs of Earth rising up out of the darkness of space, we sense that our sphere of life occupies no more than this *terra firma* and a few kilometers of air. At the same time, our sensory ground is such that we gaze out at the dark sea of "nothing-ness" that swallows the real world like a drop of water, and view it as a higher dimension. We can set out for this dark sea only by leaving land, or "this world." Although lacking any experiential knowledge of this immeasurably vast sea, we sense anew that we are within it, and that the land at our feet is but a speck in its midst. It is not that there exists a horizon that limits the sea, but rather that man's impoverished sight creates that horizon. The world of "illusion" becomes more real the more "scientific" it becomes.

A "world beyond" unquestionably opens up before man. If "this world" is man's real world, then the "world beyond" (*hi-gense*) represents an inhuman (*hi-ningenteki*) "otherworld." At that time in the past when death was clear and obvi-ous to man, the contours of "this world" were also obvious. For the world then ended or was marked off by death. Death was the lot of all men. However, if all deaths come to be universally reserved and individual deaths managed such that the death one should die no longer belongs to oneself, then "immortality" has fil-tered into the world of the dying and the other world has filtered into this world. Such infiltration turns what had hitherto been the certain real world into some-thing permeable. For example, it is as if one could now suddenly see through the everyday walls and furniture, although these do not disappear. In other words, the ground of human or rather humanistic reality—that concrete reality which had hitherto been unconditionally enjoyed—is now made slightly transparent.

Hence we are no longer faced with the question of whether to believe in "immortality" or the "otherworld." As goes without saying, people can enjoy without in any way believing the tale of *Daireikai* [The great spirit world] as the thrilling and foolish performance of a peculiar actor (assuming that the film is worth enjoying).[1] For while this "otherworld" which transcends man's horizon is still very much told by human (all too human) imagination in a narrative language that gives form to the "human," people can nevertheless somehow perceive the absurdity of this human caprice. The atemporal world of "eternity" cannot be attained by human language, which unfolds as temporalization. But it is "narrative" that effortlessly temporalizes this world, and in so doing spatializes it. Human discourse generally invokes "immortality" as another life, a life that transcends life. If, however, "spirit world" discourse is narrated on the horizon of language (which gives form to that world which must be transcended by immortality), in other words, if this discourse is narrated as an extension of the everyday world, then clearly "the next world adjoins this world." "Spirit world" discourse thus essentially reassures man in his confrontation with "immortality," regardless of how uncanny it may be. For this "uncanniness" does not transgress the limits of the imaginary, whereas "immortality" is "uncanny" because of its transformation of the symbolic order itself. "Spirit world" discourse separates and joins the "next world" and "this world" within language, while "immortality" now spills over from "this world" in which language is born.

If "immortality" is truly uncanny and otherworldly, it is because "death," which constitutes the transcendent instance as absolute and all-deciding power, diffuses without ever definitively vanishing, drifting about in an amorphous and indefinite form. As a result, the world of "immortality" is enveloped by a certain inauspiciousness. The diffusion of death loses its end (*eschatos*), which is thus given over to endless flux or floating. With the mark of a period, death concludes things and fixes being. In this way, it brings to the fore the contours of man and the human in the world. Through death, the human is fixed as the final, completed edition: it is in death that man gains place and determination, and "settles down." Death, that is, guarantees the mode of a decisive "stop." When death becomes diffused, however, there is nothing to guarantee what man's authentic way of being is, regardless of where or how he is. Everything floats in indeterminacy. What appears temporarily to be fixed is only lingering. It is this floating and helplessness that is "uncanny." In German, "uncanny" is *unheimlich*, meaning unhomely or unfamiliar—but of course this uncanniness might just be "wonder."

"Immortality" deprives us of the possibility of "settling down." Let us refuse to see this as "loss," however, and say only that "immortality" becomes nomadized.

Material Immortality

Freud regarded the "uncanny" as the "return from the external world of that which has been effaced in the inner world." What was once familiar to the ego at its dawning comes in the course of its development to be forgotten and excluded from the psychic world as impossible. When this something suddenly appears in the external world, however, man encounters the "uncanny." In this sense, the "uncanny" is at once strange and familiar. Freud invoked the doppelganger as exemplary of the "uncanny." Here the profound relationship between the "uncanny" and "immortality" is thrown into relief. What makes the doppleganger uncanny is not simply the fact that it dilutes the self, but that through its disappearance it is reborn and appears in myriad forms. Freud explained that the first doppelganger is created in childhood as "security from the extinction of the ego," and that the doppelganger represents the return of this "immortal" alter ego. The various traits that Freud noted of this "alter ego's" "uncanniness" ("undifferentiation between self and other; an open communication, substitution, and division between them; as well as the resulting nullification of identity and repetition of a single entity") accurately pinpoint the consequences of "immortality" as viewed by contemporary technology.

While these traits must be emphasized, I would like to affirm here that "immortality" is not simply a psychological matter of forgotten, irrational thoughts from childhood. Going back much further than childhood, "immortality" is the "return of the effaced" in the living body. Freud's "uncanny" is a phenomenon that appears in the individual's psychological process of development and change. Of course in Freud's case, the historical development of individual psychology is analogously extended to that of all mankind. Thus the interpretation of the "uncanny" also takes into account the entire realm of man's shared psychological makeup. This notion is at times even more boldly expressed, however, as when Freud traces back the origin of all psychic phenomena to somatic life. Freudian psychoanalysis acknowledges from the outset that psychic phenomena are not complete in and of themselves, but can function only through the introduction of an "outside." Now if, on the one hand, such acknowledgment distinguishes psychoanalysis from other theories of psychology and physiology, and, on the other, the "uncanny" is not an internal psychological representation but that which the psyche experiences on the border between the inside and the outside, then perhaps "immortality" can be seen to have a privileged link with the "uncanny" as the return of a nonpsychic (that is, corporeal or material) event that is yet related to the formation of the psychic world itself.

Since "immortality" is "at once strange and familiar" as an illusion or wish, it is all the more so corporeally. In *Beyond the Pleasure Principle*, Freud boldly traces back our understanding of psychic mechanisms from their basis in ontogeny to that of phylogeny. Yet what is at issue here is "immortality," albeit in a different form. If we understand "immortality" as the infinitization of "life," then "infinity" must endlessly transcend its limits not only outwardly but also inwardly. Thus if the entire process of life is differentially contained in view of the origins of ontogeny, Freud traces the infinity of differential folds. "Immortality" glimpses its primordial form in a material, rather than a psychological, dimension. While Freud was by no means alone in seeing the repetition of phylogeny within ontogeny, he did regard the primordial form of human life as the composite repetition of the "life" of single-celled organisms.

When an individual (as we shall provisionally call it) single-celled organism divides to become two, there is clearly a material continuity between the original individual and the two newly created ones. And yet these latter differ from the original. It can be said that the original individual has been halved, and that through this division, each half is restored as one whole. The original individual (A) thus no longer exists; in its place are two new individuals (B_1 and B_2). In other words, A disappears and B_1 and B_2 appear. This does not mean that the material that produced the original cell has disappeared, but rather that propagation and division have resulted in the development of the same life in its material base. Now is such reproduction through division "death" or "birth"? What happens to "death" and "birth" in this reproduction?

No doubt there are those who would quite lucidly find these questions to be meaningless, for what is at issue here is neither "death" nor "birth" but simply division and propagation. It is certainly true that cells stop dividing at some point. This point represents the cessation of all life activities, that is to say, "death." Yet exactly *who* is it that dies here? In observing a single cell countlessly dividing itself, several (or even all) of the cells will eventually cease dividing and stop activity—at this point who (or which) has "died"? Here "death" is no one's. It has by chance overtaken several of the multiplied cells, in other words, "death" is, from the perspective of this "multiplicity," nothing more than a partial and slight event that disappears within the propagating whole. In effect, this is literally the "immortal" world of the doppleganger. For all individuals are alter egos of others.

How then can one speak of "death"? It cannot be approached from the material standpoint of sustaining continuity through the process of propagation and division, but rather from the standpoint of "form," which gives the cell its character as individual. It is this "form" that individuates cells and gives each its "propriety." "Death" would thus be the death of that propriety. In other words, when a cell divides, the original proper cell (A) disappears to become two new proper cells (B_1 and B_2). This can be said to be the death of one cell and the birth of two new ones. Here "death" and "birth" are as yet undifferentiated, for they take place as the same event. "Birth" is already taking place when "death" takes place as disappearance. "Birth" overlaps with "death," just as "death" is enveloped by "birth." Or rather, "birth" occurs and bears the result of that occurrence, while "death" is eliminated in this event of "birth."

Clearly single-celled organisms do not just divide and propagate, but they sometimes merge to form new life. At such times, of course, "death" and "birth" are one. This is why, for example, Bataille was able to see in the union of "death" and "birth" in single-cell reproduction the primordial connection between death and eroticism. Organisms become multicellular structures and then grow even more complex through sexual reproduction. In this way, "death" first comes to be separated or, as it were, made *différant* from "birth." "Death" separates and becomes actualized as "death" when it leaves behind a result in the form of an event, that is to say, when it produces a corpse—as when multicellular reproductive organisms first leave behind a corpse following the birth of new individuals. In speaking of "death" in single-celled organisms, we must also speak of "immortality." If given a suitable environment these organisms infinitely divide, then this is in principle "immortality." Life develops continuously through division here, and there is no corpse that actualizes "death." The transformation to multicellular organisms and sexual reproduction, however, separates "death" from "birth." There is now a joint or juncture that at once divides and connects. This joint divides to create space as time and extension, and an interval is formed between "birth" and "death." It is this interval that first leaves behind a "corpse" as material which actualizes death.

This interval between "birth" and "death" is really just the individual's "life," but let us consider what happens when this "life" expands to the point of overlapping with an adjacent interval. In such case, two (or several) individual "lives" as separated by "death" overlap with other individual "lives," such that one "death" overlaps with another "life" and becomes transparent. Within this compositeness, it can be said that the individual once again recovers the continuity of "immortality." Here the "part that can become a corpse" comes to be shared by these two (or several) individuals. Yet these individuals that gain the continuity of "immortality" essentially lose their "individuality," that is, they lose the discontinuity that constitutes individuals as such and guarantees each a proper death. This continuity is not one of a primary life that flows directly between individuals, as in the case of reproduction through division, but rather a kind of secondary continuity in the form of a compositing of divided entities.

Yet this is not to say that man has never known of a continuity that mediates individual death in such a way. This continuity is language, culture, and history, as well as those ideas of communal being that embody these, such as "nation" and "humanity." The most perfect of these ideas has been that of "man," who creates himself and then completes himself as totality, and who represents the "absolute spirit" as self-identical synthesis of language, logic, and history (Hegel). In effect, it is "man" as "spirit" who is the secondary continuity that compensates for the spatiotemporal separation between individuals. Such ideal universality has embodied "immortality" within man. Yet this ideal "immortality" is a posthumous one. That is to say, the idea is made "immortal" since it remains even after the individual's death (the idea transcends the individual's spatiotemporal limitations). But what has now come within range is secondary continuity at the material, rather than the ideal, level. "Immortality" now is neither eternal life after death nor the life of spirit (or its development) as replacement for dead flesh. Even less does "immortality" resemble the dream of "eternal youth." Rather it is a composite continuity that has reached the material level. Life resides in the flesh, not in the spirit. Continuity, understood here not as that which compensates for the finitude of finite individuals but rather as that which is lived as finitude, is about to arrive from the dimension of that material life of individuals in their preconditioned deaths.

On "Brain Death"

The question of "redefining death" has been discussed for quite some time now. As is well known, the so-called brain-death debate has reexamined the traditional clinical standards of "death" as based upon respiratory and heart failure and the total dilation of the pupils, and instead focused on brain failure. As goes without saying, this does not simply involve adding scientific rigor to the clinical definition of "death." Although organ transplantation has been made possible by medical technology, the transplanting of such specific organs as the heart and liver can take place only upon the death of the donor. In other words, the prolongation of life in one person requires the death of another, in addition to the fact that the donated organ must be as "fresh" as possible. Thus a "corpse" that is "new," or not fully dead, becomes necessary. The "brain death" debate has arisen in response to this requirement. That is to say, when someone reaches the stage where he is considered dead by traditional standards, it is already too late to utilize his organs as live. It has thus become necessary to identify the "brain's death" as the "person's death." If medicine normatively identifies this as "death," then the body is hereafter a "corpse." Removing organs from a dead body does not, however, make one a murderer. If undertaken with the consent of the proper "authorities" in order to save another person from death, then organ removal does not constitute defacement of the dead but rather becomes a legal act that serves humanity and the public welfare. The attempt to "redefine death" by determining human death as "brain death" has emerged in these circumstances.

Apart from the problem of securing the transplant organs, there have in fact been not a few occasions when technology has produced a "living corpse," or "dead living body." While technological changes in living conditions have increased the likelihood of accidents, there have also been technological advances in life support, such that a new "mode of life" has emerged known as living "corpses." To be sure, by considering a person's life as human (i.e., personal existence) to be governed by the brain, brain death may come in this sense to mean personal death, and brain failure to be seen as human death. It is often pointed out that the basis for this kind of thinking reflects the traditional mind-body dualism of the West. Yet such dualism has basically represented the position of idealism in its emphasis on the "mind," or "spirit." Human life essentially resides in the spirit, and the flesh is merely an appearance that rots when it dies. It is even believed that the death of the flesh releases the spirit. In the separation of the flesh from the personality in "brain death," however, it is in fact the flesh that is saved from "death." In order that the flesh be quickly rid of the spirit so as to obtain that material resource which is not restrained by personality, man must agree that the spirit's death equals human death. Let us here set aside such questions as whether the spirit or mind is a function of the brain, or if personality is reducible to the brain's activity. In any case, if one sees the shadow of a traditional mind-body dualism in this attempt to identify "brain death" as "anthropological death," thus liberating the flesh from its limitation as "human," then this is in fact nothing more than a caricature that intentionally reverses that dualism.

In modern medicine, the most extreme instance of which is surgery, the body is treated functionally at the material level. This medicine cannot be suddenly abandoned in favor of idealism, for even organ transplantation represents a recycling of human body parts informed entirely by materialism. This is in principle no different from the exchange of parts in other types of machinery. Even if there is of course some emotional resistance to viewing the body as a set of usable "parts," this should not be singled out for reproach. Yet as these parts cannot be used after the body has completely died, one must artificially hasten the pronouncement of "death." An idealistic dualism that has long been stored away must thus be taken out, reversed, and then grafted onto a theory of mechanism, such that man's determination as spirit means that brain death equals human death. Herein lies the dubiousness of "redefining death."

This phenomenon of course gains "humanitarian" (or "humanist") legitimization through cases of universal good work, as when children or youths with incurable heart problems receive transplants from those with no hope of recovery. Here it is claimed that "brain death" must be socially recognized for the sake of "humanitarian acts of good work." Yet when those who insist upon hastening the acceptance of "brain death" further generalize its "benefits" by speaking of the "immeasurable benefits to mankind" that will accrue in recognizing brain failure as human "death," then it becomes abundantly clear what is urging on the demand for this general approval, and also what this implies. According to these people, approval of "brain death" would introduce great possibilities for medical practice.[2] They claim that it not only makes possible the harvesting of organs for those in need, but would also create general organ donors. Moreover, the "brain dead body" makes an "ideal storehouse" for organs, thus expanding the very possibilities of organ transplantation. This body would become a "(living!) factory for blood and hormones" that are difficult to manufacture artificially, and could be used as unparalleled "teaching material" in dissection and surgical training. Thus the general significance of "brain death" is that it opens the way for utilization of the human body as a material resource by sanctioning the disappearance of "personality."

"Brain death" removes the human body's "personality." The "brain dead body" is, therefore, no longer anyone; it is not "human" since it lacks personality. The greatest benefit brought about by the sanctioning of "brain death" lies in utilizing this no one's anonymous body as a "public material resource." It is said that the importance of this "benefit" is far more comprehensive than the limited question of organ transplantation. Even if death is sanctioned, however, the body is still clearly living. If "living" is found here to be an inappropriate expression bound up with an outdated view of life, then we might say instead that the body still sustains fixed metabolic activity. In any case, however, it is clear that the "brain-dead body" cannot reveal any "benefits" unless its life functions are sustained even without the control of the brain. We must naturally ask, then, if there is no such thing as dispersed life without such control of the brain, or if scattered and dispersed existence—bodily existence as such, so to speak, or the existing body—is nothing more than a usable material resource.

Material Existence

It cannot be said that man has never been treated as a thing. Whether in the case of slaves, prisoners, or victims of violent rule, he has been treated inhumanely and driven like cattle, and not infrequently been placed in the position of losing his life. But what is here treated as a thing and transformed into a means is man understood as a single existence, rather than the human body (or its parts) as a material or physiological material resource. As revealed in Hegel's master-slave dialectic, the principle of man's instrumentalization is essentially the ruler-ruled relation between existing beings, in which existence is made into a unit. In this relation, one single existence remains total (not a set of parts that can be separated and utilized) while being ruled by and transformed into a means for the other existence. To be sure, a world in which man's being is completely instrumentalized has been created, as for example in the comic *Kachiku-jin yapū* [The domestic yapoo]. But even here, instrumentalization takes place with single existence as a unit, and its motif is not technology but rather man's erotic bodily relations.

Above all, such relations of objectification or instrumentalization end everywhere with death. Death is the disappearance of existence, nullifying even the most extreme relations of subordination. The ruler loses everything in killing the ruled. It is precisely because of this that suicide may become the final means of resistance in dire situations. Yet such utilization of the human body is allowed with the sanctioning of "death." It is too late for this utilization when death permeates the entire body. Death must be partial, such that the parts to be used survive its invasion. Even if partial "death" in a bodily sense is recognized as complete "death" in a human sense, this body is seen as a material resource from which the propriety of existence has been removed. Medical technology, which regards this body as now "dead," then makes extensive use of it as "organ storehouse," "hormone manufacturing plant" and "teaching material," thereby using all manner of technology to preserve the "life activity" of its parts. Thus from the moment that the death of personal existence is pronounced in the case of "brain death," the now ownerless, anonymous, and impersonal body comes for a time to continue its "undying" existence as an "intermediate" or "in-between" being excluded from life and deterred from death, even if it cannot in the end escape dismantling.

Here, of course, we are not questioning the rights and wrongs of organ transplantation. There is no turning back from the fact that organ transplantation is technologically possible under certain conditions. But what I would like to consider are the implications of the sanctioning of "brain death" as a countermeasure against the inevitable problems bound up with it. There is of course a tremendous gap between treating these problems through the introduction of "brain death" and recognizing "brain death" as death in general. In any case, "brain death" doubles death, or submits it to *différance*, and through this *différance* comes to determine the impersonal and spiritless "neutral" or "intermediate" body, which is neither alive nor dead. This body is thus "made into a material resource" as no longer "human." Its inescapable demise is such that it releases its modicum of existence or life, which in its material dimension lacks "personality" and "spirit," while at the same time interrupting death and giving itself over to artificial "dismantling." Yet this mode of existence cannot but call to mind a significant motif it shares with several strands of contemporary philosophy.

The discourse on "existence" and emergence of "anxiety" as an important philosophical theme represented a protest against the philosophical framework of "man" as consolidated by "spirit" and determined as personal subject. The excentrism contained in the notion of "existence," which inevitably led to such expressions as "I am what I am not," reveals a complex relation in which "man" can be himself only in embracing his outside, which lacks a place within the subject that establishes itself as identical. The emphasis on "existence" also expresses the fact that man is not simply determined by spirit (essence). From this thinking of "existence" there emerged a thinking for which the subject is not formed by the awakening of consciousness, but rather first comes into being in positively taking his place as a sleeping body. This is achieved by virtue of his ability to "sleep," that is, his power to interrupt wakened consciousness. As goes without saying, this thinking is that of Levinas. For Levinas, the mode of existence of "sleep," understood here literally as the body that lacks spirit, is seen as a positive moment in the creation of the "subject." This thinking is radically "materialist," if one can say that, and extends the concept of "man" to a nearly thinglike impersonal mode of existence (however, this "materialism" is the exact opposite of mechanistic theory, which is essentially idealism). "Sleep," which is merely a needless stoppage from the perspective of spirit, here becomes an indispensable moment that constitutes "spirit" as such.

If man had previously been regarded as a personal being in the sense of subject (spirit), then the radical thinking of "existence" invariably calls attention to the instant of the "subject's demise." Such thought reveals the "duality of death." The death of the "subject" does not immediately mean the annihilation of existence. The situation man is thrown into upon this death has been explained in various ways, but at the very least subjectless "existence"—if this can even be called "existence"—is now isolated, depersonalized, and rendered powerless, given over to the vanishing darkness. This thinking attests to the fact that a possibly proper death can be experienced only by the "subject." From the moment that the "subject" is exposed to death, it loses both death and its own status as "subject." Subjectless, impersonal "existence" now loses proper death and is in fact given over to an indeterminate "non-time-space," which is nothing other than death itself.

This is a thinking that, as it were, the dying "subject" delivers from within the midst of "death" to this side of it while suffering its own disappearance. It is through such thinking that the state of impersonal existence is disclosed. The appearance of the demand for "brain death" corresponds to the concrete appearance of this state of impersonal existence in real life, which the thinking of "existence" brought to light (if such expression can be applied to a lightless dimension). It is of course true that the irreversible failure of the brain as a functioning organ belongs to an entirely different discourse from that of philosophy's "demise of the subject." The legitimization of "brain death," however, is strictly a matter for philosophy. From a functional standpoint, it is natural to utilize anything as "parts" so long as it is technologically feasible. "Brain death" must be publicly approved so as to "humanly" legitimize that which is already technologically and functionally obvious. Yet "brain death" has been presented as something that cancels out such "humanity." In other words, the recognition of "brain death" as "human" death involves not so much changing the concept of death as changing the concept of "man." The question of "brain death," then, is first and foremost a matter for philosophy rather than physiology. What is at issue in this debate is less the physiological fact of brain failure than the *thinking of* "brain death" itself.

The thinking of "brain death" distinguishes between personal being, which has a determined identity, and impersonal being, which lacks a proper personality and barely exists. This thinking can be said to run parallel to the question of the "demise of the subject." The body whose personality is erased in "brain death," which sustains certain physiological functions for a certain period of time, corresponds to that impersonal existence revealed by the thinking of the "death of the subject." However, the thought of existence, with its notion of the "death of the subject," utterly differs from the thought of "brain death" in its manner of dealing with this mode of existence. In contrast to physiology, which understands the human body strictly as a functional object (physiology never engages the question of "spirit," or at most sees it as just another function), the thinking of "existence" tries to grasp existence as already a total event. Confronted with the disclosure of impersonal existence as rendered by "brain death," this thinking of "existence" grasps it as a state of existence rather than the discarded shell of "human" demise. Just as the thinking of "brain death" presents that death as "anthropological," so too must the material conditions of this most scant of existences cross the horizon of "humanism and anthropology." It is precisely these conditions that the radical thinking of "existence" takes as unknown, and to which the reexamined "humanism" remains blind. The thinking of "brain death" tries to unreflectively grasp this troublesome reality in its "human, all too human" intent to make use of it.

The problem here is not that a certain state is called "brain death," but rather why the thinking of "brain death" seeks to make this notion generally effective. As I have stated, this thinking aims at using the (assumed) personality-less human body as a material resource. It is therefore not unreasonable if the "brain death" debate calls to mind "Auschwitz." While the "brain-dead body" is of course not intentionally produced by violence, it is still a creation of advanced technology. The Nazi concentration camps stripped man of the propriety of his personality and transformed him into a depersonalized, abstract "mass," thus achieving the most destitute conditions of existence surrounded by "death." The camps must represent the "outside" of any lived world, in which the death of man as "man" is pronounced the moment he is sent there. With the "death of man," bare existence no longer contains a "self," much less the ability to determine its fate. In other words, this "closed time-space" surrounded by "death" was for the prisoners of the camps an "undying" time-space decisively robbed of death. The "undying" human body was resolutely treated as a material resource, or a perfectly expendable object. In its exposure to the "impossibility of death," the radical thinking of "existence" must have been shaped by this historical experience. This idea appears as the "outside of the human," and would refuse to separate from human "existence" even that barest, depersonalized existence which the notion of "brain death" determines as "inhuman" material, for this represents the (most elemental) dimension of material existence without which even the "human" would be impossible. Otherwise, one could not think of the experience of the "concentration camps" in which people existed as strictly "inhuman," thus depriving all human meaning to the struggle to live and survive under such conditions.

The Negation of Death

Man has certainly exploited and developed nature in forming the human world. Thus he forms himself as the world's master, and it has been a long time since he first proclaimed, "I am the world." However, the forms of those practices that generally carve out what appears before us have not changed (if nothing appears, we search for it regardless). Going beyond everyday earthly matters, the human world now infinitely extends from outer space to quarks, from DNA to satellite communications. Heidegger saw in this extension the domination of technology throughout human activity. Yet technology bypasses "death," for it is seen as transcending "man," who lives and dies. This perhaps explains why Heidegger was in a sense blind to modern "death." In Hegel, however, human activity is from the beginning bound up with "death." For "negativity" is the power of "life" to withstand "death" and the power to rule the "other" through force of "death." "Negativity" begins and ends with "death," and is as life-sized as "man." It negates the being of things as they are, and changes those things which are not necessarily for man into human things. Hegel considered negativity the "magical power" in the formation of the human world. What light does this logic shed on modern "death"?

In a sense, negativity is like a windshield wiper that slowly turns around the axis of the subject, clearing away the surrounding darkness (nature). With each turning, the darkness is cleared away and the light of civilization floods in. Thus the world is humanized throughout. Hegel believed that negativity would dissolve itself upon this humanization, for the now-perfected human world represents the fulfillment of negativity (man) itself, and the real world is nothing other than self-realized negativity. In other words, even if the windshield wiper continues turning in the same manner, all subsequent motion is simply routinized and no longer productive of new change; rather it dutifully preserves the world in its unbroken everydayness. This point was contested by such people as Bataille, however, who claimed that history does not end and negativity is not dissolved even after completing all its duties, but drifts on as "useless negativity." For Bataille, the question of history's end appeared as a serious joke that reveals the absurdity of philosophy. In a word, negativity does not disappear (that is, man does not yet die), but only fundamentally changes its nature and continues working. Determined as action, or "labor," negativity is absolutely useful in bringing about meaning and utility, but after completing its duties and negating everything to be negated, it now becomes useless and meaningless. Nonetheless, negativity still continues working as meaningless. This is basically Bataille's objection to Hegel.

For Hegel, the windshield wiper is an entity whose duty is to sweep clean, and it is meaningless to sweep what has already been cleaned. Meaninglessness cannot be regarded as being, moreover, since real being is that which realizes its own meaning in action. But for Bataille, what is *is*, regardless of whether it is meaningless or useless. Indeed, it *is* all the more incorrigibly because of this meaninglessness. Negativity continues working, in fact, and comes to sweep clean the very human world created by the windshield wiper's first turning. It can be said that the "world wars," which both materially and spiritually destroyed the civilized world, represented an unnecessary, meaningless, and futile sweeping away of such "needless negativity." The expression "useless negativity" contains Bataille's recognition of Hegel's logic, according to which man is the once-completed negativity. Negativity does not end there, however, as it is completed only once. Bataille believed that the quality of negativity thenceforth decisively changes. He called himself "useless negativity," which is to say that "meaninglessness" exists as that which is irreducible to human meaning. This confirms that the relation between man and the world has now entered an entirely different and unknown stage, for that relation is humanly meaningless; that is, it transcends the framework of "man." It is in this world that man exists.

There yet remained something else to be "negated." While Hegelian man is essentially formed as "spirit," his corporeality (which thus comes to take negativity upon itself) is barred from the "spiritual reality" of the human world and floats like a ghost (the ghost of spirit?) with nowhere to go. Post-Hegelian thought has come to be haunted by the theme of "corporeality," but the ongoing windshield wiper that is negativity delivers an indiscriminate stroke both to the just-completed human world and to this "corporeality." As that which is irreducible to meaning, "corporeality" is excluded from "spiritual reality" and, if we can say this, is positively meaningless. This "corporeality" is once again exposed to the act of negativity as surplus labor. Since it was produced as useless waste in the first cycle of negativity that created the "instrumental world," "corporeality" can no longer be an "instrument," and instead becomes a "material resource" in the form of a usable, expendable object. In short, this second cycle is literally the process of "recycling." As a matter of fact, "waste-disposal sites" have been built on the margins of the "spiritual world" which treated the body as reusables and final disposals—human fat was made into soap, hair was used for carpets, etc. With astonishing ingenuity, the transformation of the human body into material resources was achieved. Even if we condemn this transformation as a "dehumanizing" deviation and take shelter in "humanitarianism," we can no longer escape such "recycling." This is not an exception that arose from a blending of the particular conditions of Nazism and war, but rather a situation that penetrates within the development of normal social activities. Organ transplantation is but a direct expression of this. "Recycling" is a condition of man's modern world. If man is even now seen as negativity that produces meaning and the world, then negativity must not only create "man," it must also then go on to ceaselessly negate him.

As Bataille remarked, Hegel was entirely correct, even in his mistakes. If there has been one crucial moment in the Western world, one which we could agree in principle has guided and shaped Western civilization (of course the West itself has never been unitary, but a hybridization of diverse elements), then that moment could be described as "negativity." Hegel showed that language, meaning, action, love, spirit, and history—that is, all life and death and the formation of man's modern world—develop as negativity. Even the world "after the end," of which Hegel never spoke, can be understood by this word "negativity."

In this respect, it can be said that history ends twice (twice in the sense of multiplication rather than addition), the world is realized twice, and the world's humanization is achieved twice. The "human world" is negated when negativity again cuts down the world, but perhaps "man's death" as the essence of negativity is then also negated and placed beyond his reach. In which case, "death with dignity" would be discussed according to the logic of returning human death to the dying, while human death would again be artificially determined as brain death. Human death is now not one in which the dying person dies as human. When the dying *can no longer die* in this manner, death becomes for the first time something publicly sanctioned and given. "Death" would then finally become artificial, losing its meaning as a force of beginnings and ends.

The "I" That Is Nobody

Whether "brain death" is considered human death, whether "organ transplantation" is to some extent possible, or whether life support of the "personality-less" body is a viable possibility—these are all separate issues. As I have discussed, the latter two questions show that we have reached a certain level of complex medical technology, while the first involves thinking about man's spirit, body, and death. In other words, this is a condition of human existence to which thought must respond, whether we like it or not. The thinking on "brain death" represents one such response. And yet, despite the fact that advances in technology have fundamentally changed the conditions of human existence, this thinking readily recycles a very traditional view of man, thus ultimately concealing the meaning of these changes. What Heidegger quite justifiably calls "uncanny thoughtlessness" is revealed here as a shameful and grotesque "knowledge." For Heidegger fully knew that the situation man confronts goes beyond the framework of "humanist" thought. This is not to say, however, that Heidegger capably dealt with this situation.

Medicine has sought to distance man from illness and, in its turn, death. It was at one time self-evident that the phrase "to distance man from death" referred to one man's life and death. Now, however, the extension of one life requires the utilization of another "death." The prolongation of one man's life is achieved through a partial compositing with other men, and is carried out by sacrificing the identity of the "individual" on at least the corporeal level. Here we can already glimpse a "communality" at the corporeal level of the "individual" itself.

Death was that which completed and concluded the being of the individual, constituting proper being as such. While death's postponement delays the completion of the individual, the postponement of death through present technology as well as the "immortality" envisioned therein does not simply postpone the individual's death, it also changes its identity. Such change takes place not only in the recipient, whose life is extended through organs that are not his own, but also in the donor, whose organs become, so to speak, recyclable parts. The possibility of organ transplantation is premised upon the understanding that the body itself is divisible, that its parts can at a certain level lose their propriety and be exchanged. Of course this is not to say that the universality of the concept of "organ" does not already imply this. Yet such implication (e.g., that a liver be any liver) only first took into account actual "exchangeability" through advances in technology. In order to liberate the exchanged partial body from personality and propriety, the idea emerges to assign the roles of forming man's propriety and controlling personal identity exclusively to the brain. If, however, the loss of the brain's integrating function does not result in the body's becoming mere individual-less exchangeable parts, but rather parts with their own lives (even if this now seems like a frayed bundle), then it could be said that the brain's integration is enabled by this composite of living individual parts, rather than the individual-less parts being integrated by the brain as center. Assuming it were technologically possible, moreover, organ transplantation might advance to the point where the brain itself could be transplanted, just like the heart and liver, for transplant technology makes no essential distinction between the brain and other organs.

If the praxis of organ transplantation is based on a thoroughly physiological and functional grasp of the body, then the exchangeability and compositing of the "individual" must be understood as such on a material level. In other words, man is made not through "spirit," but "corporeality": "I" am this personality not through the brain's integration, but rather in the composite nature of this body; and "my" personal identity is not a simple, invariable essence as guaranteed by the brain's identity, but rather a variable that can at any time be reorganized by this body's composite nature. "I" am nobody, and it is only through this fact that the "I" first has life. Were this not the case, it would be impossible to reclaim the experience of "impersonal existence" on the part of those who suffer "personal death" and become barely existing, expendable objects living on until their final demise.

In an essay on the world of the concentration camps as depicted in Robert Antelme's novel *The Human Race*, Blanchot examines man's appalling need to live even in the most destitute of situations. When those who survived the camps speak of the brutality of their experiences, it is not only the absolute violence of their captors that they mention, but also the conflict of naked egos among the now personality-less prisoners, which unfolded like images of hell. Under the pitiless scorn of their captors, life-and-death struggles were waged between helpless prisoners over a morsel of bread or a drop of soup. Stripped of their personality, these prisoners lost their self-respect and concern for others, for otherwise they could not have survived this "otherworld." The survivors of the camps perhaps enjoyed certain privileges or abandoned others to their misfortunes, but in any case they lived "inhumanely," and it was this that made their memories all the more unbearable (according, for instance, to Primo Levy, who committed suicide in 1984).³ For these people, being placed in inhuman conditions meant that one could only live "inhumanly." Human life in such an inhuman environment is reduced to one's most basic needs of "living" and "eating." There is of course no concern for others here, for what sustains life is only the "animal" need to live. This "primordial need" of those forced to live such an "inhuman existence" is described by Blanchot as follows:

> [This need] relates me no longer either to myself or to my self-satisfaction, but to human existence pure and simple, lived as lack at the level of need. And it is still no doubt a question of a kind of egoism, and even of the most terrible kind, but of an *egoism without ego* where man, bent on survival, and attached in a way that must be called abject to living and always living on, bears this attachment to life as an attachment that is impersonal, as he bears this need as a need that is no longer his own need proper but as a need that is in some sense neutral, thus virtually the need of everyone. "To live," as Antelme more or less says, "is then all that is sacred."⁴

As Primo Levy writes, the survivors are sometimes confronted with the cruel question of why they went on living under such conditions (the survivors themselves no doubt ask this same question). I do not know whether the prisoners of the camps remained alive through the will to live. Placed in a situation that strips away all human will, one might say rather that they survived precisely because they utterly lost their will and were reduced to a kind of pure instinct. That is, precisely because they had no will, they unthinkingly just ate whatever was placed before them. Thus Blanchot, finding these people reduced to the "most basic needs" of existence, regards such "attachment to life" as impersonal. Because, as Blanchot writes, this is no longer "my" need (for the subject that says "I" has been destroyed) but rather impersonal need, the need of this "person" who is now a naked corporeal existence "potentially bears the needs of all people," such that the life of one "person" is equivalent to the life of all "people." With these words, Blanchot affirms and "sanctifies" those anonymous, impersonal corporeal existences who lived through an inhuman situation as "inhuman" in their very impersonality. Too wretched to be remembered and too cruel to be forgotten, this "inhuman" experience has no resting place within any normal "personal existence" (survivors not only were treated "inhumanly," they prolonged their own lives as "inhumans"). It is this "fractured present" of those suffering from the "disobedient past" that Blanchot affirms without solace or deceit, and in so doing seeks to "save" these people.

Rather than deny or rationalize the "meaning" of personality-less existence (corporeal existence) from the standpoint of personality, Blanchot seeks to affirm the two in the very knot of their shifting (between the loss and recovery of personality, between personal and impersonal being). His thinking is extremely suggestive in its reflection upon another "corporeal being," in which "anthropological death" is pronounced and personality removed. If the state of personal "death" is regarded simply as "nothing" and its experience considered one of exceptional misfortune that is best forgotten, then (the time of) lost life becomes merely a meaningless and pitiable lack. "If only this misfortunate lack were *compensated* for by the fullness of a 'redeemed life'"—such is the "economy of compensation." If "lost life" represents one part of a man's life, then this lack is offset by a "redeemed life." Likewise, if "compensation" functions within social relations, then such a pure offsetting or balancing out is socioeconomically expanded through the notions of "sacrifice" and "donation." Individual existence is considered irreplaceable, and yet precisely because of this irreplaceability—in other words, death is proper, and no one can die in place of another—"death" can become a "sacrifice" and a "donation." When "death" becomes a sacrifice and a donation, it is ultimately compensated for by that other "life" that receives this favor. Otherwise, sacrifice and donation would never take place. Here, sacrifice and donation depend ultimately upon an "economy of compensation." The "propriety of death" raises the value of sacrifice and donation, and compensates for the fact that compensation is merely "compensation," thereby hiding the truth that in this "economy of compensation" even propriety can be supplemented. However, the aim of Blanchot's thinking here is not to compensate that which is lost with something else; rather it is to ensure that what was in the state of "nothingness" be "sanctified" in the present while yet remaining "nothing." Hence "what is lost (and lived in death)" is affirmed within "something else (extended life)," even as it remains "what was nothing." In other words, "what is lost" is now reborn within "something else." Here there is no "economy of compensation," for everything is saved as it is.

It is only because "I" am nobody that "I" have life—this "nobody" that supports the "I" is a corporeal existence that can be ascribed to no person, and is revealed only upon the demise of "my" personality. In discarding this "anonymous body" as "nothing," "my" present, surviving life would also be lost, for "I" am revived only in being borne by that "nothing." Confronted now with the concrete emergence of a personality-less "corporeal existence," what is to be demanded? It is not that we treat the otherwise "worthless" body (parts) as usable material resources, reclaiming the body's "meaninglessness" within "utility," thereby strengthening an inflexible "humanism." Rather we might affirm this "meaninglessness" as such, allowing it to spread within us through the compositing of the "individual" at a bodily level, thus transforming "man" himself.

We must accept the changing nature of the being of the "individual" and consciousness of "communality."

For hundreds of thousands of years, man has died in his naturally proper body. With the exchangeability of bodily parts, however, man is no longer man in his propriety. Without taking into account this "no-longer man," or man's composite being, we can only fraudulently accept the possibility of transplant technology—and hence we will be unable to "revive" that neutral body. In effect, we must seek "rebirth" rather than "compensation."

The World of "Immortality"

At the level of existence at which bodily parts become exchangeable between individuals, the compositing of the individual itself emerges within the universal reserve of death. Of course organ transplantation is not unconditionally possible. On the whole, actual transplants involve such a variety of practical constraints that every case seems unique. For man, however, the meaning of this situation as such is utterly fundamental. The exchangeability of parts renders individuality itself composite, thus changing the meaning of the event of "death," which completes the individual as absolute unit. In the world of the individual as exchangeable composite, even death comes to be cheated in the formation of new composites. Death occurs only with the individual, but this individual is now variable and recombinable.

Just as there is no death in the existence of single-celled organisms, so "immortality" returns to the human world. Yet this is not the "immortality" of everlasting "spirit," but rather a materialist "immortality" as grounded in the dimension of material life. With this return of "immortality," man is now nomadized. Such nomadization does not simply take place in man as "individual," however, as this "individual" is itself already a nomadized composite of partial lives. Levinas calls *il y a* (there is) the state of impersonal or "neutral" existence as exposed to the fear of being unable to die while dying. According to Levinas, "negativity" is no longer effective in this *il y a*, for it can only be destroyed or eradicated here. "Immortal" man as this composite of partial lives exists—if one can say this—on the surface of *il y a*. Such *il y a* is freed from the violent pursuit of "negativity" and transformed into something benign.

The image of the world of immortality is always haunted by an air of inauspiciousness. This is perhaps because immortality generally refers to that which should die, and thus the disappearance of death is at once its dispersal. When immortality is envisioned as the negation of limited life or the postponement of everlasting death, the decision on the "individual" is deferred: the "individual" is maintained as unchanging while the shadow of death grows the more death is delayed. If this world of life grows increasingly inauspicious, this is because "immortality" as the negation of death does not disturb the notion of the "individual."

The notion of "immortality" embraced here, however, represents the consequences of dissolving the "individual's" absoluteness, as the partial lives untied from the "individual" bundle both cut across and recombine "individuals." Death completes the individual and ensures its substantiality. Yet the dissolution of individual absoluteness evades death. Death is visited upon the "individual," but this "individual" is already faint. The "immortality" that now comes into view occurs not as the individual's permanence, but rather as the attenuating of a death that has lost its support. There is thus nothing inauspicious here. Just as division at the level of single-celled organisms eliminates "death" and is explained materially as "immortality," so too does the compositing of the "individual" attenuate "death."

Of course this does not mean that each individual existence is incorporated within one permanent and totalizing essence (the Other) that transcends the individual, as the individual's death is not overcome by integration within this essence. Rather such deaths are dissolved within the event that takes place on the same surface as "individual" existence in the form of a hybridization of partial beings at the material level, a relay, sharing, and compositing of the "individual."

This principle radically "de-essentializes" and nomadizes existence. Technology has now allowed this principle to come into view at the material level, but it extends to the "individual" at every level of human existence. The transformation of "death" is decisive for man, and profoundly changes the very conditions upon which we think of the human. All forms of the "individual"—corporeal, spiritual, cultural, and communal—reveal this aspect of hybridization. "Individuality" of course remains, allowing us to speak of the individual as individual. However, this individual is now rendered transparent by virtue of the composite nature of individuality itself, and this both allows for the emergence of the individual's own diverse coloring and provides for the freedom to always accept rebirth, or metamorphosis. This process is not something that has begun only now, however, for man was originally like this, even before entering upon the "humanist" impasse. Death binds the individual to an essence that is fixed to a certain truth. From the material dimension of partial lives, however, the material "immortality" that has now come into view again reminds us that man, his practices, thinking, communality, and "culture" can always be a free composite, one that is not determined by the essence of death.

Translated by Seth Jacobowitz and Takeshi Kimoto

Notes

Nishitani Osamu, "'Fushi' no wandārando," in *Fushi no wandārando: sensō no seiki wo koete* [The wonderland of immortality: Beyond the century of war] (Tokyo: Kōdansha Gakujutsu Bunko, 1996), pp. 249–296. This essay first appeared in *Gendai shisō* [Contemporary thought], August 1989.

1. This 1989 film both stars and was directed by Tanba Tetsurō. —*Trans.*

2. See, for example, the article by Morioka Masahiro and Akabayashi Akira, "'Nōshi' shintai no kakushu riyō" [The various uses of the "brain dead" body], in *Chūō kōron* (May 1988). Intended as a contribution to fruitful "calm discussion" on "brain death" by a young scholar of "bioethics" and a doctor, this essay explains the possibilities regarding those "various uses of the brain dead body" that are far more "important" (if relatively unknown) than organ transplant. Written as if exploiting a new resource, it reads like a kind of black humor parody on the benefits of "brain death." It is the naïveté of these techno-elites, who do not for one moment dwell on the uncanny *desire for "brain death"* but rather speak triumphantly only of its "benefits" for the "general public," that comes across as being so *uncanny*. It is clear that such scholars of bio-"ethics" regard "ethical problems" here simply in terms of the psychological aftercare given to those family and friends of the "brain dead body."

3. Primo Levy, *Survival in Auschwitz*, trans. Stuart Wolf (New York: Collier Books, 1961).

4. Maurice Blanchot, *The Infinite Conversation*, trans. Susan Hanson (Minneapolis: University of Minnesota Press, 1993), p.133. Emphasis in the original. [Translation slightly modified].

Chapter 5

TWO NEGATIONS: THE FEAR OF BEING EXCLUDED
AND THE LOGIC OF SELF-ESTEEM

Naoki Sakai

Another season of the concentration camp seems to be descending upon us.

Now one is all the more conscious of one's own vulnerability as a second-class citizen of the United States who could potentially be deprived of United States' nationality or the right to legal residence by official decree. What is expediently promoted in American politics and mass media today is an anxiety that America, as the last superpower of an imperial nature, has turned into the symbolic target of anticolonial vengeance.[1] This assessment, in turn, justifies the federal administration's insatiable search across the globe for signs attesting to imminent attacks by "terrorists." As long as the public buys this paranoid formula, a state of emergency can easily be linked to a global colonial war and spread throughout an entire civil population.

In reference to the *campos de concentraciones* of the Spanish in Cuba and the "concentration camps" of the English in South Africa, Giorgio Agamben gives an historical account of how the concentration camps were inaugurated around the beginning of the last century:

> [The camps were] born not out of ordinary law (even less, as one might have supposed, from a transformation and development of criminal law) but out of a state of exception and martial law. This is even clearer in the Nazi *Lager*, concerning whose origin and juridical regime we are well

informed. It has been noted that the juridical basis for internment was not common law but *Schutzhaft* (literally, protective custody), a juridical institution of Prussian origin that the Nazi jurors sometimes classified as a preventative police measure insofar as it allowed individuals to be "taken into custody" independently of any criminal behavior, solely to avoid danger to the security of the state.[2]

The concentration camp itself was a preemptive measure taken by the State to prevent threats to the security of the State from actualizing.

As Hannah Arendt assessed a half century ago, the decline of nation-state sovereignty was accompanied by the decline of the rights of man. It seems that this formula is being ascertained once again. We have to deal with more and more organizations that are neither national nor international, as class struggles and the classes themselves can no longer be integrated into or confined by the nation-form.[3] Hence sovereignty is increasingly removed from nation-states to a new kind of "super-stateness" that has neither a central republican body nor the antagonisms of class or national interests resisting the unilateral logic of the market.[4] Driven by a transnational, private, commercial understanding (as opposed to law, which must refer to a social body), this super-stateness assumes that it is in the process of producing a global civil society that represents a reign of law without the State. Since, however, there is no articulation of inter-individual to central contractuality, the reality is actually quite the opposite: a State without law. In this global State-without-law, the nature of sovereignty in its relation to the movements of the stateless multitudes follows the logic of the police. Consequently, the systemic struggle between the center and the periphery itself is aligned, or shall we say, complicitous, with the emergence of a super-state, or, quite simply, the identification of humanity in general with stateness. While asserting itself time and time again as representative of a particular national will, the United States super-state assumes the responsibility of global police for protecting all those subjected to stateness. Indeed, today's wars, launched in the name of humanity, signal the coming of an age in which the meaning of humanity itself is starting to gradually coincide with stateness.

The Gulf War set the precedent for global complicity with the new order of sovereign police, now consolidated by the wars in Afghanistan and Iraq, in which the two figures of modern central order, imperialist and statist, converged. Although the United Nations arrogated to itself the ultimate right of war and legitimate violence, which had formerly exclusively defined the power of each sovereign state, it immediately divested itself of this power by granting the conduct of the war to a private force, that of the United States and its allies. By placing itself beyond jurisdiction, this private force appropriated the power of the police, and thereby constituted itself as a state without law.

Today the top officials of the U.S. federal administration have declared themselves the most authentic representatives of humanity and the embodiment of this ultimate sovereign power. They claim the right to arrogate ultimate lawfulness to the U.S. federal authority. In other words, it is increasingly difficult to differentiate the military that protects and promotes national interests outside U.S. territory from the police that serve to regulate violence and maintain the State's jurisdiction within its territory. This is to say that the embodiment of lawfulness is in fact beyond any existent law. Therefore, these top officials have repeatedly asserted a state of exception, invoked by the state of emergency—which allows the suspension of political rights concerning personal liberty, freedom of expression, informational privacy, etc.—as an indefinite and unending condition under which we must live from this point on. They want to deliberately confuse this condition with juridical rule itself.

In such a situation as, Agamben tells us, was once referred to as the "state of willed exception,"⁵ if one is of an "alien origin" and potentially a second-class citizen, how can one survive such a condition without committing oneself to that condition voluntarily? This is a question that I could not resist posing to myself and on which I would like to concentrate in this presentation with a view to the general problem of the *poiesis* of the subject.

I will read three texts; the first two form a pair, which were published almost simultaneously. These two texts are short stories written in Japanese: "Michi" [Road], which appeared in the journal *Bungei Taiwan* [Literary arts Taiwan], and "Honryū" [Torrent], which appeared in *Taiwan Bungaku* [Taiwan literature]—both published in July 1943 in the midst of what was customarily referred to as *hijōjitai* or *hijōji* (the state of exception)—by the Taiwanese writers Chin Kasen (Chen Houquan) and Ō Shōyū (Wang Changxiong). The third text is *No-No Boy* by John Okada, a fictional piece about the experience of a Japanese-American draft resister, published initially in 1957, more than a decade after the end of the Asia Pacific War.

No doubt, what I am going to present is a comparative project. Yet it is necessary to issue a disclaimer at the outset. My comparison is guided by the analysis of schematism in the regime of translation,⁶ according to which the representation of the comparable unities between which comparison is conducted is posterior to the act of translation. Translation is often represented as a transfer of "something" from one language unity to another, between two organic unities of languages that are supposedly not implicated in one another. But it is important to note that comparison cannot be reduced to one between the presumed unities of two organic entities or—in this case—two societies postulated as organic unities. Above all, it is a matter of how comparison is represented, a matter of an assumed scheme that is rendered self-evident as a consequence of the repeated use of such representation. What I want to presage here is that my reading of these texts will not conform to this scheme or view them as representing in one way or another the societies in which they were produced. Undoubtedly it is necessary to refer to the specific social and historical conditions that enable us to make sense out of these texts. The historical and social specificities of the texts cannot be overlooked. Yet comparison is not regulated to produce some judgment about the similarities or differences between Japanese society—or Taiwanese/Chinese society?—of the early 1940s and American society of the 1950s. I refuse to equate the historical and social specificity of a text to the subsumption of it under the generalized organicity that is more often than not superimposed upon the putative spatiotemporal unity of a nation-state. Accordingly, whereas I do not deny that these were produced in the particular loci marked by the specificities of place and time, I do not regard either "Michi" or "Honryū" primarily as expressions of "Japanese reality," or *No-No Boy* as an expression of "American reality." These texts will be read under a comparative directive toward an uncovering of the general technology of imperial nationalism, a technology by means of which a subject of the imperial nation is manufactured out of so-called minority individuals.

* * *

In the first half of the twentieth century, many of the industrialized nations underwent some transformation in response to the sense of crisis in capitalism. The United States and Japan were no exceptions. Although chronologically and geopolitically the nationalisms of the two countries should be approached from different viewpoints and in separate historical contexts, they have much in common when we examine them from the perspective of imperial nationalism. My inquiry, therefore, adopts the formula of comparative imperial nationalism. (I hope that this essay will eventually be couched in a larger treatise on the formation of imperial nationalism). Since I have neither time nor space to talk about other aspects of imperial nationalism, I would like to focus on the problem of the manufacture of the subject or, to use the philosophical idiom of the 1930s, the *poiesis* of the subject, with a view to minorities, those people of "alien origins" who could be stripped of their citizenship and fundamental political rights preemptively in imperial nationalisms.

In considering how histories of East Asia prior to the end of the Asian-Pacific War had been remembered and written about in the postwar period, we cannot overlook two moments: the collapse of the Japanese empire and the colonization of Japan by the United States. Generally speaking, as far as countries under the U.S. postwar domination are concerned, histories of East Asia have been written in large measure for the sake of legitimizing the American military and political reign in the Asia-Pacific region. Let us not forget that the histories were also filed to absolve Japanese imperialism. As became glaringly obvious at the International Tribunal on War Crimes against Women, in Tokyo in December 2000, the absolution of Japanese colonial and war responsibilities constituted an essential component of American hegemony. Deliberately avoided in those histories, which apparently celebrate Japan's defeat and the democratic objectives behind U.S. policies and strategies, were questions indispensable to peoples who had suffered from the multilayered imposition of colonial domination and violence: How could colonial rule damage the colonized physically as well as psychologically? How did colonialism give rise to not only national liberation movements but also racial hierarchy? Why does nationalism exist in complicity with racism? What measures have to be taken in order to liberate the ex-colonized from colonial legacies? In addition, those histories were designed to obfuscate and disperse the issues of colonial and war responsibilities of the institutions, colonial administrators, military personnel, and cultures that required and propagated colonial violence and oppression.

These histories were not promoted by the conservative historians of the United States alone. Japanese historians and intellectuals were also instrumental in their invention, propagation, and endorsement. Unlike previous colonial rules, the American occupation administration did not rebuff Japanese nationalism; rather it put up anticolonial banners and pretended to take sides with national liberation causes; it protected and even nurtured Japanese ethnic exceptionalism. Japanese intellectuals, who could hardly endorse the military and political policies of the United States toward East Asia, were exonerated from the task of investigating the mutually reinforcing relationship between their nationalistic sentiments, which propelled their anti-Americanism emotively, and American hegemony.[7] It is in the disavowal of the two countries' colonial pasts that Japanese and U.S. nationalisms were in complicity with one another, as if intimating today's complicitous mutuality of the center and periphery under the domination of the global super-state. Furthermore, despite extremely violent encounters and interactions among many different ethnic, racial, gender, and national groups, the past was narrated only within the framework of national history, so that neither American nor Japanese historians dared to undertake the elementary examination of comparing the two imperial nationalisms in the same analytical field, using the same set of criteria. Therefore, Japanese society and its colonial strategies in the 1930s and early 1940s were frequently objects of denunciation, but scarcely studied in detail for fear that the results of such a study would reflect on America's home problems. From the outset, Japanese nationalism was by definition assumed to be an exceptionalist, ethnic particularism exclusive of other ethnicities, while American nationalism always manifests itself in its universalistic orientation toward multiethnic integration. Perhaps this is a case of collective transference, as it is brilliantly allegorized in the film *M. Butterfly*.[8]

It is a most common feature of the imperialist complex to justify the imperialism of one's own country by insisting on its exceptional traits and superiority over other imperialisms. Every nationalism, imperial nationalism in particular, presents itself as an exception. Exceptionalism is inherent in any imperial nationalism. But we cannot succumb to the temptation of exceptionalism, regardless of whether its claim is clothed in the uniqueness of an ethnicity, of the West, or of some religious tradition. This is why a comparative analysis of imperial nationalisms, together with an appropriate analysis of the psychic mechanism of denial of colonial guilt, is indispensable in view of our urgent need to find the ways to deal with the reality, in the progressive present, of a new imperialism and its effects.

In the early 1940s, systematic campaigns to mobilize local students and youths to join the military were under way, not only in Japan proper but also in the annexed territories of the Japanese empire, such as Taiwan and Korea.[9] Undoubtedly these were a response to the chronic shortage of labor in Japan, which also gave rise to a variety of social measures, including the lifelong employment system, the higher social status of women, and the forced relocation of laborers from the annexed territories to industrial centers in Japan proper and other parts of the empire. Just as the civil rights movement on the U.S. mainland could not be separated from the war going on in Indochina during the 1960s and early 1970s, integration policies—generally referred to as *"kōmin-ka seisaku"*[10]—and the integration of minorities into the nation were closely connected to the prolonged war in China.

Perhaps the most salient feature of government rhetoric can be found in its emphasis on voluntarism. The local recruits in Taiwan, the *hontōjin—bendaoren* in Beijinghua—(i.e., the islanders as opposed to the *naichijin—*or *neidiren*—meaning the Japanese from Japan proper) were supposed to have decided of their own free will to join the Imperial Forces, and to have found an anticipatory resolution to their own deaths as Japanese subjects loyal to the emperor. Publicly propagated was the fantastic scenario that these islanders wanted to be "Japanese," and therefore volunteered to die as "Japanese." It is important to note that the islanders' voluntarism was premised upon their subjectivity. Their anticipatory resolution to their own deaths for the country was appealed to as testimony of the fact that they were just as capable of patriotic action as the Japanese from Japan proper, that they were as authentically "Japanese" as the *naichijin* in respect to their subjectivity.

Citing passages from Miyata Setsuko's *Chōsen minshū to kōminka-seisaku* [The Korean masses and imperialization policies], Komagome Takeshi refers to some cases concerning imperialization policies in Korea. He notes that the Korean youths often boasted of "their being Japanese" in the 1930s and early 1940s.[11] While the governor-general's office and the Japanese army in Korea worked hard to manufacture loyal imperial subjects of the colonized population, as Miyata and Komagome both argue, they implemented a number of social reforms, but never in the direction of abolishing existing institutionalized forms of discrimination. Yet some Koreans wished to go beyond the existing discriminatory barriers by becoming "more Japanese than the Japanese from Japan proper themselves," says Komagome.[12] There was no way to conceal the obvious contradiction between what the rhetoric of national integration and imperialization claimed and the reality of institutional discrimination against the Korean population. "It would be an impossible demand: you ought to behave as loyal subjects of the emperor even though you must be aware you can never be Japanese."[13] But precisely because of this contradiction inherent in the colonial reign, it was necessary to invent a technology whereby that contradiction could be mediated for the manufacture of the subject. What was at issue was how to render it a productive moment in the *poiesis* of the imperial subject. Such desire for Japanese identity would otherwise be blocked in the subject because of the contradiction inherent in colonial reign, and yet in fantasy it could be fulfilled. This is why the management of fantasy was absolutely essential in the *kōminka-seisaku* (imperialization policies) for, in certain fantastic works, colonial discrimination could be appealed to so as to produce an insatiable desire for Japanese identity in the colonized. Thus the contradiction could be internalized in the colonized as the source that propels them toward Japanese identity.[14] Accordingly, we regard literature in Japanese in colonial Taiwan as a technology for the *poiesis* of the subject.

Nevertheless, let us not overlook the fact that the setting of a fantastic staging as background to the discriminatory distinction between the islanders (*hontōjin*) and the Japanese from Japan proper (*naichijin*) was sublated into the indiscriminate "Japanese." This scenario was played out effectively only insofar as a certain division of fantastic labor was assumed: it was to be staged with the islanders as actors and the Japanese proper as audience. The islanders were expected to act before and for the audience from Japan proper. However, it is not the islanders but the Japanese from Japan proper who were the protagonists in this fantasy.

During the period of *kōmin-ka seisaku*, Taiwanese novelists wrote such short stories about volunteer soldiers as "Shiganhei" [The volunteer soldier], by Shū Kinha (Chou Jingbo); "Michi," by Chin Kasen; and "Honryū," by Ō Shōyū. It is to be noted that the editors of the literary journal *Bungei Taiwan*, who were Japanese from Japan proper,[15] commented upon "Road," which depicts the anguish an islander intellectual experiences in the process of reaching a decision to join the military. As one editor wrote,

> Some critics might say that this is not sophisticated enough as a work of literature, but I would ignore such an evaluation. Has there ever been as powerful and honest a work describing a wholehearted enthusiasm for becoming Japanese? Has one ever talked so excruciatingly about the anxiety involved in becoming Japanese? Has the human struggle with this anxiety ever received so forceful an expression as this? This road is the road to Japan.[16]

The other editor wrote,

> Up to halfway in the script I was not really convinced. It was a bit rough. There were many incorrect uses of particles. But as I reached the latter half I felt my eyes watering. I thought that this was a great piece of literature, and I could not help sitting up straight. I wished everyone could read this work. I read it aloud. And each time I read it aloud, I found myself moved without any pretense.[17]

In respect to their literary techniques and linguistic competency, islander writers are inferior to writers from Japan proper; but in terms of their patriotic ardor, as the journal's editors insisted, they can surpass the Japanese from Japan proper. On the one hand, the Japanese from Japan proper are vastly superior to the islanders with regard to their industrial development and degree of civilization, so their civilizing positionality remains unwavering. On the other hand, they have to learn from the islanders about those virtues of honesty and sincerity that they used to possess but have now lost. The *naichijin* overwhelm the *hontōjin* with their economic and political superiority. But the *hontōjin* are more authentically "Japanese" in respect to their patriotic ardor than the *naichijin*. Summarily, this is the lesson that the editors of *Literary Arts Taiwan* wanted to discover in Chin Kasen's autobiographical short story "Road." What was wished for in this fantastic staging was that the islanders themselves should confess the desire, the fulfillment of which the Japanese from Japan proper wished the islanders to achieve. Basically, what the editors recognized in "Road" was a scenario in which the Taiwanese misrecognized the desire of the *naichijin* editors as their own, and thereby wanted to be "Japanese" by acting out the roles expected of them by the *naichijin*.

In "Road," the *hontōjin* intellectual, whose pen name is Sei Nan (Qing Nan),[18] works as an engineer in a national camphor-refinery factory in Taiwan and hopes to be promoted to the rank of full engineer, but his wishes are dashed because of the ethnic glass ceiling within the company. The protagonist, who is personally committed to the principle of equality in the Japanese nation, is portrayed as follows:

> He regarded himself as a proper Japanese. He disliked not only the word *naichijin*, but also its opposite, *hontōjin*. The texture of these words and their connotations made him feel ill at ease. He believed it foolish to regard oneself either as *naichijin* or *hontōjin*. In the first place, the self-deprecating attitude of regarding oneself as *hontōjin* was repulsive to him. He wanted to believe that he was simply a good Japanese. He did not want this belief to be called into question. He should not be forced to doubt what he wants to believe, and people must let him hold on to that belief [which should protect him from envy and self-deprecation]. It would be, he believed, stupid to cause a tragic incident out of a sense of envy or self-deprecation.[19]

Obviously, to be Japanese does not mean to be *naichijin* here. Taiwanese islanders are equally as Japanese as those from Japan proper, and to claim to be Japanese is to obtain the right to overcome the various forms of discrimination that distinguish *hontōjin* from *naichijin*. Nonetheless, Japanese nationality is not an abstract quality totally free of the past. The narrator of the novel acknowledges the weight of tradition:

> The Japanese return to their authenticity when they are aware of "the tradition of their blood." By this I do not mean that one is Japanese because one has inherited Japanese blood. What I mean to say is that Japanese are to grow up receiving the tradition of the Japanese spirit from their childhood, so that they may be able to manifest that spirit if necessary. Precisely because of this capacity, one is Japanese.[20]

Certainly, "to be a good Japanese" is not a property monopolized by the Japanese from Japan proper. As Sei Nan admits, however, it is necessary for the islanders to emulate the *naichijin* as the ideal in order to be good Japanese. Therefore, among "the *hontōjin*, the Koreans, and the Manchus," there should be many who are equipped with the Japanese spirit. They "hold onto the Japanese spirit firmly."[21] As it is not innate in them, however, they must learn it from those who have grown up with it.

Thus, the scenario outlined in "Road" accommodated two contradictory demands at the same time. On the one hand, the Japanese from Japan proper were inherently superior to the islanders. On the other, as Japanese, they were equal, regardless of their ethnicity. A similar scenario, which fulfils the wishes of one group to be recognized as superior to the other in the midst of the rhetoric of equality, might be found in humanistic ideology in general. And no doubt it is this humanistic scenario that moved the editors of *Literary Arts Taiwan* to tears.

It goes without saying that the celebration of the Japanese spirit in "Road" cannot immediately be taken as an expression of the author's conviction. Literary production was apparently conceived of as an essential part of total war mobilization, and the marks of censorship and integration policies are evident in this work, too. As the traces of censored characters indicate, this work was published only after the approval of government censors. However, this does not mean that the Japanese-language literature by *hontōjin* writers can be viewed merely as a consequence of their collaboration with the Japanese colonial authorities. For, as in "Road," we now can recognize the features of an imaginary relationship between the individual and the State there, and this imaginary relationship between minority individuals under colonial rule and the State was the very theme that the State logic of integration (whose most elaborate expression can be found in the Logic of Species)[22] pursued as its problematic. In other words, a reading of this literature might well illustrate to us how the multiethnic State's logic of integration could weave the desires of minority intellectuals and persuade them toward the policies of the empire.

Throughout "Road," however, although speaking the Japanese language and behaving like Japanese from Japan proper was not thematically problematized, the multilingual nature of Taiwanese society was hinted at here and there. It is presumed that a Taiwanese intellectual could transform himself and thereby modernize his environment by speaking Japanese and behaving like those from Japan proper.

For those who could not easily convince themselves of their Japanese nationality, the concern for national belonging inevitably oscillated between two polarities: the facticity of their immediate ethnic origin and the belonging to a national community through their commitment to ideas. Accordingly, Sei Nan is portrayed as a protagonist who tries to go beyond his fixation with ethnic origin in order to belong to the nation through his commitment to ideas. This must have been exemplary behavior among well-educated local intellectuals in Taiwan then. But at the same time, as Chen Wanyi observed about the ambiguous relationship between the Japanese nation and those elite *hontōjin* (such as former Taiwan president Lee Denghui) returning from the large cities in Japan proper,[23] the story of Sei Nan seems to vividly illustrate the ideological setting of national belonging for minorities.

Since he is not from Japan proper, Sei Nan is denied promotion to the rank of full engineer at the factory. He is betrayed by the very Japanese spirit in whose universalism he has invested so much, and as a result he is now caught in a self-destructive neurosis. He was flatly told that he did not belong in the Japanese nation. Censorship was exercised to prevent the negative images of those from Japan proper from spreading widely in the colonies, and yet how could such a description of naichijin's outright hypocrisy be allowed? The colonial authority could not disallow the symbolic expression of colonial violence precisely because literary production was a technology for the poiesis of the subject, a technology by which to manufacture the colonized as a subject who would identify with the Japanese nation. It was meant to produce an effective scenario in which, at the level of fantasy, the colonized would overcome many obstacles imposed by the reality of colonialism to evolve into a full-fledged Japanese. Only through a vivid description of these obstacles—naichijin's discriminatory attitude, their haughtiness, hontōjin's backwardness and sense of inferiority, legal discrimination, etc.—could hontōjin characters such as Sei Nan serve as the point of attachment for the colonized. Otherwise, the story would never succeed in offering the sense of reality against which the colonized could recognize the protagonist as an embodiment of their own fantasy. Engaging in the integrationist strategies of kōmin-ka, the colonial authority could not afford to remove the description of harsh colonial reality from Japanese-language literature.

Just as the humiliation of the colonized is directly represented in the sexually impotent figure of Ayuh in Chō Bunkan's (Zhang Wenhuan) "Iyatumu ge,"[24] Sei Nan's breakdown is no doubt a trope for Taiwanese humiliation throughout the colonial reign. In due course, his self-respect that was premised so much upon his membership in the nation is fatally crushed. Then he is forced to learn that, while promoting the ideal of the Japanese nation beyond ethnic particularity, the Japanese from Japan proper do not believe in it at all. Evoking a sense of guilt in the naichijin readership, the depiction of his anguish may well turn his patriotism into rebellion. Chin Kasen's narration seems to lead the reader to a fantasized argument that Sei Nan loves the country so much that, as a proper Japanese, he is fully entitled to denounce injustice in Japanese society and protest against the colonial administration. Implicitly it discloses the fundamental hypocrisy of the integrationist rhetoric of imperial nationalism and the miserable situation of minorities in which, in the final analysis, they can only demand recognition from the nation as a whole, seeking love from the pastoral power, just as a lost sheep begs for the merciful gaze of the shepherd. Let us recall that, from the establishment of the modern state at the beginning of the Meiji period until the loss of the empire in August 1945, the emotive sense of Japanese nationality was often displayed in the imperial slogan *isshi dōjin* — which implies "since everyone in the nation is embraced in the gaze of the emperor, he never ceases to care about you."[25]

In spite of the universalistic rhetoric of integration, what confronts Sei Nan is the reality of Japanese proprietarism, of a *naichi-shugi* that the Japanese nation consists solely of Japanese from Japan proper. Yet it is misleading to argue that the rhetoric of imperial nationalism, such as the Logic of Species, primarily serves to disguise the presence of ethnic and racial discrimination within the empire. For, perhaps more important, it was a response to colonial anxiety and had to be invented in order to prevent the mutiny of minorities. It was a reaction to those social antagonisms which racial and ethnic discrimination could provoke. The empire had to displace potential civil strife by appealing to the logic of national integration.

Realizing that the glass ceiling that prevented his promotion to the rank of full engineer could neither be removed nor publicly criticized, Sei Nan decides to volunteer for military service. He makes an anticipatory resolution to his own death only when he has seen that the universalistic rhetoric of national integration has unambiguously failed him. For he believes that the only way to recover his self-respect is to renegotiate his belonging to the nation, which, for the Taiwanese at that time, meant embracing the State's call for self-sacrifice and, implicitly, Japanese supremacy. But, as Avishai Margalit tells us, self-respect is not self-esteem.[26]

Instead of appealing to the option of rebellion, however, Sei Nan chooses to postulate his enemy not inside the empire but outside it. His real antagonism is displaced by an external and fantastic one between Japan and its external enemy. Among the works of Japanese literature by islander writers, Chin Kasen's "Road" is said to be one of the most accommodating with regard to the *kōmin-ka*, or imperialization, policies. Yet even "Road" does not fail to question the pertinence of such patriotic articulations as, for example, the following: "We must act to make the State accord with the way of God, and thereby prevent it from deviating from truth and justice," and "We are called upon to destroy deception, untruthfulness, and injustice within the State because these drive the nation to be alienated from the State and give rise to a separation between the two."[27] Chin Kasen shows us implicitly that when one is not allowed to "destroy deception, untruthfulness, and injustice within the State," the Taiwanese islander volunteers to be a "Japanese soldier" not because of his freedom but rather because of coercion or desperation.

What is outlined in "Road" is a fantastic mechanism in which the domestic colonial violence against minorities within the nation is displaced onto the aggressivity of nationalism and externalized into military violence against the enemies of the nation as a whole. Therefore, it is not because the rhetoric of national integration failed to actualize equality beyond ethnic and racial differences that we must denounce imperial nationalism, as exemplified in the Logic of Species. Rather, it is because those humiliated minorities regain their honor and self-esteem by displacing and externalizing the aggressivity of the nation as a whole onto outside victims. The rhetoric of national integration thereby succeeds in integrating minorities without actualizing equality for them or allowing them to fully regain not only their self-esteem (which could only be granted through recognition by their victimizers), but also their self-respect, which endows the victims with an agency capable of extending solidarity to the oppressed of another place and ethnicity. What must be called into question here is the technology of national subjectivity, in which one's belonging to the nation can be guaranteed through the anticipatory resolution to one's own death, through one's voluntary will to die for the country.

It is in this historical connection that we might appraise the political significance of Ō Shōyū's "Torrent." For "Road" and "Torrent" seem to have engaged in a severe struggle with one another, indicating different ways for minority intellectuals under Japanese colonial rule to act in response to the State's call for their voluntarism.

Whereas "Road" is written as a narrative depicting the protagonist Sei Nan's anguish through internal monologue, Ō Shōyū succeeded in giving expression to those fears and contradictions that a colonial intellectual had to live through in the form of three main characters and their conflicts with each other. The three characters are the narrator, seemingly a Taiwanese medical doctor who, having lived in Tokyo for a long time to receive his university education, returned to Taiwan to inherit his father's clinic; Itō Haruo (Zhu Chunsheng), a high school teacher of Japanese literature; and Itō's nephew, Rin Hakunen (Lin Bainian), a student at the high school where Itō teaches. Itō Haruo is portrayed as a native intellectual who is most successful in modernizing himself, receiving a Japanese education, speaking impeccable Japanese, and working tirelessly to build the Japanese spirit among native Taiwanese children. While the narrator remains unbelievably loyal to the colonial authorities' propagandistic stereotyping of Japanese culture and the *naichijin*, Ō Shōyū did not fail to include a few remarks indicating the oddity of Itō's presence. In the narrator's second encounter with Itō, a peculiar exchange takes place:

> "Welcome to our house," said my [the narrator's] mother in the national language [Japanese]. She continued, but this time in the Taiwanese language (*hontōgo*). "The rainy season has just arrived. It is unpleasant, isn't it?"

"This is my mother. She only speaks a little of the national language."
I introduced my mother to Itō.

He responded in the national language. "This is your mother? How do
you do? I am Itō Haruo. Thank you for your welcome." I was struck by a
sense of oddity. Itō would not speak Taiwanese, even on such an occasion.
Instantly I was overwhelmed by the feeling that Itō's philosophy of life was
extreme and excessively unyielding. I could not help translating his words
for my mother.[28]

What is remarkable about this story is the fact that, having chosen Japanese
literature over his medical career, Itō Haruo is not depicted as a typical seeker
of upward mobility who would collaborate with the colonial authorities simply
in order to acquire whatever economic and political gains that might trickle
down from the colonial government structure. He is married to a woman from
Japan proper and attempts to totally render every aspect of his life as Japanese.
Beyond his personal life, he believes that the entire native population in Taiwan
must be fundamentally Japanized; consequently he devotes himself to the task
of educating the young Taiwanese. Most hostile to this character is his nephew,
Rin Hakunen, who sees in Itō the very betrayal of the Taiwanese native community. He cannot forgive Itō for being ashamed of his native language, his own
family, and, particularly, his mother, in whose figure his ethnic identity is symbolically represented.

What the intense animosity between Itō and his nephew invariably discloses
is a competition between two contrasting visions of modernization. The vision
that unproblematically endorsed the figure of Itō authorizes the historical
scheme of the colonial civilizing mission, by which the cultural quality associated with the colonizing power is immediately equated with a sign of progress,
a defeat of the primitive, and the transformation of the uncivilized. The social
reality of Taiwan is constantly viewed as essentially primitive, as that which must
be radically transformed. But in this view of the primitive, the chronological
order of modernization is invariably identified with the colonial order of a civilizing mission. Consequently, the time of modernization is totally usurped by
the dichotomy between colonizer (developed) and colonized (underdeveloped). Civilizing time is, as a result, expected to run from the developed to the
underdeveloped. There are many who uphold this scheme in both the colonizing and colonized societies. Itō Haruo is typically a fictional native character
whose entire existence confirms the historical scheme of the colonial civilizing
mission from the viewpoint of the colonized. As Japan has also been modernized in this manner, Itō is a generalizable figure who could be found anywhere
in the empire, either in Japan proper or in the annexed territories.

Rin Hakunen, Itō's nephew, offers a different vision of modernization. The trope of the native mother plays an exceptionally important role here, just as in many contemporary Japanese novels centering on the theme of *tenkō*, i.e., the leftist's conversion to nationalism under state oppression. In a letter Rin writes to the narrator from Tokyo, where he has decided to pursue his college education, he argues against his uncle's modernization scheme:

> But it is my belief that, the more authentic a Japanese I become, the more self-confident a Taiwanese I should be. I have no need to be ashamed of my origin, though I was indisputably born in the South Seas. As I become familiar with everyday life here [in a Japanese metropolis], I do not necessarily look down upon the provincial styles of my home country. However embarrassing my native mother may appear, I cannot deny my affection for her.[29]

In the process of modernization, according to this vision, local social formations must be transformed. But this does not necessarily mean that the reality of local sites such as the old port town of Tanshui—which is implicitly referred to in "Torrent"—must be made identical with that of Japanese metropolises. The cultural quality of Japaneseness cannot be determined unilaterally by the Japanese from Japan proper. Rather than the predetermined archetype of the past, the Japaneseness of Japanese nationality must suggest this indeterminacy of the future in subject formation, an open-endedness that allows every ethnic group in the empire to participate in the process of self-fashioning and self-transformation. Undoubtedly such a State integrationist logic as the Logic of Species is a response to the logic of *minzokushugi*, or ethnic nationalism, as symbolically represented in the figure of Rin Hakunen. The imperial nation cannot survive unless it has a persuasive logic with which to undermine the political legitimacy of ethnic nationalism. The Logic of Species is such an attempt, but it also tries to appropriate the issues of ethnicity and cultural difference for the constitution of the imperial nation.

The Taiwanese intellectuals' authentic Japanese nationality, which was to be endorsed by their patriotism, was supposed to serve as a warranty that they were fully qualified to criticize the discriminatory attitudes of the Japanese from Japan proper against the islanders and other minorities, and to destroy the various forms of injustice in the Japanese nation-state, so as to transform the given social formation. As Tanabe Hajime conceptualized in philosophic terms, Japanese nationality should transcend ethnicity and racial differences because one's ethnic and racial identity come into being only within the movement of transcending such identity toward the actualization of the national community, as premised upon universal values. Ethnicity and race do not exist in and of themselves. They are not fully objective categories; they remain indeterminate unless they are determined subjectively. They are always moments of mediation of and in the subject. The subject here is this agent of self-transformation or self-fashioning. But because it transforms and changes itself, it exists only in self-differentiation and in the ecstatic movement of becoming other than itself.

Therefore, Tanabe introduced the distinction between subject and substratum, according to which the subject gives rise to or discloses its substratum as the original environment of itself that is being transformed in the formation of the subject. For example, a person who was born and brought up in Taiwan faces his ethnic background and manages to assert his identity of ethnic Taiwanese as his "substratum." But he can assert his ethnicity only insofar as he is a modern subject who continually refashions himself anew and reconstitutes himself as a "subject" overcoming his "substratum." Being of an ethnic origin is no hindrance to being "modern. The term "subject" meant the individual agent who participates in the active transformation of social reality, in which the subject's old self was nurtured. In this sense, the figure of Rin Hakunen exemplifies those to whom the introduction of such a universalistic rhetoric as the Logic of Species was a response. In order to mobilize a large population of varying ethnic and historical backgrounds, it was absolutely necessary for the Japanese state to invent a philosophy of the multiethnic empire, which could weave the desires of minority intellectuals and persuade them toward the policies of the empire.

Although the islanders may be less Japanese in terms of their substratum, they are fully "Japanese" as subjects in their freedom to choose to be "Japanese," to live and die according to the universal laws of the Japanese state. The scenario that had been outlined in theoretical vocabulary in the Logic of Species was now used repeatedly. Of course I am not arguing that the Logic of Species texts were cited verbatim by the government agencies in their propaganda.[30] Nonetheless, one can see how the Logic of Species could endow intellectuals of minority backgrounds with very elaborate meanings and interpretations for the anxiety and suffering which they had to undergo under colonial conditions, and encourage them toward a particular direction of historical action.

* * *

Now I would like to move on to the third text, *No-No Boy*, written mainly in English and published in 1957, twelve years after the end of the Asia Pacific and Second World Wars.

Since it was written and published after the war, it evaded wartime censorship. In addition to the many historical and social conditions that demand our attention in reading *No-No Boy* together with "Road" and "Torrent," we can discern a number of underlying problematics that all three texts address:

1. The ambivalent and unstable relationship between the narrator and his language of writing. Perhaps this is an attribute shared by all three texts, which allows me to treat them as works by those of "alien origins."

2. National belonging and the fear of losing one's nationality. How and whether one belongs to a national community presented itself primarily as an anxiety-invoking query. All these texts were written to deal with this anxiety.

3. All three refer to the historical conditions of the state of exception, or *hijō jitai*, in the early 1940s, when minority populations were systematically mobilized in the total war in both the Japanese empire and the United States.

4. Although this point was not explicitly spelled out in the cases of "Road" and "Torrent," the voluntary soldiers were potentially recruited to fight against an enemy who could well include people ethnically similar or even familially related to the soldiers themselves.[31] Voluntarism was a choice forced upon minority individuals between the two contrasting forms of collective identification: nationality and kinship.

As in "Road" and "Torrent," what is pursued throughout *No-No Boy* is the omnipresence of the State in the life of the protagonist, Ichiro. Yet at issue is not whether or not some substantive authority called the State objectively exists to regulate every aspect of life for the entire civil population. Instead, its omnipresence is meant to draw attention, above all else, to the fact that the novel's narrative is organized from such a particular point of view that, as soon as any word is uttered, every character in this novel inevitably has to engage in some dialogue with the State. When every character's utterance is already an implicit address to the State, then the State must be present everywhere in the imaginary space of this novel. This is what is meant by the omnipresence of the State.

Born in the United States and brought up by first-generation Japanese parents, Ichiro was transferred along with his family to a concentration camp. After two years there, he and other Japanese-American male prisoners of the appropriate age were drafted for military service. But Ichiro refused to to serve in the U.S. military. Consequently, he was sentenced to imprisonment and forced to spend two years as a convict.

A draft resister is a criminal, that is, one who has committed a crime against the State. Since in modern societies crime is primarily defined as a transgression of the State's law, draft resistance constitutes a criminal offence against the State just like tax evasion, extortion, and drunk driving. Unlike other criminal acts, however, to refuse the State's call for military service is a felony of exceptional gravity. It is not only a violation of the State's law but also an infringement of the very emotive bond tying the State with the totality of the national community.

Readers are expected to gradually reconstruct Ichiro's story from fragments of memories about his past and to shape a background against which his anecdotes are narrated. Like a hidden center of gravity, Ichiro's draft resistance overshadows every aspect of his life and, in due course, predetermines the horizon of these anecdotes. In other words, in this novel the reality of his "draft resistance" works as a general atmosphere within which the narration must proceed.

After serving two years in prison, Ichiro comes home to Seattle, where his parents now live. He returns from the punishment for his act of saying "no," and also from a specific history that is irredeemably engraved in the lives of his family. Yet unlike many soldiers coming home from war, Ichiro cannot expect to return to his normal life, for the past is for him something he cannot pay for in only two years. It may even appear that Ichiro does not believe he has paid for his crime. Ichiro's struggle is presented as though it were a tormenting process of personal redemption and a search for forgiveness. Thus the narrator refers to the pointless resistance of Freddie Akimoto, Ichiro's friend, who also refused to be drafted:

> Freddie was waging a shallow struggle with a to-hell-with-the-rest-of-the-world attitude, and he wasn't being very successful. One could not fight an enemy who looked upon him as much as to say: "This is America, which is for Americans. You have spent two years in prison to prove that you are Japanese—go to Japan!"[32]

The narrator continues:

> Was it possible that he and Freddie and the other four of the poker crowd and all the other American-born, American-educated Japanese who had renounced their American-ness in a frightening moment of madness had done so irretrievably? Was there no hope of redemption? Surely there must be. He was still a citizen. He could still vote. He was free to travel and work and study and marry and drink and gamble. People forgot and, in forgetting, forgave.[33]

In these passages, where the narrative voice oscillates between the narrator and Ichiro, this allusion to Ichiro's and the other draft resistors' past act as a crime and their hope for redemption cannot be sufficiently comprehended as either a description of their situation or as an analysis of their inner strife. Here the narration itself is a speech act that we may call "confession."

Confession presumes a specific power relationship between the addresser and the addressee. The addresser refers to himself, thereby erecting a boundary between his interiority, to which the others have no access, and his exterior, which is exposed to the scrutiny of others. In this instance, it is not necessary for us to preempt the interiority of the addresser prior to the performance of confession. What is at stake is that the interiority of the addresser enters the scene as a correlate of the addressee. The addressee is posited by the addresser as a special *persona* to whom his interiority—which would not be unveiled to others—is exclusively disclosed and in whom his wish for redemption is invested. In confession, the penitent discloses his or her secret, and yet confession is not a general disclosure of some secret. It must be addressed to this special person or one who occupies the position of the confessor: the addresser must solicit the attention of this person by unveiling what cannot be seen by others. In addition, there must be an asymmetry between the addresser and the addressee, for while one is urged to disclose his interiority, the other is exempt from risking such disclosure.

It may appear that the narrator of *No-No Boy* wants to assign Ichiro the position of the penitent in confession. When Ichiro is made to occupy this position, you, as reader of this narration, would then be solicited to occupy the position of confessor. You would be listening to Ichiro and, in this narrative configuration, you would be expected to play the role of one who is capable of forgiving his sin.

Here it is necessary to bear in mind that the crime Ichiro committed was neither injury nor larceny, but draft resistance. Judicially speaking, injury and larceny are both crimes against the State, but in these criminal categories it is possible to identify particular victims. And it is from these victims that the criminal must solicit forgiveness in the first place. The intelligibility of the term "forgiving" depends upon whom one can identify as authorized to forgive and, in the cases of injury and larceny, we tend to assume no serious dispute about the identity or identifiability of the one to whom debt in some form must be paid back.

However, in the case of draft resistance, from whom can a criminal expect forgiveness? By refusing the State's call for military service, whom did Ichiro offend in the first place? One cannot find any particular victim for his felony. Or the victim from whom he has to obtain redemption is the very notion of the people of the United States of America as a whole, which the State is supposed to represent.

If what is deployed in *No-No Boy* is nothing but the performance of confession, with Ichiro as addresser and the reader as addressee, that is, if Ichiro is demanding forgiveness from "you," the one who listens to this would then be put in the position of the State as such. In other words, it may appear that "you" as readers would be an embodiment of the people of the United States of America to the extent that "you" understand Ichiro as a penitent searching for your forgiveness. What is meant by the omnipresence of the State in this novel is not so much the thesis that everybody is under surveillance by the State's apparatuses. Rather it is the presence of "you" as the readers of this novelistic narrative, who receive Ichiro's address in such a manner that he is never allowed to speak unapologetically.

The narrative that is deployed along with such an asymmetrical interpersonal relationship is inevitably laced with many honorifics. Ichiro would speak to "you" from a lower position, in subordination, as if admitting your qualification as someone capable of forgiving him. Given such a power relationship, he would speak to satisfy your expectations and not offend your sensitivities. Therefore, from the outset, the narrator presents Ichiro's circumstances as if Ichiro has admitted his decision to refuse the draft to be one of utter conceit.

But for such a narrative tactic, how could he possibly talk about his refusal to serve in the military *and* his and his family's internment in the camp at the same time? The words of Ichiro, the narrator, and the novelistic text are enunciated in a network of censorship. In addition to the censorship practiced by government agencies such as those we have observed in the cases of "Road" and "Torrent," the network includes the one imposed by people upon themselves; people who build their national solidarity on a blind endorsement of the patriotic imperative that one must devote one's life to one's country, and who believe this endorsement to be the only communal ground upon which the narrator and reader can communicate. Under such conditions, neither Ichiro nor the narrator can evade the frequent use of honorific language, just as Scheherazade could not do so in A *Thousand and One Nights*, simply for the sake of postponing your philanthropic attention without which you would instantly withdraw from conversation. Let us not forget that this is the potential speaking positionality of the minority, one which minority intellectuals might appeal to under certain social and political conditions. Not only John Okada, the author of *No-No Boy*, but also Chin Kasen and Ō Shōyū had to occupy this speaking position. Like Sei Nan in "Road," must Ichiro renegotiate his belonging to the nation in order to regain his self-esteem, which means embracing the State's call for self-sacrifice and, implicitly, the white supremacy inherent in American imperialism? Or, to put it differently, one of the crucial differences between *No-No Boy* and "Road" and "Torrent" is precisely this: while Okada was allowed to make Ichiro refuse, Chin Kasen was not allowed to let Sei Nan refuse to renegotiate his belonging to the nation in order to regain his crushed self-esteem.

Consequently, a certain ambiguity is implanted in these uses of honorific language in *No-No Boy*. In the first paragraph that touches upon the notion of Ichiro's sin, it is already detectable: "The legs of his accuser were in front of him.

God in a pair of green fatigues, U.S. Army style. They were the legs of the jury that had passed sentence upon him. Beseech me, they seemed to say, throw your arms about me and bury your head between my knees and seek pardon for your great sin."[34]

This is an observation filled with the reminiscence ascribed to Ichiro in his encounter with Eto, another Japanese-American. Eto believed that he had become an authentic American because he had volunteered for military service and, for that reason, was entitled to despise Ichiro. He believed that he had regained his self-esteem, and that his affinity to national authenticity granted him the excuse to ostracize Ichiro.

What is in question in this peculiar use of the honorific? It is to tell Ichiro himself that one does not regain self-respect by increasing self-esteem. And it is to turn the form of confession into one in which the *penitent* interrogates the *confessor*. Thus the story has to begin with the negation that Ichiro uttered against the judge who condemned him to imprisonment; it has to begin with Ichiro's "no" to the representative of the State.

Is this a confession in disguise, and manipulated by John Okada in order to lure you into a trap where it is not Ichiro's sin at stake but "yours" for interning the innocent American citizens of Japanese ancestry? If not a trap, would it be then an invitation—somewhat hinted at in the kindness of Mr. Carrick, a character who is sympathetic enough to give Ichiro a job in the story—to conciliation between the American nation at large and Japanese-Americans, a conciliation in which, professing their own righteousness as well as admitting their own mistakes, each side forgives the other?

But before trying to answer these questions, let us explore Okada's attempt to incorporate the actual conditions of Ichiro's linguistic situation. The Taiwanese situation in the early 1940s was drastically different from that of the United States, but in the constant if implicit appeal to "national language" in the three texts, we can manage to remain attentive to the problematic of the dominant language in the two imperial nations.

Ichiro's parents are first-generation Japanese-Americans who cannot speak English adequately. Within his family the common language is still Japanese, but since the novel itself is written in English, the family's conversation is expressed in English, just as conversation in Minnanhua (Taiwanese) was expressed in Japanese in "Road" and "Torrent." It is feasible that Ichiro's parents' words are translated in order to be integrated into this novelistic narrative. This means that at least some part of *No-No Boy* was originally meant to be a translation, and yet, given that this work is fiction, in this translation there was no original.

The question that emerges, then, is this: can we assume that the rest of the novel is *not* translation? Is it possible to draw a distinction between translation and the original in the case of this novel? Of course I am not proposing an inquiry into John Okada's biography and family genealogy. Rather, what is in question is whether or not it is possible to determine the mother tongue of Ichiro or the narrator, the very issue of determinability as to his mother tongue. (After Taiwan's liberation from Japanese colonial rule, Ō Shōyū worked to recover the original of "Torrent" from its Chinese translation.[35] In this case, too, the relationship between the published version and its original is highly ambiguous, to say the least). In "Torrent," let us recall, Rin Hakunen is depicted as a character who believed in his mother tongue while expressing his love for his mother in a language that was not his mother's.[36] But his uncle, Itō Haruo, may not have actually believed in his mother's tongue or his mother tongue. This issue was carefully left unresolved in "Torrent." It could have been a gen- erational dispute between a generation for whom one's linguistic identity was given and another who need not take its "native language" as a source of col- lective pride. As a *gongsheng*, i.e., a successful candidate for the Qing Dynasty's government examination, did not Itō's father learn literary Chinese and write in this medium in which the determinability of his mother tongue could not be meaningfully raised?[37] This is precisely the reason why the destruction of liter- ary styles and the *genbun itchi* movement were absolutely necessary for the determinability of one's mother tongue to be addressed as an essential issue of ethnic nationalism.

Now let me shift our focus trans-Pacifically from the western shore of the Pacific to its eastern shore. In light of the problematic of ethnolinguistic iden- tity as a historical construct, we cannot evade a new question: how can transla- tion be distinguished from the original in *No-No Boy*? This distinction can be drawn only when a character is explicitly portrayed as having a particular national or ethnic language as her or his mother tongue. In modern literature, this character's and narrator's belonging to a national language is usually taken for granted. However, let me note the fact that this general assumption does not apply to *No-No Boy*.

Nearly all of the paragraphs in this novel are supposedly written in English. Except for scattered pockets of explicit translation, however, what is dominant in this text is the language of those who cannot have an exclusive relationship with a particular national or ethnic language. Their relationship to English is fundamentally unstable. Unlike the writings of such writers as James Joyce, Chinua Achebe, or Teresa Cha, Okada's writing does not manifest apparent multilingual features. Nevertheless, this novelistic text cannot reproduce a clear-cut distinction between English and Japanese, between one enclosed eth- nolinguistic identity and another. There is no symmetrical scheme between the two language unities here. Instead, the dialogue continues between those who dream of ultimately belonging to a language and those who cannot do so. The words most clearly marked as translation are those of Ichiro's mother.

> Patiently, she waited until he had spoken. "Germans, Americans, accident, those things are not important. It was not the boy but the mother who is also the son and it is she who is to blame and it is she who is dead because the son did not know."
>
> "I just know that Bob is dead."
>
> "No, the mother. It is she who is dead because she did not conduct herself as a Japanese and, no longer being Japanese, she is dead."
>
> "And the father? What about Mr. Kumasaka?"
>
> "Yes, dead also."
>
> "And you, Ma? What about you and Pa?"
>
> "We are Japanese as always."
>
> "And me?"
>
> "You are my son is also Japanese."
>
> "That makes everything all right, does it? That makes it all right that Bob is dead, that war was fought and hundreds of thousands killed and maimed, and that I was two years in prison and am still Japanese?"
>
> "Yes"[38]

In which language is this conversation conducted? If in English, then the peculiarity of his mother's syntax should reflect her lack of fluency in the language. But Ichiro was brought up by her who "opened [his] mouth and made [his] lips move to sound the words."[39] The setting of this conversation sounds rather incongruous, in the same sense that Itō Haruo's utterances with the narrator's mother do. It is his uneasy relationship to his mother's language rather than her stilted rapport with English that is tacitly indicated by the grammatical irregularity of Ichiro's mother's utterances. What we perceive in her syntax is the distance that separates Ichiro from the language to which his mother believes she belongs, namely, from his mother's tongue—which is *not* his mother tongue.

Ichiro thinks that his dependence upon his mother's language "got [him] two years in prison."[40] For him, his mother's language is not primarily a technical problem concerning language acquisition; her stifling syntax suggests her attitude toward other languages, and particularly the manner in which she figures out her relation to the image of American society as a whole. One already discerns in this suffocating attitude a hint of her stubbornness and fixation, which eventually lead her to suicide. It is an obsession with the naturalness of national/ethnic belonging and ethnolinguistic identity, as well as the total denial of her life in the United States. Though it long preceded the age of the photo-telegraphic facsimile, it was a sort of long-distance nationalism based upon the schema of cofiguration. To the extent that she denies her American-ness, she has to idealize Japan as a negative of America. As a matter of fact, the content of her Japan is supplied with the inverted images of the Japanese stereo-types as imposed upon Japanese-Americans by mainstream America. The racial hierarchy of the United States and Japan is reproduced inversely in her national belonging.

The figure of Ichiro's mother forms the polar opposite of people like Eto, who dreams of maintaining his ethnic pride by becoming "a good and loyal American." This opposition is then mapped onto the negation/affirmation axis. In this configuration, Ichiro's refusal to be drafted could easily be explained away in terms of the no/yes binary, as a rejection of assimilation and a gesture of loyalty to his mother and her country. If his "no" is accommodated in this con-figuration, his confession, which adds another "no," would then mean nothing more than a reversal, a conversion to affirmation through a double negation. The "no-no boy" would then be nothing but a yes-man. He would be nothing more than a humiliated slave trying to regain his self-esteem by desperately seek-ing the master's recognition.

Ichiro refuses to endorse his mother's persistent denial of American life; he says "no" to her. Nevertheless, this negation of a return to Japan does not result in his return to America either.

> Was it she who was wrong and crazy not to have found in herself the capacity to accept a country which repeatedly refused to accept her or her sons unquestioningly, or was it the others who were being deluded, the ones, like Kenji, who believed and fought and even gave their lives to pro-tect this country where they could still not rate as first-class citizens because of the unseen walls?[41]

By now it is evident that the ambiguity implanted in his confession prevents him from professing a coherent position with regard to his nationality and national belonging. It is not a trap, nor is it a disguise. The pursuit of national belonging cannot elude discriminatory violence in the direction of either his mother or Eto. His mother acquires a sense of national belonging at the cost of totally disavowing Japan's defeat and the death of her loved ones. Similarly, it is by deliberately overlooking the white supremacist bias inherent in American policies toward people of "alien origins" that Eto believes he will someday be an authentic American. Moreover, his blind faith in American nationalism, which reminds us of Itō Haruo's obsessive involvement in the Japanese national spirit, is sustained by public discrimination against unpatriotic Japanese-Americans like Ichiro. By displacing the discriminatory and humiliating stare of the public fixed upon him onto a publicly marked outcast like Ichiro, Eto barely manages to uphold his sense of national belonging. What I notice here is an economy of discriminatory identification with the nation, once referred to as "the transfer of oppression."

> The Negro who was always being mistaken for a white man becomes a white man and he becomes hated by the Negroes with whom he once hated on the same side. And the young Japanese hates the not-so-young Japanese who is more Japanese than himself, and the not-so-young, in turn, hates the old Japanese who is all Japanese and, therefore, ever more Japanese than he.[42]

An individual is able to feel fully embraced in a nation only as long as he is confident that he is distinct from those who are unable to belong there. Yet the definition of those who are unable to belong there is historically fluid and almost contingent. Discrimination against foreigners or those of "alien origins" is, therefore, a prerequisite for the sense of certainty in national belonging. Knowing that he would face his own death sooner or later, Kenji, a Japanese-American character who once attempted to become a "good and loyal American" by risking his own life, cannot conceal his sympathy with Ichiro. No doubt this is because Ichiro is free, even if not completely, of the obsessive desire for national identification. As Kenji says to Ichiro,

> They think just because they went and packed a rifle they're different but they aren't and they know it. They're still Japs. . . . The guys who make it tough on you probably do so out of a misbegotten idea that maybe you're to blame because the good that they thought they were doing by getting killed and shot up doesn't amount to a pot of beans.[43]

Risking one's own life for the country does not amount to a secure seat within it. One's desperate wish to be a fully integrated member of the nation will remain frustrated. As Ichiro says to himself,

> And what about the poor niggers on Jackson Street who can't find anything better to do than spit on the sidewalk and show me the way to Tokyo? They're on the outside looking in, just like that kid and just like me and just like everybody else I've ever seen or known. Even Mr. Car-

rick. Why isn't he in? Why is he on the outside squandering his goodness on outcasts like me? Maybe the answer is that there is no in. Maybe the whole damned country is pushing and shoving and screaming to get into someplace that doesn't exist, because they don't know that the outside could be the inside if only they would stop all this pushing and shoving and screaming, and they haven't got enough sense to realize that.[44]

Nobody absolutely belongs to the nation; nobody is on the inside. Potentially, everyone is a minority member. What is certain is that everyone tries to be in by expelling someone else.

* * *

As goes without saying, the transfer of oppression operates differently in the various social settings described in "Road," "Torrent," and *No-No Boy.* Yet in spite of the different viewpoints from which personal animosity is described, one can observe in all these cases a certain mechanism by means of which the national whole maintains its equilibrium. "By exercising arbitrary power on those who are below, people manage to transfer in a downward direction the sense of oppression that comes from above, thus preserving the balance of the whole."[45] Maruyama Masao, the renowned political scientist of wartime and postwar Japan, believed that the transfer of oppression was a trait particular to Japanese ultranationalism, and so he did not inquire into how this discriminatory mechanism operated together with the policies of integration promoted by the logic of the multiethnic state. Further, he deliberately evaded the question of colonialism with which the formation of the national subject was closely connected.[46] In other words, he failed to recognize the propinquity between the transfer of oppression and national belonging, the displacement of humiliation, and the manufacture of the subject. In fact, Maruyama's analysis represented a typical response by the *naichijin* (i.e., the Japanese of Japan proper) to the question of war responsibility after Japan's defeat. Whereas the *naichijin* had required the colonized people in the annexed territories in the empire to become "good and loyal Japanese" until just a few years earlier, Maruyama deliberately overlooked the fact that, soon after the collapse of the empire, the Japanese of "alien origins" were deprived of their nationality and fundamental political rights by official decrees.

In this respect, a much more politically savvy and theoretically insightful explanation than Maruyama's is given by Luke Gibbons about what often accompanies the coerced accommodation of the minority to the prevailing dominant ideology. In trying to provide some coherent elucidation as to why there have been so many instances where "the humiliated of one culture become the shock troops of another, the ignominy of the slave prompting a need to retrieve dignity and self-respect by identifying with the master's voice and the very forces that gave rise to domination in the first place,"[47] Gibbons argues that the insidious logic of humiliation inherent in the process of colonization is that "it is only at the discretion of the perpetrator that the victim regains honour and pride." Therefore, the minority, or the humiliated in these processes, has no other option but "the alienation of one's self-image to another 'superior' or more powerful adversary."

> Redemption then takes the form of heroic self-immolation—the "voluntary" reenactment of the original ordeal which led to domination and humiliation. Thus, for example, the gory spectacle of gladiatorial combat in ancient Rome . . . turned on a dramaturgy of sacrifice, in which despised slaves could regain their self-respect by audacious bravery, by staring defeat and annihilation in the face.[48]

What was acted out by Sei Nan in "Road," Itō Haruo in "Torrent," and Eto in *No-No Boy* is this scenario of heroic self-immolation: the humiliated desperately perform the expected role of patriotic subject in order to recover their self-respect by gaining recognition from their masters. In the British Empire, there thus emerged "the fearless (and fearsome) reputation of colonial cannon-fodder—the Scots, the Iroquois, the Irish, the Sikhs, the Gurkhas—in the heat of battle."[49] The United States has its own versions, with Unit 442 of the Japanese shock troops in the U.S. Army as probably the most renowned case. What enchants the minority most in their frantic endeavor to redeem their sense of honor from humiliation is often an insatiable desire to display their self-destruction beyond the pleasure principle. This explains why the colonial foot soldier so often ended up "doing the dirty work of empire, including his own self-destruction." It also explains "the tragic paradox whereby the Irish or the Scots reserved their greatest rage and bloodlust for each other, or for those who resembled them most in battle."[50]

Not surprisingly, what these three texts unwittingly disclose is that, under the threat of ostracism, minority individuals engage in various processes of negotiation about how to be accommodated in the prevailing dominant nationalism. (One thinks here of the particularly egregious case of negotiation whereby "the Irish 'became white' in the United States, compensating for their own indignities by buying into the very white supremacist attitudes which discriminated against them").[51] In reading these three texts, the following remark by Gibbons is remarkably apt:

Accommodation with the prevailing dominant ideology—hybridity under hierarchical rule—is often akin to the *ressentiment* of the humili-ated in Nietzsche's terms, forced into outward shows of servility towards the humiliator who strikes them, but inwardly seething with resentment and the thirst for revenge. What is lacking in these circumstances is not the desire but the opportunity and weapons of resistance. But it is pre-cisely this last line of defence—the domain of self-respect rather than the achievement ethic of self-esteem—which cultural humiliation extin-guishes, aiming for fully internalized loyalty to the dominant order so that the subject, literally, has no shame.[52]

What is striking about "Torrent" and *No-No Boy* is that the authors describe the struggles of the humiliated as their "last line of defence," and that, perhaps in spite of themselves, they seek to find some social space for "self-respect" rather than "the achievement ethic of self-esteem," a space which could be sus-tained neither by identifying with "the master's voice" nor by seeking recogni-tion of those who humiliated them in the first place. By refusing an imaginary solution to the problem of the historical conditions in which they were caught, they tried to remain in shame. They refused to be shameless.

Here let me briefly ponder over the conceptual distinction between self-respect and self-esteem, for which Luke Gibbons relies upon Avishai Margalit. With respect to a decent society where, in principle, people are to live without humiliation, a fundamental difference must be drawn between the concepts of self-respect and self-esteem, even though both originally derive from the affir-mation and respect entrusted to one by others. While self-respect demands that one be treated as an equal human being by another person, self-esteem is based upon the evaluation of one's achievement by others. My achievement is com-pared with others' and recognized as valuable by them, and thus I gain self-esteem. Since self-respect is rooted in self-confidence and not based upon the evaluation of my achievements, my self-respect cannot be shaken in my com-petition with others. On the one hand, I must earn, so to speak, my self-esteem by displaying my achievements to those who evaluate me, so that I cannot evade being in competition. When I hold myself high in esteem, somebody else must be held low in esteem. If I am suffering from low self-esteem, some other per-son must be enjoying high self-esteem. Self-esteem is impossible in the system in which one does not compete with others. On the other hand, self-respect does not derive from any observable or meritorious trait such as qualification and achievement, but rather from an unfounded—and anti-foundational—confidence that I will treat others as equal human beings and that others will treat me likewise. Inherently, self-respect is a matter of my attitude concerning the future. As Margalit says, "The attitude of others is built into the very concept of the value of humans which the bearer of self-respect is supposed to adopt with regard to herself."[53] Therefore, "any traits that might be used to justify respect are parasitic on our attitude toward human beings as human."[54] An empirically unfounded respect of others toward me serves as the support for my self-respect and self-confidence, and gives me the courage to endlessly open myself toward others or to expose myself to others. What is called self-respect is this courageous action, or what the seventeenth-century Confucian scholar Itō Jinsai called *ai* (love, affection).

It is by destroying the very source of courage, or *ai*, that the experience of humiliation most deeply hurts a person. Precisely because self-respect is damaged, the victim of humiliation mistakes the recovery of self-esteem for the recovery of self-respect. Although self-respect derives from the existence of another, I cannot recover my self-respect from others' immediate commendation or recognition. It might enhance my self-esteem, but I will continue to suffer from the loss of self-respect. Yet in order to recover their self-respect, the logic of integration in imperial nationalism solicits minorities, who carry the burden of historical humiliation, to identify themselves with the colonial nation and commit themselves to their anticipatory deaths. According to national humanism, a human being is first of all a member of the nation-state. Judicially, a nonnational cannot be treated as a human being, so that only those who are qualified as members of the nation are capable of recovering self-respect as a "human being." But minorities are those who are potentially people of "alien origins" who could be deprived of their nationality, just as the colonized from the annexed territories of the Japanese empire actually were so deprived. The logic of national integration of minorities in hierarchical hybridity may well promote the recovery of self-esteem. Yet in order to regain self-esteem, minority individuals would have to continue to parade their achievements and patriotic loyalty to the majority audience. This is why national integration in imperial nationalism requires a scenario whereby the minorities act out their expected roles to fulfill the desires of the majority.

Now what is allegorically invested in the figure of Ichiro, the protagonist of *No-No Boy*, should be evident: against all the odds of imperial nationalism, it is to wager a counter-scenario that a minority individual can hold onto her or his self-respect. Instead of accumulating patriotic allegiance to the nation, one could recover one's self-respect by refusing to yield to the majority's self-justification. For this refusal, of course, Ichiro is exposed to the humiliating violence of the State and denied belonging to the nation. Nevertheless, he does not relinquish his self-respect, thereby pointing out the possibility that a minority individual can evade "fully internaliz[ing] loyalty to the dominant order."

No-No Boy was published twelve years after Japan's defeat, and retrospectively offered a critical alternative to the dominant scenario of national integration as put forth by imperial nationalisms during the Asian-Pacific and Second World Wars. Unlike Chin Kasen's "Road" and Ō Shōyū's "Torrent," it was not written under tight censorship during a wartime state of emergency. In *No-No Boy*, the fictive nature of the narrative consists in the retrospective alternative hypothesis: what would I have done if I had been able to respond to the historical conditions otherwise than I actually did? Understandably, most of the Japanese-American community in the United States were hostile to the novel's publication. They accordingly ignored it, perceiving in this fiction an insult to their loyalty and national belonging, which they had managed to internalize according to the scenario of national integration by imperial nationalism.

Finally, *No-No Boy* speaks of an irreparable history, it adheres to the historical experiences of the people of Japanese ancestry in the United States during the war. It is part of a singular history that cannot be generalized. But what was disclosed through John Okada's obsession to repeat this past experience of the concentration camp in a fictional narrative was an event of encounter, in which a minority individual struggles to survive tremendous humiliation without giving up his own self-respect. The story tells us that some minorities do refuse to give up their self-respect, even if they are deprived of national belonging. Whether or not it effectively undermines the logic of subjective *poiesis* on the part of minority people according to such universalisms as the Logic of Species, however, remains to be examined.

Notes

In writing this essay, I have adopted much from two previously published articles: "Hutatsu no hitei: *No-No Boy* wo yomu" [Two negations: A reading of *No-No Boy*], in *Shisō no kagaku* [The science of thought], 125 (1990), 114–126, reprinted in *Shisan sareru Nihongo-Nihonjin* [The stillbirth of the Japanese language and Japanese people] (Tokyo: Shinyōsha, 1996), pp. 99–126; and "Nihonjin dearu koto: taminzoku kokka ni okeru kokumin shutai no kōchiku no mondai to Tanabe Hajime no 'shu no ronri' " [Being Japanese: The problem of the construction of the national subject in the multi-ethnic state and Tanabe Hajime's "Logic of Species"], in *Shisō* [Thought], 882 (1997), 5–48, translated into English as "Subject and Substratum: On Japanese Imperial Nationalism," in *Cultural Studies* 14:3:4 (2000), 462–530.

1. The document that most explicitly presents this colonial paranoia is the Bush Administration's "The National Security Strategy of the United States of America" (September 2002).

2. Giorgio Agamben, *Homo Sacer: Sovereign Power and Bare Life*, trans. Daniel Heller-Roazen (Stanford: Stanford University Press, 1998), pp. 166–167.

3. Étienne Balibar, "Les identités ambiguës," in *Les craintes des masses* (Paris: Galilée, 1997), pp. 353–371. For a discussion of super-stateness and class struggle, see Jacques Bidet, *Théorie générale* (Paris: PUF, 1999), pp. 233–306.

4. Some of the wording and expressions in the first several pages of this essay are taken from the "Proposal" for the journal *Traces*, issue 4, as composed by myself and Jon Solomon. I thank Jon Solomon for allowing me to use some expressions from the "Proposal" in this essay and for drawing my attention to Jacques Bidet's argument.

5. Agamben, *Homo Sacer*, p. 168. As Agamben writes, *"The state of exception thus ceases to be referred to as an external and provisional state of factual danger and comes to be confused with juridical rule itself.* National Socialist jurists were so aware of the particularity of the situation that they defined it by the paradoxical expression 'state of willed exception' (*einen gewollten Ausnahmezustand*). 'Through the suspension of fundamental rights,' writes Werner Spohr, a jurist close to the regime, 'the decree brings into being a state of willed exception for the sake of the establishment of the National Socialist State.'"

6. For a more detailed exposition of schematism in the regime of translation, see my *Translation and Subjectivity: On "Japan" and Cultural Nationalism* (Minneapolis: University of Minnesota Press, 1997), pp. 51–63.

7. The recent emotional response of the Japanese public to the disclosure of the North Korean kidnapping cases, which was initially provoked by rightist newspapers in September and October 2002, is ample testimony of the complicity between American hegemony and Japanese nationalism.

8. See Rey Chow, "The Dream of a Butterfly," in *Ethics After Idealism* (Bloomington: Indiana University Press, 1998), pp. 74–97.

9. Cf. Higuchi Yūichi, *Kōgunheishi ni sareta Chōsenjin* [Koreans who were turned into Japanese imperial soldiers] (Tokyo: Shakai Hyōronsha, 1991), and Kang Dokusang, *Chōsen gakuto shutsujin* [Korean volunteer student soldiers] (Tokyo: Iwanami Shoten, 1997).

10. A number of policies were implemented in order to assimilate the population in the annexed territories into the Japanese nation during the late 1930s and early 1940s. The banning of the use of local languages in mass media and on public occasions in Korea and Taiwan as well as the practice of *sōshi kaimei* (creation of the modern family and change of family names) are well known as such policies. Cf. Miyata Setsuko, *Chōsen minshū to kōminka-seisaku* [The Korean masses and imperialization policies] (Tokyo: Miraisha, 1985).

11. Komagome Takeshi, *Shokuminchi teikoku Nihon no bunka tōgō* [Cultural integration in the Japanese colonial empire] (Tokyo: Iwanami Shoten, 1996), p. 223.

12. Ibid., p. 224.

13. Ibid., p. 231.

14. This is exactly the state of affairs that Leo Ching points out in "Give Me Japan and Nothing Else!" "Unlike *dōka* [assimilation], which remained an unrealizable

ideal of colonial integration, *kōminka* necessitated an objectification of Japanization by demanding the colonized to act, live, and die for the emperor in defending the Japanese Empire. What *kōminka* entailed for the colonized, then, as exemplified in the subject construction of a good and loyal Japanese and the so-called *kōmin* literature, is the interiorization of an objective colonial antagonism into a subjective struggle within, not between, colonial identities. In other words, cultural representations under *kōminka* displaced the concrete problematic of the social and replaced it with the ontology of the personal." In *The South Atlantic Quarterly*, ed. Tomiko Yoda and Harry Harootunian, (Fall 2000), p. 780.

15. The editors of this journal were Hamada Hayao and Nishikawa Mitsuru. Nishikawa was born in a Japanese family from Japan proper, but he grew up in Taiwan.

16. Hamada Hayao, "'Michi ni tsuite" [On "Road"], in *Bungei Taiwan*, June 1943, p. 142.

17. Nishikawa Mitsuru, in *Bungei Taiwan*, p. 142.

18. Taiwanese names are romanized according to the standard pronunciation of 1957. When necessary, Japanese pronunciation is added. Due to my ignorance, I cannot romanize Chinese characters in phonetics other than that of Beijinghua.

19. Chin Kasen, "Michi," in *Bungei Taiwan*, p. 110.

20. Ibid., p. 118.

21. Ibid., p. 117.

22. For a more detailed reading of the Logic of Species, see my "Subject and Substratum: On Japanese Imperial Nationalism."

23. Chen Wanyi, "Yume to genjitsu" [Dream and reality], in *Yomigaeru Taiwan bungaku* [Resurrecting Taiwanese literature], ed. Shimomura Sakujirō et al. (Tokyo: Tōhō Shoten, 1995), pp. 389–406.

24. In *Taiwan bungaku*, 2:3 (1942): 63–102.

25. For a more detailed account of *isshi dōjin* and modern state formation, see Hirota Masaki's "Epilogue," in *Sabetsu no shosō* [The various aspects of discrimination] (Tokyo: Iwanami Shoten, 1990), pp. 436-516.

26. Avishai Margalit, *The Decent Society*, trans. Naomi Goldblum (Cambridge: Harvard University Press, 1996).

27. Tanabe Hajime, "Shi sei" [Death and life], in *Tanabe Hajime zenshū* [Complete works of Tanabe Hajime] (Tokyo: Chikuma Shobō, 1963), vol. 8.

28. In *Gaichi no Nihongo bungaku sen* [Selected Japanese-language literature from the overseas territories], ed. Kurokawa Sō (Tokyo: Shinjuku Shobō, 1996), vol. 1, p. 224.

29. Ibid., p. 247.

30. In a small number of cases, it is possible to argue that the government announcements and ordinances included direct references to the Logic of Species. For one such example, see *Daitōa kensetsu-ron* [On the construction of greater East Asia], as prepared by the Planning Agency and published by the Ministry of Commerce and Industry, 1943.

31. Some Taiwanese soldiers of the Japanese Army actually defected and crossed over to the Chinese Red Army. Cf. Chen Yingzhen, "Imperial army betrayed," in *Perilous Memories: The Asia Pacific War(s)* (Durham: Duke University Press, 2001), pp. 181–198.
32. John Okada, *No-No Boy* (Seattle: University of Washington Press, 1979), p. 51.
33. Ibid.
34. Ibid., p. 4.
35. As Chen Wanyi notes in *Yomigaeru Taiwan bungaku*, three versions of "Torrent" currently exist in Chinese: a translation by Lin Zhonglong, in *Guangfuqian Taiwan wenxue quanji* [Complete works of pre-liberation Taiwanese literature] (Taipei: Yuanjing Chuban, 1979), vol. 8; a version edited by Ō Shōyū himself, in *Taiwan zuojia quanji: Weng Nao, Wu Yongfu, Wang Changxiong* [Complete works of Taiwanese authors: Weng Nao, Wu Yongfu, Wang Changxiong] (Taipei: Qianwei Chubanshe, 1991); and finally a new translation by Zhong Zhaozheng, in *Riju shidai Taiwan xiaoshuoxuan* [Selected Taiwanese novels from the Japanese occupation period] (Taipei: Qianwei Chubanshe, 1992).
36. As far as *Minnanhua* is concerned, the situation has not changed much since then. Even today, Rin Hakunen would not be able to express in writing his love of his mother in his mother's language.
37. *Gaichi no Nihongo bungaku sen*, p. 245.
38. *No-No Boy*, pp. 41–42.
39. Ibid., p. 12.
40. Ibid.
41. Ibid., p. 104.
42. Ibid., pp. 135–136.
43. Ibid., p. 163.
44. Ibid., pp. 159–160.
45. Masao Maruyama, *Thought and Behaviour in Modern Japanese Politics*, ed. Ivan Morris (London: Oxford University Press, 1963), p. 18.
46. This issue is closely related to the problematic of Japan's postwar responsibility. The Japanese government has refused to acknowledge that many in the annexed territories, who were Japanese subjects until the loss of the Empire, were recruited or drafted to serve in the Imperial Forces. A number of lawsuits have thus been filed by former soldiers from Taiwan. Cf. Lim Kingbing, *Taiwan no kōminka kyōiku* [Nationalization education in Taiwan] (Tokyo: Kobunken, 1997). On Japan's postcolonial legacy and leftist politics toward Taiwan, see Mori Yoshio, *Taiwan, Nihon: rensa suru koroniarizumu* [Taiwan, Japan: The reactionary chain of colonialism] (Tokyo: Inpakuto Shuppankai, 2001).
47. Luke Gibbons, "Guest of the Nation: Ireland, Immigration, and Post-Colonial Solidarity," in *Traces: "Race" Panic and the Memory of Migration*, ed. Meaghan Morris and Brett de Bary (Hong Kong: Hong Kong University Press, 2001), vol. 2, p. 93.
48. Ibid., pp. 94–95.

49. Ibid., p. 95.
50. Ibid.
51. Ibid., p. 96.
52. Ibid.
53. Margalit, *The Decent Society*, p. 125.
54. Ibid., p. 124.

Chapter 6

JAPANESE NEO-NATIONALISM:
A CRITIQUE OF KATŌ NORIHIRO'S
"AFTER THE DEFEAT" DISCOURSE

Takahashi Tetsuya

I. Introduction

Here I take as my theme the discourse of Katō Norihiro. Although Katō is a literary critic and not a historian, the publication of his *Haisengo ron* [After the defeat] (Kōdansha, 1997) nevertheless established him as one of the central figures of the "historian's debate" in Japan. This book had its beginnings in an essay of the same name published in the January 1995 issue of the literary arts journal *Gunzō* [Arts group] that was written at the end of 1994—in other words, on the eve of the fiftieth anniversary of the end of World War II. I immediately published a criticism of this essay in the March 1995 issue of the same journal, thereby opening up a debate in which many others have since come to participate. It has been suggested that this discussion be called the "debate on the historical subject." Regardless of the suitability of this name, however, it seems undeniable that the debate has become one of the focal points of both the history and nationalism debates taking place in Japan today. Since I myself am one of the participants in these debates, it would be senseless on my part to attempt to provide an "objective" or "neutral" commentary thereon. Instead I would like to offer a critical analysis of Katō's discourse, which I shall for convenience' sake refer to in the following as "After the Defeat."

II. The Notion of Postwar Japan's "Personality Split"

Let us examine the basic claims of "After the Defeat" in due order.

According to Katō, Japan's defeat in World War II brought about a "personality split" in the postwar. This "personality split" refers to the opposition between the reformists and the conservatives, or those who support Japan's postwar Constitution and those who seek to revise it. The reformists represent an "outward-looking self," one that depends upon such foreign universal ideas as those contained in the Constitution, as for example democracy and human rights. In contrast to this, the conservatives are an "inward-looking self," grounded upon such traditional values as the homeland, the emperor, and the purity of the Japanese ethnos. Thus the postwar Japanese "self" is split or doubled into one that is "outward-looking" and one that is "inward-looking."

From the outset, we can discern here a highly suspect premise. Everything proceeds as if "Japan" were originally a single personality. What splits or doubles the nation's originally indivisible unity of personality is the unprecedented catastrophe and traumatic experience of the defeat. Yet on what authority can Japan's conservatives and reformists be seen as a split of what was originally one "personality," particularly when the U.S. Republican and Democratic parties and the British Conservative and Labour parties are equally seen as an opposition of two "personalities"? Katō fails to examine these essential contradictions or oppositions, for he assumes that there exists beneath them an underlying national oneness. Here already we can glimpse a typically nationalist desire to restore such oneness.

Yet Katō would not concede as much, for he believes that this national personality split must be rigorously eliminated in order for the Japanese to apologize to the Asian war victims as a unified "national subject." Katō seems to think that the nation must first become a unified subject in order to fulfill its responsibility. In the postwar period, however, Japan has been divided both *by* and *about* the defeat. For Katō, this is precisely why it remains unable to offer a true apology to the Asian victims.

Now what exactly is meant by this notion of postwar Japan's "personality split"? Exactly what kind of split has the country suffered both by and about the defeat? Generally speaking, Katō raises three points here.

III. The Problem of the "Forced Constitution"

First, Katō discusses the issue of Japan's postwar Constitution, and particularly Article Nine.

Since its enactment in 1946, Article Nine of the present Constitution has consistently been the target of intense debate. It stipulates that war must be renounced as a "means by which to settle international disputes," that Japan must to that end not maintain an army, and that the "nation's right of belligerency" is refused. In their defense of this war-renunciation clause as the centerpiece of postwar Japanese pacifism, the reformists have formed the "Constitution protection camp," whereas the conservatives, who view the article as originally forced upon Japan by the U.S. Occupation forces, are known as the "Constitution revision camp" in their constant desire to have it repealed. A paradox thus emerges in which it is the reformists who wish to "conserve" Article Nine while the conservatives are more "reformist" in their efforts to "revise" or repeal it.

Now Katō, if he is to be believed, seems to support Article Nine. Nevertheless, he disagrees with the reformists (the Constitution protection camp) in their efforts to safeguard this article. Here he sides with the conservatives in his claim that the Constitution cannot be "ours" insofar as it was originally forced upon Japan. Katō writes that this peace Constitution, which forbids the use of arms, was enforced in the context of America's overwhelming military strength. For him, this represents one of the major "distortions" of postwar Japan, and he harshly criticizes the Constitution protection camp for its "self-deception" in failing to confront this "distortion." In order to eliminate this "distortion," which marks the very beginning of postwar Japan, Katō proposes that the Constitution be "re-chosen" by means of a plebiscite. Even if this plebiscite were to result in the repeal of the war renunciation clause, as he states, it would produce the positive outcome of making the Constitution "ours" or "our own" for the first time since the war.

Here I cannot enter into a historical or theoretical discussion of the Constitution and Article Nine, but such a discussion would be unnecessary. Rather I shall restrict myself to pointing out the basic problems of Katō's argument.

First, Katō abhors the Constitution's impurity of origins as it was "enforced" by the Occupation forces, a point on which he dwells at length. His thinking falls into a fundamentalism here in insisting that all discussion of this matter is futile if the Japanese people do not now purely "subjectively" re-choose the Constitution from scratch. Although Katō himself supports the Constitution, he nevertheless finds it to be a case of "self-deception" to depend upon it insofar as it remains "enforced." He claims that it is nonsense to speak about peace in this regard, but here his words seem indistinguishable from a mere "emotional outpouring" which ignores any question of real politics.

More concretely, Katō's argument ignores, or at least makes light of, the role played by the Constitution these past fifty years in its tension with the logic of

Japan's military safety and security, as embodied in the Japan-U.S. Security Treaty framework. On the one hand, Katō supports the Constitution: "In fact, we have single-handedly just managed to hold onto this forced Constitution despite being at the mercy of various international forces." And again, "This Constitution was forced upon us. In these past fifty years, however, we have made its ideas our own and somehow decided to hold onto it . . . allowing it to take root after our own fashion." Nevertheless, he ridicules the Constitution protection camp for its "theory of assimilating the Constitution's forced character," as this runs counter to his own view that the Constitution be substantively "re-chosen." He insists that the Constitution "is not ours" insofar as its original "stain" is not wiped absolutely clean by means of a plebiscite.

Such fundamentalism can most clearly be seen when Katō encounters *present* issues of real politics. Today the principles of the peace Constitution are being flagrantly violated by such pacts as the New Guidelines for Japan-U.S. Defense Cooperation, according to which Japan must virtually automatically help the United States in times of war. Katō claims to support the peace Constitution and yet is unable to defend it without "self-deception." In response to those who call for the vigorous employment of its principles, Katō argues that the Constitution is not "ours" insofar as it is not re-chosen by plebiscite. He has only ridicule and scorn for people who criticize real politics in the name of "our" Constitution, for such behavior is mere "self-deception." As Mamiya Yōsuke correctly points out, Katō places himself on the "far side of both the Constitution protection and Constitution revision camps." From these heights he refuses in advance all concrete political judgments, thereby "making himself a politically irresponsible subject" (Mamiya Yōsuke, "Chishikijin nashonarizumu no shinri to seiri" [The body and soul of intellectuals' nationalism], in *Dōjidai ron* [On contemporary matters] (Iwanami Shoten)).

Second, Katō's notion that the Constitution be "re-chosen from scratch" appears as a kind of "philosophy of pure subjectivity" in which all trace of the other is dispelled from the origins of the "national subject." Abhorring its impurity of origins in being originally "enforced" by the U.S. Occupation forces, Katō writes that *"our choosing of the Constitution must take priority over its content"* (*Kanōsei toshite no sengo igo* [The post post-war as possibility] (Iwanami Shoten, p. 237; italics Takahashi). Or again: "It is only correct for a nation to have a Constitution that it has chosen itself, even if it be a bad one, than for it to have a good Constitution that it has not so chosen" (ibid., p. 254). While such statements may appear to be "correct" in a formalistic sense, they are not at all self-evident when seen in the context of concrete historical situations.

For example, would Katō see as "correct" a proposal to "revise" the Constitution along the lines of fascism? Would he view as superior a militarist Constitution "chosen by ourselves" over the present peace Constitution, which "we have somehow decided to hold onto these past fifty years" despite its being "enforced" by the Occupation army? Such preference for a "bad" Constitution purely chosen by "us Japanese" over a "good" Constitution that bears traces of the other represents, in fact, a pure nationalism that remains indifferent to the Constitution's actual content. Or rather, *what makes this nationalism so pure is this very indifference to content.*

The erasure of the trace of the other is not equivalent to a mere abstract manner of thought. Katō's discussion of the Constitution proceeds as if everything began with the Occupation and the defeat were strictly a defeat by the United States. What is thus overlooked is the broader historical context in which the war-renunciation clause was imposed upon Japan. For example, the text of this article appears after the final exhibit at the Beijing War Memorial against Japanese Aggression. This cannot simply be written off as an instance of China's "anti-Japanese" policy. While there is indeed here a political intent to benefit China's "national interest," people nonetheless visit the memorial out of a resolve to never again allow an invasion that was overcome only at the cost of some twenty million casualties and billions of dollars in damages. Although it is certainly true that the war-renunciation clause stemmed from an initiative by the U.S. Occupation authorities, it must not be forgotten that this clause was imposed upon Japan because of the enormous destruction and countless sacrifices in Asia brought about by its own war of invasion. Despite Japan's postwar military build-up under the terms of the Japan-U.S. Security Treaty, we can see from this standpoint that the "enforcement" of this clause has for the past half-century effectively released Asia from the threat of Japan's excessive remilitarization. In the postwar period, the memory of this "enforced" renunciation of war has long been a source of resentment against the United States and a hotbed of anti-U.S. nationalism. However, if we could deliver this historicity up to a relation with Asia as well as rigorously overcome the subordination to the logic of the Japan-U.S. Security Treaty, the memory of that "enforcement" might break out of the closed cycle of resentment and nationalism so as to become an indispensable starting point in the process of building peace in East Asia and the world.

IV. The Emperor's War Responsibility

Katō's second point concerns the Shōwa emperor's war responsibility.

The Shōwa emperor was, in the words of the Meiji Constitution, the "sovereign overseer," i.e., head of state; he was the "supreme commander," or the highest in charge, of the former army. It was in his name that Japan's "imperial subjects" waged war and carried out the invasion of Asia. Thus the emperor's war responsibility was already fully laid out, domestically as well as internationally, on a legal, political, and moral level.

With the onset of the Cold War, however, the emperor was cleared of all responsibility at the 1948 Tokyo War Crimes Tribunal as part of the, so to speak, "political cooperation" between the U.S. Occupation forces and Japan's leadership clique. Ever since, there has been little public discussion of this question. Particularly symbolic in this regard was a press conference held in 1995 to mark the occasion of the Socialist Party chairman, Murayama Tomiichi, becoming head of the Socialist-Conservative coalition government. Despite the fact that the Socialists had throughout the postwar period occupied the political center of the reformist faction (the Constitution protection camp), Murayama remarked at this press conference that the Shōwa emperor bore "no responsibility" for the war. It is in fact rare even among reformist politicians to openly acknowledge this responsibility, although it must be said that such acknowledgment might well endanger both one's political and actual life. As such, it appears somewhat simplistic for Katō to view this issue as yet another example of postwar Japan's "personality split," as if the conservatives' denial of the emperor's war responsibility could be directly opposed to the reformists' affirmation of it.

Yet Katō himself acknowledges this responsibility. This is certainly true, and so why was I originally critical of him on this point? As he writes in his original article, "The emperor is responsible for his subjects, and above all for those soldiers of our nation who died in his name. While we the Japanese people bear responsibility for the twenty million Asian dead, the emperor cannot escape partial responsibility for the three million of our nation who died" (*Gunzō*, January 1995, p. 285).

Here Katō determines the emperor's responsibility as "responsibility for his subjects," and especially "for those soldiers of our nation who died in his name." This is mistaken. Clearly the Japanese people bear responsibility for the Asian victims, just as the emperor bears responsibility for those "subjects" and "dead soldiers" who were mobilized and suffered in his name. Yet why does Katō say nothing of the emperor's responsibility for the Asian victims? Weren't all Asians killed by the "Imperial Army" (as the Japanese army was then called) sacrificed "in the name of" the emperor? The Japanese authorities at this time referred to the so-called "comfort women" as "gifts for the Imperial Army soldiers," and this explains why those women who have survived and come out seek the emperor's apology.

Katō's silence here is certainly no accident. It is fully consistent with his discussion of the emperor's war responsibility solely in terms of "moral responsibility." As he writes, "What words should we address in the postwar to the Shōwa emperor, who died without fulfilling his moral responsibility to the soldiers who above all died in his name?" (*Haisengo ron*, p. 74). If we are to interpret Article Three of the Japanese Imperial Constitution (which states that "the emperor is sacred and inviolable") as "sovereign immunity from prosecution," then it becomes impossible to question the responsibility of his actions in terms of Japanese law. The emperor's responsibility toward his "subjects" is thus reduced to a question of "moral responsibility" rather than one of legal responsibility. On the other hand, however, responsibility toward Asia is first and foremost a question of international law. Despite prevailing international opinion, the emperor was not tried as a "war criminal" at the Tokyo War Crimes Tribunal because of a combination of U.S. Occupation policy objectives and Japanese demands for the "retention of the national polity." The fact that Katō shows absolutely no interest in this matter is further evidence that he neglects this question of legal responsibility. Focusing instead solely on "moral responsibility," he claims that the emperor should have "abdicated." What concerns Katō is the fact that the emperor did not abdicate, not that he escaped judgment. As he argues, "Regardless of the sophistry of his postwar supporters, it is abundantly clear that the Shōwa emperor should have clarified his responsibility as signatory of the Imperial Declaration of War by abdicating, at either the time of the defeat, the end of the Occupation, or some other time" (ibid., p. 72).

Let us focus here on this notion of "responsibility as signatory of the Imperial Declaration of War." If Katō understands the emperor's responsibility in this manner, then he would be forced to restrict the meaning of war responsibility. For the emperor would thus be released from all responsibility for those "soldiers who died in his name" during the first four years of the second Sino-Japanese War, as this was an "undeclared war" which preceded the Imperial Declaration of War (issued on December 8, 1941). *In other words, Katō both excludes the emperor's responsibility prior to the Imperial Declaration of War and interprets his responsibility as "signatory" of this document solely in domestic terms. Through this double operation, the emperor's responsibility comes to be reduced to nothing more than a matter of moral responsibility for those "Imperial Army" soldiers who died in the so-called Pacific War.* Also, there is an obvious confusion here. Since the "three million Japanese dead" that Katō cites is the government's figure for those who died "after the China Incident," the emperor's responsibility for these dead remains at odds with his "responsibility as signatory of the Imperial Declaration of War."

Now, Katō subtly revised this point after a two-year silence. With the publication of his essay in book form, there appears without any explanation whatsoever the following change: "The emperor is responsible for his subjects, and above all for those soldiers of our nation who died in his name. While we the Japanese people bear responsibility for the twenty million Asian dead, the emperor cannot escape partial responsibility *not only for these people, but all the more* for the three million of our nation who died" (ibid., p. 72; italics Takahashi).

It seems that "twenty million Asian dead" are now added to the emperor's war responsibility. Since however the emperor is responsible "all the more" for the "three million of our nation who died," the emphasis remains on the emperor's domestic moral responsibility. Nor is there any change in Katō's notion that the emperor should abdicate as part of this moral responsibility, which introduces the possibility that responsibility toward Asia is likewise conceived only as moral responsibility. Katō leaves this question of Asian responsibility vague, but what has in any case already been established is the question of order, according to which the Japanese dead, and particularly the soldiers, are given priority over the Asian dead. This prioritizing of "our nation" can be seen throughout Katō's argument, but it is set forth most boldly in his third point, concerning the mourning for the war dead.

V. The Problem of Mourning the War Dead

For Katō, the problem of "mourning" the war dead lies at the "origin" of post-war Japan's personality split. Here, then, we enter the heart of the debate around "After the Defeat." In the "debate on the historical subject," some have regarded as mistaken those efforts to critically focus on Katō's notion of mourning the war dead, as these overlook the important issues he raises. Yet such focus may be justified when one considers the structure of his argument, in which this issue of mourning occupies the "original site" of the postwar "distortions."

What is meant by postwar Japan's personality split as concerns this question of mourning the war dead? According to Katō, the postwar reformists claim that we must apologize for the "twenty million Asian dead" killed during Japan's war of invasion. Yet these reformists ignore the issue of the "three million dead of our nation," and particularly the "dead soldiers," for they revile those who led the invasion as "defiled dead." On the other hand, the conservatives fall into the "falsehood" of ignoring the "twenty million Asian dead" and worshipping the dead Japanese soldiers at Yasukuni Shrine as "fallen heroes." If the reformists in their focus on the "twenty million Asian dead" represent postwar Japan's "out-ward-looking self," then the conservatives are the "inward-looking self" that focuses on the "three million dead of our nation," and particularly the dead soldiers. There exists a kind of "Jekyll and Hyde" split at the "origin" of postwar Japan, one that is both *of* the war dead and *by* the war dead. Like an annual event, apologies for the war are repeatedly nullified by reactions against them, as when Prime Minister Hosokawa's 1993 statement that "the war was a wrongful war of invasion" was followed by Justice Minister Nagano's remark (for which he was forced to resign) that the "Nanjing Massacre was an invention." Insofar as Japan does not overcome this personality split, it will remain unable to take responsibility for the war and offer a true apology to the Asian victims. Conversely speaking, in order to accept its responsibility and truly apologize, Japan must overcome this split and form a unified nation as subject of apology and responsibility.

What then should one do? Katō proposes that the Japanese people should not, like the reformists, focus solely on the Asian victims, but rather first of all deeply mourn the "dead of our nation," and particularly the soldiers. But what does such mourning mean? Katō says that this is to "respect" these dead and "thank" them from one's perspective as postwar Japanese (*"Haisengo ron wo meguru 'Q & A'"* [Questions and answers about *After the defeat*], in the January 1999 issue of *Ronza* [Forum]).

One should thus "thank" the dead soldiers, whom Katō describes as having "died for our nation," "died so that we could be here now." But how does this logic differ from that of Yasukuni Shrine? Katō insists there is a difference. Indeed, he says that we must first mourn and thank these soldiers so as to sever that Yasukuni logic. For Katō, it is not the case that Yasukuni logic still survives among the conservatives *despite* the reformists' efforts to apologize to the Asian victims. On the contrary, it survives *because of* these efforts, in addition to the reformist neglect of Japan's dead soldiers. The source of Yasukuni logic lies precisely in the reformists' abandonment of and contempt for those soldiers as "invaders" and "defiled dead" killed in an "unjust war." For Yasukuni's supporters, it is intolerable that the soldiers have come to be ignored in the "outward-looking official histories." Even when these supporters "forge history" and repeat such "slips" and "reckless remarks" as "The war was not a war of invasion" or "The Nanjing Massacre was an invention," Katō attributes this to their determination to somehow give meaning to the soldiers' deaths and mourn for them. Or as he puts it, "Yasukuni logic emerges from the reformist view of the war dead as its twin" (*"Haisengo ron wo meguru 'Q & A'"*).

In order to break free of this logic, one must break free of its point of emergence, i.e., the "reformist view of the war dead." Rather than neglect the dead soldiers of our nation and focus on the Asian victims, as with the reformists, one must in fact give priority to these soldiers and deeply mourn and thank them. Only then can postwar Japanese first recover their unified identity as "we Japanese," in the sense of a single undivided national subject, and truly apologize to the Asian victims. It is this that is the logic of Katō's "After the Defeat" discourse.

While differing from Yasukuni logic, the national subject of "we Japanese" is nevertheless still conceived as a *community of mourning* for those soldiers "who died for our nation" and as a *community of gratitude* for those soldiers "who died so that we could be here now."

I cannot agree with such an argument. In the following, I shall speak of Katō's argument in the order of its premises, its effectiveness, and its central idea.

VI. Odd Premises and a Questioning of Effectiveness

To begin with, let us examine the argument's premises.

First, it is unreasonable to interpret the repeated "slips" and "reckless remarks" of the conservative revisionists (including "forgery of history") as a reaction against the reformists' logic of apology to Asia. Katō's assertion that *"Yasukuni logic emerges from the reformist view of the war dead* as its twin" (italics Takahashi) is itself a "forgery of history." This logic existed before the war, which makes it impossible to speak of its emergence from the postwar reformists' view of the war dead. Dating back to the Meiji period along with the Yasukuni Shrine, Yasukuni logic promoted nationalist displays and the heroization of those who "died for the emperor" throughout all of modern Japan's wars—the Sino-Japanese War, the Russo-Japanese War, the second Sino-Japanese War, and the Pacific War. The notion of dying for the homeland (*mourir pour la patrie*) is the typical slogan employed by the modern nation state to mobilize its people for war, and Yasukuni logic is its Japanese version. It is simply that this logic still lives on in the nationalism of Japanese conservatives today.

The same thing can be said of such justification of colonial rule as is evident in the representative "slip" or "reckless remark," "It was right to annex Korea." This "Kubota's remark" aggravated the third Japanese-Korean negotiations of 1953, and yet a horrible "tradition" thus emerged in which these words were repeated some thirty times. It would be impossible to see in "Kubota's remark" a reaction against the reformist logic of apology without thereby committing a flagrant anachronism. For this represented the same defense of colonial rule as could be seen in the 1948 Finance Ministry and 1949 Foreign Ministry documents—papers which in turn marked the extension of prewar colonial rule ideology. If Katō were in fact correct, then the Japanese people must now once again "thank" those who died in the nation's wars of colonial acquisition (the Sino-Japanese War, the Russo-Japanese War, the Taiwan colonial war, and the suppression of the Korean resistance struggle) in order to break free of the discourse of justifying colonial rule.

Second, the claim that the reformists have neglected the dead of our nation and focused only on the Asian dead is entirely unconvincing. For after the war there was an overwhelming belief among the Japanese, *including the reformists*, that they themselves were the war victims, having suffered through such experiences as Hiroshima, Nagasaki, and the urban air raids. Mourning at this time was strictly for the "dead of our nation." The "National War Dead Memorial Ceremony," held every August 15 since 1963, was devoted to the "three million dead of our nation," who, as the "cornerstone of postwar peace," were given "thanks." In the prime minister's speeches, even the slightest concern for the "dead of other countries" did not appear until the 1990s, after Hosokawa and Murayama. The nonreligious Chidorigafuchi cemetery was built in 1959 as an alternative to Yasukuni Shrine, but this too was an institution in which one mourned only the "dead of our nation." Furthermore, there existed a massive imbalance in the financial support given to the war-dead families: until the early 1990s, approximately forty trillion yen was made available to the war victims "of our nation," most of which went to the families of soldiers and military civilian employees, whereas foreign payments were stopped at approximately one trillion yen, with no individual compensation. Katō's proposal that the Japanese dead, and especially the soldiers, be given priority over aliens and foreigners was thus realized some time ago.

Generally speaking, the reformists' sense of responsibility toward Asia began in the turmoil of the anti–Vietnam War movement of the late 1960s. This sentiment gradually expanded during the 1970s and 1980s, and yet it was not until the late 1980s and early 1990s, when Asian victims from various countries began suing for postwar compensation, that an actual movement was formed seeking apology and compensation from the Japanese government. Hayashi Fusao's "affirmation of the Greater East Asian War" appeared in 1963, but this was not premised upon the reformists' recognition of their war responsibility. (Hayashi's discourse represents an extension of his prewar right-wing activities as a writer of *tenkō* literature). With the exception of such figures as Takeuchi Yoshimi, the 1950s debates on war responsibility were utterly devoid of any reference to Asia. For example, a 1956 survey conducted by the *Nihon dokusho shinbun* [Japan readers' news] reveals that even "progressive" intellectuals focused on the domestic aspect of war responsibility: of a total of 181 responses, only two referred to responsibility for the invasion of Asia (Yoshida Yutaka, *Nihonjin no sensōkan* [Japanese views of war], Iwanami Shoten). The Japan Memorial Society for the Students Killed in the War (popularly known as the Wadatsumi Society) is one of the antiwar groups most representative of postwar Japan, and its activities are symbolic. This group was formed in 1950 with the goals of remembering those students who were killed as "soldiers" and of working to prevent war. After a half-century of various twists and turns, during which it overcame its focus on student-soldiers and sought to thematize the emperor's war responsibility, it finally took up in the late 1980s and 1990s the issue of these dead students' own responsibility. It should thus be clear that the Constitution protection camp can in no way be understood as mourning only the Asian dead and neglecting the dead of our nation.

Next, let us discuss the effectiveness of Katō's argument.

Katō states that Yasukuni logic can be "choked off" by "severing its emotional roots." More concretely, its adherents' "slips" and "reckless remarks" will disappear if the "three million dead of our nation," and particularly the soldiers, are mourned first. For here a logic would emerge that, as he writes, "represents 'ourselves' by containing the opposition": this would be a "logic of apology that 'assimilates' the conservatives' logic by containing the basis of such assertions within itself so as to make these conservatives unable to issue contrary assertions"—for instance, that accepting responsibility for Asia means no longer mourning the Japanese soldiers—"thereby arriving at apology."

I am unable to agree with this. Katō's claim is that "The Japanese died meaninglessly in a war of invasion, but they can still be mourned first." The conservatives' logic is that "the war was not one of invasion. If it were, then the Japanese deaths would have been in vain, meaningless." Regarding World War II, Katō's premise is that Japan's war was "unjust," "wrong," a "war of invasion." He says that "the dead of our nation" perished "meaninglessly," "in vain." Were he to state otherwise, then his claims for the priority of "the dead of our nation" would be indistinguishable from those of the conservatives. However, it is precisely this premise that the conservatives and Yasukuni supporters would find so unacceptable. The conservatives' "emotional roots" are this: "If we accept that the war was an invasion, the Japanese will have died meaninglessly, in vain. This alone is absolutely unacceptable." Such words can hardly be "incorporated" or "assimilated" by a logic that states that "The war was an invasion, and so the deaths were meaningless. Yet the Japanese must still be mourned first." In fact, the *manga* artist Kobayashi Yoshinori, whose revisionist claims are made alongside those of people like Fujioka Nobukatsu, flatly rejects Katō's argument as "masochistic." From the perspective of Kobayashi and Fujioka, even Katō is a prisoner of the "masochist view of history" by accepting responsibility for Japan's war of invasion.

What then should one do? I believe there can only be confrontation. By this I mean that we must repeat, clarify, and persuade ourselves of the judgment that Japan's war was one of invasion, in which the soldiers were each in their own way victimizers.

I would like to refer to this confrontation by way of analogy with psychoanalysis as "working through." Here, working through refers to the analytic work done in order to overcome the patient's resistance to accepting the analyst's interpretation of his past. This involves creating a critical distance vis-à-vis that past, which is achieved through recollection — regardless of how painful — and judgment. This kind of working through is necessary in order to eliminate the fierce resistance against accepting both the past invasion and the fact that the soldiers were also victimizers. What was in the past must be bravely confronted and then critically judged through one's own responsibility. To avoid this process is to ensure that the work of "mourning," which severs the domination of the past, never takes place.

VII. The "Japanese Nation" as Closed Community of Mourning

Finally let us turn to the, so to speak, central idea of Katō's proposal.

In a word, I am unable to agree with this idea because *it constructs a Japanese "national subject" as both closed community of mourning for the dead of our nation and closed community of gratitude for the dead soldiers of our nation, and this ultimately leads to the obfuscation of Japan's war responsibility.* I shall explain why this is so in the following three points.

First, the "national subject" formed by mourning only the dead "of our nation" without regard for the Asian victims necessarily excludes the memory of these latter. These victims would thus be excluded from the center of the Japanese nation's war memories, unable to encroach upon its subjectivity and identity; they would be merely inessential to Japan's national identity, such as to have no essential effect on the truth of "we Japanese." Their accusations would have no influence on the definition of "we Japanese," whose essence would remain unchanged. For this essence cannot be formed without mourning only the dead "of our nation" and ignoring the Asian victims' accusations, which we should already have seen and heard. In this sense, it must be said that Katō's argument, as it were, structurally protects Japanese national memory from the memory of the Asian other, such as to prevent the memories of those forced to work as "military comfort women," for example, from marking up the nation's interior.

This closure of the community of mourning would cause serious problems even within the Japanese nation in its legality. For example, although the roughly 200,000 Korean residents (who for various reasons became "naturalized" Japanese after the war) possess the sovereign right to demand that the Japanese government fulfill its war responsibility, must these residents therefore "thank" Japan's dead soldiers? And what of the people of Okinawa, whose memories are of being held at gunpoint by the Japanese army? It would be absurdity itself for these "Japanese citizens" to mourn those soldiers for having "died so that we could be here now." Wouldn't Katō's notion of "we Japanese" also exclude these people?

Second, the proposal that one mourn not simply the dead "of our nation" "first" but indeed the "three million" dead as a whole, serves to obfuscate Japanese war responsibility. Katō claims that the reason he insists on this point is to overcome the "division" between military and civilian dead (*"Haisengo ron* wo meguru 'Q & A'"), for the dead who were originally separated were all simply Japanese. Again, such a call for blind, indiscriminate mourning can be seen only as a pure nationalism that remains indifferent to content. For if you are Japanese, as Katō says, you must mourn the Japanese dead regardless of the circumstances of their deaths. This pure, blind nationalism is of a piece with the abstraction and emptiness of mourning those "of our nation" who died in a war with others without relation to those others. This makes all concrete mourning impossible. Concretely speaking, how can one mourn a soldier who died in the second Sino-Japanese War without any regard for the fact that he died in China, that is to say, without relation to the Chinese victims?

The American intellectual historian Dominic LaCapra examines postwar Germany's relation with its dead by means of a psychoanalytic model, and argues through the example of Hitler that the work of mourning is not a benefit to be enjoyed indiscriminately by all the dead. In effect, we must not obfuscate the differences in war responsibility among Japanese at this time by giving priority to such emotional demands as national mourning and gratitude. Mourning the dead of the victimizing nation cannot take place without judging the nature of their war responsibility. I would like to point out that Katō refers to the Japanese military dead as "soldiers," but these include many high-ranking officers below the level of general. In fact, it is odd, if not indeed impossible, to mourn equally and collectively the commander who led the Chinese invasion, the soldier who participated in the Nanjing Massacre, the boy who served in the suicide unit at the end of the Pacific War, and the girl burnt to death in Hiroshima, simply because they are all the dead "of our nation."

Third, we find the problem of "fathers" or "those close to us." Katō says the following about this "psychological" motif of his argument: "The war was wrong. Yet say one's own father killed people. There is an impulse to defend him as one's father, but this is meaningless. Nevertheless, the fact remains that he died for us, as someone who could have been loved" (Akasaka Norio shi tono taidan, "Sanbyaku man no shisha kara nisen man no shisha he" [Interview with Akasaka Norio, "From Three Million Dead to Twenty Million Dead"]).

Preceding all debate, these words can be seen as a straightforward expression of where Katō's own "emotional roots" lie. Why must we "first" mourn the dead "of our nation," and particularly the soldiers? For Katō, it is because they are "fathers"—even if they were murderers, these "fathers" died "for us," as people "whom we could have loved."

There is clearly here a confusion between the levels of family and nation. We must not superimpose the familial relation between father and child onto one's relation with the soldiers "of our nation" or the "three million dead of our nation." As is well known, the image of soldiers who "died for the homeland" as "fathers" of the nation as a whole is one of the typical representations of nationalism. In the prewar period, this image combined with that of women as the nation's "mothers" to form a view of Japan as one large family with the emperor as head. (Excluded from this view were the so-called licensed prostitutes and "comfort women.") Insofar as Katō's notion of "we Japanese" also supposes only those members who can be mourned like the "fathers" "who could have been loved" and who died "for us," it leads to an extremely closed community of family ideology. I have only one father, and so why must I treat the soldiers "of our nation" as "fathers" simply because they are the soldiers "of our nation"? I have only one father. We will become caught up in nationalist movements when we lose the ability to resist the emotionalism inherent in imagining all the dead and the dead soldiers "of our nation" as "fathers." One can only feel anxious in seeing the warm welcome extended to Katō's *Haisengo ron*, as evidenced by such comments as, "The heart-rending voice that says our defiled fathers are still fathers" or "The deliberate battle to mourn our fathers."

Next, Katō makes a remark in the heat of debate. In response to criticism of his proposal that the dead "of our nation" be mourned first, he says: "Yet speaking of this problem as one of human feelings, one naturally focuses on the pain of realizing the meaninglessness and emptiness of one's close relatives dying in a wrongful war. Here the notion of atoning for the wrongs of others emerges after this pain."

("Why do you think that?")

"Well, if for example a schoolboy were to ask his teacher why it is wrong to kill people, I think the most common response would be to say . . . wouldn't you be sad if your father were killed?" (*Asahi Shinbun* [Asahi news], August 13, 1998, evening edition)

Here as well, Katō explains the issue of the nation's wars through recourse to the individual's relation to his "father" or "those close to us." Without even mentioning people from Okinawa or those Koreans who have acquired Japanese citizenship, why must I direct the feelings I have for my family toward the dead and dead soldiers "of our nation" in general? Utterly missing here is the notion that distance should be kept from the very mindset that superimposes the images of father and family upon those of soldier and nation.

As goes without saying, I am not at all denying that those who lost their fathers and grandfathers in the war should mourn. Of course "defiled fathers are still fathers." Even those fathers who were "Class A war criminals" are still fathers from the perspective of their children, and it is natural for these latter to want to properly mourn them. I think that family and friends have the right to mourn anyone — exactly like Antigone of ancient Greece, who opposed the "law of the gods" to the "law of men" (the law of the nation) when she risked her life by violating the king's injunction and burying the exposed body of her elder brother. In fact, Japan's war dead have also been mourned "privately" in a variety of ways and places. In such mourning it would be meaningless to discuss the question of priority.

Yet this "private" mourning must not be allowed to obfuscate war responsibility. This issue can be raised even with regard to actual "fathers." In the Costa-Gavras film *The Music Box*, a female lawyer finds that her beloved father is suspected of helping in the slaughter of Jews in wartime Hungary. She defends him, convinced that he would never do such a thing. On the verge of winning the suit, however, she discovers his secret and agonizingly decides to have him indicted. In the West Germany of the late 1960s, it is said that the children's questioning of their fathers' actions during the Nazi period led to the country's struggles with its past since the 1970s. Such questioning is possible even with *one's actual* fathers who are *still living*. This is all the more reason why we must not leave unclear the judging of war responsibility and demand that one first mourn collectively the dead "of our nation" — who were the victimizers in a war of invasion — simply because they are the dead "of our nation."

VIII. Nationalism and Democracy

In the foregoing, I have clarified the three major arguments set forth by Katō Norihiro in his "After the Defeat" discourse. These points regard the Peace Constitution, the Shōwa emperor's war responsibility, and the mourning of the war dead.

We have, I believe, confirmed the existence of certain elements that make up what must be described as an index of a new Japanese nationalism, even if Katō differs from the revisionist and xenophobic nationalism that can be seen in the Liberalist historical view and the "New History Textbook Association."

As we have already seen, *Katō constructs the "national subject" that is "we Japanese" in his dual claims that (one) the Shōwa emperor should have abdicated as a sign of his (strictly) moral responsibility for the dead "of our nation," and particularly the soldiers of the "Imperial Army," and (two) the people must first of all mourn (only) these same dead "of our nation," and particularly the soldiers of the*

"Imperial Army." These two claims fully correspond to one another. What remains consistent in this logic in regard to both the emperor's responsibility and the people's mourning is the exclusion of the relation to the Asian other. Moreover, this "we Japanese" desire to make the Constitution purely "our own" regardless of its content, and hence even if it loses its quality of pacifism. *It is impossible to think of the emperor's war responsibility, the war responsibility of the Japanese soldiers and citizens, and the Peace Constitution apart from the relation to the Asian other.* Nevertheless, I cannot but be surprised at the attempt here to define "we Japanese" without relating it to this other.

Both Katō and his supporters routinely deny the charges of nationalism. As I have said, Katō is certainly not a nationalist in a xenophobic or negationist sense. In claiming that he is not a nationalist, Katō in effect means that he is neither a traditional conservative nationalist nor a Liberalist historical-view nationalist. But let us be careful here. In truth, Katō cannot not be a nationalist. In an essay on Fukuzawa Yukichi titled "'Yase gaman no setsu' kō" [A study of the "theory of strained endurance"], Katō states that the opposition between the reformists' notion of democracy and the conservatives' notion of nationalism is one of the signs of postwar Japan's personality split, whereas in the modern West, democracy was originally one with nationalism (in *Kanōsei toshite no sengo igo*). What is thus needed is to unify democracy and nationalism so as to create a *democratic nationalism*, a nationalism that is without "distortion," an originally "sound nationalism."

A democratic nationalism, or perhaps a nationalist democracy.

In a discussion of the post–Cold War global situation held in Paris at the Sorbonne, the political analyst Alain Minc referred to the series of violent incidents of xenophobia perpetrated by the neo-Nazis following German unification, and concluded that whereas German nationalism was originally an "irrational nationalism" (*nationalisme de déraison*), that of France was a "rational nationalism" (*nationalisme de raison*). Upon hearing this I was once again shocked. There is a deep-rooted belief that the nationalism of the modern West exemplifies, in its oneness with democracy, a "sound" nationalism, one that is "rational," healthy," and "normal." When France later repeated its nuclear testing in the South Pacific in the face of global opposition, I remember thinking that I had very clearly seen the dangers of "irrationality" that dwelt within such nationalism.

If we consider the case of "resistance nationalism" as adopted by those fighting against invasion and colonial rule, we realize that nationalism must not be denied in all cases. To the extent that nationalism is nationalism, however, we cannot deny that it possesses an essential tendency to fabricate a nation's oneness, homogeneity, and identity, thus excluding the heterogeneous other. If we imagine democracy as a political device through which people of different nationalities and national memories can respect one another's differences, then I think we must conceive of a *democracy without nationalism*, one that goes beyond nationalism, as precisely a democracy to come.

Translated by Richard F. Calichman

Note

Takahashi Tetsuya, "Nihon no neonashonarizumu 2: Katō Norihiro shi 'Haisengo ron' wo hihan suru," in *Sengo sekinin ron* [On postwar responsibility] (Tokyo: Kōdansha, 1999), pp. 131–159. Originally given as a seminar on March 19, 1999 in Paris at the Collège International de Philosophie.

FROM THE *HINOMARU* AND *KIMIGAYO*
TO THE SYMBOLIC EMPEROR SYSTEM

I. Introduction

Regarding the *Hinomaru-Kimigayo* legislation, Katō Norihiro has proposed that these two bills be separated: "I don't mind the *Hinomaru* legislation, but the Japanese people should not accept the *Kimigayo* legislation in its present form. If one claims that the *Kimigayo* melody has already taken root as a custom, then let us at least replace the lyrics" (*Mainichi Shinbun* [Daily news], June 28, 1999, morning edition, and elsewhere). Katō was not alone in proposing such a separation. The Japan Democratic party, wavering between support and opposition of this legislation, made a similar separation when it introduced as counterproposal only the *Hinomaru* bill. This was rejected, however. In the end, both the lower and upper houses of the Diet passed by overwhelming majority the combined National Flag–National Anthem bill as introduced by the government. From my own standpoint of opposition to the legislation of both the *Hinomaru* and *Kimigayo*, it is particularly impossible for me to overlook Katō's proposal. This proposal is intimately bound up with his "After the Defeat" argument, the same argument that I have consistently criticized in recent debates.

For Katō, the "greatest problem" stirred up by this legislation is the "existence of an inflexible viewpoint that sees all feasible proposals regarding the *Hinomaru* and *Kimigayo* issue"—as, for example, Katō's own proposal—"only as a return to nationalism. Today the most powerful support for this viewpoint is the anti–nation-state sentiment based on postmodern thought." Referring to my book *Derrida*, Katō also points out the "reversal" in the French philosopher Jacques Derrida's notion of justice, for moral issues are to be conceived not from the relation with the "'absolute other' excluded by the community," but rather from the "plural 'ordinary others'" who form the community (*Mainichi Shinbun*, May 11, 1999, evening edition).

Let me say in advance that this represents an elementary misreading of Derrida (or of my *Derrida* book), but what this misreading makes clear is an opposition between Katō and myself in the "After the Defeat" debate regarding the memory of Japan's invasion of Asia. In Katō's claim that priority be given to the plural "ordinary others" rather than to the "absolute other" excluded by the community, one can perceive his response to my criticism regarding the impossibility of speaking of "we Japanese" without focus on the Asian victims. Katō's position, which he has persistently defended, is that focus on the Asian victims can take place only after establishing "we Japanese" through mourning the war dead of our nation first. In the following, I would like to once again clarify the points of opposition between Katō and myself through a critique of his proposal that the *Hinomaru* and *Kimigayo* be treated separately.

II. Violence Against the Disobedient

First, let me explain my own basic position on this *Hinomaru-Kimigayo* issue. I am against their legislation. Prior to this legislation, I opposed the raising of the *Hinomaru* and the singing of *Kimigayo* (as the *de facto* national flag and national anthem) at various functions, particularly in the schools and educational centers. I have been extremely critical of the enforcement of these activities in the schools, which dates back to the Ministry of Education's 1985 "Notice of Thorough Implementation." My opposition derives above all from the fact that both the *Hinomaru* and *Kimigayo* were symbols of Japan's war of invasion and colonial rule.

I am unable to yield this general principle. If Japan is to make use of a *de facto* national flag and national anthem, then it should have replaced these based on reflection on the past, just as the former Axis nations Germany and Italy immediately replaced their own national flags and national anthems after the war. Even now it is not too late, as such a replacement would be highly desirable.

Would the problem disappear if Japan were to make this change? Even if a different national flag and anthem were to be adopted, I would still oppose their obligatory use in such places as schools and educational centers. The history of national flags and national anthems is inseparable from that of the nationalism, overseas wars, and imperialism of the modern nation-state. As with the French Republic's *Tricolore* and *la Marseillaise* in their representation of liberty, equality, and fraternity, national flags and national anthems reveal their force in coercing people into national unity and mobilizing violence against disobedient people and others—and this not merely regardless of which "sublime" ideals they symbolize, but rather precisely to the extent of that "sublimity" itself. Opposing *Kimigayo* "because it is not the song the people can sing from their hearts as one" is valid to a certain degree, but we must not forget the horror of making the people as a whole "as one" to their very "hearts," under one national flag and anthem, through the repetition of such collective bodily acts as worshipping the national flag and singing the national anthem.

The significance of national flags can be reduced to their function of distinguishing nations from one another in the context of international society. Compared to this, it is difficult to fully remove from national anthems their function of creating both emotional identification with the state and a sense of national unity. On the other hand, one could say from a practical point of view that national flags are more necessary, since the absence of a national anthem would mean little.

I am not absolutely opposed to Japan having for the present a de facto national flag and national anthem within the system of nation-states that currently envelops the globe. My position differs from the one described by Katō, which contents itself with idealistically denying *in toto* the currently dominant nation-state system. But we must be wary of the pressures of "nationalization" and the violence of identification as effected by all national flags and anthems; we must remain vigilant against the politics of the nation-state's symbols. Ultimately, I would also wish to keep in sight the possibility of abandoning all national symbol politics, including national flags and anthems. The *Hinomaru-Kimigayo* legislation belongs in the very worst category of such national symbol politics.

III. Who Are "We"?

Distinguishing between these two, Katō Norihiro states that the *Hinomaru* legislation is fine whereas the *Kimigayo* legislation "in its current form" is not. Why is this? In effect, he seems to say that there is no reason to replace the *Hinomaru* insofar as Japan as a modern nation-state requires a national flag, but that *Kimigayo* violates the present Constitution's principle of popular sovereignty in its reference to the "eternity of the emperor's reign." Yet there are a number of contradictions or confusions here.

As Katō writes of the *Hinomaru*, "Since we cannot deny that Japan is a modern nation, we can neither deny the existence of a national flag. Such denial would be irresponsible insofar as we presently accept as its premise this modern nation's existence. Insofar as the nation Japan must possess a national flag, we have no reason to replace the *Hinomaru*, with its negative historical image" (*Kanōsei toshite no sengo igo* [The post postwar as possibility] (Tokyo: Iwanami Shoten, 1999), p. ix).

To repeat, I am of course not denying the present existence of a modern nation, nor am I even denying the practical utility of a national flag. But it is one thing to speak of modern nations having national flags and quite another to say that Japan's national flag is the *Hinomaru*. Without any explanation whatsoever, Katō moves here from the necessity of a national flag for the modern nation Japan to the self-evidence of the *Hinomaru* as that flag. This leap of logic takes place in the context of two examples raised by Katō to illustrate the necessity of the national flag.

First, the American historian Otis Cary, surprised during the Gulf War at seeing the minesweepers of Japan's self-defense forces hoisting the Rising Sun flag when calling at Manilla Bay, asked why the prewar battle flag was being used instead of the *Hinomaru*. When his companion mentioned the Filipinos' probable dislike of that flag, Cary replied, "But they have to hoist some flag." Therefore, as Katō says, "We cannot and should not deny the national flag's existence."

The second example concerns passports. Anyone traveling abroad possesses a passport. This "means that one considers oneself a citizen of a nation." Those who carry a passport and yet claim that national flags are useless "must be described as presuming upon the nation-state's kindness." As a citizen of a nation, then, one cannot deny the national flag just as one cannot deny a passport.

This passport discussion is absurd, as it goes so far as to deprive all members of the nation-state of the right to claim that national flags are useless. Drawing forth the necessity of national flags from that of passports represents another leap of logic. At any rate, Katō's claim until this point is that one should accept the necessity of national flags. Yet from here he immediately makes the following connection: "What we thus have here is a situation that is rather difficult to explain, for while we regard the present national flag *called* Hinomaru as something negative, we nevertheless depend upon it" (emphasis Takahashi). But to say that we require a national flag is not the same thing as saying that we "depend" upon the "*Hinomaru*." What emerges from the statement that "they have to hoist some flag" is neither the necessity of that flag being the *Hinomaru* nor the appropriateness of the *Hinomaru*. Yet Katō writes that "insofar as the nation Japan must possess a national flag," "we have no reason to replace the *Hinomaru*," exactly as if the *Hinomaru's* status as Japan's national flag were an indisputable premise.

In claiming that "we" have no reason to replace the *Hinomaru*, who is this "we"? I, for one, have a reason to replace this flag. To repeat, this is because the *Hinomaru* was a symbol of Japan's war of invasion and colonial rule. Even among Japanese citizens alone, there are certainly not a few who share this same "reason," even if we are not a majority. Why does Katō write that "we" have no reason to replace the *Hinomaru*, as if every Japanese citizen were in favor of this flag?

IV. The Way to Repay the War "Debt"

Katō prepares the following explanation in response to those who share this same "reason" as myself:

> Some are of the opinion that the *Hinomaru* should be abandoned and replaced since it was a symbol of Japan's past invasion. But . . . this flag drags along a negative image because postwar Japan has not yet fully repaid its war debt. The *Hinomaru* is a symbol of this. If this national flag is a defiled one with a negative image, then postwar Japan should be asked to hold itself liable, thereby transforming the flag's image into something more positive. If the *Hinomaru* is simply abandoned, then at precisely that moment it becomes a source of distrust on the part of those conscientious people from the invaded nations.
>
> (*Mainichi Shinbun*, May 11, 1999)

According to Katō, "If Japan still drags along its war debt without having resolved the various problems of the postwar, then this is all the more reason why we must not replace the *Hinomaru*" (*Mainichi Shinbun*, June 28, 1999). Readers might be pleased to find here a clever paradox that "differs from the thinking of society's intelligentsia." Unfortunately, I can hear only sophistry in this remark.

First, given that the *Hinomaru* has remained throughout the postwar Japan's (*de facto*) national flag as if nothing had ever happened, couldn't this fact itself represent one of the nation's "war debts" and unresolved "problems of the postwar"? When the government first raised this question in March 1999, it was again endorsed by the media response of China and Southeast Asia—although this went largely unreported in the Japanese media. Let me cite one example:

There can be no doubt that the Japanese people desire a national flag and anthem. Yet history still has not taught them that the *Hinomaru* and *Kimigayo* must be excluded as unfit for these. If those nations of the world with imperial pasts continued to make use of the same national war banners, then many more nations would lodge complaints against them than against Japan.

(Singapore, *The Straits Times*, March 9 editorial, trans. Wani Yasuo)

The "source of distrust on the part of those conscientious people from the invaded nations" lies not in Japan's "abandoning" of the *Hinomaru* and *Kimigayo*, but rather in their "continued use" and attempted legislation. Katō asks what would happen if these were "simply" abandoned, and yet Japan has continued to make use of the *Hinomaru* and *Kimigayo* for the past half-century now. Italy promptly changed its national flag in 1946, and West Germany did so in 1949. There is no talk that this became a "source of distrust on the part of those conscientious people from the invaded nations." Katō would admit that both Germany and Italy went on to reconcile with their surrounding nations and become important members of the European Union, and that Germany's postwar dealings, which have gone farther than those of Japan, are acclaimed internationally. He even says that, unlike Japan, West Germany "immediately after the defeat" sought out its logic of "distortion" based on the awareness of its own "defilement," and that its "post-defeat discourse" has been the nation's "cornerstone of public opinion." Although contrary to Katō's argument, it is West Germany (which "simply" abandoned its national flag) that has repaid its war debt relatively well, whereas Japan (which has continued to make use of its "defiled flag" for the past half-century) cannot. If one highly esteems West Germany's postwar, then far from arguing that Japan "must not replace" the symbols of its invasion, should one not rather demand that they be replaced at once, even now?

Second, if we accept the logic that the *Hinomaru* not be replaced "all the more" because Japan still drags along its war debt, then there is no reason to deny this logic in regard to *Kimigayo*. The emperor's war responsibility yet remains one of the unresolved "problems of the postwar"; it is one of the highest "war debts." As such, there is "all the more reason" that *Kimigayo* not be replaced,

This anthem drags along a negative image because postwar Japan has not yet fully resolved the issue of the Emperor's war responsibility. *Kimigayo* is a symbol of this. If this national anthem is a defiled one with a negative image, then postwar Japan should be asked to hold itself liable, thereby transforming the anthem's image into something more positive. If *Kimigayo* is simply abandoned . . .

The Shōwa emperor's death rendered his war debt forever unpayable. As a "symbol of this," should Japan forever continue to make use of *Kimigayo* as its national anthem?

V. If Popular Sovereignty Were Also "Enforced"

Here Katō's argument takes a surprising turn. He opposes the legislation of the present *Kimigayo* as Japan's national anthem, claiming that its lyrics of imperial sovereignty violate the postwar Constitution's principle of popular sovereignty.

Certainly this is true. It is clear that these lyrics violate popular sovereignty, and this is the most obvious reason for opposing the *Kimigayo* legislation. Since the current National Flag–National Anthem bill combines the *Hinomaru* and the present *Kimigayo*, this in and of itself is sufficient reason to oppose it. As an intellectual issue, however, I must admit to having certain reservations about Katō's argument.

First, doesn't Katō here contradict his own intellectual position as set forth most centrally in his book *Haisengo ron* [After the defeat]? There he showed an undisguised aversion to the many antiwar declarations at the time of the Gulf War that sought support in the peace Constitution: "So then, people would not oppose the Gulf War if there were no peace Constitution?" Given that the Constitution's renunciation-of-war article was "enforced" by the Occupation army, as Katō writes, it is a matter of "self-deception" to oppose war based on the "peace Constitution." How then do his actions here differ from this? If the renunciation of war was "enforced," then popular sovereignty was also "enforced." Rather than asking, "So then, people would not oppose *Kimigayo* if there were no Constitution with its principle of popular sovereignty?" he says, "The Japanese people must accept popular sovereignty as set forth in the present Constitution." Katō even writes that the Japanese people "*won* popular sovereignty through the defeat." He does not describe such claims of enforced popular sovereignty as "self-deception."

Of course it is not my aim to make an issue of these contradictions. Rather I would like to say that even if the present Constitution was originally "enforced," there is still sufficient ground for the Japanese people now to oppose the *Kimigayo* legislation on the basis of popular sovereignty, and this would be equivalent to opposing the nation's war assistance through appeal to the war-renunciation article. This also bears upon the current problem of coping with the related "New Guidelines for Japan–U.S. Defense Cooperation" law. I would hope that Katō does not discourage those trying to reject Japan's war collaboration with the U.S. based on the war renunciation article through such charges as "self-deception."

VI. The Problem of the Symbolic Emperor System

Second, since Katō's *Kimigayo* proposal represents a halfway measure to "keep the melody but change the lyrics," after the Tokyo governor Ishihara Shintarō, the relation to the symbolic emperor system remains ambiguous. First, "I actually wanted someone who symbolizes postwar Japan, like Takemitsu Tōru, to write the song for postwar Japan," but since this was "unfeasible," Katō made the counterproposal to change the lyrics. However, it is extremely unclear why it was "unfeasible" to replace the song, including the melody. If the lyrics can be replaced, then so can the melody. There are many people who find the *Kimigayo* melody unappealing. There are also not a few Asian victims who remember only the melody. I would like to counter-propose not that we "at least replace the lyrics," but that we at least replace the song itself.

What is the ambiguity surrounding the symbolic emperor system? Let us examine Katō's proposal more closely. As he writes,

> In the government's unified opinion of June 11, the *kimi* of *Kimigayo* is interpreted to mean the symbolic emperor as opposed to the prewar "emperor as sovereign." The crucial point here, according to the government, is that the meaning of *kimi* changes from the former prewar Constitution to the present Constitution. *If that is the case*, however, then *those* lyrics must be changed. If they are not, *that difference in meaning* will go unnoticed internationally, regardless of how much the government and bureaucracy subjectively twist its interpretation of this term. The intention behind the present legislation will then be reversed. In which case, international opinion will hold that despite the Japanese people's winning of popular sovereignty through the defeat, fifty-four years later *they still chose a relation to the same prewar "emperor."*
>
> (*Mainichi Shinbun*, June 28, 1999; italics Takahashi).

To be exact, Katō's proposal here is that the *Kimigayo* lyrics be *changed to something befitting the symbolic emperor system* as opposed to the absolutist emperor system, as based on popular sovereignty. The *kimi* of *Kimigayo* "changes in meaning" from the former Constitution to that of the present, and "if that is the case," the lyrics must be changed so as to reveal "that difference in meaning" "internationally." Hence these lyrics must be changed into something that clarifies the relation to the symbolic emperor of the present Constitution rather than the "relation to the same prewar 'emperor.'"

What is being questioned here: only the stance on prewar-like imperial sovereignty or also that of the present Constitution's symbolic emperor system? Katō continues, "This matter has great significance for postwar Japan in that, following the Era Name law of 1979, it represents an even more decisive opportunity for us as Japanese citizens to legally reveal our clear intentions *to the symbolic emperor system*" (ibid.).

I agree that the present legislation can become a "decisive opportunity" for the Japanese people to reveal their clear intentions to the symbolic emperor system. For the past half-century since the war, both *Kimigayo* and the *Hinomaru* have been deeply bound up with the symbolic emperor system, all the while ambiguously dragging along the prewar memories of their status as symbols of the sacred and inviolable emperor and his "empire." (As with the "imperial pageants" of the past, observe the waving miniature *Hinomaru* flags in recent imperial visits). What is really being questioned through this issue of the *Hinomaru-Kimigayo* legislation is what to do with the symbolic emperor system: should it be maintained or discarded as Japan moves into the twenty-first century?

When Katō speaks of "legally revealing our clear intentions to the symbolic emperor system," his choice is ambiguous. He proposes that, since the meaning of the term *kimi* has changed from the prewar to the postwar, the *Kimigayo* lyrics should be replaced so as to clarify "that difference in meaning." But this represents a choice to newly approve of—or, as Katō is wont to say, "re-choose"—the present Constitution's symbolic emperor system. This is perhaps why he repeats that the problem is whether a song of prewar imperial sovereignty is appropriate: "The legislation involving the present *Kimigayo* lyrics reveals that postwar Japanese intend to re-choose as their own postwar national anthem a song that praises prewar imperial sovereignty. What is being questioned through this legislation is whether we Japanese people should do this."

In other words, what Katō's proposal boils down to here is that the *Hinomaru* legislation is fine, that this flag should rather be kept, and that the *Kimigayo* legislation would also be fine if the lyrics were replaced by something befitting the symbolic emperor system. If this is true, then it is wrong to complain that "all feasible proposals regarding the *Hinomaru* and *Kimigayo* issue, including my own proposal to separate these two, are seen only as a return to nationalism." In what sense is Katō's proposal "feasible"? It is "feasible" in view of what? Like the proposal of the Tokyo governor, Ishihara Shintarō, which he cites, Katō's proposal bears a strong affinity with neo-nationalism. If this proposal were really "feasible," then it should problematize the symbolic emperor system itself. Article One of the present Constitution clearly states that the principle of popular sovereignty takes priority over the symbolic emperor system. The "status" of the emperor as "symbol of Japan and the unity of the Japanese people" can be changed by the "will of the sovereign Japanese people."

I believe that this problem, emerging now a half-century after the war and with the twenty-first century in view, must become a "decisive opportunity" to seriously consider Japan's choice of breaking away not only from the *Hinomaru* and *Kimigayo*, but also from the symbolic emperor system, from which these two are inseparable.

VII. Pressures for a New "Imperialization"

Katō writes, "It is well known that the nation-state now has a great many problems. But this does not demand that we now deny its existence and see the national flag and national anthem as useless. What is demanded is that the nation-state become more open, that it continue trying to overcome its own closure."

Let me confirm that while I do have criticisms of the nation-state's way of being, I do not "deny" its "existence." (The nation-state's "existence" is a fact that cannot be "denied"). Nor do I claim that the national flag and anthem are immediately useless. I seek possibilities of doing away with the politics of national symbols, but at present I believe we should at least find another national flag and anthem. Now does Katō really think that his proposal to accept the *Hinomaru* and *Kimigayo* (provided that the latter's lyrics reveal "that difference in meaning" of the term for emperor) is the way to overcome the "closure" of the nation-state Japan and make it "open"? *Won't this proposal have precisely the opposite effect?*

The *Hinomaru, Kimigayo*, and symbolic emperor system are major factors that prevent contemporary Japan from becoming an "open" nation. For example, the Korean residents of Japan (both North and South Korean nationals) consist of people and their descendants who were in the prewar period appropriated into the Japanese empire and "imperialized"; yet in the postwar period they were deprived of Japanese citizenship, as unlike most cases of colonial independence they were denied the right to choose their nationality. For them, the *Hinomaru, Kimigayo*, and symbolic emperor system not only recall the history of prewar colonial rule, they are also the symbols of the "nation-state" Japan's postwar discrimination. If these Korean residents try to acquire Japanese citizenship in order to escape this discrimination, the *Hinomaru, Kimigayo*, and symbolic emperor system stand in their way as tests of allegiance. This is the structure of "naturalization" as a new "imperialization." Approximately 90 percent of the Korean resident children attend Japanese schools, in part because national universities and graduate schools in Japan refuse admittance to graduates of ethnic schools. The raising of the *Hinomaru* and singing of *Kimigayo* in the schools function as a constant pressure of "imperialization." The present legislation will aggravate this pressure even further.

Katō seems to think that even with the *Hinomaru* legislation, there should be no obligation to raise the flag at graduation ceremonies and festivals, for "these practices" should be made "more open." But he misses the point here. Even the government holds that it won't demand respect for this rule, that there will be "direction" rather than enforcement, but legislation is nothing other than giving legal justification to what is already obligatory. In past hearings and opposition movements, those who argued against the compulsory use of the *Hinomaru* and *Kimigayo* did so on the major grounds that "these had no legal basis as the national flag and national anthem." The present legislation robs us of this important authority.

As goes without saying, I do not speak for the Korean residents, nor am I using the other as an excuse for opposition so as to avoid my own judgment. The *Hinomaru* and *Kimigayo* are not only symbols of invasions for Korean residents and "those conscientious people from the invaded nations." They are also symbols of invasion for such Japanese people as myself. They are inseparable from the memory and history of the emperor system and the war. Scholars speak of the *Hinomaru* and *Kimigayo* as not simply "used" in Japan's war of invasion, but as having "brought it forth" (Komagome Takeshi). As a Japanese person of today, I oppose their legislation as national symbols. Replacing the *Hinomaru* and *Kimigayo* is one solution to the "various problems of the postwar," it is part of making the nation-state Japan "become more open, overcoming its own closure."

VIII. What "Popular Consensus" Excludes

Finally, let us examine what Katō calls the "greatest problem."

Katō refers to the "anti–nation-state sentiment based on postmodern thought," and the French thinker Jacques Derrida as one "example" thereof, as the reason that such proposals as his own are "all seen only as a return to nationalism." According to Katō, Derrida's notion of justice is "reversed." For whereas justice and morals were built originally upon the relation with the plural "ordinary others," "those others right next to oneself," Derrida approaches these from the single "absolute other" excluded by this community of plural "ordinary others." What is worse, Katō links Derrida's thought to that of "the 1970s anti–Japanese-armaments front" and the "series of industry explosion incidents"!

Doubtless there are readers who are puzzled by this sudden shift from the *Hinomaru* and *Kimigayo* to abstract philosophical discussion. Now what if we were to replace what is here called the community of "ordinary others" with the nation-state Japan, and the excluded "absolute other" with, say, the Korean residents?

> The *Hinomaru-Kimigayo* legislation is first of all an internal issue for "we Japanese," i.e., the community of "those others right next to oneself." Although decisions made by one's fellow Japanese "must invariably exclude the other," issues of justice and morals become an "anti-Japanese-armaments front" when seen from the relation with these excluded "absolutely other" Korean residents. It is important to think of these issues not from the relation to the excluded other, but rather from the advantage of "we Japanese."

Readers familiar with the "After the Defeat" debate will notice that this argument is of the same type as Katō's claim that the Japanese war dead be mourned first by "we Japanese" so as to apologize to the Asian victims.

Yet there is first of all here a misreading of Derrida. In reading Derrida, it is clear that the point of his notion of justice and responsibility is far from the opposition between the single "absolute other" and the plural "ordinary others;" rather, it is the deconstruction of that opposition (see my *Derrida*, chapter 5). In contrast to Kierkegaard's absolutizing of the relation with God as the one "absolute other," which sacrifices responsibility to such ethical communities as the nation and family, Derrida problematizes such dual analysis by claiming that "every other is the absolute other." "Every other is the absolute other." That is to say, the "absolute other" is not only that other excluded from the community. Every other, including the plural "ordinary others" and "those others right next to oneself" that make up the community, is the "absolute other" who has something unknown and unknowable to me. In this argument, Derrida parts ways with all thinking that privileges a specific other, as for example Levinas's philosophy in its tendency to see only "Jews" as the privileged other.

For "me," "every other" — the Japanese citizen others A and B and the Korean resident others C and D — is the "absolute other." Nevertheless, a stark legal borderline is drawn between A, B and C, D, such that the community of Japanese citizens to which "I" and A and B belong excludes C and D outside itself. If we do not ask if such exclusion is violent, and, if so, how violent, then the "nation-state" Japan will never "become more open."

To evoke the relation with others C and D is not to privilege the relation with the single other, and even less can it be to sacrifice in terror other others for the sake of such single other. Rather it is to focus on and re-question the violence of exclusion and difference that, although already present, is frequently forgotten and ignored.

The *Hinomaru-Kimigayo* issue precisely requires such an approach. Even when considered solely in terms of the relation with the Korean residents, it is clear that this issue must not be decided only by what is advantageous to the Japanese people. In particular, every foreign resident making a living in Japan is involved here. In deferring the relation with the excluded other *of* the nation-state while prioritizing the relation with its internal other, Katō's approach simply repeats the "people's" violence of exclusion. If the national flag–national anthem issue is one of symbolizing "we Japanese," then here as well we cannot speak of "we Japanese" without dialogue with the other *of* the nation-state.

The *Hinomaru-Kimigayo* issue has thus led us to a re-questioning of the right of "popular sovereignty" itself. Katō said that the reason for replacing the *Hinomaru* does not lie "in us." But even in the unlikely event that the Japanese people as a whole were to agree with this, should this issue be decided by "us" alone? It is certainly valid to oppose the *Kimigayo* legislation based on popular sovereignty. Yet what if such "sovereign" decision by the "people" itself were to go hand in hand with the exclusion of the voices of those "others" involved in this issue?

Those in favor of this legislation claim to be "anchored in the people," whereas those against it claim that "there is no popular consensus." Regardless of which survey one reads, there is no doubt that national opinion is divided here. Furthermore, even if a fixed "popular consensus" regarding this issue were a necessary condition, it is not a sufficient one. Those who speak of an anchoring in the people fail to see that such "anchoring" is the result of force. They ignore the fact that, even assuming that this anchoring exists, it can itself become a threat to those parties outside of the "people."

The *Hinomaru-Kimigayo* issue is not simply an issue of the national flag and national anthem. It is an issue of the symbolic emperor system, one that questions the very framework of the "nation-state" Japan. A Japanese-styled "communality" is legally guaranteed by Article One of the Japanese Constitution, i.e., the symbolic emperor system article. Insofar as this is not changed, Japanese society will be unable to realize a true "public sphere."

Translated by Richard F. Calichman

Note

Takahashi Tetsuya, "Hinomaru-kimigayo kara shōchō tennōsei he," in *Sengo sekinin ron* [On postwar responsibility] (Tokyo: Kōdansha, 1999), pp. 237–256. Originally published in *Ronza* [Forum], September 1999.

Chapter 7

IN THE FEMININE GUISE: A TRAP OF REVERSE ORIENTALISM

Ueno Chizuko

The Orient as Feminized

In *Orientalism*, Edward Said argues that Europe has continuously feminized the Orient:

> Orientalism itself, furthermore, was an exclusively male province. Like so many guilds during the modern period, it viewed itself and its subject matter with sexist blinders. This is especially evident in the writings of travelers and novelists: women are usually the creatures of a male power-fantasy. They express unlimited sensuality, they are more or less stupid, and above all they are willing.[1]

Accordingly, the Orient is related to "the separateness, its eccentricity, its backwardness, its silent indifference, its feminine penetrability, its supine malleability,"[2] all of which are also assumed to characterize femininity. Women, of course, are no more creatures of a male power-fantasy than the Orient is that of a European power-fantasy. Both of them were created by Western male discourse as "the other." Women are to men as the Orient is to the Occident; and difference attributed to them as a distinctive feature defines their "otherness."

The attribution of this difference tells us more about those who attribute than those who are attributed. Said points out that Orientalism is "a considerable dimension of modern political culture, and as such has less to do with the Orient than it does with 'our' world."[3] As Toni Morrison writes in her postcolonial criticism of a popular American *bildungsroman*—Mark Twain's *Huckleberry Finn*—the black people are a necessary shadow in the story, present for no better purpose than to set off the nobility and generosity of the "white identity."[4]

"The Orient" is a generic term to refer to non-European countries located to the east of the Occident.[5] When did it start to be related to femininity? This usage began fairly recently, from the time of the rise of European imperialism. The medieval Muslim world, which once surpassed Europe in terms of advanced science and technology and whose military power threatened it, could never be referred to by feminized metaphors. Orientalism is by no means an innocent egoism. It is a discourse of power, another name given to colonialism, which constructs "the other" as inferior. This alone is sufficient reason to feminize it, since "woman" is another name given to a land to be conquered.

In this paper, I take Japan as a particular example of Orientalism and investigate how it is represented in the gendered language of Orientalist discourse. Now, if we consider that Oriental men have been feminized, Oriental women have been doubly feminized. This double feminization complicates the situation of Oriental women when they struggle against their own men, for their femininity has already been appropriated by men themselves. In the process of constructing an Oriental counter-identity—something I am tempted to dub "reverse Orientalism"—Oriental men have exploited femininity. Building feminism is not an easy task in such a cultural context, and I am sure that the experience of Japanese feminism can shed a useful light on women's experience in other orientalized nations.

Formation of the Japanese Mind

It is easy to see that the Orientalist scheme is identical to that of gender in the structuralist paradigm of binary oppositions:

the Occident : the Orient :: men : women :: culture : nature[6]

When Europeans define themselves as masculine, how is the "feminine" identity of "the other" constructed? This may be best seen in colonized discourse. In theory, there are two possible ways for colonized intellectuals (no doubt male, as they monopolize the production of discourse) to define their own identity.

One is masculine: to reject the imposed "otherness" and compete with colonialists for "universal" values. The other is feminine: to accept the imposed "otherness" and attempt to take advantage of it. The former inevitably leads to a dangerous conflict over which side has the best claim to "universality," since universalism does not admit of plural values—namely, to what Max Weber termed "a battle among gods." However, when there is a significant power imbalance between the two parties, the inferior tends to prefer the latter strategy; which holds that "the short-term loser is the long-term winner"—a cultural irony.

As early as the Edo period, the philosopher Motōri Norinaga (1730–1801) was an example of the latter mode of adaptation. Motōri is known as one of the founders of Japanology, a doctrine opposed to the Confucian philosophy officially propagated by the Tokugawa government.

Throughout Japanese history, "Japanneseness" has been constructed in the shadow of China, and this has given it an irreducibly colonial nature. Premodern aristocrats and intellectuals were necessarily bilingual, since much upper-class written discourse was produced in Chinese, not Japanese.[7] China has always been an ethnocentric imperial state that has considered its own culture to define the borders of the fully human realm. Though sometimes conquered by nomadic tribes and once invaded by Japan, the Chinese have never questioned their own superiority and universality.[8] With this overwhelming Chinese presence as a focal point, Japan has defined itself as particular, distant, and differentiated—put more simply, as inferior to the universal standards of China.

Motōri adopted the strategic approach of cultural irony by postulating that "the Japanese mind" is different from "the Chinese mind." In "Tamakatsuma," one of the essays in his *Collected Works*, he defined "the Chinese mind" as follows:

> What I mean by the Chinese mind is not simply respect for Chineseness and a tendency to fall in with the Chinese; it is rather a state of mind by which people define, argue and judge right and wrong in this world. It is not only the state of mind of those who read Chinese literature; it is also that of those who do not read it, if they follow the same ways. Contrary to the assumption that those who do not read cannot have a Chinese mind, throughout the thousand years of history during which the Japanese people have been affected by the Chinese and followed their ways with respect, the Chinese mind has become an underlying component of the popular mind, and now appears as commonsense knowledge. Having reached this stage, even when people say that they do not act in accord with the Chinese mind, it is because they take the Chinese mind for granted.[9]

The definition that Motōri gives to the Chinese mind here is unarguable, for to him, the term is a generic one for any kind of universalistic thinking that defines right and wrong and creates rules and logic, regardless of whether the person with such a mind is literate in Chinese. He further argues:

> When you think that there is no difference in the human mind, Chinese or Japanese, and that there should be only one universal truth in the world, you are already trapped by the Chinese mind.
>
> For what they think right might not be right to us, and what they think wrong is not necessarily wrong to us. Therefore, you cannot say there is only one truth in the world.[10]

This may at first glance seem like cultural relativism, which admits that every culture has a different definition of right and wrong. After all, if the Japanese mind were to make a claim to universality, that would lead to a fatal conflict with the Chinese mind over the definition of the truth. Nevertheless, Motōri did not deny the universality of the Chinese mind—he never suggested that the Chinese mind is just one among various particularisms. Instead, the cultural strategy he applied was subtle and dangerous: he defined the Japanese mind as something differentiated from the "universal" Chinese mind. Thus he made the Japanese mind into a residual category of universalism, while at the same time rejecting universalistic thinking by naming it "the Chinese mind."

The Japanese Mind as Feminized

Hasegawa Michiko, a right-wing student of Motōri Norinaga in contemporary Japan, has claimed that his position can indeed be summed up by the phrase "cultural relativism."[11] As noted above, this is difficult. Motōri cannot be a simplistic cultural relativist because he defines "the Chinese mind" as a cultural perversion which accepts the universality of another culture, the product of the validation of China's ethnocentrism. By tagging Motōri a cultural relativist, Hasegawa fails to grasp important aspects of his argument: as Hasegawa herself points out, the Chinese mind is not the mind of the Chinese but the mind of the Japanese who accept and accord with the Chinese mind. When Hasegawa calls the Chinese mind "cultural perversion," what does this say about the Japanese mind, which is no more nor less than the child of this "perversion"?

Hence "the Chinese mind" is a Japanese product. It has worked its way into the foundations of Japanese thought and society and is long since past the point where it could have been eradicated. Given this, we can see how there has been a curious coexistence and "division of labor" between the Chinese mind and the Japanese mind in Japanese culture.

History tells us that the *écriture* of the Japanese mind was carried out in *kanamoji*, which is a Japanese script made out of Chinese characters; the term means, literally, "fake script" (as opposed to the "true" Chinese script). At the point in history when Chinese *écriture* was used for official documents, *kanamoji* were used for storytelling and poetry—that is, to express the emotions left behind after everything official had been subtracted.

Motōri is also known as a student of *The Tale of Genji*, the world's oldest novel, which was written by a court lady in the Japanese script in the eleventh century. It is easy to understand how closely the Japanese mind is related to the women's world, because women at the time were excluded from the public world and prohibited from writing in Chinese, which actually helped them develop their own literature in Japanese. While men had both the public and private spheres, women were assigned solely to the private sphere. Aristocrats and bureaucrats wrote and read official documents and poems in Chinese, then expressed in Japanese the sentiments which could not be represented in the official language. For men, the Japanese mind was thus from the outset the residue of the public sphere, and Japanese was in particular the language used to express "affairs among people" or relationships with women in the private sphere. Thus, when the idea of *écriture feminine* from French differentialist feminist thought, such as Irigaray's and Cixous's, was introduced to Japan, some people argued that there was no need to import it because it already existed in Japan in the form of women's literature from antiquity.

There is a trap in the concept of *écriture feminine* itself, for if we admit the French *écriture* as universal and feminists define it as man-made language, then this automatically leads to the conclusion that women's share is the "residue of the universal"—namely, that it must be characterized by a lack of all reason and logic and must therefore descend to the incomprehensible. *Écriture feminine* can only be defined as what is not man-made language, differentiated from and deviating from the universal language. Here is the significant parallel between the Japanese language and *écriture feminine*. This is not to say that the former resembles the latter; rather, the differentiation of the Japanese language from the Chinese language is parallel to the differentiation of *écriture feminine* from the universal (and, accordingly, masculine) language.

Modernization as Rape and the Defeat in World War II

Colonialist discourse has been familiar to Japan from the earliest stages of its cultural formation. After the Meiji Restoration of 1868, the West replaced China as the universal center. Chino Kaori, an art historian, argued in her 1994 *Nihon bijutsu no jendā* [Gender in Japanese art history] that cultural discourse on Japanese art was reproduced in this colonialist configuration for more than a thousand years. Given this background, it was relatively easy to assimilate a new Western-centered discourse to the previous discourses by substituting the West for China at the center.

The Occident—epitomized by the abrupt visit of Commodore Perry's American ships after three centuries of isolation—used military power to force Japan to open its borders. No doubt remained that the West was dominant in terms of technology and military force.

As in the case of Flaubert, who visited the Orient and later fantasized about it in feminized form through an account of his affair with an Oriental prostitute, Kuchuk Hanem, Pierre Loti wrote an opera, *Mme. Chrysantheme*, feminizing Japan in the guise of his native lover.[12] Though there were in fact some violent reactions by Japanese men, for instance at Namamugi in 1864, in which samurai from Satsuma attacked and killed a British citizen named Richardson, Japanese men have been gradually deprived of their masculinity since the samurai were disarmed.[13]

Sex serves as a path through which men can access "the other" at a deep level. Said, for instance, repeatedly points out the "almost conformist association between the Orient and sex" in European literature.[14] When obtained by force, sex is nothing but rape. At this point we become witnesses to the birth of a cliché in the minds of conservative Japanese intellectuals. In their narrative, modern Japan is symbolized as a poor woman raped by the West. The policy of opening up the country by force and imposing unequal treaties, which favored the West, seems to them comparable to rape.

This rape, the narrative continues, was reproduced in 1945, when Japan lost World War II, with the rapist this time being the United States instead of the European powers. The surrender forced on Japan by the atomic bomb was the "second threat" by the West, while the Constitution imposed by the Occupation Army is held to have colonized the Japanese nation. This logic can be used to justify starting the war with the United States: it is called self-defense, for Japan had no other way to survive. A nationalist intellectual, Hayashi Fusao (1903–1975), wrote a controversial book, *Dai Tōa sensō kōteiron* [In defense of the Great Asia War] (1964), in which "the Great Asia War" is a euphemism for Japan's invasion of Asia carried out by the Japanese Imperial Army during the war. Hayashi insists that European imperialism forced Japan to start the war.

Hasegawa, referring to this book, states that it is necessary "to see correctly the historical fact that the whole of Asia was confronted by a fatal crisis, and consequently Japan coped with this critical moment in a right way."[15] There is nothing new or original in her argument; what is astonishing is that the nationalist discourse, which is almost a cliché and which was once upheld by Hayashi, an old conservative born in 1903, has acquired a new voice in a woman, Hasegawa, born in 1946, after the war.

Hasegawa continues to argue that this rape is being repeated today in the form of "internationalization." She investigates the etymology of the term, originally defined as "to bring a country or territory under the combined government or protection of two or more different nations;" in her paraphrase, it is correctly understood as "to share a territory among imperialist powers."[16] If "internationalization" is rightly understood as being heavily political and referring to power relationships, no one can naively put forward the slogan that we should "internationalize ourselves." This political naiveté, the passive acceptance of Western justice as universal, is exactly what Hasegawa would call "the Chinese mind." The binary opposition between the Chinese mind and the Japanese mind is visible to this day, she would maintain, and this proves the enduring validity of the paradigm put forward by Motōri.

Feminism as the Chinese Mind

In 1984, during the drafting of the Equal Employment Opportunity Law—hastily slapped together in time to meet the requirement to ratify the United Nations Treaty for the Elimination of All Forms of Discrimination Against Women (hereafter the U.N. Treaty for Women), which required that existing domestic laws be fitted to the treaty—a controversial article entitled "The Equal Employment Opportunity Law is Destructive to the Ecology of Japanese Culture" appeared in the mainstream magazine *Chūō Kōron*. The identity the author assumed was simply that of "a housewife and schoolteacher." Opposing the law from the point of view of "a Japanese woman," the paper attracted public attention and caused a great controversy in the same journal. The "housewife and schoolteacher" was later proved to be an associate professor at Saitama University by the name of Hasegawa Michiko.

It seemed to Hasegawa that the Japanese government was forced to ratify the U.N. Treaty for Women unwillingly. Even worse, she saw the drafting of the Equal Employment Opportunity Law as a raped woman demanding more subordination in total ignorance of her own rape. Hasegawa was frustrated, first, with the diffident attitude of the Japanese government toward confronting the forcible "Western powers," and then with Japanese feminists who demanded the ratification of the U.N. Treaty, only to become subject to Western ethnocentrism. To her, this ignorance and naive subjugation to the values of the West was a prime example of "the Chinese mind."

Japanese feminism is often misunderstood as a Western import, and there-

fore no more than another form of Western universalism. I have already analyzed how this misunderstanding was created and whose interests it serves, and
will not go into further detail here.[17] Japanese feminism has its own *raison d'être*,
its own history, and its own voice, and the charge of being an import was created
to attack feminism by reducing it to mere Western influence. What I would like
to highlight here is the reversed gender bias of reversed Orientalism, which
complicates the situation of Japanese feminism considerably.

As I have already argued, Orientalism is gendered. Oriental men are feminized by Orientalism, and Oriental women are doubly feminized. Accordingly,
if a European man is a "real human," then Orientals should be either women
or feminized men. When Oriental women protest against their already feminized men in this doubly colonized situation, they face the frustrating alternative of either being blamed by Oriental men as agents of Western colonialists or
being forced to join the struggle against Western colonialists to build the world
envisioned by their men, which often has patriarchy as an integral part of it. In
such "anticolonialist" struggles, men always exploit women, as is the case with
Islamic fundamentalists who force women to wear veils. In Japan in the 1980s,
this exploitation took the form of a female writer criticizing the Equal Employment Opportunity Law in the name of "the ecology of culture."

In a forcible binary opposition, if you are not on our side, you automatically
become an enemy. There is a fatal oscillation between friends and enemies, and
nothing in between. In this context, the struggle against Oriental men is bene-
ficial to imperialists. It is important, however, to note that, at least in this case, a
double negative does not equate with an affirmative; "a plague on both your
houses" cannot be reduced to a blessing for one of them.

Ivan Illich and the Distortion of Gender

The doubly gendered bias in the relationship of Orientalism with feminism
comes out clearly in the tale of how Ivan Illich was accepted by (male) Japanese intellectuals in the 1980s. Known as a counter-industrial critic, Illich has a
wide influence over intellectuals in the Third World. His writings, such as
Deschooling Society (1971) and *Medical Nemesis* (1976), were widely welcomed
by anticolonial intellectuals in such countries of the margins as Australia and
Mexico, which took his work as theoretical ammunition against Western hegemony.[18] He was also influential among "progressive" male Japanese intellectuals, who were searching for counter-industrial values.

Turning his attention to the gender issue, Illich published a book entitled
Shadow Work in 1981, and a second, *Gender*, in 1982. When translated into

Japanese, both works were welcomed with enthusiasm by male intellectuals, a fact which highlighted the colonization of their minds. Western feminists either ignored Illich's work or severely criticized it. They were perfectly aware that Illich had stolen his ideas from anticolonial feminist thinkers such as Maria Mies and Claudia von Werlhof[19] and transformed them to serve a contradictory purpose.

In *Gender*, Illich creates a strange distinction between sex and gender which is totally alien to the feminist use of these terms. He defines gender as "vernacular gender" and sex as "economic sex"; the former is embedded in the indigenous culture with "ambiguous complementarity," while the latter is imposed by industrial societies on both men and women as no more than a gender role assignment, mainly for economic reasons. He stresses the oppression of the "unprecedented gender apartheid" in industrialized societies but tends to romanticize the harmonious gender complementarity in the "vernacular gender." By using the term "ambiguous complementarity," he implies a general antagonism and potential hostility between the two genders; although it remains clear that, in contrasting industrialized societies and preindustrial societies, he finds more value in the latter.[20]

The term "gender" came into widespread use among Japanese intellectuals through Illich's work. Instead of being of assistance, it put an additional burden on Japanese feminists, who had to replace Illich's biased definition of gender with a more comprehensive feminist one through public discourse.

The twisted alliance of Illich and male Japanese intellectuals who are more or less progressive (in other words, critical of industrialization) clearly explains the dilemma of Japanese feminism. Male intellectuals took advantage of Illich's idea of "vernacular gender" to justify their sexist society and exclude external interference. Look, our gender relationship is harmonious enough for us to complement each other, they said, and we have no desire for interference by Western societies. Moreover, Japanese women have been powerful throughout history. There is no need for them to be more liberated . . . [21]

Hasegawa's argument against the Equal Employment Opportunity Law fits neatly into the general scheme of these gender politics. The U.N. Treaty for Women was regarded as the "third threat" from the West, which thus forced "sexist" Japan to open up to the rest of the world. Illich was invited to be a guest speaker at international conferences and symposiums in Japan. On one such occasion Hasegawa was invited to speak as well and was anointed by Illich as an expert on Japanese gender issues.

When anticolonial discourse takes up gender in its own cultural context, it turns into an oppressive discourse that justifies the sexist status quo. In this context, Japanese feminists were blamed as agents of American imperialism and promoters of industrialism. To be honest, some women did show an uncomfortable degree of "Chinese mind." They tried to increase the external pressure by arguing that Japan was exceptionally backward in women's issues, under the assumption that the Japanese government would never change without interference from the international community.

The Birth of Reverse Orientalism

I have taken this detour to demonstrate that the familiar clichés about the feminine characteristics of Japanese culture are in fact the products of Orientalism. It is impossible to know whether Japanese culture is really "feminine" because that depends on one's definition of masculinity and femininity. Psychological gender scales show that Japanese men are more feminine than French women, but this cannot be taken as conclusive because the gender scales in question are defined in Eurocentric terms, with masculinity including such traits as self-assertiveness and individuality. Hence they produce self-fulfilling prophecies, not objective results. It is, after all, not very surprising to find that a Eurocentric gender scale defines European men as the most masculine.

It is easy enough to see the Occident orientalizing the Orient. The question here is how the orientalization of the Orient by Orientals themselves was constructed, and why. To put it in gendered terms, when the Orient is feminized by the Occident, Oriental men accept this and feminize themselves; thus European Orientalists first feminized Japan, and Japanese intellectuals assimilated this.

The construction of femininity is only possible as a residual category of masculinity. As Said points out, women are nothing but "creatures of a male power-fantasy." Woman is defined by differentiation from the center, which is the male ego, and therefore as a negative mediator of masculine identity. As the Orient is feminized, femininity is defined as inferior. How is it possible for Oriental men to accept this imposed femininity, with its definition of inferiority?

According to Motōri, "the Chinese mind" is the attitude of judging one's own culture from a "universal" point of view. Motōri performed a grand piece of sleight-of-hand in taking advantage of Orientalism to reinforce his cultural identity by contrasting the Japanese mind with the Chinese mind. If you impose your "universalism" on us, he said, we will accept it. We are only the shadow of your civilization, a residue of your universality. However, we belong to another empire, that of particularism, which you can never understand. Our sovereignty can never be interfered with by external powers . . .

This is what I call "reverse Orientalism." Most theories of Japanese particularism can be seen as versions of this. We should note again that it was the European Orientalists who imposed particularity and uniqueness on the Orient in the first place. But reverse Orientalists accepted Europeans' ethnocentric logic, reversed their discourse, and created a counter-discourse following the same logic. Certainly we are unique, reverse Orientalists claimed, and this is exactly where your universalism falls down.

Such clichés as the following are still in circulation: "Foreigners cannot understand the essence of Japanese culture"; "Japanese literature is impossible to translate into foreign languages"; and the like. Though undeniably colonial, such ideas reflect an effort to restore national pride at some level, however humble. In this sense, nationalist discourses lie within the Orientalist perspective and are no more than by-products of Orientalism, despite their self-conscious particularism. Nationalists are, in the literal sense, reactionaries—people who formed themselves in reaction to the Occident. Conservative discourses are destined to be reactionary and therefore to be products of crisis, a fact which inevitably gives them an air of tragic heroism, of comedy, or even of a farce whose action ends up being all in vain.

It is now easy for us to see how reverse Orientalism can appropriate feminized discourse on the Orient. In this context, femininity is nothing but an empty sign that implies no more than "what is not."

Psychoanalysis of the Mother-Dominated Society, Japan

Feminized discourses on Japanese culture and nationhood have been nourished by theories of Japaneseness. The representative arguments in this field are found in Doi Takeo's well-known *Amae no kōzō* [The anatomy of dependence] (1971) and Kawai Hayao's *Bosei shakai Nihon no byōri* [Psychiatry of the mother-dominated society, Japan] (1976). Most of these theories stress the strong emotional ties between mothers and sons in the Japanese household, ties considered unique to Japanese culture.

However, a strong bond between mothers and sons is not necessarily unique to Japanese culture.[22] For example, it is common also in Italian and Jewish families. Moral masochism, which characterizes Japanese mothers, is also found among Jewish mothers. There is nothing unique in the dominance of the mother within the household. Nevertheless, there is one common thing which characterizes all so-called mother-dominated societies: they are very patriarchal. Ironically, patriarchal society seems to place more value on mothers than on fathers. Jewish law defines a child born from the marriage between a Jewish mother and a non-Jewish father as a Jew, whereas a child born to a Jewish father and a non-Jewish mother is not registered as a Jew (as if patrilineality were to be distrusted, since there is always the chance that wives might commit adultery). Apart from the blood relationship, this shows that Jews believe in cultural inheritance through mothers rather than through fathers. And, as this fact highlights, reproduction of the patriarchal system is not possible without the cooperation of women.

Kawai is careful to adopt the term "mother-dominated society" and yet to avoid the concept of matriarchy or matrilineality. Though a matrilineal society is often confused with a matriarchal one, it is in fact totally different. A matrilineal society is a form of patriarchy in which the male bond is based on matrilineal kinship ties rather than patrilineal kinship ties. Regardless of the lineality, matrilineal or patrilineal, power is in the hands of men of the same kinship group. And despite all the myths and fantasies about ancient matriarchal societies, not one has ever been certainly identified by historians.

In patrilineal and patriarchal societies, women can only survive by producing sons, successors to the male line of the household. The most prudent strategy for a woman lies in controlling her sons and becoming the mother of a head-of-household in the next generation. I call this informal power of women behind the scenes "the power of the dowager." Cherishing the expectation of reaching power by becoming the mother of a patriarch in the next generation, women are willing to become accomplices in patriarchy.

In a matrilineal society, where membership in a kinship group and its patrimony is inherited through the matrilineal line, women are more likely to value daughters rather than sons because daughters are more secure members of the community than sons, who will become related to women of other lineages. Thailand is known for its matrilineality and matrilocality, with a succession rule by which the youngest daughter inherits the household of her parents, together with the obligation to take care of them. This matrilineal social structure serves as the basis for a prosperous sex industry and consequently an epidemic of AIDS in rural districts in Thailand, since prostitution is considered no more than a profitable business for women who have the responsibility of supporting their parents. Prostitution is not stigmatized in rural Thailand, and once a former prostitute goes back to her home village with money, she is welcomed as a good member of the community and marries a man in the same village. Thus the tragedy of transmission of AIDS through a mother to a young baby can occur in very remote areas in Thailand.

I bring up the case of Thailand as a matrilineal society in order to contrast it with a mother-dominated society. Mother dominance is by no means an attribute of a matrilineal society but, rather, it is the product of a patriarchal one. Mother dominance reflects the power of a mother in a patrilineal household and has nothing to do with matrilineality, much less with matriarchy. When theorists on Japaneseness, such as Doi and Kawai, argue about the psychological aspects of mother dominance and the overly close relationship between mothers and sons, which can prevent Japanese men from reaching full maturity, they are talking about harmful aspects of Japanese patriarchy, not matriarchy. As Mizuta Noriko accurately points out, "Sons dependent on mothers are no more nor less than the product of patriarchy, not matriarchy."[23]

On Bilineality

Karatani Kōjin, a postmodern literary critic who long refrained from talking about feminism, uses the term "bilineality" instead of the confusing "matrilineality" to refer to Japanese culture and society.[24] He chose this concept in order to reflect the particularity of Japanese culture and differentiate it from Western patriarchy. According to Karatani, Japanese society is unique in that it combines bilineality—the coexistence of patrilineality and matrilineality—with the lack of a well-established patriarchy, unlike Christianized Western societies. Karatani's assumption implies that the enemy of Japanese feminism cannot be a Western type of patriarchy, and that Japanese feminist strategy cannot be the same as feminist strategy in the West.

Generally speaking, Karatani's argument is correct in refuting the universalism of Western feminism. Nevertheless, it runs aground on a particularistic theory of Japanese culture, which essentializes the feminine attribute of Japaneseness.

When Karatani began to talk about gender, he immediately raised the suspicion that he would betray feminists, as had happened so many times before, with Illich and other male thinkers. Dealing with gender issues, so-called progressive intellectuals often unconsciously slip into the masculine mode. Mizuta Noriko has advanced the following explanation of why Karatani kept silent for so long.

> Karatani Kōjin has argued little about gender so far. It seems strange that he does not write about gender, but in fact is not so strange.
>
> In the latter half of the twentieth century, feminism and gender perspectives have made an undeniable contribution to social science, literature and literary criticism, posing fundamental questions that no one can avoid. In this cultural space of discourse, it is certainly mysterious why Karatani, a leading contemporary critic, has shown a lack of interest in gender issues. . . . In the meantime, all the efforts of Western literary theories, such as structuralism, psychoanalysis, deconstruction, semiotics, and new historicism, can be seen as an attempt to answer the question of

gender that was raised by feminism. It is almost impossible for him to exclude himself from this current.

Nevertheless, seen from a different perspective, the absence of gender in his writings is understandable, because all his inquiries concerning "outside," "the other," "singularity," "exclusion," "difference," "communication," and "modernity" include a gendered perspective on a deep level. Since all these themes in his research are inevitably related to gender, which is a central concern of modern thought, he does not have to refer specifically to gender.[25]

But is it really true that Karatani had no need to talk about gender because he had already argued about "the other"? Or was he simply being cautious? For any literary theorist in a North American intellectual community, it would be impossible to avoid the question of gender. Karatani is familiar with the North American literary scene, and Mizuta's description of him seems as much of a challenge as a narrative.

Karatani originally borrowed the term "bilineality" from Takamure Itsue (1894–1964, one of the most important indigenous feminist thinkers in prewar Japan, who gave enthusiastic support to ultranationalism) and her historical study of ancient matrilineality.[26] The concept of bilineality in Takamure is itself controversial, and Karatani's use of this concept has nothing to do with kinship structure. In his writings on Motōri, he calls the mixed use of Japanese and Chinese in one sentence "bilineality." This linguistic mixing finally resolved the bilingual situation, enabling Japanese to assimilate the Chinese language into the Japanese language's own structure, instead of distorting Japanese. Hasegawa argues that this mixed usage of the languages was "a successful trick to avoid the domination of Japanese by Chinese."

Karatani uses "bilineality" as a metaphor in literary criticism. However, his understanding of this concept as a kinship term is incorrect to begin with, and the concept itself is arguable at best, even in its original context. Karatani shows little interest in kinship structure; indeed, he ventures to adopt the term only because he was trying to distinguish patrilineality from bilineality, which he thinks characterizes Japanese culture.

One question remains: why does Karatani propose an idea which fits so well with the theory of Japanese uniqueness and which is, accordingly, easily captured within the framework of American revisionists who blame Japan for cultural conflicts? On top of that, by redefining "bilineality," Karatani implicitly criticizes Japanese feminism as a follower of Western feminism, since the enemy of Japanese feminism cannot be the patriarchy in a Western sense. In making "particular" Japaneseness his enemy, he even becomes patronizing, telling

Japanese feminists "to be first of all modernist" instead of adopting a postmodern strategy. By so doing, he ignores the existing discourses of feminism critical to modernity and reduces feminism itself to mere modernist enlightenment.

Feminization of the Image of the Emperor

The psychology of mother-dependent sons that characterizes Japanese masculinity has become a dominant principle of Japanese society and is symbolized by the feminized figure of the emperor as a mother. In a book on Takamure Itsue, the historian Yamashita Etsuko writes about mother dominance as a symbol of leaderless, "soft" fascism, a ruling system of interdependence in which no one takes responsibility as an individual person.[27] In this context, the Japanese imperial system is interpreted as maternal dominance.

It is doubtful, however, that the emperors have been feminized in imperial discourse throughout the history of modernization. During World War II, in particular, it is difficult to imagine that the figure of Emperor Hirohito, a military dictator, was at all feminized.

The iconography of imperial figures tells us that in the late Edo period the emperor was symbolized in a feminized mode, with cosmetics and darkened teeth like a court lady. He was a powerless center to be fed and served for survival. Moreover, the samurai class feminized aristocrats surrounding the emperor because aristocrats as a class represented cultural sophistication in manners and rituals. After the Meiji Restoration, however, a more masculine visual representation of the emperor was created, in which he dressed in military garb and sported a kaiser mustache. And with the establishment of the "nation-state" ideology before World War II, there was a division of labor between the emperor and the empress. A formulaic photo of the imperial couple, distributed to all primary schools for use in school ceremonies, symbolized them as "a strict father and a nurturing mother." This is evidence that, from 1868 until 1945, the figure of the emperor was carefully kept away from feminized imagery.

The emperor, as the center of the Great Asia Community, had to be represented as masculine. As a military dictator, he symbolized not maternal benevolence but paternal authority to ultranationalists. Mishima Yukio (1925–1970), the postwar nationalist, cultural conservative, and well-known writer who committed suicide in 1970 in the anachronistic samurai fashion, by *hara-kiri*, expressed his resentment toward the late emperor for declaring himself to be no more than a human after Japan's 1945 defeat. When Mishima demanded of the emperor why he had become a human being, resigning from the throne of God, he was definitely seeking a paternal figure, not a maternal one.

It appears to me that the modern emperor has been feminized since the six-tieth anniversary of his reign in 1986. Hasegawa was invited to a celebration organized by the right wing, where she made a speech openly referring to the emperor as the mother of the nation. Coming from a contemporary conservative intellectual, who reproduces the mainstream discourse of nationalism faithfully, it was surprising that her speech did not induce anger among authentic male nationalists.

Since the mid-1970s, it has also become popular to use another metaphor, "an empty center," as a contemporary image for an imperial system lacking all responsibility. This term, once used to berate Japanese ultranationalism, is now applied to explain the secret of the continuing survival of an old-fashioned Asian monarchy in such a highly developed society as Japan. It may be right to call the emperor an empty center if he holds a nominal position as a symbol of the unity of the nation. One prewar political scientist, Minobe Tatsukichi (1873–1948), argued to this effect in his theory of the imperial system as ruling machinery with a double-edged effect—one for the rulers, as an efficient bureaucracy, the other for the ruled, as a dictatorship. But with the growth of ultranationalism, Minobe had to resign his position in the House of Peers because of his theory. No one could correctly call the emperor "an empty center" when he exercised military dictatorship during the war.

The rise of the "empty center" discourse occurred as part of the postwar imperial system, in the context of the prosperity that followed the rapid economic growth of the 1960s, and it coincided with the transformation of the imperial figure from a military leader into a civilian. When he reached his seventies, the late emperor showed himself as a powerless, pacifist, old "grandpa." There was a corresponding rise in discourses that associated supreme nobility with this passive, powerless being who was to be fed and served by the people in exchange for his passion to accept pain for the benefit of the nation. In this context, age was identified with innocence.[28] In 1988, when he was on the brink of death, Emperor Hirohito attracted the attention of young people, who visited the imperial palace to show their empathy for his passion. One young social critic, Otsuka Eiji, observed that high-school girls at the time referred to him as "cute."[29] On his deathbed, a new folktale of the emperor was created: it was reported in a newspaper that this dying old man showed concern for the year's harvest, as if assuming a final responsibility as the highest priest of the agricultural rituals of the imperial court.

In fact, the term "empty center" is not a Japanese invention but was created by a French semiotician, Roland Barthes, who visited Japan in 1970. Based on no more than a three-week stay, he wrote a book that same year, entitled *L'empire des signes*, in which he stated,

The city which I am talking about [Tokyo] represents a precious paradox; a paradox that this metropolis certainly has a center, but an empty center. The entire city is built surrounding this prohibited area, covered with green and protected by a moat, the locus of the imperial palace where the emperor lives without being seen by anyone.[30]

The phrase "empty center" quickly became popular among Japanese intellectuals. First applied to describe the nature of the contemporary emperorship, the metaphor later became ahistorical and was used to symbolize the "essence" of the Japanese imperial system, because it provided a good explanation for the long survival of a system with an emperor in nominal authority. It should be noted, however, that there is no such thing as an ahistorical essence of the imperial system. Historians understand that the rule of the emperor took different forms in different historical contexts; in some cases it was nominal, but in other cases it was not. The newly adopted postmodern term "empty center" successfully conveys the current Japanese emperorship's ahistorical, benign, pacifist, and, accordingly, feminine nature.

Beyond the Transvestite Patriarchy

By now, we have perhaps said enough about the politics of discourse that feminizes Japaneseness. The problem is that "the Japanese mind" as opposed to "the Chinese mind"—and femininity as opposed to masculinity—are asymmetrical dualisms created and deployed by men. Better still, we can call them male discourses in a colonized situation. According to Motōri, femininity is a way of thinking and acting, a cultural attribute that can be adopted by men as well. His concept of masculinity and femininity is close to the culturally constructed concept of gender; for him, anatomy is not destiny, for men can cross the border of gender by using feminine language. This tradition of men as "transvestite" writers started back in the thirteenth century, when the aristocrat Kino Tsurayuki wrote down his personal memories of a trip in *kanamoji*, the "feminine" Japanese script used only by women of the time. In the guise of a woman writer, he began his story with the following sentence: "I will try to write a journal, as men do."

This is why I am tempted to call Japanese patriarchy "transvestite patriarchy." Even when it cloaks itself in femininity, patriarchy is patriarchy. It can never be matrilineal or matriarchal. Even worse, this female disguise makes women's situation more complicated and the struggle against patriarchy more difficult.

Is transvestite patriarchy unique to Japan? It seems to me an inevitable path for colonized male discourse to take. In transvestite patriarchy, women are doubly marginalized. In the forced alternatives of either masculine or feminine, in the frustrating oscillation between men and women dictated by gender dualism, any counter-discourse of woman against transvestite patriarchy becomes, in turn, "masculine." In just this way, in the recent past, feminized Japan exercised masculine power over its colonies such as Korea and Taiwan. We ourselves can hardly expect to avoid this trap in the future, unless we can refuse the forced alternative dictated by binary constructions and insist on a future that we ourselves define, rather than a "reactionary" mirror image of that which we are resisting.

Notes

Ueno Chizuko, "Orientarizumu to jendā" [Orientalism and gender], in *Bosei fashizumu* [Maternalist fascism], vol. 6 of *New Feminism Review*, ed. Kanō Mikiyo et al. (Tokyo: Gakuyō Shobō, 1995), pp. 108–131. This essay first appeared in English in *U.S.-Japan Women's Journal*, English supplement, no. 13 (1997), pp. 3–25, and is reprinted here (with several minor changes) with the kind permission of the author and journal.

1. Edward Said, *Orientalism* (New York: George Borchardt, 1978), p. 207.
2. Ibid., p. 206.
3. Ibid., p. 12.
4. Toni Morrison, *Playing in the Dark: Whiteness and the Literary Imagination* (New York: Vintage Books, 1993); trans. Taisha Yoshiko, *Shirosa to sōzōryoku* (Tokyo: Asahi Shinbunsha, 1994), pp. 76–77.
5. According to its distance from the European world, "the East" is divided into different categories, such as the Near East, the Middle East and the Far East. There is a real irony in the use of "the Orient" by Japanese. Prince Mikasanomiya, a younger brother of the late Emperor Hirohito and supposedly a pacifist who tried to stay away from politics, was involved in archeology. He founded the Japanese Society of Oriental Studies—meaning study of the Near and Middle East. Thus while Japanese do not care to call Japan "the Far East," it is clear that they view "the Orient" through Western eyes and therefore assume that they themselves do not belong to it.
6. This binary opposition, founded basically on the one between nature and culture, comes from the structuralist paradigm of Lévi-Strauss, which was later criticized by feminist anthropologists such as Sherry Ortner, Michelle Rosaldo, and others. See here *Woman, Culture, and Society*, ed. Michelle Rosaldo and Louise Lamphere (Stanford: Stanford University Press, 1974).
7. It might be confusing to call premodern Japanese intellectuals bilingual in a literal sense, because what they actually did was create a way of reading Chinese in

accordance with Japanese grammatical structure. Their knowledge of the Chinese language was limited mainly to its written form, and they preserved the old pronunciation of Chinese characters from the Tang dynasty (618–907). Though they did not speak or comprehend contemporary Chinese, Japanese intellectuals could always read and understand written Chinese, even as its pronunciation changed throughout history.

8. In the sixteenth century, when "barbarians from the south" (i.e., Europeans) arrived in China, took over a couple of cities in coastal areas, such as Amoy, and set up their first colonies, the Chinese government of the time found it difficult to admit that there was another spot on Earth that was on the same footing as they themselves were and that had to be dealt with as an equal. In their view, China was simply the world itself; they could not accept any heterogeneity in their space.

9. Motōri Norinaga, "Tamakatsuma," in *Motōri Norinaga zenshū* [Collected works of Motōri Norinaga] (Tokyo: Chikuma Shobō, 1968), vol. 1, p.48.

10. Ibid.

11. Hasegawa Michiko. *Karagokoro* [The Chinese mind] (Tokyo: Chūō Kōronsha, 1986), p. 24.

12. Though Loti wrote the original story of *Mme. Chrysantheme* with a happy ending, Puccini's popularized version in the form of an opera, *Madama Butterfly*, converted it into a tragedy by romanticizing Japan in the guise of an unhappy woman lover.

13. Namamugi is the name of a place near Yokohama where British soldiers landed. A group of exclusionist samurai attacked and killed one of them. Fearing possible international conflict, the Japanese government sentenced them to death by *hara-kiri*, which was performed in front of Western representatives.

14. Said, *Orientalism*, passim.

15. Hasegawa, *Karagokoro*, p. 156.

16. Ibid., p. 177.

17. Ueno Chizuko, "Nihon no ribu to feminizumu" [Japanese women's lib and feminism], introduction to *Ribu to feminizumu* [Women's lib and feminism], in *Feminism in Japan*, ed. Ueno Chizuko et al. (Tokyo: Iwanami Shoten, 1994), vol. 1.

18. Ivan Illich founded an institute in Cuernavaca, Mexico, and some of his works were translated into Spanish before they appeared in English.

19. See here Maria Mies, Veronika Bennholdt-Thomsen and Claudia von Werlhof, *Women, the Last Colony* (London: Zed Books, 1988).

20. See here my *Onna wa sekai wo sukueruka?* [Can women save the world?] (Tokyo: Keisō Shobō, 1985).

21. The Illichian school of social critique in Japan published a series of books on "vernacular gender," in one of which they invited a woman philosopher, Kawano Nobuko, to discuss the "harmonious complementarity of vernacular gender" in premodern Japan. See Kawano's "Rōdō kara mita jendā" [Gender in the perspective of labor], in *Sei, rōdō, kōnin no funryū* [Outburst of sex, labor and marriage],

ed. Yamamoto Tetsuji and Kabayama Kōichi, vol. 6 in *Series: Unplugging* (Tokyo: Shinhyōron, 1984).

22. Mother-dominance in the household is not only not unique to Japanese culture but also historical. I have argued elsewhere about the particular historical nature of mother-son ties as a modern product in Japan. See "The Collapse of 'Japanese Mothers,'" *U.S.-Japan Women's Journal*, English supplement, no. 10 (1996), pp. 3–19.

23. Mizuta Noriko et al., "Nihon bunka to jendā" [Japanese culture and gender], in *Hihyō Kūkan* [Critical space] (Tokyo: Ōta Shuppan, 1994), II-3, p. 25.

24. See Karatani's "Sōkeisei wo megutte" [On bilineality], in *Senzen no shikō* [Pre-war thinking] (Tokyo: Bungei Shunjūsha); and also Ayako Kano, "Japanese Theater and Imperialism: Romance and Resistance," *U.S.-Japan Women's Journal*, English supplement, no. 12 (1997), pp. 17–47.

   Kano referred to my original Japanese paper on reverse Orientalism, and made some critical comments which came earlier than this English version. It gives me an opportunity to respond to her. She makes two points: First, though I criticized Karatani's misunderstanding of an anthropological kinship term, bilineality, it does not work on him, as he uses the concept in a totally different way. What is to be criticized is his ahistorical essentialism on Japanese culture. Second, by attributing the femininity and semicolonized situation to Japan throughout history, I, too, end up constructing ahistorical essentialism. Concerning Kano's first point, at the roundtable discussion she referred to, I made both these points. While Karatani admitted my first point on his misuse of the technical concept of bilineality, he stuck to his idea of Japanese singularity of cultural experience. As regards Kano's second point, she is right that I was trapped by transhistorical cultural essentialism, though it was the very target I was attacking. Motōri revived the ancient chronicles and the classic literary texts so as to construct the transhistorical Japaneseness. This is exactly why nativist thinkers repeatedly come back to Motōri's texts. I could add two supplementary points to avoid misunderstanding. First, the construction of Japaneseness by Motōri is fictitious, or at least discursively performative; in addition, the formation of Japan itself is highly controversial. Second, there were actually historical moments when Japan took a masculine guise facing the other. Gendered Orientalism takes various forms in specific historical contexts, to which we should be attentive.

25. Mizuta Noriko, "Jendā no metafoa to hihyō no gengo" [Metaphor of gender and a critical language] *Gunzō* [Art group], Special Issue: "Karatani Kōjin to Takahashi Genichirō" [Karatani Kōjin and Takahashi Genichirō] (Tokyo: Kōdansha, 1992), 171–172.

26. Takamure Itsue, "Bokeisei no kenkyū" [Studies on matrilineality], in *Takamure Itsue zenshū* [Collected works of Takamure Itsue] (Tokyo: Rironsha, 1966). First published in 1938. See also Nishikawa Yūko, "Japan's Entry into War and the Support for Women," *U.S.-Japan Women's Journal*, English supplement, no. 12 (1997), pp. 48–83.

27. Yamashita Etsuko, *Takamure Itsue ron* [A critique of Takamure Itsue] (Tokyo: Kawade Shobō Shinsha, 1988), p. 237.

28. Kamata Tōji, a folklorist in religious studies, wrote a book entitled *Ōdōron* [On the aged and the young] (Tokyo: Shinyōsha, 1988), in which he traced the history of folk discourses that associate old age with innocence. In medieval Noh plays, the part of the emperor was always performed by a child actor.

29. Otsuka Eiji, "Shōjotachi no kawaii tennō" [A "cute" emperor for young girls], in *Chūō Kōron* (Tokyo: Chūō Kōronsha), December 1988.

30. Roland Barthes, *L'empire des signes* (Genève: Éditions d'art A. Skira, 1970), p. 43.

COLLAPSE OF "JAPANESE MOTHERS"

Introduction

In writing about "Japanese Mothers"—an expression that is all too often written with a capital *M*—we must begin by tentatively acknowledging their existence rather than by baldly declaring their disappearance. This paper will thus straddle the two realms of presence and absence, keeping a foot on either shore. Instead of a static group of "Mothers," timelessly present or absent, I will discuss the historical transformation of the concept of "Mothers," and the social context of that transformation.

Absence is a tempting and tenable position to take on the "Mothers" question, since the word implies a cultural representation rather than a clearly defined subgroup of actual women. "Mothers" with an uppercase *M* does not equate with "mothers" with a lower-case *m*. No person is born a mother, or even born to be a capital-*M* "Mother;" it is a role that is learned and then internalized in the process of gender socialization. Not all women give birth, so women have no absolute natural destiny to become mothers. Even the details of mothering remain undetermined, controlled neither by anatomy nor by instinct, because the experience of mothering varies widely through time and space as well as among individual women. Simplistic and reductionist theories such as sociobiology are helpless to explain this diversity and fail on many other points as well, such as the hatred a woman may feel for her children, an emotion clearly disallowed by any theory of "selfish genes." If the goal of the genes is to survive by taking an individual body merely as a vehicle, as Richard Dawkins tells in his well-known theory on "selfish genes," self-sacrifice of mothers to give a longer survival to their children, i.e., their genes, can nicely fit in his theory, and therefore reinforces the conventional stereotype of a self-sacrificing mother. In reality, however, the lived experience of motherhood includes the ambivalence of both love and hate, and women are about to break the silence imposed by "sacred motherhood" to tell of their own child-hatred and child-abuse.[1] It is not a sociobiological fate, or a predesigned control by genes, but a social norm that prohibits them from admitting the negative feeling of mothers toward children.

With no capital-M "Mothers" hardwired into human nature, transcending time and space, might we at least isolate a less universal instance—the "Mothers" specific to a particular culture? At first sight this is tempting, but it is a temptation that should be resisted. The "culture" of this approach is all too often ahistorical, exerting a deterministic force over all within its sway. Convention rather than anatomy then becomes destiny; but we are still dealing with an immutable and metaphysical force, albeit one that is more modest in scope.

Contemporary cultural criticism has carefully deconstructed the notion of "culture" itself: how it is formed, what it implies, how it affects people, what results from it—and, in particular, who operates it and who benefits from it. Only after construction of the notion of "culture" in the universe of discourse can we begin to ask questions about something called "cultural identity." Unlike the "collective gene"—or the "collective unconscious," as a Jungian might put it—"culture" is a historical product subject to constant historical change.

Historical studies on gender and sexuality have challenged even ties that seem irrevocably grounded in biological reality, such as mother-child and gender relationships, pointing out that these have undergone constant historical change and differ according to class, ethnic group, and region. Scholars of women's studies have also challenged any universal notion of motherhood defined as self-sacrifice and dedication. A French social historian, Elizabeth Badinter, has demonstrated that the intimate tie between mother and child was established only after the formation of the strongly child-centered family.[2] Seen in this new light, medieval historiography constantly testifies to the relative indifference of mothers to their children. Mothers rarely breast-fed their babies and were willing to send them to foster parents in rural villages. The mortality rate was high due to malnutrition and poor treatment, but parents cared little whether babies survived. The later decline in infant mortality, which is often attributed simply to improvement in physical circumstances, was also caused by mothers' increased care of and attention to their children.[3] Breast-feeding is now the norm for modern mothers, though it used to be regarded as a humble job for nannies and poor women.

Here I argue that motherhood is neither nature nor culture but rather a historical construct. I support this assertion by tracing the representation of "Mothers" in modern Japanese literature. The concept of "Mothers" is not an endowment from biology or fate. It came into existence during some period of the past and is thus in no sense necessary, a fact that cultural ideology tries to mask with its repression of all questions of historical origin. Despite its carefully cultivated ahistorical air and aura of being a mythical archetype or collective gene, the category of "Mothers" is a manufactured one that can be discontinued at any time. This paper concerns the market for this cultural product, and whether the concept of "Mothers" will enjoy the same consumer acceptance in the future as it has in the past.

The History of a Cultural Archetype

In *Seijuku to sōshitsu: haha no hōkai* [Maturity and loss: Collapse of "mothers"], first published in 1967, the well-known literary critic Etō Jun cites an episode from a contemporary writer, Yasuoka Shōtarō.[4] It is from Yasuoka's 1959 novel *Umibe no kōkei* [Scenes by the seashore], which consists of the childhood memories of a male protagonist, Shintarō, who is identified with the author himself. Shintarō's mother would sing a lullaby:

> Too young to know sin,
> Do you remember childhood,
> When your mom took care of you in her hand?
> Like spring rain and autumn dew,
> With tears in her eyes,
> You do not know your mom prays for you forever.

Shintarō goes on to reflect on his reaction to his mother's song:

> His mother was good at singing. . . . The song was a sort of theme song for her. She sang it again and again, until it became an unconscious habit for her. Shintarō, though, felt that the song was too insistent to move him with her feelings. Her pressure made him wonder, "Who am I as a son to this mother?"[5]

One reason Shintarō's mother becomes so attached to him is that she is not satisfied with her husband. He is a military officer, but Shintarō's mother is ashamed of his relatively low status. The close mother-son bond thus excludes the father, who is described as "shameful." Shintarō shares his mother's feelings of shame toward his father, sympathizing with her miserable life. His mother keeps telling Shintarō not to be like his father, which would be the greatest disappointment she could suffer. But who could satisfy her and meet all her demands, apart from a perfect hero of fantasy? When your life is in the hands of your husband, it becomes difficult to be satisfied with him in terms of emotion, affection, status, wealth, and even personality. Too much is at stake to consent to any departure from the ideal.

Etō points out that a sense of shame and frustration toward husbands did not exist in premodern society, where women were required to raise children to be similar to their fathers. Confined by the feudal class structure, a person born into the peasant class had no alternative but to remain there. Modernization, however, has given people the "equal opportunity" fantasy of climbing the social ladder through education, thus creating a sense of shame in those who fail to climb in society.[6]

Out of this sense of shame and frustration, Shintarō's mother tries to make an ally of her son and thus compensate for the disappointment of her life:

> The shame she feels about her husband is experienced as her own shame, as she is responsible for this wrong choice, or was fated to marry him. Though she invests a great deal of expectation in her son, the very fact that he is the son of this shameful man threatens her with future betrayal and disappointment. Even if she is fortunate enough to have a son with great attainments, unlike his father, that son will be destined to rise into another world, leaving the culture that he and his mother belonged to. Her achievement, which is embodied by the future of her son, results in her abandonment by her son, leaving her alone in the old world.[7]

Etō notes that this phenomenon is peculiarly modern and did not exist in a society of fixed classes.

Current social history of mothering has revealed a totally different view of motherhood, and has thus historicized the cultural concept of "Japanese Mothers." Mothering varied with class. Biological motherhood was the norm for upper-class women, but they were not expected to raise children by themselves. Such humble jobs as breast-feeding and washing diapers were undertaken by nannies and maids. Among lower-class women, who were mainly villagers, women of reproductive age were more producers than reproducers. Because their labor was in high demand for farming, they were not allowed to devote themselves to child rearing. In an extended household, grandparents, less productive in their old age, tended to take care of young children; otherwise, children were generally neglected while their parents were working in the fields.

Most different of all is the fact that child care required much less care and skill than it does in contemporary society. For one thing, the period of socialization was relatively short. At the age of seven, children were considered useful sources of labor: if not employed in their own households, they were sent to wealthier homes by their parents as maids or manservants, or even sold into prostitution. Second, communal motherhood and shared responsibility eased the workload of mothers, especially those who were inexperienced. Third, a high fertility rate allowed women to take advantage of their older children, usually the girls, to oversee younger brothers and sisters. Sometimes, the greater the number of children, the easier the task was for the mother. This helps to explain parents' opposition to compulsory education at the beginning of the Meiji period, for it took children away from home, thus increasing the amount of work the women themselves had to do.[8]

The construction of a new idea of motherhood took place in the Meiji period as part of the process of modernization. A young woman historian, Koyama Shizuko, has demonstrated that the concept of "mothers who educate" did not exist before this time.[9] Her careful investigation of Tokugawa Confucian texts shows that their authors did not consider education a maternal duty. On the contrary, the role of women was restricted to the mere provision of biological life; it was assumed that they were too stupid to impart anything more abstract to their offspring. Koyama discovered that Confucian ideology was itself "modernized" during modernization: the demand for a "wise mother" was added in defense of women's education at a time when it was under attack from nationalist reactionaries. Thus the slogan "A good wife and wise mother" was in fact not oppressive but progressive in its contemporary historical context.

The Making of the Modern Japanese Family

Ironically, Etō describes the cultural archetype of Japanese "Mothers" in Yasuoka Shōtarō's novel only to show how it goes into decline: Shintarō, the spoiled son, has strong ties with his mother and shares her shame over his father, identifying himself with her. At the same time, he is the object of the shame directed toward his father, since he is, after all, his father's son. It is very unlikely that he will do better in life than his father has, and Shintarō is aware of his limits, if nothing else. Precisely because his father has disappointed his mother, Shintarō is fated to disappoint her again. Hence he blames himself and at this point identifies with his father, becoming a timid son. His sense of powerless-

ness and helplessness makes him want to stay under the control of his mother—
or, rather, indulge himself in dependency on her—which satisfies his mother's
hidden agenda of keeping him under her control. Here mother and son are in
a secret alliance that excludes the father. Since the father is in any case psychologically absent, Shintarō, a Japanese Oedipus, is free from the threat of castration. He can rest comfortably in his intimate ties with his mother, which might
be called *amae* or, in a more modern, English term, codependency.[10]

The Japanese Oedipal triangle in the modern family, therefore, consists of a
disappointing father, a frustrated mother, and a weak-willed son. Up to this point
the Japanese version of modern family romance is nicely described by Etō.
However, since he does not provide the female counterpart to the Oedipal story,
let us look at such a family from the perspective of a daughter: while the mother
establishes a close relationship with her son with the expectation that he will
compensate her in the future for her disappointment in her husband, she is
rather indifferent to any daughters, assuming that they will not marry out. A
daughter thus shares with her brother the shame directed toward the father,
although, as a woman, she does not have to identify herself with him; nor does
she identify with her mother, who provides her with nothing but a role model
of angst and despair. Unlike her brother, however, she does not have even a theoretical chance of taking control of her own life. Whether or not she can escape
from her mother's fate depends on her future husband, whose personality and
attributes are largely beyond her control, as her mother's case demonstrates. Her
future is uncertain, with no promises or guarantees. Thus the Japanese Electra
becomes an irritating daughter, self-centered and present-oriented. With no
sympathy for her father or mother, and no responsibility to help right the wrongs
of their lives, the daughter becomes the most scathingly critical member of the
family.

Kojima Nobuo's well-known novel, *Hōyō kazoku* [Embracing family] (1965),
gives an exact depiction of this Japanese version of the modern family. Etō's *Seijuku to sōshitsu* provided a powerful reading of this text, which helped make it
a milestone in postwar Japanese literature. While most literary critics were
embarrassed and frustrated by Shunsuke, the antihero who tries to repair the
damage to his family and fails every time, Etō was among the few who reacted
positively to the book, which he believed succeeded in portraying the postwar
Japanese family in the process of dissolving.

In Kojima's novel, Shunsuke's family consists of a typical couple—a disappointing husband and a frustrated wife—and their insecure children. The marriage of Shunsuke and his wife, Tokiko, based on "love," is the postwar product
of a relatively egalitarian society, and they at least try to live a modern family life.
Mutual failures of communication and self-centeredness between husband and

wife are well described in a style that borders on caricature, yet these are universal traits of the modern family. Once conventional roles have been banished from the household, its members face harsh realities, only to find that the persons at their side are unknown to each other.

Shunsuke is obsessed by the idea of maintaining an ideal modern family, but behind this obsession is his desire to establish an ultimate shelter for himself, with his wife as its guardian. As long as Tokiko plays the role of *shufu*, more appropriately translated as "head of the house" rather than "housewife,"[11] and provides her husband with attention, care, and a sense of security, Shunsuke's family remains peaceful. But this peace is bought at the cost of a steadily building resentment and regret on the part of Tokiko as she plays the role of the "Mother." The peace is finally broken when Tokiko reaches the limits of her toleration and commits adultery with a young American soldier, George. Even after the truth comes out, Tokiko blames her husband, who, she claims, is responsible for causing this accident. Shunsuke, who has been trying to play the role of a family patriarch, fails ridiculously at this crisis. Afraid of losing Tokiko and, accordingly, his family, he can do nothing but helplessly tolerate her behavior. Here he acts not as a responsible, mature, adult male, but as a weak-willed son afraid of being deprived of his sanctuary. His powerlessness is thrown into sharp focus by the answer of George, his wife's lover, when asked whether *he* feels responsible: "Responsible for whom? All I feel responsible for are my parents and my country. Nothing else."[12] The irony is palpable: a young American solider from the land of individualism, and an adulterer to boot, is brought in to articulate a transcendent moral, the ideal of a father, which postwar Japan has lost.

Unlike Shintarō's mother in Yasuoka's story, Shunsuke's wife in Kojima's story no longer accepts and endures the prescribed role of motherhood. Though the closeness of the mother-son relationship is more or less a modern product, modern motherhood takes an ambiguous form. While Shintarō's mother epitomizes the "accepting mother," Shunsuke's wife represents the "rejecting mother." Shintarō's mother takes her tie with her son as fated, whereas Tokiko's link with Shunsuke is relative and unfixed, since "love" marriages are based on choice. Tokiko will not endure her frustrations forever; she tries to compensate for the inadequacies of her life through her own actions. Nevertheless, since she cannot take responsibility for her own life, she still needs someone to blame things on.

The ambiguity of the "accepting mother" and the "rejecting mother" lives within the same woman. Motherhood has become conditional, depending on what the mother's children achieve. Etō highlights the obsessive motherhood of Shintarō's mother, who would accept her son even should he become a criminal, only to emphasize the fact that it no longer exists. His intention is to show that this unconditional trust toward a mother, or perhaps better, this form of culturally constructed motherhood, has been lost forever.

Women and Internalized Misogyny

According to Etō, the loss of the concept of the unconditionally "accepting mother" is the result of women's internalization of industrialism. As a literary critic and sensitive observer, Etō does not idealize women or femininity, nor does he set women outside the historical process of modernization. As with all historical processes, men and women were both involved in modernization, although gender differences imposed different forms on the two groups. Women's desire to "catch up" with modernization is epitomized by Tokiko's hidden desire to catch up with her husband, the cause of her frustration. To her, modern life and the modern world remain a bright, glittering ideal. Since the United States symbolizes this "modern world," Tokiko will never be truly able to tolerate her husband, for when he had a chance to study abroad, he went there by himself, leaving her and their children at home. Her revenge is adultery, an act by which she takes America into her "womb" in lieu of her missed chance to penetrate its territory. Despite Shunsuke's hidden desire to have Tokiko play the role of the "accepting mother," Tokiko can no longer accept the acceptance demanded of her:

> Behind the hidden rivalry of Tokiko with her husband (itself the outcome of the co-education which American occupation policy brought to Japan) lies her subconscious desire to catch up with men. She wishes for freedom and independence, as her husband enjoys them. In turn, her envy and resentment toward her husband result in her self-humiliation. . . . In other words, she has internalized misogyny, a low self-evaluation as a mother and wife.
>
> It might be considered overly generalized if I should insist that this is the deepest sentiment imposed on women by industrial society. In a sense, however, this misogyny, internalized in women's psyches, might be universal in every modern industrial society.[13]

Nature is destroyed in the process of industrialization, and as a result women have to root out their "motherhood" as the price of participation in modern society. Women's "nature" cannot be the one sacrosanct area in the midst of this disintegration, despite men's self-centered fantasy of preserving such a shelter for themselves. Women are not just passive victims of man-made illusions but active accomplices who work together with men to promote historical processes.

Industrialization allocated to women the status of "nature" as opposed to "culture." Note that this "nature" is constructed by "culture" as its residual category. The only way women can survive in industrialized society is either (1) to accept their status as second-class citizens, or (2) to internalize misogyny, viewing themselves from an adopted male perspective. To make matters worse, women who do succeed in this internalization are defined as "neurotic" because they fail to accept their femininity. Freud said that women who "wanted to be like men" suffered from "penis envy." To a psychoanalyst, the cure is defined as inducing a female client with this mental disorder to return to where she belongs so that she can accept her predetermined inferiority. The "neurotic" woman, who by definition is already castrated by the culture, must thus castrate herself again under his guidance so as to enjoy "the happiness of the slave." Freudian theory is nothing but a product of modern family romance, and this is why it has become so expert at explaining women's misogyny as a form of "neurosis." But it cannot pretend to be a universal interpretation because both Freudian theory and its romantic roots are themselves products of the modern era.[14]

Japanese Motherhood and the Ajase Complex

One of the earliest Japanese students of Freud, Furusawa Heisaku, asserted that the Oedipal complex could not be universal and proposed an alternative model, which he called the "Ajase complex," as early as the 1930s.[15] The term is borrowed from ancient Buddhist legends. Ajase was the name of an arrogant tyrant in the time of the Buddha. Like Oedipus, he killed his father and usurped the throne. He put his mother in jail and did not feed her well, since she persisted in remonstrating with him about his evil deeds. She suffered from the deeds of her son but considered them something she herself should feel guilty about. When Ajase found his mother tormenting herself with blame, he came to realize what he had done to her. By identifying himself with his mother, though not with his father, he became mature and responsible. Thus the tale of Ajase provides a model of growth by which an immature son can become an adult man.

Furusawa developed this concept in response to his doubts about classical Freudian theory, according to which the initial pre-Oedipal stage of close relationship between a mother and son is obstructed by a third person, the father. As the legitimate possessor of his wife's sexuality, the father does not tolerate his son's incestuous desires, and threatens him with the possibility of castration. Unable to compete with his grown father, the son represses his desire for the mother (which forms his subconscious) and identifies with his father (or phallic symbol, in Lacanian terms) hoping to get a substitute for the mother in the future. In the process of growth, the son successfully internalizes his father's prohibition and establishes a phallic order that forms his "superego." The problem lies in trying to apply this model to the Japanese situation, with its absence of strong, potentially castrating father figures. To do so seems to predict that the son will fail to develop a superego, and will thus be doomed to immaturity and moral weakness.

Furusawa's theory of the "Ajase complex" is an attempt to show how, without the interference of their fathers, Japanese men can grow morally in relation to their mothers. As "accepting mothers," Japanese mothers tolerate anything evil you have done and suffer for your deeds. If you do not succeed in life, it is your mother who is blamed and tortured by your father for her failure. She demonstrates her pain, and her endurance of it, before your eyes. In this process you internalize your mother's, rather than your father's, discipline, which eventually gives rise to the Japanese counterpart of a superego. Furusawa was trying to explain how the Japanese could be as ethical as Westerners, even though the process of psychological development varied with cultures.

Furusawa's theory seems to work well in the case of the relationship between Shintarō and his mother. However, a self-made film critic by the name of Satō Tadao questioned the continuing validity of this model, based on his observations of the contemporary TV dramas of the 1960s and 1970s.[16] He observed the historical transformation of women, who in larger and larger numbers were declining the role of self-sacrificing mother. Japan had passed into the age of Shunsuke and Tokiko, with women more self-centered, seeking their own benefit and comfort. In common with Etō, Satō declared this historical process irreversible and irresistible.

It might seem easy to blame women for their lack of morality and responsibility, but men are not qualified to do the blaming, because they have abandoned their responsibility by their absence. In *Katei no yomigaeri no tame ni: Hōmu dorama ron* [For the revival of the family: On home dramas], Satō asks what will happen to Japan in the future if the nation loses the moral foundation of self-sacrificing mothers. Whatever the answer to that question, by the end of the 1960s the process of change had relegated Furusawa's theory of the Ajase complex to the status of a historical footnote.

Alternate View on Amae: A Cultural Critique

In August 1993, the University of British Columbia held a conference on *amae* in modern Japanese literature with the participation of the well-known psychiatrist, Doi Takeo, who proposed the idea of *amae*, or codependence, as the key to understanding Japanese culture. At that conference Tsuruta Kinya made an important comment that was either neglected or ignored, though it touched on a point both important and, in retrospect, obvious: though *amae* is understood as mutual codependence, no one has ever theorized about it from the side of the supplier of *amae*. *Amae* has always been analyzed from the standpoint of the person who receives tolerance, generosity, and self-sacrifice from the other party. As long as this emotional supply is maintained, the person who receives it can keep his or her "sweet" relationship, and it is easy to imagine that loss of the source of its supply will be a painful experience. But how does this relationship look to the other party, whose participation and cooperation are essential? Is it such a "sweet" experience to be emotionally exploited, to give endless forgiveness and tolerance on demand? Upon examination, this seemingly mutual codependence is revealed to be one-sided. This is particularly significant because the asymmetrical relationship of codependence often involves questions of gender relations.

We can get an idea of the answer to these questions by looking at recent studies of pathological codependence. Amy Borovoy, a young anthropologist, conducted a survey among wives of alcoholic men in Japan.[17] Alcoholism is known to be a mental disorder, and being the wife of an alcoholic is also considered a mental disorder. Alcoholism is an addiction, like other drug addictions, driven by feelings of insecurity and an identity crisis. Wife-of-an-alcoholic-man syndrome, as it is called, is also a kind of addiction, an addiction to the sense of being needed and depended on, again based on insecurity and an identity crisis. Between the two there is thus a perfect match between the depending and the depended-on. This forms a vicious cycle in which both parties are trapped; although a form of "codependency," the relationship is hardly mutual because the roles cannot be reversed. There are alcoholic women, but the husband-of-an-alcoholic woman syndrome is virtually unknown. Women's alcoholism tends to lead to family disintegration and divorce because there are few men who will stay in such a marriage.

Just as alcoholic men have formed a mutual-assistance group named Alcoholics Anonymous, so their wives have formed a similar group for mutual support. Since violence often goes with alcoholism, they often get beaten by their husbands, sometimes beaten to death. Despite repeated violence they rarely run away; when they do they usually come back home, by choice, not force, remaining in the vicious cycle. These women are aware of their problem and their need for help, yet they cannot help themselves.

Based on her survey and participant observation of the support group, Borovoy found a continuity between ordinary women and the wives of alcoholics. This is hardly to be wondered at, since the wives themselves are ordinary women, not alcoholics. They tend to play the role of the cultural ideal of "wife" to an extreme, and end up becoming addicted to being depended on. Borovoy named this cultural ideal *sewa nyōbō* (the caring wife) — a wife who assumes the role of a mother and provides limitless care, attention, generosity, tolerance, and forgiveness. These wives need to keep someone dependent on them and, because dependency is the key source of their identity, they are inclined to work against the other party becoming independent. This is similar to the overprotection of children by Japanese mothers, which ends up spoiling children and making them more arrogant and self-centered.

Borovoy sees the cultural ideal of *sewa nyōbō* as a means to exploit female identity and sexuality. Because a nature of caring and nurturing is so deeply embedded in feminine identity, such a woman's greatest fear is being deprived of someone to take care of. Needless to say, this "nature" is not a nature these women were born with, but one that has been constructed by "culture."

Feminism and Transvestite Patriarchy

It was not until 1970, with the rise of the so-called second-wave feminism, or Women's Liberation, in Japan, that women began to question the dilemma generated by the acceptance of low self-evaluation and self-internalized misogyny. Japanese feminism rejects this dilemma, not motherhood *per se*, focusing not on women but on man-made society, that is, patriarchy. It is patriarchy that has created this dilemma in which some women oppress others, thus acting as agents of patriarchy themselves:

> Japan is often described by the cliché "mother-dominated society." This in turn is often misunderstood as indicating matriarchy. However, we have little if any firm evidence in the past, let alone the present. Matriarchy is a red herring: "mother dominance" in Japanese society must be seen as an aspect of patriarchy, in which the "Mothers" represent male fantasies and re-present patriarchal thought. It is these "Mothers" who teach their sons to reproduce patriarchy in the next generation. "Transvestite patriarchy" might be the best name for it: male dominance hiding behind the skirts of the "Mothers." It is a form of male dominance which

keeps its female agents, the "Mothers," between itself and its victims, so that these "Mothers" can absorb the resentment of their sons and the aggression of their daughters. Since it is able to deflect hostility from itself to its female agents, "transvestite patriarchy" is more difficult to identify and overcome than more direct versions of male dominance.[18]

Feminism has challenged Freudian theory, since the only alternative to such a challenge is to accept meekly the status of a second-class citizen. To be sure, feminist psychoanalysts such as Julia Kristeva have tried to create a female version of psychological development that would be less oppressive. In this they have partially succeeded, but their perspective has remained limited to that of the daughter, while that of the mother has been consistently neglected. For example, Kristeva, who is a mother herself, proposed an idea of "abjection," through which a child sees her mother in the confrontations that are a part of the process of development. This is fine enough from the perspective of the child, but what mother would be comfortable with "abjection," if she were aware that she was being cast in such a negative light?

Sons and Daughters of the Japanese Modern Family

As long as the cultural ideal of "Japanese Mother" is successfully reproduced, the theory of *amae* can survive. But I am tempted to predict that this part of Japanese culture is facing a reproductive crisis and a barren future.

As a distinctive literary critic, Etō has the sensitivity to select the works that mark major turning points in cultural history. Among them have been controversial texts such as Murakami Ryū's *Kagirinaku tōmeini chikai burū* [Almost transparent blue] (1976); Tanaka Yasuo's *Nantonaku kurisutaru* [Somewhat crystal] (1981); and Yamada Eimi's *Beddo taimu aizu* [Bedtime eyes] (1985) in the 1970s and 1980s—works of which Etō himself has always been more supportive than critical.

These works are representative of the children who have refused maturity and embraced instead the distinctive traits of "irresponsible sons" and "irritating daughters." This historical change is more evident in the case of women, who now do not hesitate to take advantage of men and society for the sake of their own welfare. Since society offers them only a limited set of alternatives, they have reason to be increasingly frustrated and present-oriented.

Here we see the sons and daughters of Shunsuke and Tokiko in *Hōyō kazoku*. They are concerned exclusively with themselves. These children, now in their thirties and forties, are the historical product of postwar Japan, where the family has dissolved into a chance collection of individual people. Their first priority is their own material and mental welfare; little time is left over to maintain the family. Divorce and single parents have become common, and any stigma attached to them has largely disappeared.

In the late 1980s, these spoiled children became parents themselves. This third generation of the Japanese modern family, the grandchildren of Shunsuke and Tokiko, took as their cultural heroes figures from popular comic magazines. For instance, Tsumugi Taku, a woman comic writer well known to the mass audience, wrote a story entitled Hotto rōdo [Hot road] (1986–1987) about the daughter of a family headed by a single mother. Haruki, age sixteen, joins a group of young motorbike gangsters and gets involved with their leader, Yoshiyama, age eighteen. Yoshiyama cares nothing for his life and will take any risk simply to drive as fast as he wishes. Because of her insecurity and emptiness, Haruki shares her boyfriend's despair, but her divorced single mother, belonging to the baby-boom generation, is too immersed in herself to notice her daughter's delinquency. Living on the money her wealthy ex-husband sends, she has nothing to worry about but her latest love affair. Trying to catch her attention, Haruki one day says to her mother, who is waiting for her latest lover to arrive, "If only you could behave like a mother."

The children of this third postwar generation are all too aware of how fragile the family is. But since, as young children, they cannot survive without a family, they are extremely conscious of any symptom of family disorganization. They may even invest a great deal in maintaining their family by voluntarily assuming the role of "good child." They are self-aware enough to understand that they are playing a "family game," and by playing that game, they force their parents into compliance with its rules. For them, the family is no longer a secure shelter they can rely on without question, but an ongoing project that must be managed and even negotiated.[19]

The Rise of New Motherhood

The current popular literature is full of frank accounts of women's experiences during pregnancy and mothering. Popular women's comic writers, such as Uchida Shungiku and Tajima Miruku,[20] talk openly about their experience of pregnancy and mothering; about the sexual desire of pregnant women; about the physical pleasure of being suckled during breast-feeding; about hostile emotion toward babies; and about their own self-centeredness and conflicting demands. Contemporary women are allowed public expression of their negative feelings toward their children, or even toward having a family at all, without fear of retaliation. They talk about and even publish accounts of their personal experiences of child abuse. None of this fits within the received model of motherhood, yet none of it has worse consequences for its authors than a flurry of criticism and some free publicity.

The shock and criticism that these accounts can still evoke tell us that the cultural code of "Mothers," which has dictated to women what they should and should not feel when bearing and raising children, still retains some of its old force; the relative mildness of the reaction, compared with the drastic sanctions that such accounts would surely have earned in earlier times, shows to what extent the cultural ideal of "Mothers" has decayed. Until recently, a woman who became a mother felt as the code would have her feel and blamed herself for her weakness if she transgressed it. Now the boundaries of the permissible have become much wider. Some women writers, like Kōno Taeko in Yōji gari [Child hunting], have sketched a nightmare of child-hatred out of their hostile feelings.[21] But it is precisely the ghost of the old "Mothers" ideal which gives her visions their disturbing quality. Once this ghost is dispelled, child-hatred will become no more than one of many emotional reactions possible to the biological mother.

Motherhood is neither nature nor culture. It is a historical product, subject to historical change. Can the old ideal of Japanese "Mothers" be maintained in the present? Or is it already gone beyond all hope of recovery? Only by a further deconstruction of these "Mothers" can we hope to propose answers to such questions.

Notes

This essay by Ueno Chizuko was first published in U.S.-Japan Women's Journal, English supplement, no. 10 (1996), pp. 3–19. It is reprinted here (with several minor changes) with the kind permission of the author and journal. A subsequent Japanese translation, titled "Josō shita kafuchōsei: 'Nihon no haha' no hōkai" [Transvestite patriarchy: Collapse of "Japanese Mothers"], has appeared in Ueno Chizuko ga bungaku wo shakaigaku suru [Ueno Chizuko's sociologization of literature] (Tokyo: Asahi Shinbunsha, 2000), pp. 103–128.

Author's note: This paper was originally a keynote speech at the Conference of "Mothers" in modern Japanese literature held at the University of British Columbia, Vancouver, Canada, in August 1995. I would like to thank Professor Kinya Tsuruta for his organization and invitation to the conference, all the participants who gave me comments and suggestions, and Dr. Gary Arbuckle for his professional editing of my paper.

1. Tachibana Yūko, *Kodomo ni te o agetaku naru toki* [When you want to abuse your children] (Tokyo: Gakuyō Shobō, 1992).
2. Elizabeth Badinter, *L'amour en plus* (Paris: Librairie Ernest Flammarion, 1980).
3. Phillippe Ariès, *L'enfant et la vie familiale sous l'ancien régime* (Paris: Plon, Editions de Seuil, 1960); and Edward Shorter, *The Making of the Modern Family* (London: Basic Books, 1975).
4. Etō Jun, *Seijuku to sōshitsu: haha no hōkai*. First published in 1967 by Kōdansha; new edition in 1988 by Kawade Shobō; paperback edition in 1993 by Kōdansha.
5. Yasuoka Shōtarō, *Umibe no kōkei* (Tokyo: Kōdansha, 1959), as cited in Etō, *Seijuku to sōshitsu*, pp. 11–12.
6   High social mobility is an important element that marks modern society, in which children do not inherit the status and profession of their fathers. Thus modern children continuously face a question that premodern children were never asked: "What are you going to do when you grow up?"
7. Etō, *Seijuku to sōshitsu*, p. 14.
8. At the beginning of the compulsory education system, in order to encourage girls to go to school, the local government introduced a "nanny class," where girls could take babies to the classroom while studying.
9. Koyama Shizuko, *Ryōsai kenbo to iu kihan* [A norm of good wife and wise mother] (Tokyo: Keisō Shobō, 1991).
10. The well-known concept of *amae*, proposed by the Japanese psychiatrist Doi Takeo, is too often used to characterize Japanese culture. (See Doi's *Amae no kōzō* [The anatomy of dependence] (Tokyo: Kōbundō, 1971). It requires careful examination for the following reasons: first, *amae* should be translated as "codependence" but not as "interdependence;" and second, as I discuss later, this codependence is based on an asymmetrical power relationship, which can by no means be mutual.
11. See my "Genesis of Urban Housewife," in *Japan Quarterly* 34, no. 2 (1987).
12. Kojima Nobuo, *Hōyō kazoku* (Tokyo: Kōdansha, 1965), as cited in Etō, *Seijuku to sōshitsu*, p. 66.
13. Etō, *Seijuku to sōshitsu*, p. 64.
14. It should be noted here that the impact of so-called second-wave feminism, which started in 1970 in Japan, goes beyond the scope of modern misogyny, though it is often misinterpreted as a "catching-up" strategy for women to be like men. Second-wave feminism shaped itself as counter-industrial thought from the beginning. Feminism questioned modernity, which imposed on women the status of second-class citizens. For further arguments, see my "The Japanese Women's Movement: The Counter-Values to Industrialism," in *Modernization and Beyond: The Japanese Trajectory*, ed. G. McCormack and Y. Sugimoto (Cambridge: Cambridge University Press, 1988); and "Nihon no ribu" [Japanese women's liberation movement], introduction to *Ribu to feminizumu* [Lib and feminism], volume 1 of *Series: Feminism in Japan*, ed. Ueno Chizuko et al. (Tokyo: Iwanami Shoten, 1994).

15. Okonogi Keigo, *Moratoriamu ningen no jidai* [The age of moratorium] (Tokyo: Chūō Kōronsha, 1978).

16. Satō Tadao, *Katei no yomigaeri no tame ni: hōmu dorama ron* [For the revival of family: On home dramas] (Tokyo: Chikuma Shobō, 1978).

17. Amy Borovoy, "Sewa nyōbō to sono rinri: arukōru izonshōsha 'kazoku miitingu' nite" [The politics of self-sacrifice: Meeting for families of alcoholics in Japan], in *U.S.-Japan Women's Journal* 20 (1996), pp. 56–68.

18. Ueno Chizuko, "Orientarizumu to jendā" [Orientalism and gender], in *Maternalist Fascism*, vol. 6 of *New Feminism Review*, ed. Kanō Mikiyo et al. (Tokyo: Gakuyō Shobō, 1995), p. 123.

19. Ueno Chizuko, *Kindai kazoku no seiritsu to hōkai* [The rise and fall of modern family] (Tokyo: Iwanami Shoten, 1994).

20. Uchida Shungiku, *Watashi tachi wa hanshoku shite iru* [We are procreating] (Tokyo: Bunkasha, 1994); Tajima Miruku, *Watashi tenshi, anata akuma* [I as an angel, you as a devil] (Tokyo: Fujin Seikatsusha, 1992).

21. Kōno Taeko, *Yōji gari* [Child hunting] (Tokyo: Naruse Shobō, 1976).

Chapter 8

COLONIALISM AND MODERNITY

Ukai Satoshi

Introduction

What happened? What is happening? When did *it* begin? When did *it* end? Or has *it* yet to end?

When we substitute the two words "colonialism" and "modernity" for the word "it" in each of these sentences, what kind of feelings arise in our hearts and what kind of thoughts come to mind?

Furthermore, in each of these cases, how do the feelings that arise in our hearts and the thoughts that come to mind overlap, and how do they diverge?

But who is this "we" that is referred to here? Is it not the case that who "we" are is indeed announced by the ways in which the various feelings and thoughts both overlap and differ from each other in their contents, qualities, and intensities? Without examining this fact, is it not impossible for one to obtain any kind of knowledge and, first of all, knowledge about oneself?

The discipline called Postcolonial Studies constantly and often unconsciously revolves around these questions. We could say that it is fated to maintain its productivity as a discipline only by continuing to revolve insistently around these questions. For colonialism and modernity, rather than having determinable beginnings and ends, and thus being objectifiable as "historical periods," are phenomena which by their nature are forbidden to end, and hence ought to be called "events" in the strongest sense of the word.

Even this two-in-one "event" is proper, in the way that any event is proper. It is first of all—and perhaps eternally—connected with one proper name, which is, of course, the name Europe. This means that, contrary to outward appearances, both colonialism and modernity are not *entirely* common nouns. In other words, they are not entirely translatable. In these two Latinate words, for example, there remains a reserve of latent meaning even if translated into Japanese as *shokumichishugi* and *kindai*. Does one not see here the enigma of Europe: its nonidentical identity; its "essence" that makes the nonidentical its identity; its "essence" that makes its essencelessness its essence?

This is a question that should be asked repeatedly, apart from all the "images" that are woven around the name Europe. To put it differently, it is a question that attaches itself inseparably like a shadow to every question that is asked anywhere about anything. The attempt to respond to this question, or at least to recognize the necessity of this question, is definitely not a local concern limited to "Europeans," let alone an example of a Eurocentric attitude. How can colonialism be thought through without at the same time asking this question? Fifty years ago, for example, this question was already on the horizon of thought of a writer who was seeking the cause for failure of a certain non-European nation-state's experience of modernity. As Takeuchi Yoshimi writes in his 1948 essay "Chūgoku no kindai to Nihon no kindai" [Chinese modernity and Japanese modernity]:

> I do not know if the European invasion of the Orient was based upon the will of capital, a speculative spirit of adventure, the Puritan spirit of pioneership, or yet another instinct for self-expansion. In any event, it is certain that there existed in Europe something fundamental that supported this instinct, making the invasion of the Orient inevitable. Perhaps this something has been deeply intertwined with the essence of what is called "modernity." Modernity is the self-recognition of Europe as seen within history, that regarding of itself as a self distinct from the feudalistic, which Europe gained in the process of liberating itself from the feudal (a process that involved the emergence of free capital in the realm of production and the formation of personality *qua* autonomous and equal individuals with respect to human beings). Therefore, it can be said that Europe is first possible only in this history, and that history itself is possible only in this Europe. History is not an empty form of time. It includes an infinite number of instants in which one struggles against obstacles so that the self may be itself, without which both the self and history would be lost. Sim-

ply being Europe does not make Europe Europe. The various facts of history teach that Europe barely maintains itself through the tension of its incessant self-renewals.[1]

As the title suggests, the point of Takeuchi's essay is to present the qualitative difference between Chinese and Japanese modernity. In this case, the stance toward Europe, i.e., whether or not there was resistance, is made the standard of judgment. At the time of his writing this essay, Takeuchi did not yet refer to the non-Western world that included China and Japan as "Asia," but rather as the "Orient." He represented from a particular history-of-civilizations perspective the necessity of the "Orient's" "resistance" and "defeat" in relation to Europe, and attempted to find in the Chinese writer Lu Xun—and through him in China itself—the form of "resistance" required of this historical necessity. In order for the "Orient" to attain "modernity," it must pass through a "resistance" grounded upon the self-awareness of "waking up from a dream to find no path to take."[2] Of course this view was required in order to illuminate contemporary Japan at the same time, which, according to Takeuchi's thinking, had pursued the path of modernization without passing through this kind of "resistance." Japan had thereby met the destruction of "August 15," yet had even then been unable to deeply understand the fact of "defeat" because of this lack of "resistance."

In its turn toward modernity, Japan bore a decisive inferiority complex vis-à-vis Europe. (This inferiority complex was the result of Japanese culture's superiority). It then furiously began to chase after Europe. Japan's becoming Europe, as European as possible, was conceived of as the path of its emergence. That is to say, Japan sought to emerge from slavery by becoming the master—and this has given rise to every fantasy of liberation. Today's liberation movements are so permeated by this slave nature that they cannot fully free themselves from it.[3]

These words were written by a Japanese intellectual just after the collapse of the colonial empire of Japan—the first non-European nation-state in world history to have carried out colonial rule on a large scale over a long period of time. Given that many events occurred in the years since, above all the struggles for independence and revolution in the former European colonies in Asia, Africa, and Latin America as well as the difficulties that followed, what kind of light can these words shed on the question of the mutually determinative nature of colonialism and modernity? Here I would like to cast this text, which is usually discussed in the concrete but limited context of Japanese and East Asian modernity, into the general question of colonialism and modernity. And for the sake of a very preliminary consideration, I would like to take up two indices from the above quotations. The first is the character of Takeuchi's understanding of Europe in the first quotation, the other is the function of the opposing concepts of "master" and "slave" (which are placed in a structural relation with such other concepts as "self" and "subject"). In the first section of this essay, I will begin from the former index and compare the discourse on Europe by twentieth-century European intellectuals with research into the history of (European and Japanese) colonialism. In the second section, I will look at the discourse of a colonial intellectual from the period of independence struggles in order to analyze how the opposing concepts of "master" and "slave" functioned in the work of theorizing anticolonial struggles. Based on my examination of these two indices, I will in the third section suggest that questions of colonialism and modernity, as well as questions concerning the essence of Europe, must necessarily disrupt the thought that depends on this master/slave dichotomy.

I. What Is Colonialism?

"Simply being Europe does not make Europe Europe." This sentence, taken from Takeuchi Yoshimi, can mean various things that go beyond the author's intention. The author tried to say that "the invasion of the Orient" was a necessary process for the self-realization of Europe, whose essence is self-expansion. This sentence, however, can suggest not only this kind of external expansion of Europe but also an essential inner difference within Europe. Anticolonial thought has almost always existed in Europe, even though it has had various limits and in the end lacked the force to change the direction of history. For example, in the turmoil of the French Revolution, fierce opinions both for and against abolishing slavery and colonies were exchanged in the National Assembly. The philosophy of English utilitarianism, as exemplified by John Stuart Mill and Adam Smith, had a large influence on the French discussions of abolishing colonialism.[4] Or again, for German thinkers at the beginning of the nineteenth century, when their country had no colonies to begin with—and was not even a nation-state—colonialism was still the "vice of others." In particular, it is worth drawing attention to the fact that both Kant and Fichte had deeply anticolonial philosophies.[5]

It was surprisingly late that the ideology of affirming colonialism as the "white man's civilizing mission" gained mass consensus in the contemporary sense, which goes beyond the bounds of intellectual discourse as analyzed by Edward Said in his *Orientalism*, and which presupposes compulsory education and the establishment of the mass media. This happened both after Europe entered the stage of imperialism and after World War I, that is to say, around 1930. In 1930 France celebrated one hundred years of its possession of Algeria, and in the following year held an international colonial exhibition. The representation of colonialism from the side of the colonizers shows its most typical discursive form at this time.

The first "value" of colonialism is "progress." "Progress in the world, that is to say, the exploitation of latent wealth, is the best justification for colonial activity," and "Colonialist ideology is equated with the development of humanity." In the historical section of the International Colonial Exhibition, colonial activity was represented as a single continuity, from the crusaders to the beginning of the twentieth century.

The second "value" of colonialism is "morality." Seen from this perspective, the acquisition of colonies is more a duty than a right. When this moral consciousness takes the form of a "civilizing mission," it has a doubly religious character. In addition to the fact that the activities of Christian missionaries had always been at the front line of colonial activities, the "empire builders," i.e., the military and colonial bureaucrats who were the actual parties involved in conquest and rule, were also the owners of a deep ideology that might even be called colonial mysticism. Furthermore, such ideology always sought its expression in "action." This "action" had to be expressed through the efforts of the colonialists, who were "creators of an energy that emerged from this land of energy that is France." In the discourse from this period, "action," "energy," and "effort" were always connected with masculine virtues. Colonization is invasion and conquest. According to the words of then Prime Minister Pierre Laval, "all the children of France received the most virile of lessons from the Colonial Exhibition."[6]

This exhibition was greeted with enthusiasm by all political forces in the Third Republic, with the exception of the Communist Party. Hardly any objections were raised, even among writers and artists, with the exception of the surrealists. Even the poet and critic Paul Valéry praised it as "magnificently organized."

. However, in the critiques of civilization and in the discussions of Europe that Valéry wrote during this same period, one can catch a pessimistic echo suggesting that he was not able to affirm colonialism without reservation. At this time, one of the main factors that established the consensus about colonialism in France was the wide public recognition of the strategic importance of the colonies during World War I. The colonies were suppliers of strategic resources and, above all, suppliers of soldiers. After a large number of colonial soldiers lost their lives on the battlefield, the words, "The Colonies' efforts were worthy of the homeland" became a cliché of French journalism.[7]

Unlike Gide, who became inclined to anticolonialism after witnessing the conditions of forced labor in the Congo, Valéry's doubts about colonialism did not come from so-called humanistic motives. For Valéry, who grasped World War I as Europe's "crisis" and as the beginning of its decline, the future consequences of colonialism for Europe could not possibly have been considered uniformly bright.

When the Sino-Japanese War and the Spanish-American War broke out at the end of the nineteenth century, Valéry realized that world history was witnessing the appearance of nation-states that pursued their interests independently of Europe and yet through institutions and technologies that Europe invented. As the first to grasp a portent of the coming age, Valéry stated the following in the preface to his 1931 *Reflections on the World Today*:

> This finite world, of which the internal bonds do not cease to multiply, is also a world which is increasingly equipping itself. Europe laid the foundations of science, which has transformed the life and multiplied the power of those who own it. But by its very nature it is essentially transmissible; it is of necessity reduced to universal methods and recipes. The powers it gives to some can be obtained by everyone else. . . . Thus the artificial inequality of powers on which European predominance was based for three hundred years is tending rapidly to vanish.[8]

The struggle to divide up the world among the European nation-states that had reached the stage of imperialism (the "Great Powers") lacked a unified "politics" suitable for the ideal of Europe. Therefore, Europe was now facing extinction as a geographical and spiritual entity with clear contours because of colonialism, that is, because of Europe's globalization. In Valéry's understanding, as long as Europe lacked a "politics of spirit" that went beyond the individual and material interests of each nation-state, colonialism could only become a fatal mistake. As a "European," he knew painfully well that the chance for such a "politics" was already lost forever.

In principle, those who dominate others in the name of universality cannot maintain those relations of domination forever. One must either put an end to domination after the other has been assimilated and become equal with oneself, or one must take down the banner of universality and end the domination that has now lost the foundation of its legitimization. The experience of colonialism in fact did not take either of these paths, but tore apart the colonized through the dual pressures of assimilation and exclusion. Because of these pressures, the path of political liberation for the colonized inevitably suffered distortions.

Let us look at the example of Algeria. Even after Algeria was declared a

French possession by the king's ordinance of July 1834, the inhabitants of this country, i.e., the Arabs or Berber Muslims and Jews, were for a period of time placed under the jurisdiction of religious laws. While in 1864 the "natives" at last became legally "French" and gained the "right" to perform such public duties as military service, they were second-class citizens still deprived of various rights, beginning with the right to vote. In 1870, only Jews among the "natives" were given citizenship through a government ordinance called the Crémieux Decree, which was named for the colonial governor at the time. After World War I, following the deaths of many Algerian soldiers, the path to French citizenship for Muslims was finally opened in 1919, as if in compensation. However, because the achievement of citizenship was to be accompanied by the renunciation of religious rights, almost no practical effects arose. Participation in the "universal" was only allowed on the condition of renouncing the "culture" of the colonized, which was regarded as "particular." Then, in the age of the popular front, the granting of civil rights without the renunciation of religious rights was for the first time proposed for those Muslims who had supposedly sufficiently assimilated through military service, or by having credentials in a profession. Finally World War II began, and once again with a large number of Algerian soldiers participating in the battle to liberate France, the government ordinance of 1944 came at long last to guarantee suffrage to those living in Algeria (that is, for both colonists and "natives"), regardless of origin, race, language, or religion. Yet this too was a discriminatory system that aimed to protect the interests of the colonists by distinguishing between Muslim and non-Muslim electorates. This situation continued until the beginning of the Algerian War in November 1954. The history of civil rights in colonial Algeria unfolded under French rule which, lasting for over a century, was based on the principle of assimilation. The collapse of French rule over Algeria was more than anything proof that politicosocial equality among ethnic groups is in principle unrealizable in a colonial situation.[9]

In the past, Yanaihara Tadao pointed out that there were many commonalities between Japanese and French colonialism.[10] Unlike England, France possessed a large colony across the Mediterranean Sea in North Africa, and, like Japan at the time (which possessed Korea across the Japan Sea and claimed "Manchukuo" as a dependency), France had adopted the policy of unifying the colonies and the homeland into a bloc. This was called homeland extensionism, and its principle was assimilationism. British-style colonial rule belonged to a different model in that it paid attention to local cultures and recognized a certain degree of self-governance on the part of the "natives." Yanaihara examined French assimilationism in terms of the three areas of tariffs, suffrage, and education, and thought that the policies of Japan and France were fundamentally similar concerning tariffs and education. Yet in regard to suffrage he wrote, "In Japan this problem has been abandoned without being resolved," and pointed out the deviation of Japanese colonialism from the French-style ideal, which touted the granting of civil equality in exchange for assimilation. As seen above, however, France too was unable in the end to resolve this problem, at least in Algeria.

Yanaihara's view of Japanese colonial policy (and especially its education policy) as assimilationist was long accepted. Recently, however, Komagome Takeshi's *Shokuminchi teikoku Nihon no bunka tōgō* [The cultural integration of the Japanese colonial empire] has radically reexamined this point.[11] Komagome draws attention to the fundamental clash of opinions that arose within the Japanese government at the time of the annexation of Taiwan in 1895 as well as the subsequent process of determining policy for rule. In 1897, Nogi Maresuke, the governor general at the time, submitted a "proposal" that opposed applying the Japanese Imperial Constitution to Taiwan. In opposition to this, Ume Kenjirō, the chief of the Legislative Bureau, refused to recognize any grounds for differentiating Taiwan from Okinawa and Hokkaidō, and advocated the adoption of a policy that would anticipate the implementation of suffrage and conscription for Taiwan as well. It is thought that this opposition reflected the opinions of the Englishman W. M. H. Kirkwood and the Frenchman M. J. Revon, both of whom were then advisers to the Ministry of Justice. However, it was Nogi's policy, which was based on Kirkwood's opinion paper, that came to be adopted.

> Frequently, Japanese and French colonial rule are simply compared as "policies of assimilation." However, the choice of not extending substantial parts of the constitutional system to Taiwan shows that in fact the line of Kirkwood and Nogi was adopted. Furthermore, we should bear in mind that the grounds for justifying this kind of policy of rule was of course not universalistic natural law philosophy, but rather the dogma of the Emperor system. As seen in Nogi's assertion, Emperor-system dogma *clearly distinguishes between the "inside" and "outside" of the nation-state of Japan and functions as a logic that impedes fluidity*.[12]

It is true, as Yanaihara pointed out, that the position of "national language" (Japanese) education in colonial educational policy shared fundamental elements with that of French language education in the cultural policies of French colonialism. In Japan's case, however, the logic of exclusion through "consanguineous nationalism" as represented by Hozumi Yatsuka worked very powerfully. If we take the example of suffrage as the institutional index of "homeland

extensionism," the application of the Election Law for the House of Representatives and the House of Councilors was not actualized for Taiwan or Korea
until April 1945, during the very last stages of the Asia-Pacific War, as compensation for the strengthening of the conscription system.[13]

Komagome's work accurately traces the supplementary relationship between
two principles for dealing with different ethnicities during changes in Japanese
colonial policies. This relationship involved the language-based "principle of
inclusion" and the blood-based "principle of exclusion," whereby the latter is
privileged over the former. As such, his work presents us with rich clues for our
project of elucidating the interrelationship between colonialism and modernity.[14] Here, however, I would like to point out that, when compared with the
previous example of Algeria, the internal contradictions of assimilationism in
Japanese colonialism cannot necessarily be considered a problem particular to
Japan. That is, the terrible contradiction that forced upon the colonized a "double bind"[15] situation, in which "on the one hand you are different from the
'Japanese,' while on the other hand you are an 'Imperial Subject,'" also worked
at the very heart of French colonial policy. Even though this contradiction
included many irreducible differences, it is perhaps characteristic of the colonial situation in general, whether of the French or British style. Moreover, this
"double bind" situation is something that *the rulers must "share" asymmetrically*. Was this not precisely what Valéry grasped in his acute consciousness of
"crisis" as a "European"?

II. The Aporia of Decolonization

Valéry, of course, was not able to examine this asymmetrically "shared" "double
bind" from the two sides of the colonizer and the colonized, the colonial
suzerain and the colony. In this context, he could only play the role of the
melancholy witness of European self-consciousness, which reproaches itself for
not having carried out its "responsibility" as ruler, even while destined to be a
ruler. It was with the progress of colonial liberation struggles starting in the 1950s
that it finally became clear exactly how, in concrete terms, this situation had
torn apart the spirit of the colonized on the "other shore" and in the "outer
regions." Among the works produced at this time, the work of Frantz Fanon has
a certain exemplarity. This is because Fanon, a psychiatrist from the French
colony of Martinique, pursued with deep insight a perspective for transforming
the ethnic and racial relations that had been determined in the colonial situation. He pursued this insight on the basis of a self-analysis in which, employing
European theoretical discourse however creatively transformed, he analyzed his

own "existential" crisis while facing racial discrimination. It is no coincidence that Fanon, in the process of this work, went further back than his contemporary Sartre and focused attention on Hegel, specifically the movement of self-consciousness that seeks recognition, i.e., the so-called "master-slave" dialectic as described in the *Phenomenology of Spirit*.

In a section titled "The Negro and Hegel," located in the latter half of "The Negro and Recognition," which is the seventh chapter of his *Black Skin, White Masks* (1952), Fanon comments directly on a passage from Hegel's text.

> Man is human only to the extent to which he tries to impose his existence on another man in order to be recognized by him. As long as he has not been effectively recognized by the other, that other will remain the theme of his actions. It is on that other being, on recognition by that other being, that his own human worth and reality depend. It is that other being in whom the meaning of his life is condensed.
>
> There is not an open conflict between white and black. One day the White Master, without conflict, recognized the Negro slave.
>
> But the former slave wants to *make himself recognized*.
>
> At the foundation of Hegelian dialectic there is an absolute reciprocity which must be emphasized.[16]

Here Fanon is speaking specifically about the situation of French blacks, in other words his own situation, in which the system of slavery was abolished by the suzerain without any struggle. More generally, however, we could say that he is taking on the fundamental difficulty of transforming the relationship between ruler and subjugated as formed by colonization—especially in its assimilationist forms—into the mutual recognition that Hegel discusses. What happens to the slave's desire for recognition when, in contrast to Hegel's scenario, recognition is not obtained through struggle but rather unilaterally awarded, or when the master merely recognizes the slave but does not in turn desire to be recognized by him? Is this not precisely the situation of the colonized, driven into the "double bind" of assimilation and exclusion? When placed in this kind of situation, how can the slave achieve self-consciousness? Since in Fanon's dialectic the slave cannot find the moment of his liberation in labor by immersing himself in the object, as with Hegel, what remains for him but the desire "to become like the master"?[17]

In a section titled "The Negro and Adler" that precedes this reading of Hegel focusing on the relationship between the colonizer and the colonized, Fanon analyzes the relationships among Martinicans, i.e., the relationships among the colonized. In Martinique, since everyone tries to upstage the other using the white man as standard, mutual recognition cannot take place and fellow countrymen cannot aim for "communication between people."[18] This is not the result of a "dependency complex" unique to the colonized, as asserted by the psychoanalyst Octave Mannoni. Rather it is an effect of French assimilationist education that transforms the Martinican into a white man at the level of the psyche. "The Martinican is a man crucified. The environment that has shaped him (but that he has not shaped) has horribly drawn and quartered him; and he feeds this cultural environment with his blood and his essences."[19] It was through Hegel that Fanon tried to elucidate the essence of this assimilationist education, of which he himself was a product.

However, for blacks (who were "historically . . . steeped in the inessentiality of servitude"[20]) the possibility of negating and sublating their negative existential conditions through the mediation of labor was closed off. In order to effect "the transformation of subjective certainty of [one's] own worth into a universally valid objective truth,"[21] the only path remaining was to assert one's "alterity of rupture"[22] amidst the struggle to "go beyond life."[23] But at such a time, can this struggle still be said to share the premises or goals of Hegel's "absolute reciprocity"? It is here that we can see the early signs of the emergence of theories of colonial liberation and revolutionary violence that Fanon, who later participated in the struggle for Algerian liberation, would develop in *The Wretched of the Earth* (1961):

> The zone where the natives live is not complementary to the zone inhabited by the settlers. The two zones are opposed, but not in service of a higher unity. Obedient to the rules of pure Aristotelian logic, they both follow the principle of reciprocal exclusivity. No conciliation is possible, for of the two terms, one is superfluous.[24]

> The natives' challenge to the colonial world is not a rational confrontation of points of view. It is not a treatise on the universal, but the untidy affirmation of an original idea propounded as an absolute. The colonial world is a Manichean world.[25]

For Fanon, it is in decolonization that "the 'thing' which has been colonized becomes man during the same process by which it frees itself."[26] Revolutionary violence gives birth to "new men" and "consists of reintroducing mankind into the world, the whole of mankind."[27] For Fanon, a "new humanism"[28] would dissolve the divisions among the colonized, as analyzed in "The Negro and Adler" in *Black Skin, White Masks*. The unity of the people would thus be realized, at least during the liberation struggle, through the generation of a "national culture" that is the daily struggle itself. But this was a perspective that could be achieved only by presently abandoning the reconstruction of the horizon of "absolute reciprocity" with the master (the colonizer), by rejecting "one-sided recognition," and by choosing a recalcitrant "alterity of rupture." We cannot make our primary task here the reexamination of the range or possibility of Fanon's theory of violence and his "new humanism." As a preparatory step, however, let us confirm what we can see in Fanon's philosophical transformation from an initial emphasis on the importance of the Hegelian presupposition of "absolute reciprocity" to its abandonment in *The Wretched of the Earth*. It is the aspect of those difficulties that the colonized must inevitably face in the process of decolonization. Fanon's attempt to break through the "double bind," aporia, and "pathless" condition that colonialism had assigned to the colonized did not leave behind any easy "paths," applicable methods, or "answers" to questions for those who followed. On the other hand, after Fanon any idea of "rehabilitating" the notion of "absolute reciprocity" as a presupposition or goal, and of using the logic of modernity to "solve" the "problem of ethnic nations" in the postcolonial period, would be only a repressive idea theoretically and practically fated to end in bankruptcy or self-deception. In this sense, Fanon's texts expose in the form of a truly exemplary "questioning" the extreme consequences of colonialism as well as the limits of modernity. It is precisely because of this that these texts are irreplaceable as theoretical testimony, worthy of our constant return and re-questioning.

III. Colonialism as Repetition Compulsion

> The slave refuses to recognize the fact that he is a slave. He is a true slave when he thinks that he is not a slave. And he reveals the full extent of his slavishness when he becomes a master, for at that time he subjectively views himself as no longer a slave.[29]

Takeuchi Yoshimi drew this insight from Lu Xun's allegory "The Wise Man, the Fool, and the Slave." Here, of course, the "master" refers first of all to modern Japan and particularly to that spirit which supported colonial rule and the war of invasion. Takeuchi sought what he believed was hopelessly lacking in Japanese modernity in Lu Xun's "resistance," which did not take as its standard of liberation the "humanism" of European modernity. For now I will leave open the question of the results of Takeuchi's endeavor, along with the question of Fanon's "new humanism."

In terms of our question of colonialism and modernity, it is noteworthy that in this sentence Takeuchi himself apparently fails to draw one of the logical conclusions of his statement. Shortly after the previous quotation, Takeuchi continues: "As Lu Xun writes, 'The slave and the master are identical.' Lu also writes, 'The tyrant's subjects are more violent than the tyrant himself' and 'He who enslaves all others as a master would himself be content as a slave.' The slave is not liberated when he becomes the master."[30]

There follow after these words a few lines that I quoted near the beginning of this essay, which sharply critique the "nature of Japanese culture" that misapprehended "its own Europeanization" as "liberation." Seen in this context, it is self-evident that Europe is posited as "master." Yet if, as Lu Xun says, "The slave and the master are identical," then even the "master" of Japan, i.e., Europe, cannot be simply a "master" but must also be a "slave." If we suppose that this is the case, what kind of agreement or disagreement can be found between this understanding and Takeuchi's understanding that "Simply being Europe does not make Europe Europe"? Furthermore, how should this understanding be positioned in relation to Valéry's sense of "crisis" upon discovering that Europe lacked a "politics of spirit" befitting the "master" of the world? On the other hand, how should it be positioned in relation to Fanon's sense of aporia when he realized that it was impossible to use the European logic of the master-slave dialectic to solve the contradictions that arose from European colonialism? Would this situation simply become more complicated if we introduced the voice of an Algerian-born Jew at the place where the voices of a Frenchman, a Martinican, and a Japanese—as well as a Chinese quoted by the Japanese—intersect and resonate? Or would a certain clue for elucidation thus become visible? As Jacques Derrida recounts of his own linguistic experience in a recent work, *Monolingualism of the Other* (1996):

> For contrary to what one is often most tempted to believe, the master is nothing. And he does not have exclusive possession of anything. Because the master does not possess exclusively, and *naturally*, what he calls his language, because, whatever he wants or does, he cannot maintain any relations of property or identity that are natural, national, congenital, or ontological, with it, because he can give substance to and articulate (*dire*) this appropriation only in the course of an unnatural process of politico-phantasmatic constructions, because language is not his natural possession, he can, thanks to that very fact, pretend historically, through the rape of a cultural usurpation, which means always essentially colonial, to appropriate it in order to impose it as "his own." That is his belief; he wishes to make others share it through the use of force or cunning; he wants to make others believe it, as they do a miracle, through rhetoric, the school, or the army.[31]

Derrida is not multilingual. The only language that he can speak fluently is French, his "mother tongue." In the city of Algiers, where he was born and raised, however, this French language was always the language of the other, which sought its norms in another country, i.e., France. From this the following proposition arises: "I have only one language and it is not mine."[32] As we previously saw, for the Jews in Algeria who rapidly assimilated into French culture after they were given French citizenship in 1870 through the Crémieux Decree, it would be difficult to find a language other than French for which they could claim historical legitimacy. Both Hebrew and Arabic are unnatural as authentic spoken languages. However, Derrida does not stop here but continues thinking. Is this situation of his own community, in which no relation to any language can be said to be natural, really that exceptional? In fact, is it not the case that there is no one who can naturally or innately "possess as their own" a language, even their "mother tongue"? Conversely, then, is this not why the love for and pride in one's "mother tongue" can become so fierce and sublime? And is this not the case with any element that constitutes identity, not just language? The colonizer coerces the colonized to assimilate into his culture, but is this really the colonizer's culture? Is it not the case that the colonizers themselves are, in the first place, those who have been assimilated, and whether in order to forget the pain of their own process of assimilation or to avoid remembering it, they try to force that culture on the other as if it were "their own possession"? Is it not the case that at the origin of colonial violence there is an originary nonidentity between the colonizers themselves and their culture, and that in order to avert their eyes from this abyss, they try to inculcate in others the belief of their oneness with this culture by means of various speech acts and by creating the conditions that can support the establishment of these speech acts, and that it is through the other's belief that they try to believe in their oneness with that culture themselves?

Can it not be said that Derrida's hypothesis is a translation, one that has passed through a distant and different circuit of experience and thought, of those words of Lu Xun's, "The slave and the master are identical"? Or rather it may be that the possibility of all "resistance" dwells in the fact that these two experiences and thoughts, while in a sense saying the same thing, are not entirely translatable into each other. In any case, in Derrida's thought colonialism does not begin between Europe and its outside. It has always already begun (and is moreover not finished) in the "inside" of Europe's geographical boundaries and in the midst of its history. Europe itself is in a sense a colony, and this is why colonialism constitutes its essence.

In fact, it is interesting to look at the kinds of arguments that were used to determine assimilationism in French colonial policy. Arthur Girault, a major theorist of the French colonial legal system from the 1890s to the 1930s who was involved in numerous policy decisions, wrote in 1894:

> We must consider the temperament and aptitude of the colonizing nation. Self-government suits Anglo-Saxons. We French are Latin. The influence of Rome formed our spirit over the course of many centuries. We cannot escape this obsession, and to deviate from the path traced by this idea is to force our nature. The only thing we can do, and therefore should do, is assimilate.[33]

Here, assimilationist colonialism itself is regarded as continuing the tradition of the Romans, who once conquered Gaul, Spain, and North Africa, spreading their language, religion, and customs. In other words, the "nature" or identity of France and the French is explained through ancient colonialism—Rome's colonization of the regions and ethnic groups of what was later called Western Europe—and modern colonialism is defined and justified as this ancient form's continuation, imitation, and, indeed, *repetition compulsion*.

Here, perhaps, what Takeuchi Yoshimi meant by his view that "Simply being Europe does not make Europe Europe" is being voiced from the reverse side. According to Girault, the movement of "freedom," in which Europe's "self" ceaselessly maintains itself at the same time that it transcends itself, is driven by an "obsession" that was implanted through centuries of colonization. Since this movement is now "our nature," and so cannot be "forced," one can only "force" others through assimilation. It is probably no coincidence that such a sentiment was declared precisely at the time when colonial policy was being determined. Conversely, Takeuchi's understanding that "modernity is the self-recognition of Europe as seen within history, that regarding of itself as a self distinct from the feudalistic, which Europe gained in the process of liberating itself from the feudal" still seems to me too limited, because of historical constraints, by modern Europe's official self-representations. This limitation must influence the content of the concepts of "self" and "subject" in these sentences—sentences that are striking in the motion of tenacious re-questioning that goes forward and backward, as well as in their dense textuality that came from a literal groping in the dark. For when the "slave and master are identical," the "self's" regulation or domination, i.e., the definition of the "self's" "master" as "subject," also demands a careful yet fundamental rethinking. Takeuchi depended on these concepts of "self" and "subject," but did not their situation determine and in a sense limit the breadth of his thinking about such things as nationalism, the Japan-Asia relation, and even "resistance"?

Takeuchi/Lu Xun, Valéry, Fanon, Derrida—each of the thinkers discussed in this essay experienced and thought through colonialism and modernity at a specific time and place, and from a specific standpoint. Not one of them was able to command a bird's-eye view of the situation in its entirety. The question concerning the interrelation of colonialism and modernity, perhaps even more than any other, can be thought only in the midst of multiple voices. And it may be that today this is what it means for "us" or "me" to *think*; in short, to remain within the unending "event"—the two-in-one event of colonialism and modernity—and attempt to define one's own "proper" place, in a groping and infinite series of forward steps, while allowing these multiple voices to echo in one's ears.

Translated by Lewis E. Harrington

Notes

Ukai Satoshi, "Koroniarizumu to modaniti," in *Tenkanki no bungaku* [Literature at the turning point], ed. Mishima Kenichi and Kinoshita Yasumitsu (Tokyo: Minerva Shobō, 1999), pp. 206–226.

1. Takeuchi Yoshimi, "Chūgoku no kindai to Nihon no kindai" [Chinese modernity and Japanese modernity], in *Nihon to Ajia* [Japan and Asia] (Tokyo: Chikuma Bunko, 1993), pp. 12–13; trans. Richard F. Calichman, *What Is Modernity? Writings of Takeuchi Yoshimi* (New York: Columbia University Press, 2005), p. 54.

2. Ibid., p. 38; Calichman, p. 70. Translation slightly modified.

3. Ibid., p. 43; Calichman, p. 72.

4. See Yves Benot, *La révolution française et la fin des colonies* (Paris: La Découverte, 1987).

5. "If we compare with this ultimate end [the Third Definitive Article of a Perpetual Peace: The Obligation of Universal Hospitality] the *inhospitable* conduct of the civilised states of our continent, especially the commercial states, the injustice which they display in *visiting* foreign countries and peoples (which in their case is the same as *conquering* them) seems appallingly great. America, the negro countries, the Spice Islands, the Cape, etc. were looked upon at the time of their discovery as ownerless territories; for the native inhabitants were counted as nothing." Immanuel Kant, "Perpetual Peace," in *Kant: Political Writings*, ed. Hans Reiss, trans. H. B. Nisbet (Cambridge: Cambridge University Press, 1991), p. 106.

   "As time went on, a kind fortune preserved it [the German nation] from direct participation in the conquest of other worlds—that event which, more than any other, has been the basis of the development taken by modern world history, of the fates of peoples, and of the largest part of their ideas and opinions. Since that event, and not before, Christian Europe, which hitherto, without being clearly conscious of it, had been one, and by joint enterprises had shown itself to be one—Christian Europe, I say, has split itself into various separate parts. Since that event, and not before, there has been a booty in sight which anyone might seize; and each one lusted after it in the same way, because all were able to make use of it in the same way; and each one was envious on seeing it in the hands of another." Johann Gottlieb Fichte, *Addresses to the German Nation*, ed. George Armstrong Kelly (New York: Harper & Row, 1968), p. 191.

6. C. Coquery-Vidrovitch, "La colonisation française: 1931–1939," in *Histoire de la France coloniale III: Le déclin* (Paris: Armand Colin, 1991), pp. 9–26.

7. See C-R. Ageron, "L'exposition coloniale de 1931—mythe républicain ou mythe impérial?" in *Les lieux de la mémoire, I. République*, ed. Pierre Nora (Paris: Gallimard, 1984).

8. Paul Valéry, *Reflections on the World Today*, trans. Francis Scarfe (New York: Pantheon Books, 1948), pp. 24–25.

9. See L-A. Barriére, "Le puzzle de la citoyenneté en Algérie," in *Plein Droit*, vols. 29–30 (November 1995).

10. Yanaihara Tadao, "Shokumin seisaku yori mitaru Nichi-Futsu" [Japan and France as seen through colonial policy] (1937), in *Yanaihara Tadao zenshū* [Complete works of Yanaihara Tadao] (Tokyo: Iwanami Shoten, 1963), vol. 5, pp. 303–308.

11. Komagome Takeshi, *Shokuminchi teikoku Nihon no bunka tōgō* (Tokyo: Iwanami Shoten, 1996).

12. Ibid., p. 38. Emphasis in the original.

13. Ibid., p. 42.

14. While the distinction between "modernity as civilization" and "modernity as ideology" that Komagome introduces is another important argument in relation to the theme of this essay, I cannot touch upon it here. Please see ibid., p. 370 and below.

15. Ibid., p. 231.

16. Frantz Fanon, *Black Skin, White Masks*, trans. Charles Lam Markmann (New York: Grove Press, 1967), pp. 216–217. Emphasis in the original.

17. Ibid., p. 221, note 8.

18. Ibid., p. 213.

19. Ibid., p. 216.

20. Ibid., p. 219.

21. Ibid., p. 218.

22. Ibid., p. 222.

23. Ibid., p. 218.

24. Frantz Fanon, *The Wretched of the Earth*, trans. Constance Farrington (New York: Grove Press, 1963), p. 38.

25. Ibid., p. 41.

26. Ibid., pp. 36–37.

27. Ibid., pp. 36, 106.

28. Ibid., p. 246.

29. Takeuchi, *Nihon to Ajia*, p. 43; Calichman, p. 72.

30. Ibid.

31. Jacques Derrida, *Monolingualism of the Other; or, The Prosthesis of Origin*, trans. Patrick Mensah (Stanford: Stanford University Press, 1998), p. 23. Incidentally, Yi Young-suk, who has analyzed linguistic policy in Japan's colonial rule of Korea, makes the following observation: "While language cannot be a mere 'form of social life,' neither can it be an entirely indigenous and untransplantable custom. Even if a spirit of loyalty to the Emperor resides in Japanese at birth, there is not a single Japanese that is born speaking Japanese. Moreover, language, unlike other ethnic customs, can be learned even by foreigners given the proper education. Language becomes language for the first time through the mediation of the 'inside' and 'outside,' 'nature' and 'artifice.'" *"Kokugo" to iu shisō* [The ideology of the "Japanese national language "] (Tokyo: Iwanami Shoten, 1996), p. 261.

32. Derrida, *Monolingualism of the Other*, p. 25.

33. Arthur Girault, *Principes de colonisation et de législation coloniale* (1894), vol. 1, p. 107. Cited by Jacques Thobie in *Histoire de la France coloniale, II-L'apogée* (Paris: Arman Colin, 1991), pp. 299–300.

REFLECTIONS BEYOND THE FLAG: WHY IS THE *HINOMARU* FLAG "AUSPICIOUS/FOOLISH"?

It has been six months since the National Flag and Anthem Law was enacted.[1] During this time, not a day has passed in which I have not returned, as if compulsively dwelling on a nightmare, to the question of what kind of event the 145th regular session of the National Diet had been.[2] Who and what kind of ideology within the government had conceived of the event? What kinds of maneuverings between political parties had made it possible? What kind of a dynamic both inside and outside the Diet had given rise to it? Moreover, what has been the nature of our society that would allow such an event to occur, and what kind of future does it foretell? We are standing in a place where we must very painfully rethink all these questions from step one. This event has awakened in us a sense of crisis so deep as to render invalid whatever understanding we had about our society and historical period. Everyone greeted the event with a certain amazement. Or rather, everyone seemed unsure how to greet this amazement.

Such clichés as "return to the dark ages" or "anachronism" are here defensive reactions to this amazement. That thinking which must reflexively spew forth such words is indelibly marked by progressivism. War, fascism, totalitarianism — these have all continued to be our objects of knowledge in the space-time of the postwar period. We are thus convinced that we are already beyond them. Or rather, we are so anxious that we need to believe this in order to maintain our emotional stability. If we remain at such a level today, however, it is clear that we can no longer render accurate historical judgments. Hence we must first relearn how to greet this amazement.

> The tradition of the oppressed teaches us that the "state of emergency" in which we live is not the exception but the rule. We must attain to a conception of history that is in keeping with this insight. Then we shall clearly realize that it is our task to bring about a real state of emergency, and this will improve our position in the struggle against Fascism. One reason why Fascism has a chance is that in the name of progress its opponents treat it as a historical norm. The current amazement that the things we are experiencing are "still" possible in the twentieth century is *not* philosophical. This amazement is not the beginning of knowledge—unless it is the knowledge that the view of history which gives rise to it is untenable.[3]

If we replace the words "twentieth century" with "twenty-first century," this sentence will become a warning for us who today live under the National Flag and Anthem Law. Walter Benjamin is of course not recommending apathy or *ataraxia* in place of amazement here. Rather, what he is saying is that those who have belonged on the side of the majority, or those who believed they were in the majority and are therefore now frightened by the "state of emergency," should turn their "amazement" into an awareness that there have always been those for whom such a state is the norm. These people should thus forge connections with the "tradition" of "oppressed" minorities. According to Benjamin, it is only in this way that we can think in real terms about a "true state of emergency," that is, a "state of emergency" for the ruling class, and hence improve our position in the struggle against fascism.

The enactment of the National Flag and Anthem Law has forced us once again to remember just how many minds and bodies were tormented and even killed in the name of that flag and anthem in Japan, its colonies, and all the territories occupied by the Japanese military. Since this work of remembering is still weak, we must devote all our efforts to strengthening it, including confronting the forces that hinder it. Yet such indispensable remembering is not in itself "a memory as it flashes up at a moment of danger," or a "true image of the past" that "can be seized only as an image which flashes up at the instant when it can be recognized and is never seen again," as Benjamin says elsewhere in the same text.[4] As premised upon the tenacious work of remembering, we must seize the moment in which the image of the past "*unexpectedly* appears to the historical subject."[5] If we do not grasp this image, the "true state of emergency" will not come into view.

There were two ways of thinking within the movement against the National Flag and Anthem Law, and at times these were in conflict within the same person. The first was that the *Hinomaru* and *Kimigayo* should be replaced by another flag and anthem; the second was that any national communality as symbolized by a flag or anthem should be rejected. The greatest common factor of the various opposition movements was the recognition that the compulsory use of any flag or anthem would be an invasion of "freedom of thought and conscience," as putatively guaranteed by Article 19 of the Constitution.

Since the enactment of the National Flag and Anthem Law is clearly the first stage of an undesirable revision of the Constitution, the opposition movement has naturally focused on the contradictions between the present Constitution and the (compulsory use of) this flag and anthem. As this movement bears a strong affinity with essentially progressivist trends, however, any thinking of such a framework in fixed terms makes it difficult for us to seriously heed Benjamin's warning. In order to articulate a long-term resistance against the National Flag and Anthem Law, we require another movement within this movement, one which, while sustaining the opposition to the *Hinomaru* and *Kimigayo*, would readily shake up the formalistic limits of the opposition consensus. Although we are in the midst of an unmistakable crisis, it is our urgent task to now begin "to seize hold of a memory as it flashes up at a moment of danger."

"While the *Hinomaru* flag might be acceptable, the *Kimigayo* anthem is not." Regardless of how widely this sentiment was shared, many people sought in it a foothold for the movement in its opposition struggle. We can cite the reasons for this: the *Kimigayo* lyrics openly glorify the emperor, its melody is largely incompatible with contemporary music tastes, and one can easily imagine the pain of being forced to sing it. In fact, there has even appeared the ridiculous middle position of supporting the *Hinomaru* and opposing the *Kimigayo*. As Kanō Mikiyo has remarked, however, it is not the same thing to claim that the "*Kimigayo* is more of a problem than the *Hinomaru*" as it is to say that "*Kimigayo* is the more dangerous." Rather the opposite is true. At ceremonies, it is the flag (and not the anthem) that panoptically determines the spatial arrangement of the participants. Above all, fans in soccer stadiums already well attest to the fact that it is possible to love the *Hinomaru* as an extension of postwar sensibility, provided that one is blasé about whom the *kimi* (or "you") of *Kimigayo* refers to and that one forget Japan's war and invasion. When we seek a point of contact with the masses as based on a sense of unease with the *Kimigayo*, we become absorbed by the movement's unwitting progressivism. We thus succumb to the temptation of overcoming the situation at the mountain's lowest point, to use an old-fashioned expression. Benjamin would certainly see here an opening for fascism.

In other words, the "true image of the past" that we require will not appear if we refuse the difficulty of confronting the *Hinomaru*. I would thus like to begin by seeking out images of the *Hinomaru* that were discussed and put into print precisely because of this moment of crisis.

> In Shōwa 14 [1939] I lived in China's Shandong Province. One summer day my two younger brothers and I explored a barbed wire enclosure on the outskirts of town. There I saw a huge black mass in a large hole that seemed to be about ten meters in diameter. It was a mountain of corpses. I also realized that the black color was really a swarm of flies. Upon raising my head, I saw the *Hinomaru* waving in the breeze. Even after sixty years, I still remember how frighteningly beautiful the flag was against the dazzling sky. Since then I can no longer simply believe in anything that appears beautiful. This year I visited Shandong and learned that the site was an execution ground.[6]

During the continuing struggle over the National Flag and Anthem Law, it was this sixty-nine-year-old man's letter to the editor that left the greatest impression on me. Until then I had foolishly believed that only poetry and songs spoke of the *Hinomaru* as beautiful. I had been caught up in the schematic belief that ethical judgments tend to become paralyzed through the intervention of aesthetic experience. These calmly written lines told me that there are moments when the *Hinomaru* is truly "frighteningly" beautiful, and that, nonetheless, or rather precisely because of this—for the flag can be so beautiful only under such conditions—the memory of this beauty had not so much rendered one's sense of ethics dormant as instead become the core of an absolutely indelible mistrust of aesthetic experience in general. Understood literally and in a very strict sense, the inability to simply believe in "anything that appears beautiful" must be extremely saddening. The *Hinomaru*, which caused someone such loss, is after all no arbitrary sign. It is a flag that is cursed in its very design. Something in this letter can convince one of this. From that point onward I began to pay attention to those aesthetic judgments regarding the *Hinomaru* as expressed by the wartime generation.

Next I will present the remarks of three intellectuals. Born in the 1920s, these men all oppose the National Flag and Anthem Law. Their intellectual and literary work continues to furnish us with a rich legacy for thinking about future forms of resistance. The following quotations are not intended critically, but are presented merely as an index.

> It is said that in Okinawa there are special feelings about the *Hinomaru*, but these differ depending upon the before and after of the island's return to Japan. Okinawans are swayed by such political conditions.

That is, the flag's design is in itself virtually meaningless. It is precisely for this reason that one can attribute any meaning to it. The fault lies less in the *Hinomaru* than with the political attitude of those who use it. . . .

I like the flag's design. As a national flag, it might even be the best in the world. If we change it, then this new design might again be criticized in the future if there is a worsening in political conditions.[7]

It is outrageous that the *Hinomaru* and *Kimigayo* could be legalized in the Diet. Speaking from my own biased tastes, I rather like the design of the *Hinomaru*, but the *Kimigayo* does nothing for me.[8]

I do not dislike the *Hinomaru* design. In fact, I rather like it. But it is quite repelling that the Diet would pass the *Hinomaru* and *Kimigayo* into law.[9]

In a sense, these remarks can be considered exemplary of intellectuals in their sharp distinction between aesthetic and political judgment. Nevertheless, I could not but feel ambivalent in learning that these thinkers, who are otherwise so different in their thought and sensibilities, shared the same "personal" (Yoshimoto seemed especially aware of this point) and affirmative opinion regarding the *Hinomaru* design. Despite the fact that these intellectuals do not, to say the least, support the political order, their remarks could nonetheless be read by bureaucrats and establishment politicians as a guarantee that the "excellence" of the flag's design would be fully exploited so as to suppress resistance against the National Flag and Anthem Law. Herein lies an unavoidable task for us. Is it not the case that the ruling class's "state of emergency" will appear in Japan only when we break through, rather than avoid, that which is seen as the flag's "excellent" design?

It is true that the *Hinomaru* is more easily accepted than the *Kimigayo* because it is an icon, and thus, as Ōshiro says, open to any number of meanings and interpretations. Yet there is a limit to such interpretations. Or rather, there exists an immutable core here without which the flag's "excellence" would not emerge, regardless of its "excellence" as an icon in general. In a word, this core is the implicit notion or belief that no better icon exists as an embodiment of the name Japan. A historical concatenation has been formed according to which any change in the national flag would have to be accompanied by a change in the nation's name. This is what the establishment calls "fixity." The movement to disobey the National Flag and Anthem Law must thus embrace two poles: the minimal plan to oppose coercion in the name of "freedom of conscience" and the maximum plan to rethink Japan's very name. It seems to me that a communality that cannot be symbolized by any flag or anthem can go beyond idealism and gain concreteness only by enduring the tension between these two poles while concurrently staging guerilla warfare against *this* flag (and *this* anthem) at the level of sensibility.

Here we should pay more attention to Amino Yoshihiko's repeated insistence, in his remarks on the National Flag and Anthem Law, that the name Japan is not immutable.[10] Of course, even Amino doesn't believe there is any immediate opportunity to change this name. Yet it is more productive to regard his current speaking out on this issue, which no one had ever seriously discussed before, as a sign of our times rather than as reflective of his own intent. For now that the National Flag and Anthem Law has been passed, it is only the name Japan that remains to be legalized, that is, the naturalness and noninstitutionality of this name still continues to be fabricated in negative form. In fact, there is no guarantee that this name will survive beyond the clear limits of Japan's assimilation policies and the imminent collapse of the masses' monoethnic nation fantasy.

Of course, the structure of embodiment of the name Japan through the *Hinomaru* is by no means simple. There is an odd discrepancy between this name and icon, one that is premised upon supplementarity. There lies at the origin of this name the historical fact or narrative according to which Prince Umayado [Prince Shōtoku], in the year 607, at the time of the first embassy to the Sui dynasty, sent a letter to the Sui emperor, Yangdi, "from the Son of Heaven in the land where the sun rises to the Son of Heaven in the land where the sun sets." This episode is well known, if rarely recalled. In recalling it today, however, we can sense with unusual clarity that this name originally involved seeing oneself from the perspective of the other, because of which the trace of the other forever remains. Even if in such texts as the *Kojiki* the name is written as *Nihon* and read as *Yamato*, the Chinese reading of *Nihon* or *Nippon* historically became the rule and the Japanese reading *Hinomoto* the exception. Here, too, we may note an awareness of China. As soon as this name became iconized by the *Hinomaru* design, however, the trace of the other, the relation with the Chinese mainland and the East Asian power structure of the early seventh century were all utterly effaced. The self-centered forgetting that this name desired but could not achieve itself was realized by the icon of the *Hinomaru* design.

That sensibility which regards the *Hinomaru* design as "excellent" is perhaps not unrelated to this unique correspondence between name and icon. The sensibility that finds the *Hinomaru* "refreshing" is perhaps apt to lead to one that feels "refreshed" when those regarded as "other" disappear from the horizon of historical consciousness. (Apparently some local residents thrust the flag at Aum Shinrikyō members, as if it were a charm against evil spirits). Precisely because of this, however, there can also be a sensibility that abhors the *Hinomaru* design. Such abhorrence can be seen in the history of Japanese expression, even if this represented a minority view.

It was in the midst of the opposition to the National Flag and Anthem Law that I came across a number of passages on the *Hinomaru* in the later works of Tanigawa Gan. I might not have paid so much attention to these texts had I read them at a different time. Upon examination, however, it struck me that the distaste for the flag on the part of this man, who was also born in the 1920s, was deeply rooted in his intellectual formation.

> Speaking of eggs, I recall one night I complained to Saitō Yoshishige, "Why couldn't Takiguchi Shūzō break with such round forms? He writes of boiled eggs and those white rice-flour dumplings of the Bon festival." Saitō's reply was as calm as ever, "Because he's a surrealist." Indeed, Japanese surrealists love "circles." Nothing irritates my Japan resident[11] nerves so much as that vague lump that floats lightly on the scene like an island or the sun and moon. When I see it, my heart cries out that it's the symbol of *Ilbon* [i.e., the Korean reading of "Japan" — *Ukai*]. What an unwitting display of imperialism, with as much logic as a block of tofu! The terror of the "circle," the *Hinomaru's* demon-child! The problem with this flag is that there is only a circle, which in its form is completely closed. This is not so much a question of history as one of sensibility. At least Duchamp's urinal contained an opening. How obtuse that no artist has remarked upon this difference![12]

This is a passage from Tanigawa's open letter to the Korean artist Lee Ufan. The red circle, which was originally supposed to iconize the sun, merges in the *Hinomaru* with the "nation's form," i.e., the imaginary projection of equivalence between national spirit and national territory ("like an island or the sun and moon"). The periphery's provocative speech act to the center which stated, "The sun appears from your point of view to rise near me" was translated iconographically, abstracting the complex shape of the Japanese archipelago and erasing the distance between sun and land, in keeping with the religious fiction of the emperor system. Tanigawa responds appropriately to the violence of this move. For him, the sense of "auspiciousness/foolishness" that was projected onto the *Hinomaru* had thoroughly permeated Japan's avant-garde art. The flag's relation to Japanese exclusionism could thus no longer be reduced to the historical context in which the flag had been used; rather it must be critiqued immanently or structurally at the level of "sensibility."

> First of all, the "circle" is a differential in the universe's humor, it's a mandala container. Isn't it rude to thrust an empty red Tupperware container at someone and say, "Please take this"? Even Zen monks try to leave

imperfections in the "circles" of their scroll paintings. Pure frozen humor is not humor. It is simply empty, without self-definition or other people. In the theory of surrealism, however, there are no criteria by which to critique this as art. The incontinence of humor will certainly be seen if we seek a "sublime point" at the boundary of deep consciousness between sleep and wakefulness. If someone insists that even frozen or closed humor is still humor, and that the national flag represents a kind of austere humor, then we wouldn't know what to do with the autistic child that is the *Hinomaru*. Surrealism is unable to go beyond this flag.[13]

If the "circle" represents the humorously shrunken form of the universe, then it might be a container but it would belong to no one. The "auspiciousness/foolishness" of the *Hinomaru* lies in the conviction that someone would smile if one painted this container red and presented it with the words "This is me." We have here the terror of that which is literally "empty." Let us place alongside this understanding the frivolous argument of the supporters of the National Flag and Anthem Law, for they shamelessly rely on a kind of formalistic symmetry that states, "To honor one's own national flag and anthem is to learn the international etiquette of respecting the flags and anthems of other nations." In the context of the flag, however, such pathetic insensitivity to the other must be critiqued "as art." Unable to find the criteria for this critique in surrealism, Tanigawa sought it instead in the "awakened work" of those anonymous artists who, on the basis of their class consciousness, gave birth to Korean Yi dynasty folk painting ("life painting").

> Japanese artists are poor at standing against any dazzling and painful brightness, for they regard anything that cannot stay consumed as deviant. Their "deconstruction" is not a form for awakening, but rather a confession of intoxication. This is the sole reason they could not understand the meaning of the Korean itinerant painters' awakened work on dream utility.[14]

Tanigawa even makes reference to the *Hinomaru* in his last work, a series of childhood recollections titled *Kita ga nakereba Nihon ha sankaku* [Without the north, Japan is a triangle] (1995). In the chapter "Handmade *Hinomaru* Flags," there is a depiction of a group of elementary-school students parading with flags, as took place prior to the distribution of the "red ink mimeographed *Hinomaru* flags" in 1931 at the time of the Manchurian Incident.[15] Tanigawa recalls that this parade, in which the irregular size and colors of the red circles clearly reflected the children's life conditions, was "a bit ethnic and anarchistic."[16] But the episode that most closely corresponds to the *Hinomaru* discussion in his letter to Lee Ufan is to be found in the two chapters directly related to the book's title, "Without the north" and "A circle or triangle."

In 1933 (Shōwa 8), when the typhus outbreak was so severe that even meals were eaten inside mosquito nets, the Tanigawa brothers encountered a "young girl." Upon being rebuked by one of the brothers for eating a piece of fish with her hands, the girl "rolled her eyes mischievously" and in a "cheery voice" replied, "Without the north, Japan is a triangle!" These words made a strong impression on the young Gan.

> Without the north, Japan is a triangle! It is of course impossible to accurately reproduce the kind of shock I received from this phrase when only ten years old, so I must make use of my faculty of reason.
>
> First, I was certainly surprised by the claim that Japan's proper shape was that of a quadrilateral. For when the word *Japan* echoed in my head, I had always thought of it as a circle.
>
> The arc of the archipelago and Ryūkyū islands that stretch from the northeast to the southwest. Even if Karafuto and Chishima could somehow be gathered therein, any consideration of how to simplify this territorial form (which includes both Korea and Taiwan) would iconographically run up against the Korean peninsula. Hence the circle that rolls up these contradictions into a dumpling. I imagine that this is the Japanese people's inner *Hinomaru*.[17]

Tanigawa's understanding of the *Hinomaru* was thus an extremely idiosyncratic one, bound up with the memories of particular events and people from the poet's biography. As goes without saying, it is not easy to "revive" this thinking within the collective work being undertaken today by another generation, one that opposes the National Flag and Anthem Law. Tanigawa himself early on abandoned the possibility of translating his own oppositional dream into the logic of politics, and withdrew from the scene in the mid-1960s. In trying to put into historical perspective the significance of the 1999 passage of the National Flag and Anthem Law, however, I think it is worth recalling the shift in Tanigawa's own understanding of the situation, which he cited at the time as the main reason behind this withdrawal, and his predictive "hypothesis of a single world power." For it seems that Tanigawa had already largely seen through the essence of our present state of "globalism," as can be seen for example in his text "Waga soshiki kūkan" [Our organization space] (1964).

> The logic of nation-states is such as to increasingly purify them as economic units, but no matter how desperately nations fight one another this

apparently radical "multipolarization" is firmly held under the control of
the global market in its growing unification. What can be predicted and
inferred from this fact? The first question that arises is whether it is appropriate to consider the various monopolies, which either separate or join
the nation-state units, as the "moribund and highest stage" of private
property. Just as one must stand atop a mountain to see even higher peaks,
so too do we still hope for the highest peaks of private property. While revolutions in nations A, B and C may have displaced private property onto
a kind of state monopoly, there is no sign that nation-states will now begin
to die out. Instead there is a strengthening of nation-state logic and the
birth of a spellbinding new world system, consisting of complementary
relations between those nation-states gathered around the global market.
How far will this new system expand? I suspect it will soon swallow up
China and its neighbors as well as those revolutions in nations L, M and
N that will take place in the crevices of the scramble for markets. It will
then grow into a *single world* power. How can we assert that the day will
not come when we realize that the world federation or government,
which beginning with Einstein represented the dreams of so many, was in
fact the highest form of private property?

In our inner world, at least, there is nothing fundamental that keeps us
from making such predictions and inferences. Indeed, we can already see
the nude figures of men and women competing with one another under
a single global rule, surrounded by the signs of ninety-four nations. This
"peaceful" scene is surely the annunciation of the future cruelty that flows
back to us.[18]

This last passage hints at the Tokyo Olympics. I was nine years old at that
time, which is about the age when Tanigawa received the revelation that "without the north, Japan is a triangle." It was then that the *Hinomaru* and *Kimigayo*
most inundated my life. With the 2002 Japan-Korea World Cup two years away
now, what kind of legacy is possible for Tanigawa's remarks on national flags,
and the *Hinomaru* in particular, as we try to organize resistance against the
National Flag and Anthem Law? How can his words be connected to Benjamin's image of the "true state of emergency"?

"The king of the instant is dead."[19] This is Tanigawa Gan's well-known declaration of the death of modern poetry. Yet Benjamin's "image which flashes up
at the instant when it can be recognized and is never seen again" requires the
intervention of the poetic, not as a genre so much as a method of cognition. This
requirement must be emphasized all the more in our struggle over the flag and
the anthem. But it is precisely this vein that the movements in Japan have

allowed to dry up over the past thirty years. This, more than the latest public survey figures, arouses an even deeper anxiety over the future direction of our resistance. It is not difficult for the ruling class to propagate and surround us with the "legal" flag and its various partial images (red balls and circles). At such times we must see with "awakened" eyes why the *Hinomaru* is the *Hinomaru*. The only sensibility that can teach resistance how to breathe is that which extends its feelers of existence toward the others of this other-less symbol and their future image.

Moreover, the episode from Tanigawa's childhood shows us that what he calls the "inner *Hinomaru*" can be ruptured and transformed by certain words. "Without the north, Japan is a triangle." Herein lies one of the origins of his poetry. We can today feel it in our skin that the fight against the National Flag and Anthem Law not only must involve resistance against the state power of one nation, but should also potentially contain a vector of resistance against any "single world power." Tanigawa was the first to shudder at that which is openly threatening us today. Even though his 1960s declaration of the death of poetry was closely related to his "hypothesis of a single world power," he still did not completely abandon the dream for words. On the contrary, he seems to have retained until his death an infinite trust, bordering on religious belief, in children's ability to invent words. Likewise, Benjamin refused until the end to abandon his "belief" in a "weak Messianic power," the power of salvation as contained in words.[20]

1933, 1946, 2000. The enemy has not stopped winning. Yet within this accumulation of defeat and the heaps of rubble — and only here — there must lie concealed those words and images that could disturb the stable supplementarity between name and icon, Japan and the *Hinomaru*. We must seek these out with the eyes and ears of children who have not yet been stained by the "auspiciousness/foolishness" of the *Hinomaru*.

Translated by Lewis E. Harrington

Notes

Ukai Satoshi, "Hata no kanata no kaisō: naze Hinomaru wa 'omedetai' no ka," in *Impaction* (March 2000), no. 118, pp. 28–38. (Ukai is utilizing here both senses of the word *omedetai*, meaning "auspicious" and "foolish." — *Trans*).
1. The National Flag and Anthem Law was approved in the National Diet on August 9, 1999, and went into effect on August 13 — *Trans*..

2. This session was scheduled to run from January 19 to June 17, 1999, but was extended until August 13 of that year. During the session a coalition government was formed between the ruling Liberal Democratic Party, the Liberal Party, and the New Komeitō Party, and numerous bills were passed into law with little or no debate on the basis of the sheer numerical superiority of the coalition government. The other key laws passed dealt with the security alliance with the United States and the strengthening of Japan's ability to participate legally in overseas military operations, an expansion of the permissible bounds of wiretapping, and the revision of the Resident Registration Law.—*Trans.*

3. Walter Benjamin, "Theses on the Philosophy of History," in *Illuminations*, ed. Hannah Arendt, trans. Harry Zohn (New York: Schocken Books, 1969), p. 257. Emphasis in the original.

4. Ibid., p. 255. Translation slightly modified.

5. Ibid. Translation slightly modified; emphasis Ukai.

6. From a letter to the editor by Kamino Yōzō in the "Watakushi to Hinomaru-Kimigayo" [The *Hinomaru-Kimigayo* and myself] series, in *Asahi shinbun* [Asahi News], July 22, 1999.

7. Ōshiro Tatsuhiro, "Watakushi to Hinomaru-Kimigayo," in *Asahi shinbun*, July 10, 1999.

8. Yoshimoto Takaaki, *Watakushi no "sensōron"* [My "discourse on war"] (Tokyo: Bunkasha, 1999).

9. Ōnishi Kyojin, "Shihon, kokka, rinri" [Capital, state, ethics], a discussion with Karatani Kōjin in *Gunzō* [Art group] (January 2000).

10. See his "Kasai rettō no rekishi no naka ni 'Hinomaru-Kimigayo' wo oite miru—'Nihon' to iu kokumei, tennō no shōgō, soshite 'Hinomaru-Kimigayo'" [The *Hinomaru-Kimigayo* as seen in the history of the Festoon Islands—The name "Japan," the title of emperor and the *Hinomaru-Kimigayo*"], in *Kōron yo okore! "Hinomaru-Kimigayo"* [Let's have some public debate! The *Hinomaru-Kimigayo*] (Tokyo: Tarōjirōsha, 1999) and "Kokki, kokkahō watakushi wa shitagawanai" [I won't obey the National Flag and Anthem Law], in *Sekai kinkyū zōkan "Stoppu! Jijikō bōsō"* [Urgent special issue of *World*: Stop the runaway Liberal Democratic, Liberal, and New Komeito parties!], no. 688 (November, 1999), pp. 56–64.

11. The term *zainichi* usually refers to Korean residents of Japan, but is here used ironically—and following its literal meaning—to signify simply "Japan resident."—*Trans.*

12. Tanigawa Gan, "Shūrurearesumu to Hinomaru" [Surrealism and the *Hinomaru*], in *Gokuraku desuka?* [Paradise?] (Tokyo: Shūeisha, 1992), pp. 92–93.

13. Ibid., pp. 93–94.

14. Ibid., p. 97.

15. Tanigawa Gan, *Kita ga nakereba Nihon ha sankaku*, in *Tanigawa Gan no shigoto II* [The Works of Tanigawa Gan, vol. II] (Tokyo: Kawade Shobō Shinsha, 1996), p. 451.

16. Ibid.

17. Ibid., pp. 466–67.

18. Tanigawa Gan, "Waga soshiki kūkan," in *Purazuma no zōkei* [The creation of plasma] (Tokyo: Ushio Shuppan, 1984), p. 313. Emphasis in the original.

19. Tanigawa Gan, "Kokubunsha-ban atogaki" [Afterword to the Kokubunsha edition] (1960) of *Tanigawa Gan shishū* [Tanigawa Gan poetry collection], in *Tanigawa Gan no shigoto II*, p. 471.

20. Walter Benjamin, *Illuminations*, p. 254.

Akutagawa Ryūnosuke (1892–1927), short-story writer and essayist known for his social criticism; author of *Kappa* (1927) and "In a Grove" (1922).

Arai Hakuseki (1657–1725), Confucian scholar who played a central role in forming government policy under the Tokugawa Bakufu.

Blue Stockings Society, a group formed in 1911 around the literary journal *Seitō* and its founder Hiratsuka Raichō. The goal of the group was to develop women's literary talent, but it encountered considerable social opposition and ostracism.

Chin Kasen, aka Chen Houquan (1908–1999), Taiwanese writer whose short story "Road" (1943) was written during the period of Japanese colonization.

Doi Takeo (b. 1920), psychoanalyst and major theorist of *Nihonjin-ron* discourse on Japanese uniqueness; author of *The Anatomy of Dependence* (1971).

Etō Jun (1933–1999), literary and social critic whose writings focus on such figures as Natsume Sōseki and Kobayashi Hideo.

Fanon, Frantz (1925–1961), Martinican thinker, educated in France, whose analyses of racism and colonial violence are contained in such works as *Black Skin, White Masks* (1952) and *The Wretched of the Earth* (1961).

Fujioka Nobukatsu (b. 1943), professor of education at Tokyo University and one of the central figures of the nationalist "liberalist view of history" movement; works include *The History That Textbooks Don't Teach* (1996).

Fukuzawa Yukichi (1835–1901), social reformer, author, and educator, one of the leading advocates of Japan's "civilization and enlightenment." Founded Keiō University in 1868.

Furusawa (Kosawa) Heisaku (1897–1968), psychoanalyst trained in Vienna, where he met Freud; known for his formulation of the "Ajase complex," focusing on the mother-child relation.

gesaku, a broad term used to refer to fiction produced during the century prior to the opening of the Meiji period in 1868. This fiction is largely known for its humor and parody.

Girault, Arthur (1865–1931), French government official who helped formulate legislation in France's colonies.

Gotō Shinpei (1857–1929), bureaucrat who held various high-level posts in the Japanese government, foremost among which were chief of Civilian Administration in Taiwan (1898–1906) and first president of the Manchurian Railway (1906).

Hasegawa Michiko (b. 1946), professor of philosophy and comparative thought at Saitama University; member of Japanese historical revisionist movement.

Hayashi Fusao (1903–1975), one of the leading writers of the proletarian literature movement of the 1920s; noted for refusal to renounce his *tenkō* after the war. Cofounder of second *Literary World* journal.

Hiromatsu Wataru (1933–1994), philosopher whose theoretical interests included Marxism, materialism, and epistemology. Author of *On "Overcoming Modernity"* (1989).

Hozumi Yatsuka (1860–1912), conservative legal scholar generally credited with representing Meiji imperial sovereignty on the basis of the Japanese family-state.

Illich, Ivan (1926–2002), theorist of radical ecology movement popular in the 1970s, known for his critique of modernity and its various institutions, such as education and medicine.

Inoue Tetsujirō (1855–1944), philosopher, government official, and professor at Tokyo University who sought to preserve Japanese tradition and promote reverence for the emperor.

Ishibashi Tanzan (1884–1973), journalist, economist, and politician who briefly served as prime minister from 1956 to 1957.

Japanese Romantic School (Nihon roman-ha), a group of nationalist writers and critics affiliated with the *Japanese Romantic School* journal (1935–1938), whose leading members included Yasuda Yojūrō and Kamei Katsuichirō.

Kachikujin yapū [Thedomestic yapoo], *manga* first released in 1970 by Ishinomori Shōtarō depicting a world of science fiction in which whites employ blacks and Japanese people as slaves.

Katō Norihiro (b. 1948), literary critic and professor of modern Japanese literature at Meiji Gakuin University whose books include *In the Shadow of America* (1985) and *After the Defeat* (1997).

Kawabata Yasunari (1899–1972), novelist and winner of the Nobel Prize in Literature in 1968 whose works include *Snow Country* (1948) and *The Sound of the Mountain* (1952).

Kawai Hayao (b. 1928), Jungian psychoanalyst and scholar of clinical psychology whose writings encompass such topics as religion, fairy tales, and Japanese culture.

Kawakami Tetsutarō (1902–1980), critic, scholar, and cotranslator (1934) of Lev Shestov's influential *Philosophy of Tragedy*; organized "Overcoming Modernity" symposium.

Kino Tsurayuki (872–945), aristocrat poet who helped compile the imperial *waka* poetry collection *Kokinshū*; author of the *Tosa Diary*.

Kitamura Tokoku (1868–1894), poet and essayist who developed a notion of subjective interiority based on humanist values; associated with the first *Literary World* journal.

Kobayashi Hideo (1902–1983), influential literary and social critic whose major works focus on Dostoevsky, van Gogh, Mozart, and Motoori Norinaga; cofounder of the second *Literary World* journal.

Kobayashi Yoshinori (b. 1953), manga artist known for his extreme nationalist political views, as expressed in such works as the 1993 *Declaration of Haughtiness*.

Kojima Nobuo (b. 1915), writer whose work has explored the changing nature of family relations in postwar Japanese society; author of *Embracing Family* (1965).

Kōno Taeko (b. 1926), writer known for her depiction of such topics as sadomasochism and trauma. Her short fiction has been collected in the volume *Toddler-Hunting and Other Stories* (1996).

Konoe Atsumaro (1863–1904), aristocrat statesman who served as chairman of the House of Peers and president of Gakushūin University; father of Konoe Fumimaro.

Konoe Fumimaro (1891–1945), court aristocrat who served as prime minister from 1937 to 1939 and again from 1940 to 1941. Committed suicide shortly after Japan's defeat.

Kyoto School (Kyōto gakuha), the group of philosophers and other intellectuals centered around Nishida Kitarō and Tanabe Hajime at Kyoto University in the 1920s and 1930s.

Loti, Pierre (1850–1923), French novelist whose works are notable for exoticizing foreign cultures; author of *Madame Chrysanthemum* (1887).

Lu Xun (1881–1936), pioneer of modern Chinese literature whose works enormously influenced Takeuchi Yoshimi; was the subject of Takeuchi's early writings.

Maruyama Masao (1914–1996), leading political scientist and intellectual historian in postwar Japan; major works include *Studies in the Intellectual History of Tokugawa Japan* (1952) and *Thought and Behaviour in Modern Japanese Politics* (1969).

Masaoka Shiki (1867–1902), writer and poetry critic noted for his reform of haiku poetry and introduction of *shasei*, or "sketching," form of writing.

Miki Kiyoshi (1897–1945), philosopher and critic whose thought represented a synthesis of Marxism and early Heidegger; helped organize the government commission known as the Shōwa Research Association.

Minobe Tatsukichi (1873–1948), scholar of constitutional law renowned for his "organ theory" (*tennō kikan setsu*), according to which the emperor was seen as an organ of the State.

Mishima Yukio (1925–1970), novelist who became involved in Japanese right-wing movement and committed ritual suicide; works include *Confessions of a Mask* (1949) and *The Temple of the Golden Pavilion* (1956).

Miura Gorō (1847–1926), military officer who became Japanese minister to Korea; infamous for having ordered the assassination of Queen Min.

Motoori Norinaga (1730–1801), scholar of Japanese classics and representative writer of the Tokugawa school of National Learning (*kokugaku*).

Murakami Ryū (b. 1952), novelist whose first work, *Almost Transparent Blue* (1976), won the prestigious Akutagawa Prize for literature.

Murayama Tomiichi (b. 1924), politician who headed the Socialist Party and served as prime minister from 1994 to 1996.

Nakamura Mitsuo (1911–1988), literary critic, scholar of French and Japanese literature known for his intellectual biographies of such figures as Futabatei Shimei, Tanizaki Junichirō and Shiga Naoya.

Nakano Shigeharu (1902–1979), poet, novelist, and critic, leading figure of the proletarian literature movement. Helped found the New Japanese Literature Association in 1945.

National Flag and Anthem Law, controversial law passed in August 1999 that establishes Japan's national flag and anthem as the *Hinomaru* and *Kimigayo*.

Natsume Sōseki (1867–1916), one of the founders of modern Japanese literature in his capacities as novelist, scholar, and critic; author of such works as *The Young Master* (1906) and *Kokoro* (1914).

Nishida Kitarō (1870–1945), foremost philosopher of modern Japan, founder of the Kyoto School; taught at Kyoto University from 1910 to 1928.

Nishitani Keiji (1900–1990), Kyoto School philosopher and professor of philosophy at Kyoto University who participated in both the "Overcoming Modernity" and "World-Historical Standpoint and Japan" symposiums of 1941 and 1942.

Nitobe Inazō (1862–1933), Christian writer known for his book *Bushidō, the Soul of Japan* (1899). Served as under secretary general of the League of Nations from 1920 to 1927.

Nogi Maresuke (1849–1912), army general famous for capturing Port Arthur during the Russo-Japanese War (1904–1905); committed suicide, with his wife, following the death of the Emperor Meiji.

Ō Shōyū, aka Wang Changxiong (1916–2000), Taiwanese writer whose short story "Torrent" (1943) was written during the period of Japanese colonization.

Okada, John (1923–1970), Japanese-American author of *No-No Boy* (1957).

Okakura Tenshin (1862–1913), disciple of Ernest Fenollosa who advocated a return to traditional Japanese art. His pan-Asianist views are expressed in his English-language book *The Ideal of the East* (1903).

Ōnishi Kyojin (b. 1919), writer whose masterpiece, *Divine Comedy* (1980) required two decades to complete.

Ōoka Shōhei (1909–1988), postwar novelist and critic most remembered for his antiwar novel *Fires on the Plain* (1952).

Ōshiro Tatsuhiro (b. 1925), Okinawan novelist awarded the Akutagawa Prize for Literature in 1967 for his work *Cocktail Party*

Ranke, Leopold von (1795–1886), German historian whose meticulous research and analyses can be seen in his *History of the Popes* (1834–1839); set forth notion of "moral energy" later incorporated by the Kyoto School.

Saigō Takamori (1827–1877), one of the leaders of the Meiji Restoration whose unsuccessful rebellion against the central government in 1877, known as the Seinan War, forced him to commit suicide.

Sakaguchi Ango (1906–1955), one of the central figures of the postwar *burai-ha* literary faction, whose works are noted for their rebellious, parodistic tone; author of the essay "On Decadence" (1946).

Sakuta Keiichi (b. 1922), sociologist whose writings on Japanese culture can be found in such works as *Reconsideration of Shame Cultures* (1964).

Shiba Ryōtarō (1923–1996), historical novelist whose immensely popular works include *Clouds Above the Hill* (1968–1972).

Shimomura Toratarō (1902–1995), Kyoto School philosopher and participant in the "Overcoming Modernity" symposium; noted for his writings on science, history, and art.

Shiratori Kurakichi (1865–1942), professor of history at Tokyo Imperial University and pioneer of the field of "Oriental History."

Spencer, Herbert (1820–1903), English thinker who sought to apply the scientific notion of evolution to the realm of philosophy and ethics; author of *Principles of Psychology* (1855).

Tajima Miruku (b. 1958), *manga* artist whose works include the 1992 *I Am an Angel, You Are a Devil*.

Takamure Itsue (1894–1964), prewar feminist thinker who articulated a notion of the "mother self," whose communality was opposed to that of the individual self.

Takemitsu Tōru (1930–1996), composer whose prolific works have met with enormous critical success, both in Japan and abroad; wrote the scores for such films as *Woman in the Dunes* and *Ran*.

Takeuchi Yoshimi (1910–1977), critic and sinologist who introduced Lu Xun's works in Japan, criticized Western imperialism in Asia, and formulated concept of resistance (*teikō*).

Tanabe Hajime (1885–1962), leading Kyoto School philosopher who succeeded Nishida Kitarō at Kyoto University; developed notion of the logic of species.

Tanaka Yasuo (b. 1956), novelist and politician whose works include *Somewhat Crystal* (1981) and *Our Era* (1986).

Tanigawa Gan (1923–1995), poet and critic whose texts have focused on the margins of Japanese society; author of *The Myth of Democracy* (1960).

Taut, Bruno (1880–1938), German architect of the "New Objective" school who lived in Japan from 1933 to 1936.

Tokutomi Roka (1868–1927), a Meiji-era writer whose extremely popular works included *Nature and Life* (1900) and *Footprints in the Snow* (1901).

Tosaka Jun (1900–1945), Marxist philosopher who studied under Nishida Kitarō, whom he later criticized along with the Kyoto School as a whole for their rightist political tendencies; author of *On Japanese Ideology* (1935).

Tsumugi Taku (b. 1964), popular *manga* artist, particularly in the mid 1980s, whose works center on the experiences of juvenile delinquents.

Tsumura Hideo (1907–1985), film critic who participated in the "Overcoming Modernity" symposium; author of *Film and Criticism* (1939).

Uchida Shungiku (b. 1959), *manga* artist and novelist whose stories recount the events in the lives of female office workers; author of the 1994 *We are Procreating*.

Uchimura Kanzō (1861–1930), leading Christian thinker and activist educated in the United States who criticized Western missionaries for their colonialist attitudes.

Ume Kenjirō (1860–1910), high government official who had studied law in Europe and helped established the Japanese Civil Code; first president of Hōsei University.

Yamada Eimi (b. 1959), novelist whose works explore racial and sexual issues; books include *Bedtime Eyes* (1985) and *Trash* (1991).

Yanaihara Tadao (1893–1961), Christian pacifist writer and educator who became president of Tokyo University after World War II.

Yasuda Yojūrō (1910–1981), nationalist leader of the Japanese Romantic School who wrote on German aesthetics and traditional Japanese culture; editor of the journals *Cogito* (1933–1944) and *Japanese Romantic School* (1935–1938).

Yasuoka Shōtarō (b. 1920), fiction writer and critic whose work *A Melancholy Pleasure* (1953) earned him the Akutagawa Prize for Literature.

Yoshida Shigeru (1878–1967): politician who served for two terms as prime minister, the first very briefly in 1946 and the second from 1948 to 1954.

Yoshimitsu Yoshihiko (1904–1945), Catholic theologian and participant in the "Overcoming Modernity" symposium, where he argued for a return to medieval spirituality.

Yoshimoto Takaaki (b. 1924), poet and literary critic known for his concepts of the people, emotion, and authentic communality.

Zenkyōtō (All-Campus Joint Struggle Council), student movement during the 1960s and early 1970s that protested against such issues as the Vietnam War and the Japanese university education system.

CONTRIBUTORS

Ehara Yumiko (江原由美子). Born 1952 in Yokohama. Dropped out of the graduate program in Sociology at the University of Tokyo in 1979, but later received her Ph.D there in 2002. Teaches Sociology and Women's Studies at Tokyo Metropolitan University. Works include *Seikatsu sekai no shakaigaku* (1985); *Jōsei kaihō toiu shisō* (1985); *Sōchi toshite no sei shihai* (1995); *Feminizumu no paradokkusu* (2000); and *Jendā chitsujo* (2001).

Kang Sangjung (姜尚中). Born 1950 in Kumamoto. Received his advanced degree in Political Science at Waseda University and teaches Political Thought at Tokyo University. Books include (1986) *Futatsu no sengo to Nihon* (1995); *Orientarizumu no kanata he* (1996); and *Nashonarizumu: shikō no furontia* (2001); (*Max Weber to kindai*).

Karatani Kōjin (柄谷行人). Born 1941 in Hyōgo prefecture. Earned his Master's degree in English Literature at Tokyo University in 1967. Head of the Research Institute for International Cultural Sciences at Kinki University. Principal works include *Han-bungaku ron* (1979); *Tankyū I* (1986); *Tankyū II* (1989); *Origins of Modern Japanese Literature* (Duke University Press, 1993); and *Architecture as Metaphor: Language, Number, Money* (MIT Press, 1995).

Nishitani Osamu (西谷修). Born 1950 in Aichi prefecture. After receiving his M.A. in French Literature at Tokyo Metropolitan University, he continued his

Contributors

studies at the University of Paris VIII. Teaches French Studies at the Tokyo University of Foreign Studies. His books include *Fushi no wandārando* (1990); *Sensō ron* (1992); *Yoru no kodō ni fureru: sensō ron kōgi* (1995); *Ridatsu to idō: Bataille, Blanchot, Duras* (1997); and *Sekaishi no rinkai* (2000). Has translated works by Blanchot, Bataille and Levinas.

Naoki Sakai (酒井直樹). Born 1946 in Kanagawa prefecture. Earned his Ph.D. in Japanese Studies at the University of Chicago in 1983. Teaches Japanese Literature and History at Cornell University. Works include *Voices of the Past: The Status of Language in Eighteenth-Century Japanese Discourse* (Cornell University Press, 1991); *Shizan sareru Nihongo Nihonjin* (1996); *Nihon shisō toiu mondai: honyaku to shutai* (1997); and *Translation and Subjectivity: On "Japan" and Cultural Nationalism* (University of Minnesota Press, 1997).

Takahashi Tetsuya (高橋哲哉). Born 1956 in Fukushima prefecture. In 1983 received his Ph.D. in Philosophy from the University of Tokyo, where he now teaches. Among his books are *Gyakkō no rogosu: gendai tetsugaku no kontekusuto* (1992); *Kioku no echika: sensō, tetsugaku, Auschwitz* (1995); *Derrida: datsukōchiku* (1998); *Sengo sekinin ron* (1999); and *Rekishi/shūseishugi* (2001).

Ueno Chizuko (上野千鶴子). Born 1948 in Toyama prefecture. Received her advanced degree in Sociology from Kyoto University. Teaches Sociology and Women's Studies at Tokyo University. Major works include *Shihonsei to kaji rōdō* (1985); *Onna ha sekai wo sukueru ka* (1986); *Sukāto no shita no gekijō* (1989); *Kafuchōsei to shihonsei* (1990); *Kindai kazoku no seiritsu to shūen* (1994); and *Nashonarizumu to jendā* (1998).

Ukai Satoshi (鵜飼哲). Born 1955 in Tokyo. Attended Kyoto University for his graduate studies in French Literature and Thought. Teaches French Studies at Hitotsubashi University. Works include *Teikō he no shōtai* (1997); *Tsugunai no arukeorojī* (1997); and *Ōtō suru chikara: kitaru beki kotoba tachi he* (2003). Has translated books by Jean Genet and Derrida.

INDEX OF NAMES